Drone Strike–
Analyzing the Impacts of Targeted Killing

Mitt Regan

Drone Strike– Analyzing the Impacts of Targeted Killing

palgrave
macmillan

Mitt Regan
Georgetown University Law Center
Washington, DC, USA

ISBN 978-3-030-91118-8   ISBN 978-3-030-91119-5   (eBook)
https://doi.org/10.1007/978-3-030-91119-5

This Palgrave Pivot imprint is published by the registered company Springer Nature Switzerland AG
The registered company address is: Gewerbestrasse 11, 6330 Cham, Switzerland

ACKNOWLEDGMENTS

I have been fortunate to have generous assistance from several people who helped me refine and strengthen the analysis in this book. Alexander Billy was invaluable in patiently and clearly guiding me through the latest social science research methods, which enabled me to conduct a more rigorous assessment of the quantitative studies that I describe in the book. Asfandyar Mir graciously shared his expertise in quantitative empirical research, insights from his field work in the Afghanistan–Pakistan region, and his deep knowledge of Al-Qaeda, its affiliates, and groups associated with it.

I'm also grateful to many distinguished people who took the time to read and offer insightful comments on portions of the manuscript, or to discuss many of the ideas in it: Peter Berger, Dave Blair, Dan Byman, Joe Chapa, Neta Crawford, Mary DeRosa, Ohpir Falk, Michael Gross, Luke Hartig, Bruce Hoffman, Todd Huntley, Marty Lederman, Larry Lewis, Bryce Loidolt, Paul Lushenko, Dan Mahanty, Tamir Meisels, Seumas Miller, Nancy Sachs, Sarah Sewall, Rita Siemion, Chris Woods, John Williams, and Katherine Zimmerman. I also benefited from conversations with several individuals familiar with targeted strike operations who prefer to remain anonymous.

In addition, I appreciated the opportunity to begin to develop the framework for this book while working on a project on *Global Terrorism and Collective Responsibility: Redesigning Military, Police and Intelligence Institutions in Liberal Democracies* funded by the European Research

Council and headed by Seumas Miller. None of the people I mention should be assumed necessarily to agree with the views that I express in this book, and any errors are mine alone. Finally, I'm indebted in more ways than I can recount to Nancy Sachs for her love and support throughout this project and our lives together.

CONTENTS

LIST OF TABLES

CHAPTER 1

Introduction

BACKGROUND

In November 2001, President George W. Bush met with Yemeni President Ali Abdullah Saleh in the White House and delivered a blunt message. The US wanted Yemen to arrest Qa'id Salim Sinan al-Harithi, "bin Laden's top lieutenant in the country and the head of al-Qaeda in Yemen."[1] Harithi had been involved in planning the attack on the USS *Cole* in Aden harbor in Yemen a little over a year earlier, which killed 17 Americans and wounded 39. He was continuing to engage in planning attacks against US persons. Saleh suggested it might be difficult to meet Bush's request because "[t]he tribes in these areas are very difficult."[2] Nonetheless, he agreed to do his best.

Saleh tried contacting tribal leaders to urge them to turn Harithi over or to convince him to turn himself in. These efforts were unsuccessful. On December 17, 2001, he ordered military operations in areas where he thought Harithi might be located. Eventually, tanks, personnel carriers, and a helicopter reached a village where Harithi and an aide were hiding. Officers told a young sheikh in charge of the village that they had no quarrel with residents and were interested only in the suspect.

Harithi, however, had invoked "the tribal and customary code of law that held sway across much of Yemen, stressing his shared heritage in appealing for refuge. Once the pledge was given, the tribe was honor-bound to protect him."[3] Most of the tribesmen knew Harithi and his

© The Author(s), under exclusive license to Springer Nature
Switzerland AG 2022
M. Regan, *Drone Strike–Analyzing the Impacts of Targeted Killing*,
https://doi.org/10.1007/978-3-030-91119-5_1

1

aide personally, who had been living with them for two weeks. The sheikh refused to turn the men over. As the two sides confronted one another, a Yemeni fighter jet shattered the sound barrier with a large boom. "Convinced they were under attack, the villagers scrambled back inside the thick-walled mud structures, pulling out missile launchers and rocket-propelled grenades from private arsenals."[4] The battle was over in minutes. "Scattered around the burning personnel carriers lay the bodies of nineteen dead soldiers. Nearly two dozen others were bleeding from shrapnel wounds, and thirty-five more had been captured."[5]

In the confusion, Harithi and his aide slipped out of the village. Over the next year he remained free and continued to plan attacks. These included one on the US embassy in Yemen's capital of Sana'a, which was aborted when explosives detonated prematurely and killed an Al-Qaeda member. Another was a suicide attack that destroyed a French oil tanker and killed one of the crew. The US was monitoring a series of phone numbers it had linked to Harithi, but Harithi avoided talking on the phone and relied on couriers and face-to-face meetings.

Finally, on November 3, 2002, Harithi used one of the numbers and a truck-mounted listening device in Kuwait intercepted the call. The NSA and a US–Yemeni task force in Sana'a confirmed the location, and they relayed the information to a CIA team across the Red Sea at a drone base in Djibouti. It took the US less than four hours for a Predator drone armed with two Hellfire missiles to get within its sights a car in which Harithi was riding back from an Al-Qaeda meeting in the desert east of Sana'a. A strike on the car was authorized as soon as it was isolated on the road. The first missile missed, but the second struck the car and it exploded in flames. Harithi and five men in two cars, one a native of Yemen with US citizenship, were killed and one survived.

For the US, the strike on Harithi was a perfect illustration of the potential of a new instrument of counterterrorism that was precise and surgical. Advanced technology allowed the US to locate its target and conduct a strike based on real-time video of unfolding events. The strike occurred in an isolated area and killed members of Al-Qaeda without harming any civilians. It was far more efficient than the bloody military operation in pursuit of Harithi a year earlier that had been so costly. In a rare step, the US publicly announced the strike to serve notice of its new capability.

From that date in November 2002 to the present, the US has conducted hundreds more strikes outside active theaters of combat against either pre-identified targets, or against persons identified as active militants who are members of Al-Qaeda or forces associated with it. With the recent return of the Taliban to power in Afghanistan and possible reemergence of a safe haven for Al-Qaeda leadership, drone strikes are likely to be a significant component of what the US now calls an "over-the-horizon" approach to counterterrorism.[6]

What insights can we gain from evidence on the impacts of the US strike campaign, and on similar campaigns in other contexts, on whether and when to rely on targeted strikes in the future? US operations have sparked intense debate about whether strikes are lawful or unethical, whether they are effective in combatting terrorist groups, and how much harm they cause to civilians. One unfortunate feature of this debate is that parties on both sides often tend to make sweeping factual claims. Only rarely, however, does either side attempt to provide empirical evidence to support them. When they do, they tend to be selective in pointing to research that supports their view. Patrick Johnson and Anoop Sarbahi observe, "As the debate over the use of drones for counterterrorism efforts intensifies, participants resort to anecdotal evidence to support their positions. This is unfortunate, as unmanned aerial vehicles (UAVs) and their lethal targeting capabilities will likely remain a critical aspect of current and future counterterrorism efforts."[7]

How effective have drone strikes been as a counterterrorism instrument, and what have been their impacts on innocent civilians? The aim of this book is to help answer these questions by reviewing and evaluating quantitative and qualitative evidence on the effects of US targeted strikes on terrorist groups and civilians outside war zones. Greater clarity on empirical questions will not by itself resolve a debate that has an important normative dimension. That debate, however, should not occur in an empirical vacuum. Understanding what targeting is and is not able to accomplish, and at what cost to whom, can help ensure that policy decisions and normative judgments are as fully informed as possible.

DRONE STRIKES

While the vast majority of drone operations have been in theaters of combat, strikes that occur outside such areas are the most controversial. A large number of strikes outside war zones have been conducted by drones, but some have been carried out by other aircraft such as fighter planes. This book discusses US strikes outside war zones carried out by all platforms, but focuses mainly on the characteristics of drone operations.

This focus is because the asserted precision of these platforms has been the basis for the claim that strikes provide a "surgical" option that is much less destructive than using conventional military forces against terrorist groups when law enforcement operations infeasible.[8] As John Brennan, then-counterterrorism advisor to President Obama, said in 2012, "By targeting an individual terrorist or a small number of terrorists with ordnance that can be adapted to avoid harming others in the immediate vicinity, it is hard to imagine a tool that can better minimize the risk to civilians than remotely piloted aircraft."[9]

Another reason to focus on drones is that some argue that they can be the future weapon of choice in addressing the threat of transnational terrorism. The argument is that the persistence of ungoverned spaces and weak or failed states, combined with modern communications technology, may enable transnational terrorist groups to find safe havens from which to launch attacks against numerous states. The US targeted killing program has been premised on the belief that strikes can serve as a precise weapon against terrorist groups that capitalize on these opportunities, while minimizing harm to innocent civilians. One goal of this book is to use research on targeted killing, with particular focus on the US experience, to gain insight into whether this underlying rationale for targeted killing is well-founded. This is an urgent question because the list of countries with armed drones is expanding rapidly.

US strikes outside war zones have occurred in mainly three countries. These are Pakistan, with most of these in the Federally Administered Tribal Areas (FATA), Yemen, and Somalia. The latter two countries have experienced some periods of armed conflict, but determining when strikes have been in support of combat operations in those countries is difficult, and data do not reflect this distinction. The discussion of Yemen and Somalia therefore is of all strikes in those countries.

Strikes have been carried out against identified high-level leaders of terrorist organizations, but also against mid-level commanders; persons with specialized skills such as bomb-making; persons in the process of carrying out a planned terrorist attack that has been detected by intelligence; and "signature strikes" against groups of persons regarded as engaged in hostilities, such as by participating in training camps, or being members of armed units on patrol or convoys on the way to engage in hostilities.

The Legal and Ethical Debate

It is important to have a basic understanding of the legal and ethical debate about targeted strikes in order to appreciate the relevance and significance of the empirical material that I describe in the following chapters. As a legal matter, the US takes the position that it is engaged in an armed conflict with Al-Qaeda and associated forces, and that members of these groups are "combatants" under the law of war who are legally presumed to pose a threat to the US or US persons abroad. I use the term "law of war" to refer to what is known as the Law of Armed Conflict (LOAC) or International Humanitarian Law (IHL), because enemy combatants are presumed always to pose a threat, and may be killed at any time without first attempting to capture them. The US interprets the law of war to permit this wherever a combatant is engaged in furthering the war effort, even if that location is not part of an active theater of combat. The law of war also permits unintended civilian casualties in an operation as long as they are not excessive in comparison to the military benefits that the operation is anticipated to provide.

Since 2013, the US as a matter of policy, although not law, has adopted a more restrictive legal approach to operations in what it calls areas "outside of active hostilities." Under the Obama administration, that policy provided that even if someone is an enemy combatant, they may not be targeted unless they pose a "continuing imminent threat" to the US or to US persons and capture of them is infeasible.[10] In addition, it required that there be near certainty of no civilian casualties before a strike could occur. The Trump administration relaxed the continuing imminent threat standard to permit strikes against a larger set of targets, but preserved the requirements that capture of the target be infeasible and that there be near certainty of no civilian casualties. The US reserves the legal right, however, to use force under the laws of war against someone it deems an enemy combatant participating in hostilities, or someone it considers an imminent threat to the US, regardless of where that person is located.

The US also argues that drone strikes are ethically justified because they defend the US from terrorist attacks while causing less destruction, and taking fewer lives, than invasive military operations in areas where relying on conventional policing operations against terrorists is infeasible. It argues that this may be the case when a terrorist group is committed to and capable of attacking the US, is continuously engaged in planning and coordinating such attacks, and cannot be easily interdicted by local police or military forces. This scenario may arise because a group operates in an area over which a government cannot exercise control, or where the government tacitly supports a group's activities. In these cases, strikes ostensibly provide a targeted way to prevent terrorist attacks that otherwise might kill large numbers of innocent persons.

Critics argue that the law of war does not apply outside theaters of active combat. They argue that in these locations, states must follow more restrictive law enforcement standards based on human rights law, which generally permit the use of lethal force only if it is necessary to save someone's life, and only if capture is infeasible. Furthermore, critics argue, even if the US permits strikes outside war zones only against persons who pose an imminent threat to the US or US persons, the US defines imminence too expansively. It assumes that some members of Al-Qaeda pose an imminent threat even in the absence of intelligence about a specific attack that is being planned. This authorizes killing not someone who actually poses a threat, but who may do so in the future.

Some critics also argue that targeted strikes are ethically problematic because their effectiveness in reducing the risk of attacks in the US is uncertain and speculative, while the harms they inflict on populations where they occur are concrete and substantial. Still others argue that drone strikes create an ethical risk because they make it too easy to rely on force instead of other measures to address the threat of terrorism. On this view, the impacts that strikes cause should be compared not with the impacts of a military invasion, but with non-kinetic alternatives that might be pursued if strikes were not readily available.

Organization of the Book

The chapters that follow attempt to inform these debates with empirical findings on the impact of targeted strikes on terrorist groups and civilians. Part I, consisting of Chapters 2 through 4, examines research on the impact on terrorist groups of strikes other than by the US. Chapter 2 discusses methodological challenges in attempting to determine such impacts, and recent refinements in empirical methods that aim to meet these challenges. Chapter 3 discusses the Israeli experience with targeted killing during the Second Intifada beginning in late 2000, the period in which Israel has relied most heavily on this measure. It reviews research on the effectiveness of the targeting campaign, and considers whether it offers any lessons both for the US and for reliance on targeted strikes more generally.

Chapter 4 examines studies of large databases on leadership targeting operations against a large number of terrorist groups over the last several decades. These operations focus on killing the top leaders of a terrorist organization as a means to weaken and even eliminate the organization. US strikes have had a broader set of targets, but the US has regarded operations against top leaders as especially valuable. Research on leadership targeting campaigns therefore may shed some light on whether this assumption is warranted.

Part II, consisting of Chapters 5 through 8, examines the impact of US strikes against Al-Qaeda and groups associated with it. By Al-Qaeda I mean Al-Qaeda top leadership, commonly known et al.-Qaeda Core (AQC), as well as groups formally affiliated with it, such as Al-Qaeda in the Arabian Peninsula (AQAP) and Al-Shabaab in Somalia. By groups associated with Al-Qaeda, I mean groups that are not formal affiliates but that may collaborate with it. An example is the Tehrik-i-Taliban Pakistan (TTP), and the Jemaah Islamiyah in Indonesia, the latter of which received funding from Al-Qaeda to conduct bombings in Bali in 2002 that killed 200 people.

The US also has conducted several targeted strikes against the Islamic State, or ISIS, in recent years, but this book for the most part does not discuss the impacts of these operations. There is no empirical research on the effects of strikes against ISIS that is comparable to the extensive body of work on strikes against AQ. In addition, a large percentage of strikes against ISIS have occurred in war zones, whereas the focus of this book is on strikes outside such zones. Nonetheless, there is reason to think that the conclusions in the book about the impacts of strikes at least broadly apply as well to strikes against ISIS.

Chapter 5 describes how US targeted strike operations against Al-Qaeda have evolved in Pakistan, Yemen, and Somalia. It then describes the legal and policy standards that have guided US operations in areas outside of what it calls "active hostilities." This includes a discussion of both the criteria for conducting a strike and the process for deciding whom may be targeted.

Chapter 6 describes and assesses the findings of quantitative research that has been done on the effects of US strikes on Al-Qaeda and associated forces in the Middle East and Africa. Chapter 7 reviews qualitative evidence of such effects drawn from interviews, Al-Qaeda correspondence, and other sources. Chapter 8 assesses what the quantitative and qualitative research tells us about the immediate and long-term effectiveness of the US targeting campaign, and how these lessons should guide future deliberations about whether and how to use targeted strikes against Al-Qaeda and other terrorist groups.

Part III, consisting of Chapters 9 through 11, analyzes the effects of targeted strikes on civilian populations. Chapter 9 discusses the challenges in obtaining accurate data on civilian deaths and injuries caused by strikes, which include conditions in strike locations and US government secrecy about strikes. It then reviews estimates by nongovernmental organizations and the US of civilian casualties caused by strikes, and trends that can be discerned from these figures.

Chapter 10 examines the concept of strike precision, and the features of the drone strike process that can both enable and impair it. It discusses the wider processes within which the execution of a strike is embedded, and the extent to which the US has effectively organized them in order to meet its own standard of near certainty of no civilian casualties from strikes outside of areas of active hostilities. As this discussion makes clear, focusing simply on the drone platform itself is insufficient to achieve genuine precision. Rather, meeting this standard requires an institutional, not simply a technological, solution.

Chapter 11 goes beyond deaths and injuries to discuss other physical, social, and psychological impacts of strikes on local populations. It then examines research on the effects of strikes on local population attitudes. The aim of the latter analysis is to enable a determination of whether any strike success is outweighed by local population resentment, and to evaluate the claim that such resentment creates more terrorists.

The concluding chapter reviews the findings discussed in previous chapters and offers conclusions about the impacts of US targeted strikes on Al-Qaeda and associated groups, and on civilians. It also discusses some findings from the research on Israeli targeted strikes and leadership targeting studies insofar as these may inform future use of strikes. The broad outlines of these conclusions are set forth in the next section.

CONCLUSIONS

Research findings on the impacts of strikes on Al-Qaeda and associated groups are not uniform, but they do permit some reasonable conclusions. First, substantial qualitative evidence indicates that intensification of strikes in Pakistan, mainly in the FATA, beginning in 2008 significantly weakened AQC, which had concentrated there after the US invasion of Afghanistan in late 2001. Strikes killed several experienced and capable leaders; impaired to some extent AQC's ability to plan and coordinate transnational attacks because of restrictions on communications and travel that AQC imposed in order to avoid attacks; and deprived AQC of its safe haven in the FATA. The most striking evidence of this comes from contemporaneous correspondence between AQC members, but other sources provide support for this finding as well. Qualitative evidence also indicates that strikes in Pakistan disrupted the operations of the TTP.

Second, weakening AQC did not seriously weaken Al-Qaeda as a whole nor reduce the total number of attacks by the Al-Qaeda network. This reflects the fact that AQC's role in the network has been to provide general guidance rather than operational direction. Affiliates and associated groups have never required AQC approval to conduct attacks, but have had broad autonomy in deciding where and when to do so based on their assessment of local conditions. This finding of the effect on the total number of attacks by Al-Qaeda also is consistent with leadership targeting research that concludes that targeting leadership of well-established, religiously oriented groups that are not organized in hierarchical fashion, or dependent on a charismatic leader, has no impact on a group's survival or the rate of attacks that it conducts.

Third, there is good reason to conclude that weakening AQC contributed to reducing the risk of AQ attacks in the US and the West. It is difficult to isolate the effect of strikes from the impact of numerous defensive counterterrorism measures that the US and other Western countries have adopted since 9/11. Quantitative studies do not shed much light on this question, but qualitative evidence indicates that AQC has persistently focused on attacks in the US and the West, that its ability to plan and coordinate such attacks on its own was seriously impaired by the loss of a safe haven in the FATA, that AQC has focused local struggles in recent years in an effort to reduce pressure from US targeting of the group, and that it faces some challenges in communicating efficiently with a larger network because of procedures designed to minimize the risk of detection and strikes.

Fourth, targeted strikes now against AQC may not make a significant contribution to reducing the risk of major attacks in the US and the West. The earlier success in the FATA was a product of particular circumstances that reflected the distinctive importance and influence of AQC at that point in Al-Qaeda's history, and the resources it had to plan, organize, and attempt attacks in the US and the West on its own behalf. Top leadership now can provide general guidance but few other resources, and must pursue the goal of attacks against the "far enemy" by attempting to persuade affiliates to conduct them. Some affiliates may attempt to do so, but the concerns of many are mainly local, and they must devote considerable time and resources dealing with conflicts in their home locations.

It is possible that strikes could help ensure that AQC does not regain enough strength and influence within Al-Qaeda to pose a serious threat to the US. There is no useful empirical research on this issue, however, which means that this impact is speculative. In addition, as Chapter 8 discusses, using strikes in this way would require considering serious legal and ethical questions.

Assessment of the value of strikes against AQC could change if leadership regains a safe haven, such as in Afghanistan with the Taliban back in power. Even so, the US would face substantial challenges in conducting strikes in Afghanistan because of limited intelligence sources and because the Taliban is unlikely to serve as a cooperative local partner. These conditions also are likely to increase the risk of civilian casualties, as illustrated by the drone strike based on faulty intelligence that killed ten innocent civilians in Kabul in August 2021.

While many Al-Qaeda affiliates tend to focus on local concerns, some have plotted attacks in the US that either failed or were intercepted. These attempts may indicate that some local groups are developing the capacity on their own to coordinate attacks in the US and the West. Studies suggest that strikes may weaken a particular group that poses an especially serious threat by reducing its ability to conduct attacks for some period of time. A more enduring decrease in the risk of attacks, however, may require meaningful political reforms in countries where terrorist groups operate in order to limit their appeal to the local population. This is likely to be quite difficult to achieve for one country, much less for an entire region. In the absence of such steps, the US likely would be engaged in a process of periodically conducting strikes to temporarily reduce risk, with the knowledge that it probably will be necessary in the future to do so again. A more modest approach to achieve long-term reduction of risk to the US may be to use strikes to inflict enough damage on a group to convince it to eschew attacks in the US and focus solely on local concerns. This also would require grappling with legal and ethical questions.

With respect to the impacts of strikes on civilian casualties, the US has regularly claimed that the precision of drone strikes results in few if any casualties. It has consistently, however, underestimated civilian casualties compared to estimates from other sources. The US has adopted several measures in recent years that have enabled it to refine its targeting process. These, along with revised targeting standards, helped reduce casualties substantially in the 2013–2020 period compared to 2002–2012. Even since 2013, however, the US has not met its standard of near certainty of no civilian casualties outside areas of active hostilities.

The US has demonstrated that it can reduce civilian casualties when it makes a concerted effort to do so across all relevant operational entities. Such efforts, however, have been fitful, and the US has not institutionalized them. That is, it has not systematically and consistently sought to identify the root causes of casualties, to use that information to revise operations, and to disseminate lessons learned from these experiences across all agencies and organizations involved in the use of force. The importance of these steps underscores that drone strike precision is not simply a function of technology, but of the organizational processes put in place to deploy that technology. The failure to institutionalize efforts to minimize civilian casualties has prevented the US from consistently meeting its own civilian casualty standard.

It is very difficult to obtain information that provides a representative indication of the effects on civilians beyond deaths and injuries. Individual stories indicate that strikes can cause civilian property damage that leaves people homeless and without means of subsistence, and cause their displacement, but there is no systematic evidence of how widespread this impact may be. There is also evidence that strikes can disrupt social life by reducing the willingness of people to gather together. One impact of this can be weakening local informal processes for resolution of disputes. Evidence on psychological effects of living in areas with drone strikes is largely anecdotal, suggesting varying levels of distress. There is no reliable information on how widespread this may be, but it seems plausible to believe that a persistent drone presence would cause some anxiety.

Finally, evidence generally indicates that there is strong local opposition to and resentment of drone strikes in the areas in which they occur. The most rigorous research does not, however, support the claim that this opposition translates into greater support for terrorist groups and increases in terrorist recruitment. Opposition to strikes and resentment of the US nonetheless can impair the effectiveness of counterterrorism and counterinsurgency operations, and needs to be taken into account in a full assessment of the impact of targeted strikes.

These empirical findings on the impacts of strikes should inform legal and ethical decisions about whether, when, and where to conduct them. Decision-makers need to make a clear-eyed assessment of their potential and their risks, as well as how these should inform legal and ethical deliberation. It is important to appreciate that understanding the empirical evidence on the impacts of strikes does not in every case yield a simple and straightforward determination of uncontested "facts." As the chapters make clear, empirical findings inevitably rest upon a set of assumptions that inform interpretation of the evidence. In this sense, analysis is never purely "objective" in the sense of being free of human judgment. Ideally, however, analysts will make their assumptions clear so that others can take them into account in reviewing their conclusions.

The fact that human judgment is unavoidable does not mean that all analysis is simply the reflection of subjective preferences that cannot be subject to rigorous assessment, or that any claim is just as good as another. Some findings, compilations, and conclusions are more defensible than others.

My conclusions may both please and displease critics and supporters of targeted strikes. This may lead them to take issue with portions of my analysis. I welcome this prospect, and have provided as much information as possible so that others can review the evidence and draw their own conclusions. It is important to dive in and wrestle with the empirical evidence that we have, and do our best to derive guidance from it, rather than proceed on the basis of unexamined assumptions. In an age in which belief in the value, and even existence, of such evidence may seem chimerical, my hope is to help us identify and draw on at least some pool of shared knowledge to inform deliberation about issues that implicate our deepest values.

NOTES

1. Johnsen, G. D. (2012). *The last refuge: Yemen, al-Qaeda, and America's war in Arabia* (p. 91). W. W. Norton.
2. Id.
3. Id. 95–96.
4. Id. 96.
5. Id. 96–97.
6. Pettyjohn, S. (2021, November 7). Over-the-horizon does not have to mean next door. *Lawfare*. https://www.lawfareblog.com/over-horizon-does-not-have-mean-next-door.
7. Johnston, P. B., & Sarbahi, A. K. (2016). The impact of US drone strikes on terrorism in Pakistan. *International Studies Quarterly, 60*(2), 203–219, 203. https://doi.org/10.1093/isq/sqv004.
8. Dilanian, K. (2011, June 29). U.S. counter-terrorism strategy to rely on surgical strikes, unmanned drones. *Los Angeles Times*. https://www.latimes.com/politics/la-xpm-2011-jun-29-la-pn-al-qaeda-strategy-20110629-story.html.
9. National Public Radio. (2012, May 1). *John Brennan delivers speech on drone ethics*. https://www.npr.org/2012/05/01/151778804/john-brennan-delivers-speech-on-drone-ethics.
10. White House. (2013, May 23a). *Fact sheet: U.S. policy standards and procedures for the use of force in counterterrorism operations outside the United States and areas of active hostilities*. https://obamawhitehouse.archives.gov/the-press-office/2013/05/23/fact-sheet-us-policy-standards-and-procedures-use-force-counterterrorism.

Empirical Research on the Effectiveness of Targeted Killing

CHAPTER 2

Cause and Effect in Targeted Killing

This chapter provides an overview of research methods that attempt to determine the effectiveness of using targeted killing to combat terrorist groups. The chapters that follow in the remainder of Part I describe studies that apply these methods to specific targeting campaigns. Chapter 3 examines Israel's targeting program, primarily during the Second Intifada beginning in late 2000. Chapter 4 reviews analysis of leadership targeting campaigns using large databases on terrorist groups stretching back several decades.

Part II of the book focuses on the US targeting program. Chapter 5 provides an overview of the program, Chapter 6 reviews quantitative studies, Chapter 7 examines qualitative material, and Chapter 8 offers conclusions on the effectiveness of the US targeting campaign based on the combined quantitative and qualitative evidence.

In social science terms, studies of targeting impact attempt to determine causality. They treat a targeted strike or set of strikes as an independent variable, and measurements of terrorist activity afterward such as attacks and fatalities from them as dependent variables. The goal is to determine if targeting causes any changes in terrorist operations. Increasing scholarly interest in this topic reflects greater reliance on targeting in counterterrorism campaigns in the twenty-first century.

Proponents of targeting argue that it can remove key individuals and thereby reduce a group's ability to engage in terrorism because of the

© The Author(s), under exclusive license to Springer Nature
Switzerland AG 2022
M. Regan, *Drone Strike–Analyzing the Impacts of Targeted Killing*,
https://doi.org/10.1007/978-3-030-91119-5_2

skilled people that a group loses, and because a group anticipating future strikes will take measures to avoid them that divert its energies and make attacks more difficult to organize. Proponents also argue that targeting is more discriminating than conventional military operations when it is necessary to use force.

Critics argue that targeting overstates the importance of particular individuals to terrorist groups. As Audrey Kurth Cronin asserts, targeting is based on the tendency of states "to view the enemy in their own terms, as a hierarchically structured group that is directed by a leader."[1] Many groups, however, are structured as networks that are not reliant on specific individuals. Some also have standard procedures that enable them to readily replace leaders whom they lose. In addition, critics maintain that targeting is not as precise as proponents claim. It can cause harm to innocent persons that fuels retaliatory attacks, increases terrorist recruitment, and generates local resentment that can undermine the larger mission.

This chapter discusses the challenges that traditional social science approaches face in trying to evaluate these claims by drawing conclusions about causality. It then describes recent analytical approaches that attempt to approximate a randomized control trial, which is generally regarded as the best method for establishing causal relationships. This discussion provides a useful foundation for the analyses of studies on the impacts of targeted killing on terrorist groups in the chapters that follow.

Overview of Empirical Research

As the discussion of specific studies will indicate, research on the impact of targeting on terrorist groups reaches different conclusions. This may be for several reasons. One important one is of course differences in the historical, political, and cultural context in which terrorism and counterterrorism occurs. As Chapter 4 describes, studies that examine large databases attempt to identify variables that are common among terrorist groups and counterterrorism campaigns.

Another reason for dissimilar conclusions is that differences in the availability of data, as well as the use of different conceptual models, may lead scholars to measure the impacts of targeting in different ways. Post-strike terrorist attacks and fatalities can be measured more easily, for instance, than effects on morale or organizational structure. Scholars also may use different time periods over which to measure the metrics they choose.

Finally, different findings may reflect different methodological approaches. Some scholars rely on traditional studies of correlation, but the admonition that correlation does not establish causality is axiomatic in social science. Techniques have emerged in recent years that attempt to enable conclusions about causality, but these have not been widely adopted in targeted killing research. The use of different methods thus may explain different conclusions. As the following chapters describe, it also means that we can place more confidence in the results of some studies than others.

In the next two sections, I discuss differences that may result from the use of different metrics and different methodological approaches.

Metrics

Studies that aim to determine the effect of targeted strikes must rely on some indication of terrorist activity to measure this effect. Because of the clandestine nature of terrorist groups, access to data can be limited. For example, a terrorist network may orchestrate an attack but not want to reveal its role to shield itself from scrutiny, or may claim responsibility for activity it did not conduct. In some cases, it may not be possible to determine who is responsible for an attack. In addition, government agencies may not release information if it would compromise security activities or sources and methods of intelligence. For these reasons, data may be incomplete and not entirely accurate.

Even when data are reasonably reliable, there is disagreement on which metrics best capture terrorist activity. These may include the continuation or demise of a terrorist group within some period after the loss of its leadership, or the number of terrorist attacks, the lethality of attacks, or the percentage of successful attacks after targeting operations. For instance, Jenna Jordan describes a terrorist group as inactive if it has not engaged in any attacks for two years.[2] Bryan Price criticizes this approach, suggesting that a group may take more than two years to recover.[3] If so, the group may be dormant but not defunct. Alternatively, a group may continue for more than two years but engage in many fewer attacks than it did before suffering decapitation.

There is no consensus on what counts as success in measuring the effects of targeted killing on terrorist groups. Some scholars use the demise of a group, while many others use the number and lethality of attacks, or the rate of successful and unsuccessful attacks. Relying on attacks and deaths likely reflects the relative ease with which these outcomes can be measured. Other variables, however, may provide a fuller indication of the effect of targeted killing. These could include, for instance, greater difficulty in recruiting individuals for leadership positions, a loss or increase in morale and commitment, or a loss or increase in local support for a group. It is much more difficult, however, to measure these possible effects.

The use of different metrics thus accounts for some of the variety of conclusions that scholars draw. As the next section describes, an even more important difference among studies is the extent to which researchers use methods that permit robust inferences about causality.

Challenges in Determining Causality

Ideally, to determine if a strike caused a change in a terrorist group we would need to determine what would have happened to the group if it had not been targeted, and compare this with any changes that occurred after the strike. In other words, we would need to imagine a counterfactual world in which the strike did not occur. Only then would we be warranted in making a claim about causality.

For this reason, as Patrick Johnston observes, "[C]redible causal inferences cannot be made from studies that only examine cases in which opposing leaders were captured or killed."[4] Stephanie Carvin, however, underscores how difficult such counterfactual analysis is in studying targeted killing: "Essentially, it is challenging, if not impossible, to say what would or would not have happened if the policy of targeted killing had not been carried out or if a given situation would have ended differently."[5] The discussion below explains why this is the case and describes approaches that attempt to meet this challenge.

The standard method for making warranted causal claims in empirical research is what is known as a randomized control trial. This involves assembling a group of subjects who are comparable with respect to characteristics that might affect the causal outcome that we are attempting to determine. Thus, for instance, a group might consist of a random sample of persons with a particular disease, and the aim of the trial is to determine whether an experimental drug is effective in treating it. The sample rests on the statistical principle that there is likely to be a random distribution among the group of other characteristics that are likely unrelated to the outcome of interest.

Persons from this group are then randomly assigned to a "treatment" group that receives the drug and a "control" group that does not. The latter group may receive a placebo or may continue with conventional care. Random assignment to each group ensures that receiving treatment is "exogenous" rather than "endogenous." This means that the severity of a person's disease does not cause them to receive treatment. If it did, we could not rule out the possibility that if the condition of the persons in the treatment group worsened, this was caused by the severity of their disease rather than the ineffectiveness of the treatment. In other words, we would not be able to draw conclusions about whether treatment caused changes in disease condition.

Random assignment to a treatment or control group thus ensures that two groups are comparable in all relevant ways except for receiving treatment or not. Using a statistically valid sample of persons in a large group who are assigned to the smaller treatment and control groups ensures that the distribution of observable characteristics that might affect the course of the disease, such as age, sex, pre-existing conditions, and severity of the disease will be random. This controls for potential causal factors other than the treatment, which allows us to infer that any difference in the course of the disease between the two groups is caused solely by the treatment.

The assumptions involved in conducting a randomized control trial therefore are that:

1. the researcher has randomly selected individuals into treatment and control groups from a statistically valid sample of persons for whom we think treatment might make a difference;
2. individuals across the two groups have comparable relevant traits and experiences; and
3. the only intervention in the two groups that occurs during the period of observation is that one group receives a treatment.

Social scientists generally are not in a position to use randomized control trials, but engage in "observational" studies of events that have already occurred. Much research aims to assess causes of various forms of social behavior or conditions, such as political beliefs or poverty, in which it is not feasible to assemble a population with comparable relevant characteristics, randomly assign them into treatment and control groups, and rule out all reasons for differences in the relevant outcome except for the treatment.

In addition, there may be ethical concerns about conducting randomized controlled trials on human subjects. In attempting to determine the effects of child sexual abuse, for instance, it would be indefensible to subject one group of children to sexual abuse in order to determine if those children behave differently from a control group not subjected to it.

If we consider the conditions for a randomized controlled trial, we can see that targeted strikes do not satisfy them. First, groups in the "treatment" group of being targeted and in the "control" group of not being targeted likely were not assigned to those categories by random selection. Groups are not targeted solely independent of characteristics that affect their behavior, such as their capacity to engage in attacks. As a result, there may be a variety of covariates—that is characteristics of the target group—that both influence their selection for targeting and their activity after it. Strikes thus may be what is called "endogenous" rather than "exogenous."

If this is the case, it is hard to determine the causal impact of strikes because we don't know if strikes cause changes in attacks or if attacks cause changes in strikes. Randomly targeting one group and not another would mean targeting a group for reasons that have nothing to do with the gravity of the threat that it poses. Taking life simply to establish a treatment and control group obviously would be unethical. We therefore must find some other way to establish the equivalent of a counterfactual group.

In addition, there may be unobserved variables apart from targeting that affect the number and lethality of post-strike terrorist attacks or other measures of outcomes. These may be features of terrorist groups, such as changes in personnel, tactics, or strategy that are unknown to researchers. Two groups are unlikely to be identical except that one is targeted and one is not. As a result, no group can serve as a complete counterfactual that indicates what would have happened to the targeted group had it not been targeted—that is, had it been selected as the "control" group rather than the "treatment" group. This makes it very difficult to isolate the causal effect of targeting from the effect of other variables.

Challenges in conducting randomized control trials mean that social scientists generally must conduct observational studies instead. That is, they take the world as it is and try to determine what causes what, rather than attempting to construct a world in which causal relationships are clear. Traditionally, social science has compiled data on events and attempted simply to establish correlations, rather than causal relationships, between them. This involves charting changes in an independent variable that is regarded as a possible cause and a dependent variable that has been affected by it.

Researchers then use methods to determine the likelihood that changes in the dependent variable occurred by chance rather than because of the effect of changes in the independent variable. While correlations cannot warrant claims of causality, they can be suggestive of the possibility of a causal relationship between the independent and dependent variable. At a minimum, correlations may provide a necessary, although not sufficient, basis for establishing causality.

In research that examines the relationship between changes in an independent variable X and a dependent variable Y, findings are expressed in a simple linear, or bivariate, regression in the form $Y = \beta X + \mu$. In this equation, β represents how much Y changes with a one-unit change in X. The data rarely, however, indicate that that βX always results in the same amount of change in Y. $Y = \beta X$ therefore is the best estimate of the likely predicted change in Y. The symbol μ represents what is known as the error term. This reflects other unobserved variables that produce a change in Y in addition to βX. If we knew these, we could add them to the equation and precisely predict outcomes for Y.

Multiple regression analysis involves using techniques that attempt to isolate the correlation between hypothesized independent variables and the dependent variable, while multivariate regression analysis includes additional dependent variables. In each case, the aim is the same: to determine the extent to which changes in one or more independent variables are correlated with changes in one or more dependent variables. As with bivariate regression, in each case there will be an error term μ that reflects unobservable variables that account for changes in Y that are not captured by the regression equation.

Analyzing correlations in this way was the dominant approach to observational studies in social science for many years. As researchers emphasize, correlation does not mean causality. That is, establishing a correlation between changes in X and changes in Y does not allow us to say that X causes Y. Unlike in a randomized control trial, it is not possible to arrange a counterfactual state of the world in which everything is the same for the study population except for the absence of the independent variable.

Omitted variable bias is always a potential concern in a study that analyzes correlations. It is possible in such a study that one or more variables that are not included in the regression as independent variables affecting Y are correlated with X. This means that the regression will not express the independent effect of X on Y, but will over- or underestimate it. To use a simple example, a regression that examined the effect of amount of education (X) on earnings (Y) would not have as much explanatory power as one that included parents' income (Z), since the amount of parents' income is correlated with a person's level of education and has its own effect on earnings. Ideally, a regression will include all variables potentially correlated with X, so that the error term and X are uncorrelated. There is always a possibility, however, that the error term is correlated with X, because that term reflects unobservable variables that cannot be included in the regression since they are unknown.

Another limitation of conventional regression analysis that makes claims of causality problematic is, as the discussion above describes, that the ostensible independent variable may be endogenous. In some cases, it may be equally plausible to claim that changes in what is assumed to be the independent variable are in fact a result of changes in the assumed dependent variable. For instance, one may posit that an individual's level of trust contributes to better overall health. It is possible, however, that the relationship goes in the opposite direction: better overall health leads persons to be more trusting.[6] This is also known as the potential for reverse causality. The fact that the two variables are correlated does not necessarily illuminate which produces effects on the other.

These difficulties suggest, as one prominent political scientist has put it, that "the traditional empirical methods have pushed observational data to their limits."[7] The next section discusses efforts to move beyond these limits.

Identification Strategies

In response to the limits of studies focusing on correlation, research based on observational studies in the last two decades has been involved in what has been called an "identification revolution."[8] This consists of the development of "identification strategies," which represent "approaches that allow random assignment of the causal variables of interest (such as field, laboratory or survey experiments), or at least that employ approaches to observational data that make causal inference possible."[9] These approaches reflect efforts to identify conditions that provide some confidence that the independent variable produces results comparable to those that would occur with random selection of a treatment and control group.

An example of a study in this vein is recent work by Melissa Dell and Pablo Querubin that examines the effects of US bombing in the Vietnam War on local population security and political allegiance.[10] As the authors acknowledge, practical and ethical constraints preclude random bombing. Bombing locations therefore are endogenous. That is, they reflect considerations that are correlated with the dependent variables of interest. It is reasonable, for instance, to assume that differences in the level of threat and support for the Viet Cong influenced decisions about which locations to bomb, while at the same time bombing was designed to affect those characteristics.

Dell and Querubin discovered, however, that Secretary of Defense Robert McNamara implemented a Bayesian algorithm that relied on 169 questions on the security, politics, economics, and civic life of Vietnamese hamlets to calculate a local security score on a quarterly basis. This metric determined the location of bombings. Specifically, a continuous score from one to five was computer-generated for each hamlet before being rounded to the nearest whole score. Hamlets with a score of one had the greatest likelihood of being bombed, with the probability decreasing as scores increased. These numbers played a significant role in determining which hamlets would be bombed, and were calculated solely for this purpose.

Dell and Querubin focus on locations with scores just above and below the cutoff. They assume that these groups are very similar because of the small difference in scores, but one hamlet effectively is a treatment group that is bombed, while the other is a control group that is not. Locations marginally below the cutoff thus had an exogenously higher probability of receiving treatment than those just below it. Otherwise, all other features relevant to the security situation in each hamlet should be comparable.

In examining hamlets just below and just above each of the numerical thresholds, they find that bombing changed discontinuously at each threshold. This confirms the importance of the hamlet score in bombing decisions, and that it is reasonable to treat hamlets just above the threshold as a valid control group for those just below it.

An example helps illustrate the identification strategy. Consider two villages, A and B. Let Village A receive a score of 4.49, while Village B is assigned a score of 4.51. Given the rounding to the nearest whole number, the computer calculation assigns Village A a score of four and Village B a score of five. Despite being only marginally different, Village A is more likely to be bombed than Village B. When Village A is bombed and Village B is not, the former becomes the treatment group and the latter the control group.

Dell and Querubin include hamlets only once in the sample; when a village appears within a cutoff range determined by the data, this is the only time it either receives or does not receive treatment. Effects are then measured by comparing conditions in the treatment and control hamlet after bombing. This strategy avoids the endogeneity risk that whether a hamlet is near a threshold in one quarter is affected by whether it is below the threshold in the previous quarter, and thus potentially subject to bombing. Based on a wide range of data, the authors conclude that "[b]ombing increased VC military and political activity, weakened local government administration, and lowered non-communist civic engagement."[11]

This study combines rich information on US military operations, combined with methods designed to enable inferences about causality that have potential policy implications. In this respect, it can provide a general template for research that seeks to enable causal claims about the effects of targeting operations on terrorist groups.

Two other identification strategies are what are known as difference-in-differences and propensity score matching. Difference-in-differences is a quasi-experimental design that seeks to identify a trend in the dependent variable prior to a treatment that is as closely identical as possible for a treatment and a control group.[12] So, for instance, assume that attacks by Group One and Group Two increase by 5% each year. Now assume that Group One loses a leader from a targeted strike. In the year after the strike, the rate of Group Two attacks continues to increase by 5% but the rate of increase in Group Two attacks is 7%. This permits the inference that had Group One not been targeted its attacks would have increased by only 5%, which means that the strike increased its rate of attacks by two percentage points.

Researchers must defend the assumption that the trends for each group would normally remain constant for the foreseeable future. In graphical terms, this would be depicted as below. Group One is represented as P, and Group Two as S. The *number* of strikes by each group is on the Y axis, and the assumed "normal" *trend* in the number of attacks for each group in the absence of any change of circumstances is represented by the uniform slopes of each from Time 1 to Time 2.

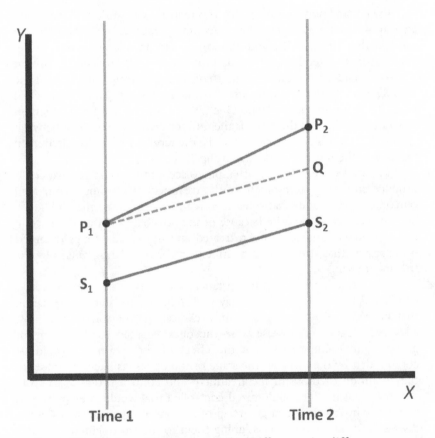

Source https://en.wikipedia.org/wiki/Difference_in_differences

Under "normal" circumstances, we would expect that the trend line for Group One (P) from Time 1 to Time 2 would be the dotted line that ends at point Q at Time 2, and for Group Two (S) the line that ends at $S2$. This represents a constant difference in the trend in attacks between the two groups that we expect if neither group suffers a targeted killing or some other significant change.

At some point between Time 1 and Time 2, however, there is a targeted killing against a leader of Group One (P). In the graph, this results in an increase in the rate of attacks that Group One conducts, so that the slope from Time 1 to Time 2 is from $P1$ to $P2$ rather than from $P1$ to Q.

How do we know, however, that this increase wouldn't have happened anyway without a targeted killing? Assuming appropriate conditions are satisfied that Groups One and Two are similar in relevant ways, we can assume that the trend line of Group One from Time 1 to Time 2 without a strike would be the same as the trend line of Group Two from Time 1 to Time 2. Group Two, in other words, represents the counterfactual state of a world in which Group One did not suffer a loss from targeting. The effect of the loss therefore is the difference in the trend line between Q and $P2$. In this case, in other words, the targeted killing resulted in an increase in the rate of attacks by Group One.

Propensity score matching attempts to account for variables that could produce an inaccurate estimate of the treatment if we simply compared outcomes among units that received a treatment and those that did not.[13] Such inaccuracy could arise because of the possibility that a difference in the dependent variable between treated and untreated groups is caused by a variable that also predicts treatment rather than being caused by the treatment itself.

In the targeting context, for instance, the average number of attacks conducted by a terrorist group may well influence the decision to target that group. This would be as if in a clinical trial persons at the most advanced stages of a disease were the ones assigned to the treatment group. Our attempt to isolate the effect of the treatment would be confounded by the fact that the stage of the disease is likely to influence the condition of those in the treatment and control group apart from the treatment itself. A randomized controlled trial would control for this possibility by selecting a large group of persons at different stages of the disease, and then randomly assigning them to the treatment and control group.

Propensity score matching attempts to mimic this random assignment in observational studies. For instance, in an observational study on the effects of smoking, the "treatment" effect of smoking estimated by simply comparing people who smoked to those who did not could be biased by any variables that are correlated with smoking, such as socioeconomic status, age, and gender. A study that seeks to isolate the effect of smoking will need to mimic a random allocation of subjects to the "control" and "treatment" groups, by ensuring that members of each group are comparable with respect to these characteristics. If they are, as measured by propensity scores, the groups are regarded as suitable for comparison for the purpose of determining the impact of smoking.

In the targeting context, one would select two groups as similar as possible with respect to ideology, resources, organizational structure, length of time in existence, intelligence networks, and other features that might affect their activity. If an operation could use targeted killing to remove a leader from one group but leave in place a comparable leader in the other group, there would be a plausible basis for inferring that the strike caused any difference in activity after the strike between the two groups.

CONCLUSION

Arguments about the impacts of targeting on terrorist groups are basically claims about causality. As this chapter describes, observational studies in social science have traditionally focused on correlation, with the explicit admonition that correlation cannot establish causality. Methodological developments in social science over the last few decades attempt to provide more robust inferences about causality than this approach. As the discussion of the studies in the following chapters indicates, however, a relatively small amount of the research on the effects of targeted killing attempt to employ such methods. The following chapters will describe the studies that have been conducted, and will take into account the different methodologies that they use in assessing the conclusions that they reach.

NOTES

1. Cronin, A. K. (2011). *How terrorism ends: Understanding the decline and demise of terrorist campaigns*. Princeton University Press.
2. Jordan, J. (2009). When heads roll: Assessing the effectiveness of leadership decapitation. *Security Studies, 18*(4), 719–755. https://doi.org/10.1080/09636410903369068.
3. Price, B. C. (2019). *Targeting top terrorists: Understanding leadership removal in counterterrorism strategy*. Columbia University Press.

4. Johnston, P. (2012). Does decapitation work? Assessing the effectiveness of leadership targeting in counterinsurgency campaigns. *International Security, 36*(4), 47–79, 48–49. https://doi.org/10.1162/isec_a_00076.

5. Carvin, S. (2012). The trouble with targeted killing. *Security Studies, 21*(3), 529–555. https://doi.org/10.1080/09636412.2012.706513.

6. Giordano, G. N., & Lindström, M. (2015). Trust and health: Testing the reverse causality hypothesis. *Journal of Epidemiology and Community Health, 70*(1), 10–16. https://doi.org/10.1136/jech-2015-205822.

7. Tucker, J. (2013, June 14). Is theory getting lost in the "identification revolution"? *Monkey Cage.* https://themonkeycage.org/2013/06/is-the ory-getting-lost-in-the-identification-revolution/.

8. Id.

9. Id.

10. Dell, M., & Querubin, P. (2017). Nation building through foreign intervention: Evidence from discontinuities in military strategies. *Quarterly Journal of Economics, 133*(2), 701–764. https://doi.org/10.1093/qje/qjx037.

11. Id. 760.

12. Girma, S., & Gor, H. Evaluating the foreign ownership wage premium using a difference-in-differences matching approach. *Journal of International Economics, 72*, 97–112. https://www.sciencedirect.com/science/article/abs/pii/S0022199606001139.

13. Stuart, E., Huskamp, H., Duckworth, K., Simmons, J., Song, Z., Chernew, M., & Varry, C. (2014). Using propensity scores in difference-in-differences models to estimate the effects of a policy change. *Health Serves Outcomes Research Methodology, 14*, 166–182. https://link.springer.com/content/pdf/10.1007/s10742-014-0123-z.pdf.

CHAPTER 3

Israeli Targeted Strikes

BACKGROUND

Israel has periodically engaged in targeted killing over the course of its history.[1] Audrey Kurth Cronin estimates that over several decades before 2000, Israel killed likely targeted 50 or fewer terrorist leaders.[2] All attacks during this period were outside Israel and the Occupied Territories. The intensity of violence during the Second Palestinian Intifada beginning in late 2000, however, caused a significant escalation of Israeli targeting operations, which included targeting in the Occupied Territories for the first time.

Particularly devastating both physically and psychologically was a substantial increase in suicide bombings. "At the height of the Second Intifada," Daniel Byman says, "there were more suicide bombings in a week than in all of 1996."[3] Hamas played a prominent role in the uprising, although several other Palestinian groups such as the Palestinian Islamic Jihad (PIJ) and the Al-Aqsa Martyrs Brigade participated, some of which were affiliated with Hamas.

Because much of the research on Israeli targeting uses Palestinian suicide bombings as a dependent variable, the table below depicts information on these attacks from October 2000 to April 2006, the period in which they were used most extensively. The data are taken by a database compiled and graciously shared by Ophir Falk. Dr. Falk describes the data as "gathered from Israeli Security Agency Reports, Israel's office

© The Author(s), under exclusive license to Springer Nature Switzerland AG 2022
M. Regan, *Drone Strike–Analyzing the Impacts of Targeted Killing,*
https://doi.org/10.1007/978-3-030-91119-5_3

Table 3.1 Palestinian suicide operations during the Second Intifada

Year	Number of suicide bombings	Number of persons killed	Number of persons injured
2000	4	0	4
2001	37	93	864
2002	59	218	1469
2003	27	146	773
2004	14	58	336
2005	6	23	233
2006	4	15	109

Source Falk Suicide Bombing Database (2015)

of Foreign Affairs, and detailed databases, including those concerning suicide attacks worldwide compiled by Ami Pedahzur. These databases were consolidated with the database generously provided by Prof. Ariel Merari."[4] Some of the studies described below may use slightly different data, but the differences are not substantial (Table 3.1).

Israel was unprepared for suicide bombings on such a large scale. As one official described, "[W]e had no solution for it, neither in combat doctrine nor weaponry."[5] Prime Minister Sharon did not want the Israeli Defense Forces (IDF) to occupy areas under Palestinian control to conduct arrests, but preferred to rely on Palestinian officials to conduct them. As Israel's frustration with Palestinian Authority reluctance to do this increased, the targeting program was substantially expanded under the coordination of the Israeli Security Agency, known as Shin Bet.[6]

The table below provides annual information on these targeting operations, which reflects calculations based on a database compiled by Dr. Falk and co-author Amir Hefetz, whose research is described later in this chapter.[7] Data used by other researchers in the studies described below may vary to some extent. As Falk and Hefetz describe, their data are based on information from (Table 3.2):

leading media search engines (e.g., LexisNexis), governmental and nongovernmental organizations (i.e., Israel Security Agency, the Palestinian Human Rights Monitoring Group; the International Policy Institute for Counterterrorism; B'tselem, the Israeli Information Center for Human Rights in the Occupied Territories; the Public Committee against Torture in Israel; and the Palestinian Society for the Protection of Human

Table 3.2 Israeli targeted killing operations, November 2000–2010

Year	Number of targeted strikes	Targeted person fatalities
2000	10	10
2001	40	30
2002	57	59
2003	45	43
2004	22	42
2005	9	23
2006	13	22
2007	7	12
2008	6	9
2009	3	4
2010	1	1

Source Calculations based on Falk and Hafetz Targeting Database (2015)

Rights and the Environment) and personal communications with decision makers and other researchers. Data from the aforementioned sources were researched again, and their accuracy was verified by reports appearing in the news media as well as professional literature.[8]

Falk and Hefetz found that 74% of strikes did not cause any unintended deaths—that is, persons other than the intended targets. Of those cases in which such deaths occurred, 68% of them resulted in one death. The remaining cases vary in the number of unintended deaths from one or two (36 cases, 17%), up to 14 (one case, 0.5%). Falk and Hafetz note, "In the latter, the targeted killing of Hamas leader Shalech Shadeh in Gaza on 22 July 2002 resulted in a death toll of 14 unintended deaths and a subsequent judicial inquiry."[9]

The principal aim of targeting was to reduce the number of suicide bombings. Simon Pratt maintains, however, that there were three distinct stages of the campaign that reflected different assumptions about how this aim could be accomplished.[10] Pratt says that the first stage, from the rise in suicide bombings beginning in fall 2000 to the end of 2001, was designed to signal to the Palestinians that Israel would escalate its response to the increase in bombings. The assumption was that "[t]he death of a few activists was unlikely to significantly affect the operational capacity of Palestinian organizations, but it would serve as an effective act of political communication."[11]

Pratt also notes that targeting at this time concentrated on "preemptive killings" designed to interrupt planned attacks.[12] As Ronen Bergman describes, during this period targeting focused on "'ticking time bombs,' people who either were working on planning an attack or about to carry out an attack, or who were directly involved in such behavior."[13]

The second stage, beginning at the end of 2001, responded to problems with focusing solely on individuals directly involved in perpetration of an impending attack.[14] The first problem was that it was difficult to identify targets within a large universe of individuals who did not fit any specific profile. In addition, identifying a prospective attacker did not ensure the ability to stop an attack. While a planned attack in progress could be monitored at each step, "Israel could not operate openly inside hostile Palestinian-controlled territory. And by the time the bomber reached Israel, it was generally too late."[15] Finally, even if successfully targeted, individual bombers could be replaced relatively easily.

Israel therefore shifted to targeting the "ticking infrastructure" that enabled the suicide attacks.[16] This included "recruiters, couriers, and weapons procurers, as well as people who maintained safe houses and smuggled money—an entire organization overseen by commanders of regional cells, above whom were the main military commanders, themselves subordinate to the political leaders of the organizations."[17] These people were not as easily replaced with skilled people as the bombers themselves. As Bergman notes, those killed "would be quickly replaced by those next in line, but over time, the average age dropped, as did the level of experience as younger and younger people filled the ranks."[18]

Officials turned to legal advisors to determine the scope of permissible targeting, which led to the establishment of a set of legal criteria. Daniel Reisner, head of International Law for the Israeli Defense Forces (IDF) at the time, described the standards that governed the selection of a target. These were based on the law of war in some respects, but were more restrictive in imposing limits based on law enforcement standards.

The criteria were that: (1) the intended target is a combatant in the armed conflict; (2) arrest of the target is not feasible; (3) senior civilian officials must approve the operation; (4) efforts must be taken to minimize civilian casualties; (5) the strike occurs in an area not under Israeli control; and (6) the target is deemed a future threat to commit terrorism, not simply someone who has engaged in terrorism in the past.[19] Israel first presented the names of proposed targets to the Palestinian Authority, with a request that they be arrested. If the Authority refused to act, Israel then determined if it would be able to effect an arrest itself. If not, an operation against the target was planned.[20] Approval by the Prime Minister was required both to permit planning a targeting operation against an individual, and later to conduct the strike.

Finally, the third stage, beginning in early 2003, marked the expansion of permissible targets to include Palestinian political leaders, with the goal of deterring attacks by making leaders fear for their lives.[21] This reflected concern that, while Israel by that point was able to stop more than 80% of planned suicide bombings, the number of attempted bombings was continuing to increase.[22] According to Bergman, this raised the specter that "over time, terrorist groups would learn from each individual defeat and would adapt and get smarter and tougher, leading to a potentially endless escalation in a potentially endless war."[23]

The assumption was that "what the leaders of the jihadist terror organizations wanted their followers to do—suicide attacks—would take on a different dimension when a price tag was attached, namely their own lives."[24] Furthermore, Israeli officials did not accept the distinction between political and military Palestinian leaders for many individuals. As one official put it, "The leaders who are called 'political' are involved in everything. They lay down the policy and issue orders about when to carry out attacks and when to hold back."[25]

Israeli strikes during the Second Intifada were conducted by snipers, Apache helicopters firing laser-guided missiles, fighter planes with bombs, booby-trapping cars or phone booths, or installing land mines along the routes of suspected terrorists.[26] Between October 2000 and July 2007, Israel carried out 134 operations on 218 designated targets. During that period, the monthly targeting rate varied between zero and six, with the exception of June 2003 when it increased to ten. Some 25% of these were against relatively high-level leaders, while 75% were low-level militants.[27]

In the study described below by Falk and Hafetz, the authors identified a total of 213 strikes between November 2000 and November 2010. In 158, or 74%, of these there were no civilian deaths. The 55, or 26%, of strikes in which there were such deaths range from one or two in 36 cases (17% of strikes and 65% of strikes with civilian deaths), up to 14 in one case.[28] Some 69% of the 159 targeting attempts between September 2000 and April 2004 were in the West Bank, with the remainder in Gaza.[29] The percentage in the West Bank declined sharply after that because of Israeli occupation of that area in Operation Defensive Shield, and the construction of a separation fence between it and Israel.

EMPIRICAL RESEARCH

Determining the impact of Israeli targeted killing on terrorism prior to the Second Intifada is quite challenging. First, Israel generally did not then acknowledge engaging in such operations, which makes it difficult to determine how many occurred. In addition, the goals of targeting likely varied from intercepting specific threats to weakening terrorist groups to reducing the threat of attacks. Devising metrics to determine whether a particular strike accomplished one or more of these goals is difficult. Moreover, to the extent the targeting was intended to serve broad aims in an ongoing political conflict, it is difficult to isolate its impact from a multitude of other factors that have shaped the course of that conflict.

By contrast, Israel's acknowledgment of targeting during the Second Intifada permits identification of individual strikes. In addition, the main immediate goal of targeting was to reduce the risk of suicide bombing. This makes it feasible to attempt to analyze the extent to which targeting achieved this purpose. For these reasons, empirical research on Israeli targeting operations has focused on the period between 2000 and 2008, and on whether there was any relationship between targeted strikes and the number and lethality of Palestinian attacks in general and suicide bombings in particular. The discussion below describes these studies and their findings. They are organized in reverse chronological order below so that the reader can appreciate how some studies relied on earlier ones.

Kaplan, Mintz, Mishal & Samban (2005)

Edward Kaplan, Alex Mintz, Shaul Mishal, and Claudio Samban analyze the rate of suicide bombings in Israel from 2001 through 2003, along with the number of targeted strikes and arrests of terrorist suspects over the same period.[30] Israel relied mainly on targeting to respond to bombings from 2001 through late March 2002, but, as noted, thereafter combined this with military operations in the West Bank that focused, among other things, on arrests of those suspected of involvement in suicide bombings.

The authors found that suicide bombings increased rapidly during the period of reliance on targeting, but decreased significantly once Israel shifted its focus to arrest of terrorist suspects. The authors suggest that the data are consistent with a "terror stock" model, which regards suicide bombing attempts as dependent on the number of persons available to plan and execute such attacks. "Increases in the terror stock," the authors maintain, "thus reflect the recruitment of new terrorists, whereas decreases occur due to Israeli tactical actions or because of suicide bombings themselves."[31] The authors model the terror stock as changing daily based on these dynamics.

The authors find that while 1.8 terror suspects are killed per targeting operation, the terror stock increases by 6.8 for each strike. They suggest that this is because strikes "motivate recruitment to the terror stock."[32] Kaplan et al. argue that this difference between lethal strikes and arrests makes sense when conceptualizing terrorist organizations as networks. While targeted killings serve only to remove individuals who are nodes in such networks, arrests enable interrogation of suspects, which could lead to the discovery of links to more nodes in the network. The authors conclude that "offensive military measures are unlikely to prove effective against suicide bombings."[33] They describe Operation Defensive Shield in 2002 in the West Bank as inaugurating the policy of preventive arrests that they regard as effective.

While Operation Defensive Shield did expand the opportunity to make arrests, it also was the largest Israeli military offensive since the Six-Day War in 1967. Israel called up 30,000 reserves in the Israeli Defense Forces (IDF), placed Yasser Arafat under siege in his compound, and conducted ground troop incursions into six major cities. A UN investigation reported that 497 Palestinians were killed during the operation, and the World Bank estimated $361 million worth of property damage in the West Bank. It thus seems reasonable to characterize Operation Defense Shield as not simply consisting of preventive arrests. Any analysis would need to distinguish the effect of such arrests from other components of the operation.

In addition, Charles Kirchofer notes that a terror-stock model does not consider functional differences among various members of a terrorist organization, which may affect its ability to engage in attacks. "Not all members of the organization," he says, "are equally capable."[34] Kirchofer also argues that having a larger stock does not automatically mean more attempted attacks. As he notes, "Hamas carries out far fewer attacks now than it did during the Second Intifada, but the reason for this is not because it has fewer militant members. Hamas makes strategic and tactical decisions. It is not simply a machine for converting recruits into attackers."[35] These considerations suggest some caution in assessing the findings of this study.

Kaplan, Mintz & Mishal (2006)

Edward H. Kaplan, Alex Mintz, and Shaul Mishal rely on the data set described immediately above to test a series of models designed to estimate the effects of targeted killing and arrests on monthly Palestinian suicide bombing attacks and Israeli responses from January 2001 to December 2003.[36] The authors describe these models as "more flexible than those that Kaplan et al. (2005) considered, and they do not rely on the terror-stock assumptions made previously."[37] Their models in this study treat the suicide bombing attack rate in a given month as a function of Israeli tactics in the current and prior months. The goal is to determine whether targeted killing and arrests have different impacts on the likelihood of increases or decreases in the number of suicide attacks, along with the marginal impact of each measure on the timing of future attacks.

While targeted killings and arrests separately did not provide good fits with the authors' data, including both in the model was strongly predictive of suicide bombing attempts. A targeted killing in a given month was associated with a 9.6% increase in the suicide attack rate in that month. This translates into an increase of 2.34 times the prevailing monthly rate. Thus, if the mean suicide attack rate was 3.33 per month, the model predicts that an additional killing would lead to roughly eight more suicide bombing attacks both in that month and in succeeding months. Exactly how many succeeding months is unclear, but the authors describe it as "many, many months."[38]

On the other hand, a marginal increase in arrests in a given month was associated with a 3.1% reduction in the rate of suicide bombing in that month. The authors calculate that this translates into a reduction of 0.8 suicide bombing attacks in that month and the months that follow. Kaplan et al. note that the number of arrests in their data (316) is much greater than the total number of targeted killings (75). Thus, although the counterproductive impact of a single targeted killing is greater than the benefit of a single arrest, "the sheer volume of such arrests had a substantial effect."[39] The authors conclude that "preventive arrests, and not targeted killings, were more responsible for the decline in suicide-bombing attacks in Israel between March 2002 and April 2004."[40]

The authors acknowledge the possibility of other contributing explanations for outcomes. Israel began constructing a security fence in the West Bank in mid-2002, which may have affected the rate of attacks. By the end of the study period, however, only about one-quarter of it had been completed. They also note that border closures and curfews may have affected attacks resulting from infiltration from the West Bank. They suggest that the timing of such measures likely correlated with arrest operations, so that it is difficult to separate out the contribution of each measure. Finally, they acknowledge that their study does not differentiate between targeting political leaders and targeting others. With a few exceptions, however, Israel did not begin targeting political leaders until the summer of 2003, near the end of the study.

Byman (2006)

Daniel Byman analyzes the intensified use of targeted killing by the Israeli government during the Second Intifada from 2000 to 2005.[41] The program during this period targeted both leaders and mid-level persons with specialized skills who were regarded as terrorist members of Palestinian organizations. Relying on figures from the National Memorial Institute for the Prevention of Terrorism (MIPT), Byman examines the extent to which Israel's targeting campaign affected the number of fatalities from Hamas attacks.

While the number of attacks increased from 19 in 2001 to 179 in 2005, the number of Israel deaths from such attacks declined over the same period from 75 to 21. The attack lethality rate rose from 3.9 deaths per attack to 5.4 in 2002, and then declined to 0.98 in 2003, 0.33 in 2004, and 0.11 in 2005. Byman argues that targeted killing contributed to this decline because "the number of skilled terrorists is quite limited. Bomb makers, terrorism trainers, forgers, recruiters, and terrorist leaders are scarce... When these individuals are arrested or killed... new recruits will not pose the same kind of threat."[42]

Byman argues furthermore that "Palestinian terrorists' own demands and actions have testified to the impact of Israel's targeted killing campaign. Again and again Palestinian groups have insisted on an end to the policy."[43] In 2004, after a lethal strike on the leader of Hamas' political wing Abdel Aziz Rantisi, for instance, the organization announced that it had appointed a new leader but would not publicly name him. In 2005, Hamas declared that it would accept a cease-fire if Israel would suspend its targeting operations. Byman also notes that the effectiveness of targeting depends on conducting it at a rapid pace. Between 2000 and 2005, Israel successfully targeted 203 persons who were mainly members of Hamas, the Palestinian Islamic Jihad (PIJ), and the Second Martyrs Brigade.

Byman acknowledges that attributing reductions in Palestinian violence to targeting alone is not warranted, since Israel employed several other counterterrorism tools during his study period. These enabled Israel "to arrest suspects previously beyond their reach, greatly increasing the intelligence available and disrupting many terrorist cells."[44] Given the simultaneous use of these tools, it is difficult to isolate the exact cause of declines in fatalities. This is true, although, as some studies below describe, these measures were used mainly in the West Bank. This may make outcomes in Gaza a clearer indication of the impacts of targeted strikes.

Hafez & Hatfield (2006)

Mohammed Hafez and Joseph Hatfield examine the effect of Israel's targeted strikes on the number of Palestinian attacks from September 29, 2000 to June 16, 2004.[45] They find that during that period, Israel killed 151 Palestinian political leaders and military commanders at various levels. The authors conduct a multivariate regression to determine whether targeted killing alone or in combination with offensive military operations affects the number of successful and unsuccessful attacks. The authors consider intervals ranging from one to four weeks between targeting and Palestinian attacks.

They find no statistically significant correlation between targeting and the number of attacks. Nor, contrary to a second hypothesis, do such strikes tend to increase attacks.[46] They find that Israel's ability to foil attacks increased substantially over the study period, but that targeting did not make a significant contribution to this. Defensive measures, they speculate, may be more responsible than targeting for the decrease in the rate of successful attacks.

Finally, the authors find that targeted strikes in combination with offensive military operations do not significantly reduce attacks. Despite such measures, "attacks continued virtually unabated."[47] This provides support, they suggest, for attributing the decline in the rate of successful attacks to defensive measures. Hafetz and Hatfield maintain that defensive measures can have the effect of reducing opportunities for terrorists to engage in violence, while targeted killing "can do little to influence opportunities for violence, unless they target actual 'ticking bombs' on their way to conduct an attack."[48]

This study is commendable for its effort to isolate the effect of targeting apart from other counterterrorism measures. As with other studies that rely on regression analysis without using an identification strategy, however, its findings do not provide the level of confidence in causal explanations that could arise from using such a strategy.

Zussman & Zussman (2006)

Asaf Zussman and Noam Zussman note that most empirical studies attempt to assess the effectiveness of targeting by comparing the number of terrorist incidents before and after strikes.[49] They suggest, however, that this approach may not be appropriate in analyzing Israel's targeting program because of the many other counterterrorism measures that Israel has used simultaneously with targeting. They thus seek to use what they call an "indirect test" to evaluate the effectiveness of targeting.[50] Based on the view that terrorism had a significant adverse macroeconomic effect from the fall of 2000 until the time of their study, they argue that the Israeli stock market should react positively to news of effective counterterrorism steps but negatively to news of counterproductive ones.

The authors review 159 Israeli attempted targeting attempts directed at members of Palestinian terrorist organizations from September 2002 to April 2004. These resulted in the deaths of 317 individuals, almost 80% of whom were members of terrorist organizations. The study established the seniority of each target and whether the individual belonged to the political or military wing of the organization. They characterize political leaders as primarily responsible for political and spiritual guidance, while military leaders as responsible mainly for planning operations, recruiting, training, arming forces, and conducting attacks.

Zussman and Zussman hypothesize that the death of a senior military leader has more potential to disrupt terrorist operations than the death of a political leader, while attempts to kill a senior political leader trigger greater motivation for retaliation. They therefore expect that the successful targeting of a senior military leader is more likely to be followed by a decrease in terrorism than the successful targeting of a senior political leader. The death of a low-ranking terrorist is likely to have a fairly small effect on both the capability of the organization and its motivation to retaliate.

Zussman and Zussman run several regressions in which the dependent variable is the daily percentage change in the Tel Aviv 25 stock index. They find a strong correlation between attempted targeting of senior political targets and a decline in the index of between 0.7 and 1.1 percentage points. They also find a strong correlation between attempted targeting of senior military leaders and an increase in the index of between 0.5 and 0.7 percentage points.

The authors find that if the target is a Fatah military leader, there is a significant negative effect on the market compared to targeting leaders of other organizations. They attribute this to the fact that Fatah was the ruling party in the Palestinian Authority during the period under study, so that such strikes threatened political stability. Finally, they find that the effects of targeting on the market persisted for between a few days and a few weeks, rather than reflecting a sharp change followed by an immediate reversion to the prior value.

The authors also compare the responses of the Palestinian stock market to targeting of senior political leaders, and of senior military leaders, which were similar to the reactions of the Tel Aviv market. The Palestinian market reacted even more negatively to targeting attempts against senior Palestinian political leaders, and responded positively to targeting attempts against senior Palestinian military leaders, although the response was not statistically significant.

This study is an interesting attempt to differentiate the effect of targeting attempts from other counterterrorism measures by using a metric of effectiveness other than terrorist activity. It is based on the idea that "terrorism can be viewed as a form of economic warfare," and the assumption that market activity reflects optimism or pessimism about the future based upon perceptions of the likely effectiveness of targeting different types of individuals.[51] While this is theoretically possible, perceptions of effectiveness are of course not the same as actual effectiveness.

Jacobson & Kaplan (2007)

Daniel Jacobson and Edward Kaplan test the predictive power of a model that assumes that Palestinian suicide bombings and Israeli targeted killings are responses to the use of these tactics by each other.[52] This game theoretic model posits that Palestinians seek to maximize the net payoff from suicide bombings, conceptualized as the number of casualties resulting from such attacks minus the costs of planning them and the deaths of those who conduct them. For the Israeli government, the payoff is the number of Israeli and Palestinian civilian lives saved, minus civilian lives lost from targeting and increases in terrorist recruitment in response to successful targeting. Their data for 2001–2003 indicate about one Palestinian civilian death per targeting, and 5.5 Israeli citizens killed per suicide bombing attack.

The calculus for Palestinians is to determine the number of attacks that will maximize their payoff without inducing Israel to respond with a targeted killing operation. Israel must determine whether the anticipated number of suicide bombing attacks warrants targeting to prevent or at least reduce the number of deaths from such attacks, while considering the effect on Palestinian recruitment. Based on a targeting success rate of 50%, the authors find that the government can withstand up to 2.46 attacks before it is necessary to respond with targeting. Based on different assumptions reflected in various other models, the analysis suggests that, notwithstanding the recruitment effect and its potential to increase suicide attacks, targeted killing in some cases can be an optimal counterterrorism measure in terms of saving total Palestinian and Israeli civilian lives.

The authors acknowledge that the models assume perfect information on both sides, and that it would be worthwhile to relax this assumption in future analysis. In addition, they treat terrorists as a homogenous group, even though they note that there are significant differences among them. They nonetheless suggest that the results of their models indicate that game theory may be useful in analyzing the effect of different counterterrorism measures.

Kober (2007)

Asa Kober examined the effect on Palestinian suicide bombing attacks of Israel's use of targeted killing against members at all levels of Palestinian organizations between September 2000 and April 2004.[53] Kober categorized targeting in several ways, such as against low-level, military, political, and religious officials. He maintains that targeting military leaders was not effective in reducing violence by Hamas. Some 75% of military targets, he indicates, were "low-level local military leaders or operatives," who were easily replaced.[54]

Kober notes that attempted Palestinian suicide bombing attacks increased from 54 in 2001 (34 successful), to 167 in 2002 (55 successful), to 209 in 2003 (25 successful). In 2004, the number dropped to 130 (14 successful). He also notes that the number of Hamas attacks increased from 19 in 2001 to 34 in 2002, 46 in 2003, and 202 in 2004, declining slightly to 179 in 2005 (most of which were in the first half of that year before Hamas agreed to temporarily suspend hostilities).[55]

Kober does acknowledge the sharp decline in successful suicide bombings beginning in 2002. The percentage of attempted bombings that were successful fell from 62% in 2001 to 33% in 2002, 8% in 2003, and 9% in 2004. He suggests that targeting nonetheless was not necessarily responsible for this decrease, since much of it may have been attributable to Israel's launch of Operation Defensive Shield in the West Bank in late March 2002.

Kober argues, however, that strikes against Hamas' political leaders in August 2003, March 2004, and April 2004 appear to have influenced the organization's decision to unilaterally suspend hostilities in June 2004. He also notes that Hamas discontinued rocket attacks on Israel in September 2005 after a warning that continuing the attacks would result in strikes against political leaders.

Kober does not provide any empirical basis for his claim that targeting military leaders was ineffective other than to note the increasing number of attacks during the first few years of the Second Intifada, and to refer to Kaplan, et al.'s quantitative study described above finding that targeted strikes are associated with an increase in suicide bombing attempts. A study that attempts to identify any different effects of targeting military and political leaders ideally would examine variables such as attempted and successful attacks, and fatalities from attacks, separately for the period during which Israel targeted only military leaders and the period when it expanded its targets to include political leaders. The limitations of this study thus suggest caution in drawing inferences about causality from it.

Jaeger & Paserman (2009)

David Jaeger and M. Daniele Paserman examined the period from September 20, 2000 to January 15, 2005 in order "to estimate empirically whether suicide attacks generate a violent Israeli response and whether targeted killings lead to changes in Palestinian violent behavior."[56] The study aims to test the "assertion that the Palestinians and Israelis are engaged in a perpetual causal tit-for-tat cycle of suicide attacks and targeted killing."[57] They focus on weekly data on fatalities from targeted strikes and suicide bombings, controlling for several variables that reflect the potential influence of the varying intensity of the conflict.

The authors conclude that targeted killing of Palestinian leaders results in a decline in Israelis killed in suicide attacks in the first week after a targeted killing. Evidence is especially strong that the number of such fatalities declines from attackers originating in the district where the targeted killing occurred. On the other hand, the number of targeted killings aggregated over longer two-, four-, eight-, and twelve-week intervals is not correlated with subsequent Israeli fatalities from suicide bombings.

At the same time, there is no evidence that targeted killings result in increases in Israeli fatalities from suicide bombings.[58] This is consistent with the authors' earlier analysis of patterns of Israeli and Palestinian fatalities from all sources, which found "strong evidence that the Israelis react in a significant and predictable way to Palestinian violence against them, but no evidence that Palestinians react to Israeli violence. This stands in contrast to the idea that the Israelis and Palestinians are engaged in a 'tit-for-tat' cycle of violence."[59]

The authors express confidence in the ability of their analysis to provide support for conclusions about causality. This is because "conditional on the total number of [suicide] attacks, the number of successful attacks is as good as random. Whether an attack is successful or not (in terms of Israeli fatalities) is at least partially a function of chance," since just over half of suicide attacks were successful.[60]

They also acknowledge the potential for omitted variable bias, noting that whether Israel is more likely to close its borders or increase its level of alertness following violence emanating from the West Bank and Gaza may affect their findings. They attempt to control for this by "including the fraction of checkpoints that were completely closed as a measure of Israeli vigilance," although they are able only to do so from October 2003 onward because data were not available until then. Controlling for this "has only a very minor effect on the other coefficients in the regression."[61] They argue that the fact that the impact of targeting on Israeli fatalities is especially strong in districts in which the targeting occurred lends further support to the claim that targeting reduces short-term Israeli fatalities due to its incapacitation effect.

The authors find that Israel "responds to both suicide attacks and other Israeli fatalities with lethal force in a regular and predictable way, with each successful suicide attack leading to approximately seven additional

Palestinian deaths, and each Israeli death caused by other means leading to about one additional Palestinian death."[62] They find no relationship, however, between such targeting and failed suicide attacks.

The authors also analyze the number of successful and unsuccessful suicide attacks after targeted strikes, which constitute what they call "intended" attacks. They estimate that that intended attacks increase when there are up to 3.2 targeted killings in the previous month and decline with a larger number of successful strikes. They conclude, "[W]e find some evidence of an inverted-U shaped relationship with targeted killings, suggesting that at low levels of targeted killings the vengeance factor dominates and Palestinians are driven to intensify their efforts to respond violently; at higher levels, however, the incapacitation or deterrent effect dominates, and the overall level of Palestinian violence diminishes."[63]

Jaeger and Paserman conclude that their study does not provide support for the claim that suicide attacks and targeted killings follow a never-ending retaliatory pattern. "Israel clearly reacts to suicide attacks," they say, "but targeted killings would appear to *reduce* subsequent Israeli fatalities."[64] They acknowledge that their evidence suggests that targeted killings lead to increases in attempted attacks, "but this activity does not seem to lead to increased levels of Israeli fatalities."[65] They attribute this decline in fatalities to weakening of Palestinian capabilities rather than increased Israeli vigilance and defensive measures.

Falk (2015)

A study by Ophir Falk, whose database of targeted killings is described above, finds that Israeli targeted strikes reduced suicide bombing fatalities from late September 2000 to March 2009.[66] The study also examines the impact of targeting in Gaza compared to the West Bank, since targeting was the main tactic Israel used in the former. Finally, the study assesses the impact of targeting political/ideological leaders compared to other militants.

Falk's independent variable is the number of strikes in each month, with the number of targeted killings within a month recorded as one observation. The dependent variable is the number of suicide bombing fatalities within the first 50 days after a month in which a strike occurs, from 50 to 100 days after the month, and from 100 to 150 days afterward. The first increment of 50 days is based on information from experts that it takes about this much time to organize and execute an attack after a targeted killing.[67]

Strikes took place in 101 of the 111 months in the study period, with a total of 213 targeted strikes. A strike occurred in Gaza in 54 months, or 53.4% of the 101 months. About 8% of the months had political/ideological leaders as targets.

Falk finds that the number of suicide bombing fatalities decreased after targeted strikes most strongly immediately after a targeted killing, for up to 50 days. Any effect on fatalities then gradually decreased over time. "This was particularly evident," Falk notes, "for cases of targeted killing in Gaza and subsequent suicide bombing originating out of Gaza."[68] The highest increase in fatalities following targeted strikes occurred in 2001–2002, while the greatest decreases in fatalities were spread out from 2000 to 2007. The largest declines followed strikes in July 2001 and March 2004. While it is difficult to isolate the effect of targeted killing from other counterterrorism measures in the West Bank, such measures largely were already in place in Gaza. Falk thus regards that area thus as a particularly useful focus for determining the impact of targeting.

Falk found that the targeting of senior political/ideological figures had the most effect in terms of reducing suicide bombings. The deaths of five of six prominent leaders from 2000 to 2006, all in Gaza, were followed by a decrease in suicide bombing fatalities. Falk regards this as consistent with qualitative evidence that Palestinian groups were especially concerned about the targeting of political/ideological leaders. Hamas, for instance, he notes, demanded a stop to targeted killing as a condition for ceasing rocket fire directed at Israel in 2012. Falk concludes, "[T]argeted killing did not end the conflict or achieve peace... But it did have a clear effect on subsequent suicide bombing fatalities."[69]

Kirchofer (2016)

Charles Kirchofer analyzes Israel's attempts to target major Hamas leaders between 2000 and 2007.[70] His analysis relies on qualitative evidence of the timing of successful targeting operations and differences in the extent to which Hamas retaliated for them. He argues that any reduction in suicide bombing attacks following a strike reflects not simply disruption of terrorist group operations, but the role of targeting as an instrument of what he calls "compellence," or coercion.[71] This seeks to induce a party to change its behavior, rather than to deter it from changing the status quo. Targeted killing, says Kirchofer, is "always an escalation and therefore signals a change in the status quo. In other words, the actual use, as opposed to the threat, of targeted killing is compellent, not deterrent."[72]

Kirchofer maintains that this framework sheds light on why targeting sometimes increased and sometimes reduced Hamas violence over this period. Targeting that occurred when Hamas regarded itself as exercising restraint, such as adhering to a cease-fire, encouraged the group to retaliate. This is because there was no incentive not to, since its most important leaders already were being killed. Targeting in this case did not serve as a deterrent. When violence already was high, Hamas reduced attacks in the hope that targeting would decrease. In this case, targeting served as a compellent.

In support of his claim, Kirchofer quotes Ziad Abu Amr, a member of the Palestinian Legislative Council who was involved in cease-fire negotiations with Hamas in 2003:

> I think the attempt on [Hamas leader Abdel Aziz] Rantissi's life [on June 10, 2003] was a catalyst of some sort. Especially when certain intelligence came to the Palestinian side to the effect that Israel was determined to liquidate all the Hamas leaders. And I think the Hamas leaders and we, too, took that very seriously. And I remember I asked... are you better off with your leaders around, is Hamas better off with its founders and top leaders around, or do you think this is irrelevant? If you think it is important... I think we have to do something political about it right now.[73]

Kirschofer notes that with the eventual death of important leaders Rantisi and Sheik Ahmed Yassin in 2004, Hamas carried out just two suicide attacks in 2005 and in 2006 "announced it was halting suicide bombing altogether."[74] He acknowledges that various security operations in the West Bank may have contributed to Hamas' agreement to a cease-fire. Nonetheless, he concludes that "[t]he rapid shifts in Hamas' behavior observed in the immediate aftermath of the targeted killing of each of its political leaders all strongly suggest that targeted killings were affecting Hamas' decisions."[75] Kirchofer does not, however, provide detailed data on Hamas attacks surrounding the targeting of the various leaders that he discusses, which makes it difficult to assess his claim.

Abrahms and Mierau (2017)

Abrahms and Mierau combine empirical methods with case studies to assess the impact of targeted strikes in the Israel-Occupied Territories area from 2000 to 2004.[76] Chapter 6 will discuss the portion of their study that discusses strikes in Afghanistan and Pakistan. Their dependent variable is the percentage change in the proportion of attacks against military versus civilian targets fourteen days after a successful strike. They find that successful strikes are followed by statistically significant redirection of terrorist attacks from military to civilian targets within the two weeks after the strike, while unsuccessful strikes have no effect on attack targets.

The study examines 130 attempted strikes on the "leaders of the most lethal Palestinian groups during the Second Intifada."[77] The authors say that their analysis "excludes targeted killing attempts against non-leaders." They do not specify how they define leaders, but note that they rely on the determination of seniority by Zussman & Zussman, whose study is described above.[78] Of these attempts, 110 were successful. The analysis examines whether there was a change in the proportion of attacks against military versus civilian targets 14 days after a successful strike. The authors find that attacks on military targets drop by 50% during this period, indicating that a successful strike has a "substantively important impact on tactical decisions of Palestinian groups."[79] They do not find that a successful strike against the leader of one group affected behavior of other groups.

Abrahams and Mierau argue that successful strikes deplete the ranks of experienced leaders who are more strategically discriminate, which enables lower-level group members who are less skilled and strategic to conduct attacks. This in turn may harm a group by eroding its political support because of public outcry over the deaths of innocent civilians.

Given the use of more varied counterterrorism measures in the West Bank than in Gaza, it would have been useful to differentiate strikes by location. In addition, the authors maintain that whether or not a strike is successful depends on factors unrelated to terrorist group characteristics, which allows them to use successful strikes as a treatment group and unsuccessful ones as a control group. This effort to employ an identification strategy is commendable, but questions nonetheless remain about whether the success of a targeted strike is in fact purely random. If not, the success of a strike will not be wholly exogenous, thus limiting the strength of inferences of causality.

Falk & Hefetz (2019)

Ophir Falk and Amir Hefetz examine 213 successful Israeli targeted strikes against members of Palestinian groups in the Occupied Territories between November 9, 2000 and November 17, 2010 to examine whether strikes in which civilians were killed had an effect on the subsequent number of, and fatalities and injuries from, Palestinian suicide bombings of Israeli targets.[80] The periods following the targeted strikes were organized according to up to 49 days, 50–99 days, and 100–150 days after each strike. The authors aggregated the number of targeted strikes carried out 25 days before and 25 days after the targeted strike in order to control for potential multiple counting effects and to enable them to test the separate effect of several strikes occurring within a brief period of time.

There were no civilian casualties in 158, or 74%, of the 213 strikes. The authors found higher numbers of suicide bombings, and fatalities and injuries from them, following a strike that caused civilian deaths than one that did not. In the first two time periods encompassing 0–99 days, suicide bombings and casualties were significantly higher following a strike resulting in such deaths.

The authors find that fatalities and injuries are the same regardless of whether a strike is in the West Bank or Gaza. However, "the number of suicide bombings out of Gaza was similar whether there were unintended [civilian] deaths in the targeted killing or not."[81] The increase in the number of suicide bombings after a strike in the West Bank was four times greater than the increase following a strike in Gaza.

The authors thus conclude that targeted strikes are most effective in combating suicide bombing when they result in no civilian casualties. They acknowledge that factors other than casualties from targeted strikes may affect subsequent suicide bombings, such as "arrests, roadblocks, fences and barriers, or a change in political setting."[82] As the discussion above of Falk's study mentioned, for instance, Israel launched a major military offensive into the West Bank during the Second Intifada.

By contrast, "in Gaza, targeted killing was the only practical method used in the time in question. There was a fence in place prior to the time in question and the use of other means such as roadblocks, house demolition, and arrests were much less practical, if at all."[83] Falk and Hefetz maintain that data from Gaza therefore provide especially strong evidence of increases in casualties from terrorist attacks when strikes cause civilian casualties. They suggest that the lack of any statistically significant relationship between strikes with or without civilian casualties in the *number* of suicide attacks may be due to the relatively small number of such attacks in that territory.

Jordan (2019)

Jenna Jordan's recent book *Leadership Decapitation: Strategic Targeting of Terrorist Organizations* draws on empirical research on leadership targeting and terrorist group activity to identify circumstances in which such targeting is likely to be effective.[84] Jordan defines decapitation to include both killing and capturing leaders, whom she defines as "top leaders and members of the upper echelon."[85] The book includes discussions of large terrorist group databases, as well as of Hamas, Peru's Shining Path, AQ, and the Islamic State (ISIS). This chapter discusses the portion of her book on Hamas. Chapter 4 discusses her analysis of decapitation of terrorist groups in large databases, while Chapter 6 describes her work on Al-Qaeda and ISIS.

Jordan analyzes 81 Israeli "decapitations," which include *both* arrests and targeted strikes, against high-level leaders of Hamas from 1988 to 2010.[86] She defines a leader as "either the top leader of an organization or a member of the upper echelon who holds a position of authority within the organization."[87] Jordan's dependent variable is the number and lethality of all types of Hamas attacks. Based on a year-by-year comparison of decapitations with Hamas attacks, she concludes that decapitations have not been effective in impairing the operational capacity of this group.

Jordan describes the early years of the conflict between Israel and Hamas as ones in which Israel relied mainly on arrests of operatives and low-level members of the organization. As described earlier, with the beginning of the Second Intifada in the fall of 2000 and increases in suicide bombings, Israel responded with an increase in its targeting operations. Below are the figures for the main years of the Second Intifada on which Jordan relies in arriving at conclusions about the impact of targeting during that period.[88] In some cases, the numbers represent estimates of figures on graphs whose values are not specifically identified in the discussion in the book.

Arrests/Deaths
Hamas leaders
2000: 1 arrest/1 death
2001: 4 arrests/6 deaths
2002: 5 deaths
2003: 13 deaths
2004: 3 arrests/7 deaths
2005: 3 arrests/1 death
2006: 2 arrests/1 death
2007: 2 deaths
2008: 0

Hamas attacks/Fatalities
2000: 1 attack/0 deaths
2001: 31 attacks/125 deaths
2002: 31 attacks/204 deaths
2003: 34 attacks/102 deaths
2004: 14 attacks/30–41 deaths[a]
2005: 13 attacks/4 deaths
2006: 19 attacks/10 deaths
2007: 37 attacks/76 deaths
2008: 10 attacks/8 deaths

[a]Page 109 says there were 30 deaths from attacks in 2004, while page 111 says there were 41

Jordan notes that trends in Hamas attacks could be due to factors other than successful targeting. As the data indicate, the most intensive decapitation operations against high-level Hamas leaders in her data were conducted between 2001 and 2007. The lethality of attacks by Hamas declined from 2002 to 2006, with an increase in 2007, followed by declines in the number and lethality of attacks thereafter. Jordan acknowledges that Hamas' attacks generally became less lethal after targeted strikes intensified beginning in 2001, but suggests that this may be attributable in part to the construction of a separation fence in the West Bank in 2003. In addition, she says that the data indicate that Hamas "was able to continue its activities in the face of repeated attacks against its leadership."[89] In other words, her dependent variable is the ability of Hamas to survive and conduct operations, rather than the number and lethality of attacks. This is what leads her to conclude that decapitations were ineffective.

Jordan suggests that during the first eight years of the Second Intifada through 2008, "a decline in targeting efforts coincided with a decline in the number of attacks carried out by Hamas."[90] Since her comparison is between targeting and Hamas attacks in the same year, however, this does not seem to be the case throughout this period. For instance, targeting declined from 10 to 5 from 2001 to 2002, but attacks remained the same. Targeting again declined from four to three from 2005 to 2006, but attacks increased from 13 to 19. Finally, targeting declined from three to two operations from 2006 to 2007, but attacks increased from 19 to 37.

There were two years in which there were declines in both targeting and attacks, two in which there were declines in targeting but increases in attacks, one year in which there was a decline in targeting but attacks remained the same, and one year in which there was an increase in targeting and an increase in attacks. It thus seems more plausible to say that there was no pattern in the effect of targeting on the number of attacks. This is consistent with Jordan's ultimate conclusion that targeting was "not effective in hindering the group's operational capacity,"[91] at least as measured by Hamas' ability to continue to engage in attacks.

As described above, other studies conclude that targeting was effective because of its association with fewer fatalities from attacks. Those who regard this as a better metric of effectiveness thus will disagree with Jordan's conclusion. In addition, Jordan's reliance on annual data makes it difficult to evaluate any causal claims compared to studies that focus on briefer periods or periods surrounding individual strikes to derive estimates. There is no indication of the distribution of either decapitations or attacks during each year, nor an indication of how their timing relates to other major counterterrorism initiatives during the year. In addition, without reliance on an identification strategy it is always possible that targeting may not be exogenous. It could be, for instance, that any decline in Hamas attacks in a given year causes a lower number of targeting operations in that year, rather than vice versa.

Jordan notes that her set of 81 decapitations "is by no means the universe of cases," but she does not indicate the criteria by which they were selected.[92] This could be a problem in comparing annual decapitations and annual attacks if the distribution of the decapitations is not representative of their distribution over the study period. Finally, it would have been helpful to differentiate data for Gaza and the West Bank, since there were several counterterrorism measures in the latter that may make trends in Gaza a better indication of the specific impact of targeting. These considerations set some limits on the ability to draw robust conclusions from her study about the effect of Israeli decapitation.

The study nonetheless could provide a useful analysis of the evolution of Hamas based on Jordan's theory of organizational resilience. As she suggests, "instead of carrying out large scale attacks and suicide bombings, Hamas focused on building tunnels in the aftermath of the Second Intifada."[93] Jordan regards this "substitution effect" as indicative of resilience in response to targeting that preserved Hamas' organizational capability.[94] Unlike others who focus on the lethality of attacks or on the number and lethality of suicide bombings, Jordan regards the inability of targeting to degrade this capability for adaptation as indicative of its ineffectiveness.

CONCLUSION

Evaluating the impact of Israeli targeted killing on Palestinian terrorist groups during the Second Intifada is challenging. Israel undoubtedly hoped that targeting might serve broader purposes, but its immediate goal appears to have been to reduce the number and lethality of suicide bombing attacks. Many studies therefore use these metrics as the dependent variables in their analysis. Most studies use as their independent variable the number of targeted killings against members at all levels of Palestinian groups, rather than high-level leaders.

There appears to be general agreement that the number of militant attacks of all types increased during 2000–2004, which was the most intensive period of targeting. There was a significant decline in suicide bombing attempts and fatalities, however, beginning in 2003. In addition, the rate of fatalities per attack began to decline in 2005 and continued through 2008.

Determining Effectiveness

Some studies that conclude that targeting was effective base their conclusion on a comparison of rates of targeting with the number of suicide bombings and fatalities over their period of study. While suggestive, this approach does not provide a robust basis for causal inference. Other studies attempt more detailed analysis of the impact of targeting by examining periods surrounding individual strikes. Falk, for instance, found that targeting was most substantially connected to a decline in fatalities from suicide bombings for up to fifty days, with the effect gradually decreasing over time. Jaeger and Paserman found that targeting resulted in a decline in suicide bombing fatalities in the first week after a strike, but were not associated one way or the other with the level of fatalities beyond that. Falk and Hefetz found an increase in the number of suicide attacks and fatalities after strikes that resulted in civilian casualties compared to strikes with no such casualties.

Assessments of targeting effectiveness will differ depending on whether one focuses on the number of terrorist attacks or on fatalities resulting from them. On the one hand, one might say that the increase in the number of attacks of all types for several years indicates that targeting did not reduce the capacity of groups to launch attacks and may have increased their motivation to do so. On the other hand, one could argue that the decline in fatalities indicates that targeting was successful in reducing the risk to Israelis by weakening the groups' ability to conduct successful attacks. On this view, "the *motivation* and *intention* to carry out attacks has not substantially changed. What has changed is the *capability* of terrorist organizations to carry out significant attacks."[95]

In addition to the decline in fatalities, the decline in the number of suicide attacks beginning in 2003 provides some support for this theory insofar as these types of attacks require especially complex coordination. One might also argue that this decline, and the decline in fatalities from them, achieved Israel's primary goal because of the particular physical and psychological damage caused by these types of attacks.

A challenge in inferring causality, however, is that a variety of measures other than targeting likely influenced the rate of fatalities to some extent. The separation wall in the West Bank, for instance, may have reduced opportunities for significant attacks within Israel, while increased security patrols and deeper intelligence infiltration of groups may have reduced the number of successful attacks and deaths resulting from them.

Jaeger and Paserman attempt to account for these factors by controlling for Israeli vigilance and defensive measures. They conclude that the decline in suicide bombing fatalities reflected the incapacitation effect of targeted killing rather than other counterterrorism measures. Falk suggests that Gaza provides a good opportunity to determine the separate impact of targeting because "a Gaza fence was in place before the examined period, very few arrests were carried out in the area during that time and targeted killing was used practically in isolation as a countermeasure for suicide bombings."[96] He examines data separately for Gaza and the West Bank, and finds that the decline in fatalities was "particularly evident for cases of targeted killing in Gaza and subsequent suicide bombing originating out of Gaza."[97]

To what extent was targeted killing ineffective or even counterproductive because it triggered retaliatory lethal violence by Palestinians? One can point to what appears to be a retaliatory attack in response to a specific targeted killing, but this may not be indicative of underlying patterns. Kaplan and his colleagues argue that the number of suicide bombings during 2001 through March 2002 reflected the recruitment of 6.8 new terrorists resulting from each targeted killing operation. They claim that the decline in suicide bombing after this point resulted from a decline in targeted killing, as Israel shifted focus to conducting more arrests. There was still, however, significant targeting activity after March 2002 through 2004, a period of decline in suicide bombings. In addition, of course, causality could run in the other direction: fewer suicide bombings caused Israel to engage in fewer targeted killings.

Jaeger and Paserman conducted a more detailed analysis that concluded that attempted suicide bombings increase when there are up to 3.2 strikes in a month, but decline after that, although there is a decrease in fatalities from such attacks in the week following a strike. When strikes increase above 3.2 a month, however, attempted attacks decrease. They argue that targeting thus appears to create a desire to retaliate, but that increased targeting can offset this because it can weaken the ability to do so and deter future attacks. This is consistent with Jacobson and Kaplan's game theoretic model, which finds that targeted strikes may be effective in reducing terror attacks in some circumstances despite any increase in terrorist recruitment that may result from such strikes.

Targeting Political Leaders

What about the effect of targeting leaders as opposed to operatives? Hafetz and Hatfield's study of targeting high-level leaders found no statistically significant correlation between targeting and the number of suicide attacks. Zussman and Zussman found that targeting political leaders led to a decline in Israeli and Palestinian stock markets, while targeting military leaders led to an increase.

Other research and evidence, however, suggest that targeting political leaders may have had an impact on suicide attacks. Kirchofer, for instance, mentions the observation by a member of the Palestinian Legislative Council who was involved in cease-fire negotiations with Hamas in 2003 that the unsuccessful targeting of Abdel Aziz Rantisi, the leader of Hamas' political wing, made a significant impression on Hamas leaders. Kirchofer notes that with the 2004 deaths of Rantisi and Hamas founder Sheik Ahmed Yassin, Hamas carried out just two suicide attacks in 2005 and 2006, and then announced a halt to them altogether.

Kober concludes that targeting political leaders was effective and targeting military leaders was ineffective, although he does not rely on any quantitative empirical evidence for his claim. As does Kirchofer, he suggests that the targeting of Hamas political leaders induced that organization to seek a cease-fire in 2004. In addition, Falk finds that the deaths of five of six prominent political/ideological leaders from 2000 to 2006, all in Gaza, were followed by a decrease in suicide bombing fatalities in the 50 days following their deaths.

Bergman provides some qualitative support for the claim that targeting Hamas political leaders helped achieve a decline in suicide bombing. By the time Rantisi was killed in April 2004, he says, Israeli targeting of political leaders "had successfully thrown Hamas into a state of shock and confusion."[98] As other researchers have noted, Hamas appointed a successor to Rantisi but would not publicly disclose his name for fear that he would be targeted.

Bergman reports that two weeks after Rantisi was killed, General Omar Suleiman, the Egyptian intelligence minister, met with top Israeli officials to convey Hamas' willingness to halt suicide attacks if Israel ceased targeted killing.[99] Israel refused because it feared that a truce would only enable Hamas to regroup and regain strength. When three more Hamas leaders were killed, Suleiman approached Israel again in mid-June to note that Hamas had unilaterally ceased suicide bombings, and to reiterate the request for a halt to Israeli targeting. This time, Israel accepted the offer.[100]

Assessing the claim that targeting political leaders led to a decline in suicide bombing is challenging because of the difficulty in isolating the impact of this tactic from various other developments during the conflict. Ideally, an analysis would use an identification strategy that enabled construction of a counterfactual in which use of this tactic was the only difference between two scenarios.

Devising such a strategy is well beyond the scope of this chapter. Short of this, a very rough approach is to review data on suicide bombings before and after significant leadership targeting events. In chronological order, these arguably are: (1) the attempted targeting of Rantisi on June 10, 2003; (2) the successful targeting of Ismail Abu Shanab, the leader of Hamas' political wing, on August 12, 2003; (3) the unsuccessful attack on top Hamas leaders at the house of Abu Ras on September 6, 2003; (4) the successful targeting of Hamas founder Sheik Ahmed Yassin on March 24, 2004; and (5) the successful targeting of Rantisi on April 17, 2004.

Beginning with the first event, relying on Ophir Falk's detailed database of individual suicide bombings, up to the day of the attempt on Rantisi there had been 14 suicide attacks in 2003. These averaged one every 11.5 days. After the attempt on Rantisi in June there were 12 attacks the remainder of the year, which occurred on average every 17 days. This could provide a crude indication that the attempt contributed to a decline in suicide bombing. On the other hand, two bombings that occurred after the attempt were especially deadly. One attack on August 19, 2003 resulted in 24 deaths and 114 injuries. A second on October 4, 2003 caused 21 deaths and 58 injuries.

A second event was the targeted killing on August 12, 2003 of Ismail Abu Shanab, a founder of Hamas, the leader of its political wing, and a main spokesman in the Arabic and foreign media. Bergman says that Hamas was "deeply rattled" by his death, because it had regarded him as "off-limits."[101] To determine a response, Hamas founder Yassin called a September 6 meeting of Hamas' military and political leaders at the home of Dr. Marwan Abu Ras, a major religious figure in Gaza and a member of the Palestinian Legislative Council.

Israel learned about the planned meeting and regarded it as an opportunity to target a substantial portion of top Hamas leadership. The original plan was to drop a bomb on the house, but that was rejected after determining that it would risk causing too many civilian casualties in a nearby apartment building. Intelligence then indicated that the meeting would be held on the third floor of Ras's residence. Officials determined that firing a missile through the window of the building would avoid civilian casualties in the neighboring building. After the missile strike, Israel learned that the meeting was on the ground floor, and Hamas leaders emerged without injury.[102]

Focusing first on the death of Shanab, there were 19 suicide bombings from the beginning of 2003 until his death, for an average of one every 11.8 days. After his death, there were seven during the remainder of the year, averaging one every 20.1 days. This could suggest that his targeting was associated with a reduction in suicide bombing activity. At the same time, the two especially deadly attacks in 2003 described above both occurred after his death.

With respect to the attempted targeting of Hamas leadership at the meeting in Abu Ras's house, there was a suicide bombing three days after the attempt that killed nine Israeli soldiers and injured 18. Bergman regards this as retaliation for the attempted targeting, as well as for targeting other Hamas leaders. "Hamas was flailing," he says, "lashing back at Israel."[103] At the same time, there had been 20 suicide bombings up to that point in the year, which averaged one every 12.5 days. After the attack, there were six in the remainder of the year, which averaged one every 19.3 days. This included one that caused 21 deaths and 58 injuries.

Turning to the targeted killing of Yassin in March 2004, there had been seven suicide bombings that year up until the day of his death, which averaged one every 12 days. There were ten such bombings in the remainder of the year, which was an average of one every 28.2 days. Finally, up to the day of the successful strike against Rantisi a few weeks later, there had been eight suicide bombings, or one every 13.5 days. In the remainder of the year there were nine, averaging one every 28.7 days.

These data at least suggest that targeting political leaders may have contributed to a decline in suicide bombing, although much more refined analysis would be necessary to establish this. It is worth noting, however, that while the rate of suicide bombings slowed in the remainder of 2003 after Shanab's death in August 2003, it had returned in the first three months or so of 2004 to the rate in 2003 prior to his death. To the extent there was an impact, it thus may not have been enduring until the deaths of Yassin and Rantisi in 2004.

Finally, one must consider the possible impact of Yasir Arafat's death on November 11, 2004. As Bergman describes, "Mahmoud Abbas (Abu Mazen), who was appointed to replace [Arafat] as president, and the new Palestinian prime minister, Salam Fayyad, who had close ties to the American administration, launched a determined campaign against terror. Even the skeptical heads of the Shin Bet admit that the Palestinians became serious about stopping terrorism after the arrival of Abbas and Fayyad."[104]

Political Impacts

Efforts to assess the impact of targeted killing during the Second Intifada must also consider that this period was only one phase in a conflict between Israel and the Palestinians that has lasted many decades. That conflict has involved complicated political dynamics between Israel and various Palestinian groups, as well as among the latter groups themselves. Even if Israel used targeting for a relatively narrow objective during the Second Intifada, that tactic necessarily would have had broader effects on the course of this conflict that are difficult to identify and measure.

Ronen Bergman, for instance, suggests in his lengthy, detailed, and at times quite critical history of Israeli targeted killing that targeting was effective in reducing the threat to Israel from suicide attacks during the

Second Intifada. Operations to conduct extensive arrests and construction of a separation barrier in the West Bank, he says, also had some effect on such attacks. The attacks ceased, however, he concludes, "only after a massive number of targeted killings of terrorist operatives and... the assassination of terrorist leaders."[105] "Thanks to its streamlined targeted killing apparatus," he says, "the Israeli intelligence community triumphed over something that for many years had been considered unbeatable: suicide terrorism."[106]

On the other hand, says Bergman, "[t]he targeted killing campaign also did a great deal to further marginalize and delegitimize Israel in the eyes of the world."[107] With respect to the killing of Abu Shanab, he notes, "the international community did indeed make a distinction between attacking military operatives and political operatives. The Abu Shanab assassination sharpened the international debate about Israel's actions."[108] UN Secretary General Kofi Annan, for instance, condemned the targeting, stating that it was an unlawful "extrajudicial killing" of a senior Hamas leader.[109]

This is but one example of the possible wider effects of targeted killing on the conflict between Israel and the Palestinians. Attempting to identify these effects is important but enormously challenging, and is well beyond the scope of this chapter. My aim here is to describe research whose focus is more limited in the hope that this will contribute to a more informed assessment of the effects of targeted killing during the Second Intifada, and perhaps the use of targeted strikes more generally.

Finally, it is worth noting that, even if it may have achieved the objective of reducing the number and lethality of suicide bombings during the Second Intifada, Israeli targeting did not seriously weaken Hamas. As Jenna Jordan describes, Hamas was a relatively mature bureaucratic organization with considerable popular support. This enabled it to be resilient even in the face of leadership decapitation. While Hamas eventually discontinued the use of suicide bombing, it continued to engage in other actions against Israel. In addition, of course, it assumed governance authority over Gaza in the 2006 Palestinian Parliament elections, and has continued to be a significant factor in the ongoing relationship between Israel and the Palestinians.

Broader Lessons

Even if one regards Israeli targeting during the Second Intifada as on balance effective, this may have been aided by the fact that both Gaza and the West Bank adjoin Israel. This enables Israel to deploy "a robust intelligence network in the Occupied Territories, efficient[ly] shar[e] information among government units, and maint[ain] an entire apparatus of sensors, strike aircraft, and military forces ready to act quickly."[110] The availability of reliable human intelligence in particular may have been crucial to the ability to identify, locate, and target individuals.

In addition, the names of Palestinian group leaders at various levels generally were readily available, which made it easy to identify them as possible targets. Furthermore, while Israel sometimes used drones, its access to the Occupied Territories enabled it also to use less destructive devices such as snipers, close-range helicopters, and explosives with a relatively small blast radius in some cases. All these advantages may not be available to states that engage in targeting remote areas in distant locations in which they have a minimal ground presence.

In addition, states that contemplate targeted strikes against transnational terrorist groups are unlikely to be involved in the kind of ongoing political negotiations between Israel and groups representing Palestinians that formed the larger backdrop of the Second Intifada. In such cases, it is unlikely that states will be able to use strikes as a bargaining chip in the way that Israel eventually may have done in convincing Hamas to cease its support for suicide attacks.

Israel conducted targeting at an especially rapid pace, averaging almost one operation per week from 2001 through 2003. This suggests that targeting may need to be persistent to have any significant effects. Such a campaign requires ongoing extensive intelligence operations that feed into targeting decisions. Significant assistance and cooperation from local authorities will be important in this process. This poses challenges for targeting in areas with uncooperative governments, or without an effective governing authority, which are likely to be exactly those areas that provide safe havens for terrorist groups.

The next chapter moves from studies of a particular campaign to research on databases of a large number of terrorist organizations and leadership targeting operations against them. This will enable us to consider whether we can draw general lessons from experience with a large number of diverse groups over several decades.

NOTES

1. Bergman, R. (2018). *Rise and kill first: The secret history of Israel's targeted assassinations.* Random House; David, S. R. (2003). Israel's policy of targeted killing. *Ethics & International Affairs, 17*(1), 111–126. https://doi.org/10.1111/j.1747-7093.2003.tb00422.x.
2. Cronin, A. K. (2011). *How terrorism ends: Understanding the decline and demise of terrorist campaigns* (p. 29). Princeton University Press.
3. Byman, D. (2011). *A high price: The triumphs and failures of Israeli counterterrorism* (p. 311). Oxford University Press.
4. Falk, O. (2015). Measuring the effectiveness of Israel's 'targeted killing' campaign. *Perspectives on Terrorism, 9*(1), 1–26, 8. https://www.jstor.org/stable/2629732.
5. Bergman, 493.
6. The agency was called the General Security Services until 1996.
7. Falk, O., & Hefetz, A. (2017). Minimizing unintended deaths enhanced the effectiveness of targeted killing in the Israeli–Palestinian conflict. *Studies in Conflict & Terrorism, 42*(6), 600–616. https://doi.org/10.1080/1057610x.2017.1402429.
8. Id. 604.
9. Id. 605.
10. Pratt, S. F. (2013). "Anyone who hurts us": How the logic of Israel's "assassination policy" developed during the Aqsa Intifada. *Terrorism and Political Violence, 25*(2), 224–245, 240–241. https://doi.org/10.1080/09546553.2012.657280.
11. Id. 231.
12. Id. 230.
13. Bergman, 498.
14. Bergman dates the beginning of this policy to the end of 2001. Id. Pratt describes the second phase as one of "institutionalization," which included seeking legal advice on authority to target, and says that it began at the beginning of 2001. Pratt, 231. He does not discuss, however, the expansion of targets that Bergman says characterized a second phase.
15. Bergman, 498.
16. Id.
17. Id.
18. Id. 500.
19. Himes, K. R. (2016). *Drones and the ethics of targeted killing.* Rowman & Littlefield. Kindle 1115.
20. David, S. R. (2002, September). *Fatal choices: Israel's policy of targeted killing* (p. 115). BESA: The Begin-Sadat Center for Strategic Studies, Bar-Ilan University. https://besacenter.org/wp-content/uploads/2002/09/msps51.pdf.

21. Pratt, 237; Bergman, 542.
22. Bergman, 539.
23. Id.
24. Id. 542.
25. Id. 539.
26. Hafez, M. M., & Hatfield, J. M. (2006). Do targeted assassinations work? A multivariate analysis of Israel's controversial tactic during Al-Aqsa uprising. *Studies in Conflict & Terrorism, 29*(4), 359–382, 362. https://doi.org/10.1080/10576100600641972.
27. Pratt, 228.
28. Falk, O., & Hefetz, A. (2017).
29. Kober, A. (2007). Targeted killing during the Second Intifada: The quest for effectiveness. *Journal of Conflict Studies, 27*(1), 76–93, 82. https://journals.lib.unb.ca/index.php/JCS/article/view/8292.
30. Kaplan, E. H., Mintz, A., Mishal, S., & Samban, C. (2005). What happened to suicide bombings in Israel? Insights from a terror stock model. *Studies in Conflict & Terrorism, 28*(3), 225–235. https://doi.org/10.1080/10576100590928115.
31. Id. 228.
32. Id. 231.
33. Id. 233.
34. Kirchofer, C. (2016). Targeted killings and compellence: Lessons from the campaign against Hamas in the Second Intifada. *Perspectives on Terrorism, 10*(3), 16–25, 19. https://css.ethz.ch/en/services/digital-library/articles/article.html/169c2bcb-5b01-40b5-86c4-2eff8a2801b9.
35. Id.
36. Kaplan, E. H., Mintz, A., & Mishal, S. (2006). Tactical prevention of suicide bombings in Israel. *Interfaces, 36*(6), 553–561. https://doi.org/10.1287/inte.1060.0242.
37. Id. 554.
38. Id. 558.
39. Id. 557.
40. Id. 560.
41. Byman, D. (2006, March/April). Do targeted killings work? *Foreign Affairs, 85*(2), 95–111. https://doi.org/10.2307/20031914.
42. Id. 104.
43. Id. 104–105.
44. Id. 105.
45. Hafez & Hatfield.
46. Id. 371.
47. Id. 378.
48. Id. 379.

49. Zussman, A., & Zussman, N. (2006). Assassinations: Evaluating the effectiveness of an Israeli counterterrorism policy using stock market data. *Journal of Economic Perspectives, 20*(2), 193–206. https://doi.org/10.1257/jep.20.2.193.
50. Id. A194.
51. Id.
52. Jacobson, D., & Kaplan, E. H. (2007). Suicide bombings and targeted killings in (counter-) terror games. *Journal of Conflict Resolution, 51*(5), 772–792. https://doi.org/10.1177/0022002707304814.
53. Kober.
54. Id. 83.
55. Id. 85.
56. Jaeger, D. A., & Paserman, M. D. (2009). The shape of things to come? On the dynamics of suicide attacks and targeted killings. *Quarterly Journal of Political Science, 4*(4), 315–342, 317. https://doi.org/10.1561/100.00009013.
57. Id.
58. Id. 332.
59. Jaeger, D. A., Klor, E., Miaari, S., & Paserman, M. D. (2012). The struggle for Palestinian hearts and minds: Violence and public opinion in the Second Intifada. *Journal of Public Economics, 96*(3–4), 354–368. https://www.sciencedirect.com/science/article/abs/pii/S0047272711001708.
60. Jaeger & Paserman, 327.
61. Id. 332.
62. Id. 340.
63. Id. 339.
64. Id. 340.
65. Id.
66. Falk.
67. Dr. Falk has noted that this estimate is specific to the Israeli-Palestinian setting, and may differ in other areas.
68. Id. 118.
69. Id. 21.
70. Kirchofer.
71. Id. 16.
72. Id. 23.
73. Id. 20–21.
74. Id. 21.
75. Id. 21–22.
76. Abrahms, M., & Mierau, J. (2015). Leadership matters: The effects of targeted killings on militant group tactics. *Terrorism and Political Violence, 29*(5), 830–851. https://doi.org/10.1080/09546553.2015.1069671.

77. Id. 833.
78. Id.
79. Id. 836–837.
80. Falk & Hefetz.
81. Id. 606.
82. Id. 610.
83. Id.
84. Jordan, J. (2019). *Leadership decapitation: Strategic targeting of terrorist organizations.* Stanford University Press.
85. Id. 206, n. 59.
86. Id. 93–123.
87. Id. 99.
88. Id. 100–101.
89. Id. 102.
90. Id.
91. Id. 103.
92. Id. 99.
93. Id. 112.
94. Id. 113.
95. Morag, N. (2005). Measuring success in coping with terrorism: The Israeli case. *Studies in Conflict & Terrorism, 28,* 307–320, 311 (emphasis in original). https://www.tandfonline.com/doi/abs/10.1080/105761 00590950156.
96. Falk, 19.
97. Id. 18.
98. Bergman, 556.
99. Id.
100. Id. 557.
101. Bergman, 543.
102. Id. 543–546.
103. Id. 547.
104. Id. 562.
105. Id. 563.
106. Id.
107. Id. 564. The US initially was critical of the campaign, but changed its position significantly after 9/11.
108. Id. 542.
109. Id. 543.
110. Byman, 100.

CHAPTER 4

Leadership Targeting Studies

The impacts of targeted strikes on terrorist groups will depend in important ways on the particular political, military, and social contexts in which strikes occur. While acknowledging this, some scholars attempt to determine if we can derive any general lessons from analyzing large databases that contain information on killing or capturing terrorist leaders. This research focuses on targeting of top leaders, unlike some studies that analyze the effects of strikes on a wider set of targets. Studies use as dependent variables group survival for a period of time after a decapitation, number of attacks following a decapitation, or both.

GROUP SURVIVAL AS DEPENDENT VARIABLE

Price (2019)

In his book *Targeting Top Terrorists*, Bryan Price examines 207 terrorist groups from 65 countries that were active from 1970 to 2008 to determine whether decapitation through killing or capturing the top leaders or coleaders of these groups affected the likelihood they would dissolve within two years afterward.[1]

Of these groups, 131 suffered at least one decapitation, with 87 groups having one, 30 suffering two, 15 having three, and three suffering four leadership losses. Price also analyzes the effect of the loss of a leader due to

© The Author(s), under exclusive license to Springer Nature Switzerland AG 2022
M. Regan, *Drone Strike–Analyzing the Impacts of Targeted Killing*,
https://doi.org/10.1007/978-3-030-91119-5_4

death from natural causes or accidents, resignation or leaving the organization, entering the political process, or accepting a cease-fire. Altogether, there were 299 cases of leadership change in his study. Price relies on survival analysis, which focuses on the extent to which different variables influence what is known as the "hazard rate," or the risk that an entity under analysis will cease to exist.[2]

Price uses three models to examine the effect of decapitation on the risk of group dissolution within two years, controlling for group size, ideology, whether a group had at least one ally or rival, and variables designed to measure a state's counterterrorism capacity and its authoritarian or democratic character. His analysis indicates that groups that suffer a decapitation are 3.62–6.7 times more likely to end than groups that do not.[3] In two of the three models, religious groups are about 45% less likely to end than nationalist/separatist groups, which were used as the baseline comparison.[4] Price notes that this finding is statistically significant only at the 10% level, but is consistent with other research.

Price also finds that if a group has at least one ally or rival, this reduces its hazard rate by up to 52% and 39%, respectively. He attributes this to the need for a state to devote its resources to countering multiple groups, rather than being able to focus on only one. The one state variable that was statistically significant was GDP per capita, which was a proxy for state counterterrorism capacity. Increases in this figure were associated with increases in the hazard rate of 47–53%.

The timing of a decapitation was highly significant. If it occurred in the first year of a group's existence, that group was 8.76 times more likely to dissolve within two years than a group that did not suffer a decapitation. In the second year, a group was 8.16 more likely to end. At ten years, the effect of the decapitation was cut in half, and by twenty years Price suggests that the decapitation may have no effect. As he concludes, "[T]he longer it takes for the state to remove a terrorist leader, the less impact it will have on the group's mortality rate."[5] The study also finds that a group is more than three times as likely to end if it suffers a second decapitation.[6]

Price examines the effect on the hazard rate of three different types of decapitation: capturing, killing, and capturing and then killing a leader. Each type increases the hazard rate, but the impacts among them were not statistically significant. In addition, the study analyzes the loss of a leader due to decapitation compared to other reasons for such loss, such as illness, and found no statistically significant difference between decapitation and other sources. That is, the effects of losing a leader from decapitation are no different from losing one for other reasons. Losing a leader for any reason increases the hazard rate for a group by over 6.5 times than for groups that do not experience this loss.

Price acknowledges the risk of endogeneity and selection bias based on the possibility that groups that suffer from decapitation are those that are less capable than others. Their demise thus may reflect this weakness rather than the effect of decapitation. To control for this risk, Price examines groups who lost leaders for reasons other than decapitation. He finds that groups that lose their leaders because of illness and accident are 2.5 times more likely to end in groups that do not. As a result, he maintains, "This is a story about leadership and the loss of leadership, not a story about incompetent or inept groups."[7]

One policy implication of his study, Price concludes, is that a state should consider devoting more resources to leadership targeting as early in the lifecycle of a group as possible. He suggests that this is because an individual leader's personal characteristics are more important at this time. Over time, groups may develop organizational structures and procedures that enable them to be more resilient to decapitation. This is consistent, he notes, with Jenna Jordan's argument that a group's level of bureaucratic organization will increase its ability to survive decapitation.

Price is reluctant to offer specific policy recommendations because of the limitations of his study. While he attempted to control for relevant variables, he admits that the clandestine nature of terrorist organizations creates an especially significant risk of omitted variable bias.[8] Second, his study does not distinguish between cases in which a state specifically targets a group's leader and those in which the leader is killed or captured as part of a larger operation.[9] Nonetheless, he regards his study as a useful point of departure for further analysis, and concludes that "although counterterrorism officials do not have the luxury of conducting controlled clinical trials in the counterterrorism field, more can be done to rigorously evaluate different tactics to see what works, what does not, and in what optimal combination and sequence they should be employed."[10]

Tominaga (2019)

In an especially sophisticated study, Yasutaka Tominaga analyzes the effects of repeated decapitation of top leaders of militant organizations from 1970 to 2008.[11] He observes that many militant groups are subject to repeated targeting, which could have a cumulative effect over time. Assessing the effectiveness of such campaigns is challenging because targeting decisions rely on considerations such as the number, lethality, attack targets, and types of attacks that groups conduct, which themselves are likely to be responses to targeting.[12] In other words, terrorist group activities at Time One can cause targeting at Time One; group activities at Time Two both reflect the effect of targeting at Time One and can cause targeting at Time Two, etc. This means there is a dynamic relationship between targeting and group activities, in which targeting and group activities can serve as both cause and effect on an ongoing basis during a targeting campaign.

As Tominaga explains:

> [S]uppose that a particular militant group frequently attacks military targets. Its intensity may urge the authorities to conduct leadership targeting, which successfully degrades the militant group's capacity in conducting attacks against the military. However, with now-low capability, the new leadership shifts to targeting civilians using suicide operations. Given the heavy civilian casualties incurred, the authorities are now required to repeat targeting against the new leadership. . .

> In this example, the intensity, target type, and attack type are all pretreatment variables that affect the authorities' decision to execute the targeting policy, but they are also posttreatment variables in that those factors changed after the first leadership targeting and became the context for the next.[13]

Tominaga says that research typically controls for variables such as group activity that can affect targeting, in order to avoid endogeneity. The problem with using this "single-shot frame" to analyze repeated targeting, however, is that these variables *also may reflect the causal impact of previous targeting.*[14] As the author notes, "numbers of militant attacks, severity of attacks, target type, and attack forms all predict subsequent leadership targeting. Targeting policies, conversely, also predict the subsequent characteristics of violence."[15] The result is that analysis that controls for militant activity may understate the effects of targeting. It also can lead to estimates of the impact of targeting on a set of groups that is a combination of those that have and have not been affected by targeting, which results in a misleading estimate.

Tominaga employs analytical techniques designed to avoid this problem. He examines the number of targeting interventions against a group each year over the course of its life, with time-varying variables for each group consisting of the number of and casualties caused by attacks; the number of suicide bombings; and the number of attacks against general government, diplomatic, military, and police targets.

The aim is to estimate the causal effect of repeated leadership targeting on ending a group. In the study, the year of an organization's death could range from 1958 to 2008. Outcomes include the predicted remaining years of an organization and its survival rate when subjected to repeated targeting, reflected in the "hazard rate" of a group. This represents "the risk of organizations being terminated within a given time after exposure to leadership targeting."[16] The analysis also analyzes the effect of repeated targeting on these outcomes based on whether targeting occurred in the first or second half of an organization's life. Finally, Tominaga includes organization- and country-level variables: the size and ideology of a group, its military capability, and the democratic level of the targeting country.

Tominaga notes that studies of the effects of targeting on the likelihood that a militant group will end generally code a group as being targeted until the end of the observation periods. Since, however, the data in this study provide information on "the leadership targeting status for each militant group for each year or panel dataset," an analyst can estimate for a given year the hazard rate of a group "depending on the intervention status each year and the cumulative numbers of targeting interventions."[17] This enables assessment of the cumulative effect of targeting on a group.

One significant finding is that from zero to two targeting interventions against a group increases its predicted survival years. As Tominaga says, "in effect, the group becomes more resilient."[18] With a third and fourth targeting however, "the predicted survival years of the group drop sharply."[19] Similarly, as the number of targeting interventions increases, a group's survival rate significantly declines. Tominaga suggests that these data "show that repeated targeting policies do work to eliminate militant organizations, but success requires repetition and patience."[20]

A second finding is that the effect of targeting on group longevity depends on how early in a group's life targeting occurs. Tominaga calculates the midpoint of a group's lifespan and then counts the number of targeting operations before and after this point. This is designed to assess the impact of targeting "when organizations are still young and when they are mature."[21] The data indicate that in the first half of a group's lifespan, "a single decapitation increases groups' survivability, but successive targeting policies significantly shorten their predicted survival years."[22] After the midpoint, however, the data indicate that successive targeting either has no effect or could increase a group's predicted survival years.

Tominaga says that evidence of the second effect is inconclusive given the wide confidence interval, but "it seems valid to argue that executing additional decapitations against firmly established militant organizations does not hasten their elimination."[23] Thus, "[a] clear policy suggestion derived from the analysis is that, to disrupt militant organizations, successive targeting policies are required soon after a group's inception; 'wait and see' is not a good strategy and may even have an adverse effect in countering militant groups."[24]

Tominaga argues that these findings reflect the potential for targeting both to enhance and reduce the resilience of terrorist organizations. On the one hand, research establishes the possibility that "removal of militant leaders motivates existing members and induces more popular support, leading to not only increased motivation but also greater human and material resources."[25] Repeated targeting, however, can weaken the organization and decrease its chances of survival. It can signal that authorities "are well-equipped to identify militant groups and determined to take tough action against them."[26] As Tominaga acknowledges, we can't know in advance when a group has reached its midpoint, so "the key for repeated interventions to be effective is to execute successive interventions as soon as a group emerges."[27]

As Tominaga notes, this study examines the impact only of targeting top leaders. It also does not include data on groups still functioning at the time it was conducted, some of which represent significant current terrorist organizations. Nonetheless, the article incorporates a methodological approach that has great potential to refine analysis of the impacts of targeting on militant groups.

Cronin (2011)

Audrey Kurth Cronin's *How Terrorism Ends: Understanding the Decline and Demise Of Terrorist Campaigns* conducts qualitative case studies of strategies against several dozen terrorist groups drawn from the more than

800 groups in the Memorial Institute for the Prevention of Terrorism (MIPT) Terrorism Knowledge Base.[28] Cronin argues that a terrorist campaign involves three key actors: the terrorist group, the government, and the audience. Understanding how terrorism ends, she says, requires understanding the dynamic interaction among all three in a given situation.[29]

Cronin finds that "six patterns in the decline and ending of campaigns emerge from the history of terrorism: (1) capture or killing the group's leader, (2) entry of the group into a legitimate political process, (3) achievement of the group's aims, (4) implosion or loss of the group's public support, (5) defeat and elimination by brute force, and (6) transition from terrorism into other forms of violence."[30]

Cronin defines decapitation as capturing or killing the top leaders or operational leaders of a terrorist group.[31] Her case studies of capture include the Shining Path, the Kurdistan Worker's Party, the Real Irish Republican Army, and Aum Shinrikyo. Cases involving killing a leader involve Abu Sayaaf in the Philippines, the Russian campaign against Chechen leaders, and Israeli targeted killings.

She maintains that a crucial consideration in determining whether removal of a leader will end a terrorism campaign is not simply how reliant a group is on a leader, but "the effects of his removal on potential supporters of both the terrorist campaign and the counterterrorist operation."[32] She finds that arresting a leader damages a terrorist group more than killing him, especially when the leader can be prevented from communicating with the group after arrest and can be "paraded in humiliation before the public."[33] This can reduce support for a leader by treating him as a criminal rather than a revolutionary. She finds that killing the leader of a group that has widespread support, however, is ineffective or counterproductive. "Cases where a group has halted a campaign following the killing of the leader are difficult to find," Cronin says.[34]

In light of these findings, Cronin considers whether decapitation is likely to result in the demise of Al-Qaeda and concludes that it is not. She acknowledges that killing Osama bin Laden and Ayman Zawahiri in the 1990s might have accomplished this because of the role of these two leaders in catalyzing the movement and shifting its focus to attacks in the West. Al-Qaeda has evolved since then, however, into an entity in which local groups are able to exercise initiative and are not dependent on particular leaders to conduct their operations. This conclusion is consistent with research by Price and Tominaga described above that finds that leadership targeting is most effective in the early years of a group.

An approach more promising in reducing popular support for Al-Qaeda, Cronin suggests, is to exploit the differences among the diverse groups under its banner. These groups have a variety of goals, many of which focus on local rather than global concerns, as well as different understandings of Islam. In addition, publicizing the harm that Al-Qaeda inflicts on Muslims could reduce their support in the Islamic community. The backlash in Iraq in response to Al-Qaeda leader Abu Musab al-Zarqawi's brutal attacks on Muslims whom he considered heretics, for instance, led to an uprising of the Muslim community against Al-Qaeda in that country.

While the discussion here focuses on Cronin's analysis of leadership targeting, her book provides a number of rich case studies that provide thoughtful analysis of the potential of several other strategies to combat terrorism. Her emphasis on terrorism and counterterrorism as a competition for public support also offers a valuable conceptual framework for evaluating the likely effectiveness of different counterterrorism strategies. Cronin defines effectiveness as the end of a terrorist campaign, and she reasonably concludes that the use of decapitation against Al-Qaeda is unlikely to cause the demise of the group. As the following chapters discuss, it is worth considering whether strikes against Al-Qaeda leadership have helped accomplish more modest goals.

Langdon, et al. (2004)

Lisa Langdon, Alexander Sarapu, and Matthew Wells examine 19 terrorist and insurgent organizations that suffered 31 cases of leadership loss through the leader being killed, captured, or dying of natural causes.[35] The study focuses in almost all cases on groups with one leader, although some were included that relied on a "central cluster of leaders."[36] The groups spanned a considerable period of time, dating from the time of the colonial Peruvian group Tupic Aramu in 1780 to groups still in existence. They also encompassed groups with a wide range of aims, from Christian Scientists and the Mormon Church to the Irish Republican Army. The study examined whether following a leadership loss a group disbanded, became less or more radical, or continued essentially unchanged. Any change lasting less than two months was not included in the analysis.

Of the 18 groups whose leader was killed, seven continued generally as before, six disbanded, and five became less radical. Of the 11 whose leader was arrested, seven continued as more or less the same, two disbanded and one each became more radical and less radical. The two whose leader died of natural causes continued essentially unchanged. Thus, in 23 of 31 cases a group survived, and in 16 of 31 cases, a group continued as usual. Killing a leader was more effective than capture; including cases in which a group became less radical afterward resulted in finding that killing a leader was successful in 11 of 18 cases, compared to three of 11 cases for arrest. The authors acknowledge, although they do not control for the possibility, that in some cases killing a leader may have been part of broader operations against the group.

Examining group characteristics, the study finds that only one of the 11 religious groups ceased operations. Of nine groups that suffered internal disputes prior to the loss of a leader, seven survived. Five of the latter broke into competing factions, with the strongest faction eventually prevailing in continuing the work of the group. In the two groups that conducted strict purges that did not allow for any internal dispute, the emergence of factions resulted in the demise of the group. The authors suggest that "groups that have allowed some level of debate and dissent are inherently more adaptable in the face of internal challenges and are thus more likely to emerge from a schism."[37] Finally, the authors find that, while the existence of a clear line of succession helps a group survive, the absence of one does not necessarily doom it to end.

The findings of this study are intriguing in suggesting relatively limited impact on a group by killing its leader. The wide range of groups in the data set, however, along with the small number of cases of leadership loss, limit the ability to draw broader lessons from it. In addition, the analysis does not rely on statistical techniques designed to isolate the impact of different variables, nor on an approach that permits strong inferences about causality.

TERRORIST ATTACKS AS DEPENDENT VARIABLE

Tominaga (2018)

Tominaga utilizes data from his 2019 study described above to examine the impact of killing or capturing top leaders or coleaders on: (1) groups losing such leaders (2) neighboring groups in the same country, and (3) allies of groups suffering such decapitation.[38] He seeks to determine if decapitation has effects beyond any effects on the group that is targeted. Understanding such "diffusion of benefits," he says, can enable policymakers to maximize the impact of counterterrorism measures.[39] This focuses on the extent to which decapitation may be an effective counterterrorism measure because of its deterrent effect, apart from whatever damage it may inflict on a group that is targeted.

Tominaga uses the first decapitation as the treatment, with the dependent variable the number of annual domestic and transnational attacks following decapitation. He utilizes a difference-in-differences approach. As Chapter 2 describes, this identifies groups with comparable pre-treatment trends in rates of attacks, even though the number of attacks they conduct may differ. Assuming that such parallel trends exist, the impact of decapitation arguably should be reflected in the difference between the rates of attacks by groups that do and do not suffer decapitation. Groups not subject to decapitation thus serve as a control group that furnishes a counterfactual indicating what the treated (decapitated) group would have done had it not been subject to decapitation.

Tominaga finds that targeted killing resulted in an increase in attacks by targeted groups in the year of decapitation of between 39 and 60%. Decapitation through capture does not affect domestic attacks but increases transnational attacks by 75% in the decapitation year. These backlash effects continue for one year after decapitation. Tominaga suggests that such increases may reflect the desire of a targeted group to "demonstrat[e] to the population whose support it seeks that the organization is undiminished, through either maintaining or increasing their level of operations."[40]

Tominaga then examines effects on neighboring groups. He finds that capture of a group's leader results in a 22% decline in attacks by neighboring groups in the decapitation year and 33% in the year afterward. This effect lasts between two and three years after the decapitation year. By contrast, targeted killing of a group's leader has no effect on attacks by neighboring groups. The author suggests that decapitation through capture has this second-order effect because capturing a leader generally is far more difficult than killing one. He says that "the cost and risk incurred in targeted capturing and the determination it conveys clearly signal a deterrer's capability and willingness to other would-be aggressors. This changes militant groups' perceptions and their cost–benefit calculation of taking further action."[41]

The study finds that neither targeted killing nor capture significantly reduces allied groups' operations. Targeted capturing does have a significant effect, however, on neighboring allies in the same country. In the year after decapitation, attacks by these groups decrease by 54%, and is still 47% lower than one year before decapitation in the third year following it. Tominaga suggests that this is because the capture of a leader creates concern on the part of allies in the same country that authorities will gain information about their operations that places them at greater risk. By contrast, more distant allies are less likely to have significant information about the targeted group.

Tominaga maintains that it is therefore crucial in estimating the effects of decapitation to consider the extent to which a group engages in domestic and transnational attacks, the number of other groups operating in the same country, and the alliances that a group has with other groups. Focusing on these considerations leads him to conclude that there are two circumstances in which leadership decapitation can reduce the overall level of militant attacks.

The first is when several militant groups conduct attacks mainly against domestic targets. In this case, capturing a leader typically reduces attacks by other groups in the same country, but does not increase attacks by the targeted group. Tominaga argues that this is because the difficulty of capture operations enables a state that captures a leader to signal its resolve to other groups.[42]

The second instance of second-order effects is that capture of a group's leader can produce an even larger decrease in attacks by a neighboring group that is an ally of the group that is targeted. In this instance, deterrence occurs not only through signaling but because of concern by the ally that the captured leader may provide information that will compromise its operations, such as the location of hiding places.

By contrast, Tominaga says, targeted killing causes an increase in attacks by the targeted group without any deterrent effect on neighbors and allies. "Contrary to capturing leaders," he notes, "killing them yields no information about neighboring groups, and the lower costs and risk generate weaker signaling of capability and determination."[43] The consequences of killing or capturing a leader thus can be significant when effects on other groups that are not targeted are considered.

Tominaga's study is an especially notable effort to draw on methodological approaches that attempt to provide a counterfactual control group to support claims about causality regarding decapitation. His research is well-designed to test a specific theory about the effects of decapitation, which can provide guidance for decision-makers on targeting operations. It also makes a useful contribution to the theoretical literature by focusing on signaling as a potential instrument of targeting operations.

Mannes (2008)

Aaron Mannes reviews data on 71 terrorist groups active between 1968 and 2007.[44] He identifies 56 instances of decapitation by either killing or capturing the leader or second in command of a group, with 28 cases of each. The data set also includes 21 groups that lost leaders because of deaths from other causes. A group is required to have committed at least 10 attacks over its history to be included. Mannes' source of information is the MIPT Terrorism Knowledge Base. He notes that this database includes slightly over 34,000 incidents, but that a little over 24,000 of these are not attributed to a specific group. There are several cases in which a terrorist group lost a leader more than once, but only the first loss was counted as a decapitation.

The dependent variables in the study are the number of attacks and fatalities from them, with comparison between two and five years prior to decapitation and two and five years afterward. Mannes classifies groups into several categories, including most notably religious, nationalist/separatist, and communist/socialist. He also includes a variable to capture cases in which decapitation is part of a broader offensive against a group, such as mass arrests or targeting of several other important leaders in addition to the top two.

Mannes notes that terrorist activity may decline for many reasons distinctive to a group. He therefore includes in his model what he describes as comparison groups in an effort to provide a firmer basis for inferences of causality. He does not, however, provide details about the characteristics of these groups. This makes it difficult to determine the extent to which they can serve as a genuine counterfactual that would support causal claims.

Mannes says that many tests in his study do not result in statistically significant outcomes "due to the relative paucity of data on terrorist activity."[45] While not statistically significant, his model predicts a decline of 22 attacks in the five years after compared to the five years before a decapitation, and a decline of 28 attacks between these periods when decapitation is part of a larger crackdown.

One statistically significant finding is that fatalities from attacks by religious groups increase by 56 five years after decapitation compared to five years before. This figure increases to 73 when the leader of a religious terrorist group is killed rather than arrested. Mannes also finds that when a religious group loses its leader for the second or third time, the number of attacks within two years after the most recent loss is greater than the two years before. He speculates that this "may reflect situations in which the strikes take place in the midst of hostilities," such as between Israel and Palestinian groups.[46]

Mannes concludes that "the general decline in incidents when groups are subject to decapitation strikes indicates that the strategy may be useful in certain circumstances."[47] However, "the limited effect of the decapitation strategy, particularly on fatal attacks by terrorists groups, raises doubts about its overall efficacy."[48] Furthermore, as the data on religious groups indicate, decapitation may in fact be counterproductive in some cases.

Mannes considers possible explanations for the finding regarding religious groups. He says that the most violent religious groups "operate on a large scale and have extensive bases of support among the population."[49] Arguably, the ability to conduct large-scale operations is correlated with the quasi-bureaucratic form of organization that Jordan regards as enabling a group to withstand decapitation. Jordan also considers strong community support as valuable for the same reason.

Second, Mannes suggests, it may be that during periods of extreme violence when decapitation is likely, "the most violent elements within a religious terrorist group will also rise to the fore."[50] This is similar to claims in some studies described in Chapter 6 that decapitation may empower lower-level members who are less discriminate than top leaders.

BOTH GROUP SURVIVAL AND ATTACKS AS DEPENDENT VARIABLES

Jordan (2019)

In one chapter of her book on leadership targeting described in Chapter 3, Jenna Jordan analyzes a database that she compiled of 180 organizations that were targeted with decapitation (which she defines as either killing or capturing) between 1970 and 2012.[51] In the first stage of her analysis, she removes the nine most active groups so that their activity would not skew the results and analyzed them separately. Jordan then conducts regression analyses to determine the impact of several variables on three dependent variables: a group's conduct of attacks one year and two years after a decapitation, and its survival for two years following a decapitation.

The variables Jordan analyzes are the size, age, and type of an organization; the gross domestic product, population, and "polity score" of the country in which the group mainly is based; whether decapitation is through death or arrest; and whether the decapitation is of the top leader or a member of the upper echelon of an organization. The types of organizations are left-wing, right-wing, religious, separatist, and Islamist. The polity score represents where on a spectrum from autocratic to democratic the regime falls in the country in which a group mainly is based.

Jordan first conducts bivariate analysis of the relationship between individual independent variables and the three dependent variables. This indicates that religious, Islamist, and separatist groups are less likely to stop attacks after decapitation than other groups. Right-wing groups have a high probability of not carrying out attacks after decapitation, and left-wing groups are most likely to dissolve after two years. Surprisingly, the largest groups (more than 1000 members) and the smallest (fewer than 100) are most likely to discontinue attacks, but the largest groups are least likely to end, while the smallest groups are most likely.

The youngest groups from one to five years old are 100% likely to conduct no attacks one year and 75% two years after a decapitation. Surprisingly, however, the oldest groups, twenty years and older, are next most likely to conduct no attacks, with 40% conducting no attacks after one year and 51% after two years. In addition, the oldest groups are most likely to collapse after one or two years, while none of the youngest groups are likely to do so. When she conducts separate analysis using group existence as a dependent variable, however, she finds that younger groups are more likely to fall apart after one or two years than older groups. On balance, then, older groups appear more resilient to decapitation as measured by group survival.

Jordan conducts multivariate analysis to discern the interaction among the variables. With respect to ceasing attacks after one year, Jordan's first model indicates that groups between 1000 and 5000 members are least likely to cease attacks, and that killing rather than capturing a leader is correlated with ceasing attacks. Right-wing groups are more likely to fall apart after an instance of decapitation, while separatist groups are more resilient.

Jordan's second model, which includes all statistically significant variables from the first model and a variable for whether a group is Islamist, also found that no size category is associated with ceasing attacks, with groups over 10,000 and between 500 and 1000 least likely to do so. She suggests this indicates that once a group reaches 500, it becomes resilient. Finally, holding other variables constant, Islamist groups are more likely to continue attacks than non-Islamic ones.

Jordan then examines variables connected with a group's conduct of an attack in the second year after decapitation.[52] In her first model, data indicate that "a group has a higher probability of not conducting attacks in a two-year period if the leader is killed."[53] Larger groups are more likely to conduct attacks than smaller ones, and separatist and Islamic groups are more likely to carry out attacks than non-separatist and non-Islamic ones, respectively. In her second model including GDP, population, and polity type, killing rather than arresting a leader is more likely to result in ceasing attacks, while left-wing and Islamist groups are least likely to cease attacks.

Jordan's last multivariate regression analyzes when decapitation was likely to result in the collapse of a group within one or two years after a decapitation. She finds that the results generally are consistent with the analyses of attacks. Younger groups are more likely to dissolve than older ones, and Islamist and separatist groups are less likely.

Jordan then conducts a separate analysis of her database that is designed to identify a control and treatment group to assess the impact of decapitation on the frequency of attacks. The control group consisted of groups suffering no decapitation ("nontargeted"), while the treatment groups were groups suffering a decapitation, before and after the decapitation ("targeted groups"). The analysis includes information on whether the rate of attacks for groups in each category was decreasing, flat, or increasing in a year. Based on data on attack activity, she then calculates the probability that the rate of attacks in the following year will decrease, remain flat, or increase. The results do not indicate any clear pattern, although groups over 1000 members and targeted Islamist groups generally are likely to increase attacks after decapitation.

Jordan then examines whether decapitation has an effect on a group's probability of its dissolution, and finds that it does not. She acknowledges that work by Bryan Price, described above, concludes that decapitation lowers a group's survival rate. She notes, however, that Price's data go through only 2008 while hers extend to 2016. Price also includes leadership losses from several sources, while Jordan focuses only on whether a leader is killed or arrested.

Finally, Jordan analyzes activity by the nine largest groups that she removed for purposes of the database analysis described above. These are Al-Qaeda in the Arabian Peninsula (AQAP), Al-Shabaab, Basque Fatherland and Freedom (ETA), Boko Haram, Kurdistan Workers' Party (PKK), Liberation Tigers of Tamil Eelam (LTTE), New People's Army (NPA), Taliban, and Tehrik-i-Taliban Pakistan (TTP). Based on her specific identification of the TTP, her reference to the "Taliban" presumably is to the Afghan group. She plots yearly attacks conducted by each group in comparison to yearly decapitation against each. Jordan says that five organizations generally had an increase in activity after decapitation: AQAP, Al-Shabaab, Boko Haram, the NPA, and the Taliban. The chapter does not provide precise data on decapitation nor the number of attacks, but a graph in the Appendix depicts the general annual level of attacks.[54]

Jordan concludes the chapter by stating that the data indicate that, while decapitation is effective in some cases, it does not result in a decline in activity by many of the most dangerous and lethal organizations. In addition, it may result in an increase in attacks by many of the largest organizations, as well as by Islamist and separatist groups. As an organization grows larger, it develops the networks and support systems necessary to replenish both members and leaders. It also is more likely to become structured more bureaucratically, with a division of labor based on specialization.

Jordan uses different approaches to analyze her database of terrorist organizations and the impact of leadership decapitation on them. Each approach has some limitations. The regression analyses, for instance, do not account for the possibility that targeting is endogenous, nor do they control for other counterterrorism measures that may influence group activity. The examination of attack frequency uses groups that have not suffered a decapitation as a counterfactual, but does not provide details that would enable an assessment of whether the groups are comparable to treatment groups. Finally, her analysis of the nine most active terrorist groups charts annual attacks over time, but does not attempt to assess the impact of individual decapitations.

At the same time, the findings from these different approaches are generally consistent. At a minimum, they provide support for the claim that decapitation will not necessarily adversely affect a terrorist group. As Jordan indicates, there are a variety of factors that are likely to influence effectiveness. The chapter therefore is valuable in suggesting that decision-makers must engage in detailed analysis of the characteristics of a group in order to determine whether decapitation will be useful against it.

Johnston (2012)

Patrick Johnston's research examines successful and unsuccessful decapitations of the top leaders of insurgent organizations in the course of counterinsurgency campaigns from 1975 to 2003.[55] Johnston's inclusion of unsuccessful attempts reflects his concern that studies of decapitation generally examine cases in which opposing leaders were killed or captured, without any rigorous attempt to determine what would have occurred in the absence of such operations.

Johnston identifies 118 decapitation attempts, of which 46, or 39%, were successful. He analyzes the effects after successful and unsuccessful decapitation attempts, indicated by whether the conflict ended, as measured by the decline in violence below a minimal threshold; whether it ended on terms favorable to the counterinsurgency campaign; the number of insurgent attacks; and the number of fatalities.

Johnston acknowledges that decapitation attempts may not be exogenous but may depend upon a group's activity, which makes the direction of causality difficult to establish. As he observes, failure to consider this makes it "difficult to identify whether decapitation explains the outcomes of interest, or whether other factors that make decapitation more likely to occur actually drive the relationship."[56]

Johnston argues that the success or failure of an attempt is random, which provides a basis for drawing inferences about the effect of successful attempts. "To the extent that chance plays a role in the outcome of operations," he says, this can help determine if "organizations whose leaders were captured or killed would have fared differently had their leadership remained intact."[57] He finds support for this claim in the fact that the variables that he uses in his analysis do not predict whether an attempt will be successful, except for the total population of the country in which a campaign occurs, which he acknowledges could be a confounding variable.[58]

Johnston's regression analysis estimates the impact of successful decapitation on the dependent variables. Johnston finds that decapitation increases the probability of the conflict ending by 27 percentage points. States were 32 percentage points more likely to prevail on favorable terms in years in which decapitation occurred than years in which attempts failed. Once the type of attempt and the region are considered, decapitation is associated with decreased fatalities, and a successful attempt is associated with a lower number of attacks.[59]

As Johnston notes, his identification strategy does not use a control group not suffering decapitation that is otherwise comparable to one that does, but relies on the ostensibly random occurrence of successful and failed attempts. The effects of failures, however, could account for the more positive outcomes associated with successful decapitations. For instance, they may generate resentment that worsens hostile conditions, decreasing the likelihood of conflict termination or increasing the number of attacks and fatalities.[60]

Johnston attempts to address this issue by using propensity score matching to provide a better assessment of differences in outcomes connected with successful and unsuccessful attempts. He relies on observable group characteristics to predict decapitation strikes, and uses characteristics with the greatest predictive power to identify groups that are comparably likely to be the target of decapitation attempts. He uses observable characteristics to predict decapitation strikes, and then stratifies the sample into control and treatment groups that are balanced on observables. This enables Johnston "to compare similar years with and without decapitation strikes as if they were similar treatment and control groups."[61]

The study finds that a successful decapitation is associated with a 28-percentage point increase in the probability of conflict termination in the year in which it occurs, and a 29- or 30-percentage point increase in the probability that a state would prevail on favorable terms. Johnston also finds little evidence of what he calls a "blowback effect" producing negative outcomes in response to failed decapitation attempts.[62]

The study then compares outcomes on ideological versus identity-based groups. The former includes groups animated by political doctrine, while the latter includes ethnic or religious groups. Johnston's data indicate no difference between these types of groups with respect to the effect of leadership decapitation. Nor did he find that effectiveness was related to the age of a group.

Finally, relevant for the assessment of targeted killing specifically, Johnston finds that killing insurgent leaders is likely to be more effective than capturing them. His data indicate a significant relationship between operations resulting in leadership deaths and both an earlier end to a conflict and a state victory. Johnston cautioned, however, that "this probability was consistently estimated at around 25 to 30 percent – a far cry from the silver bullet many look for when they analyze leadership decapitation."[63] He concludes:

> although decapitation is likely to help states' overall efforts against militant organizations, other factors will also matter greatly in most cases. In other words, decapitation is more likely to help states achieve their objectives as an operational component within an integrated campaign strategy than as a stand-alone strategy against insurgent and terrorist organizations.[64]

Like Jordan, Johnston focuses only on killing or capturing top leaders, but his data end with 2003 while hers extend to 2012. His thus excludes most of the major targeting campaign conducted by the US against Al-Qaeda and its affiliates. Unlike Jordan, he does not suggest a theoretical framework for analyzing the effectiveness of targeting and thus, for instance, does not include a variable such as size as an indication of a group's organizational structure and potential reliance on individual leaders. With these limitations in mind, his work represents a careful attempt to address challenges in inferring causality with regard to decapitation.

Rowlands & Kilberg (2011)

Dane Rowlands and Joshua Kilberg analyze the impact of removing leadership in 249 terrorist groups in the period 1970–2007.[65] Their model differentiates groups according to four organizational structures. Those characterized as having a "market" structure are highly decentralized and lack any formal leadership. Those that are "all-channel" feature a flattened structure in which all members are connected with one another.

Two more hierarchical structures are the hub-and-spoke and the bureaucratic. The former, which the authors suggest characterizes Al-Qaeda, have an identifiable leadership but rely more on local commanders than on centralized control. Finally, bureaucratic groups are highly structured and specialized, and rely on routine processes. The authors suggest that the Palestine Liberation Organization is an example of such a group. Of the 249 groups in the sample, 170 ended operations during the sample.

Rowlands and Kilberg examine the effects on these groups of the loss of a leader or a senior commander when that person is killed, captured, suffers an accidental or natural death, or is sent into exile. They assess whether after the loss of a leader or senior commander a group ends sooner than their model predicts it normally would, and whether a group conducts fewer attacks than their model projects it ordinarily would over a one-, two-, and three-year period afterward.

The model also incorporates the age of a group; whether it is left- or right-wing, or nationalist; and includes religious motivation as the base case. The authors also include a variable to measure economic and political conditions of the state that is a group's main base of operation, and whether a group is in decline as measured by the ratio of the average annual number of attacks in the previous three years to the historical average of the group.

Their basic model finds that the age of a group does not affect its probability of termination and, surprisingly, that increasing a group's size by one level is associated with a 1.2% increase in the likelihood of termination in a given year. The authors note, however, that it is difficult to obtain data on group size on an annual basis, which means that this finding "will require further exploration."[66] Overall, their analysis "does not provide any compelling evidence that targeting leadership has any significant effect on the ending of a group," regardless of organizational type.[67]

The findings with respect to the number of attacks are more complex. Because market-structured groups generally lack formal leaders, the data on attacks by them are not very meaningful. With all-channel organizations, killing leaders or senior commanders does not reduce the number of attacks, "because they are less reliant on centralized command structures."[68] Indeed, killing a leader is associated with a 2.8 increase in attacks the year afterward, and killing a commander is associated with an increase in attacks by almost two times in the year afterward, and almost 2.4 times the year after. The authors suggest that capturing or exiling these leaders or senior commanders is likely to be more effective in reducing attacks.

Leaders are more important in a hub-and-spoke organization. Killing, capture, or exile of a leader is associated with a significant decline in attacks in the following year, as well as in the year after for killing and exile. The capture of a senior commander is also associated with fewer attacks two years later, but the effect is barely statistically significant. The authors conclude that leaders play an important coordinating role in these organizations, and organizations lack a hierarchical structure that makes them resilient.

The authors' findings, however, are at odds with research described in Chapter 6 that strikes against Al-Qaeda leaders are not associated with declines in overall attacks by the group. This may be because they classify the group as a hub-and-spoke organization, whereas Jenna Jordan and others argue that it has quasi-bureaucratic features that boost its resilience.

Finally, for bureaucratic terrorist groups, the killing, capture, or exile of a leader has no significant association with subsequent attack frequency. If such groups lose a leader from natural causes or accident, however, attacks decline by almost 95% in the first year and 40% in the second year. The authors say, "[T]he multiple and possibly contradictory effects of internal competition for promotion, incentives for reprisal, and operational capacity might be intermingling at this important (but less critical) level of leadership."[69]

Rowlands and Kilberg conclude that, with the possible exception of a hub-and-spoke organization, tools other than decapitation, "such as negotiation (however unpalatable to a government) or opening avenues for conversion into legitimate political participation, may be far more effective, especially over the longer term."[70] This is consistent with Cronin's research on the various ways in which terrorist activity by a group may end. The authors' study necessarily has limitations that are inherent in analysis that does not attempt to identify a counterfactual. It provides a useful focus, however, on the role of organizational structure in affecting the impact of leadership loss on terrorist groups.

CONCLUSION

What are the most robust lessons we might draw from studies of targeting that focus on large databases of terrorist organizations? Research tends to focus on two outcomes: the survival of a group after suffering a decapitation and the number of attacks it conducts after such an event. With respect to group survival, Johnston finds that successful decapitation increases the likelihood that a conflict will end. Price finds that the loss of a leader for any reason increases the likelihood that a group will end, but that the effect of decapitation does not differ from other forms of loss. Neither Jordan nor Rowlands and Kilberg find any relationship between decapitation and group survival. Langdon, et al. find that in 23 of 31 cases a group continued after decapitation.

Because large databases aggregate terrorist groups with different characteristics, focusing on group-level variables is likely to provide more insight into the effect of targeting on group survival. Tominaga finds that targeting a group early in its lifecycle decreases its probability of survival, while targeting at a later stage has no effect or could even increase its chances of survival. This is consistent with the findings of Jordan and of Price that younger groups are likely to end sooner than older groups as a result of leadership losses. Jordan and Price also find that larger groups are more resilient to leadership losses, with Jordan suggesting that a group becomes more durable once it surpasses 500 members.

Jordan finds that Islamist and religious groups are less likely to dissolve after decapitation, consistent with Price's finding that religious groups are more resilient than nationalist or separatist groups. Rowlands and Kilberg also find in their basic model that religious groups are more durable. Finally, with respect to the relative impact of killing versus capture, Johnston and Jordan both find that killing has more impact on group survival.

The most notable findings regarding group survival thus are that younger and smaller groups are more vulnerable to dissolution from decapitation than other groups, and religious groups are less vulnerable. Tominaga suggests that older groups are likely to be more adaptive because of their experience with targeting. In addition, older and larger groups may be more likely to have the kind of quasi-bureaucratic structure and community support that Jordan argues increases resilience. Finally, Price's finding is also intriguing that losing a leader for any reason, not just decapitation, increases the risk of dissolution. More research that examines this possibility could have important implications for policymakers.

It is more difficult to extract lessons on the effect of targeting on terrorist group attacks than its impact on group survival, given the divergent findings on the former issue. The finding of increases in attacks by Islamist groups, and fatalities by religious groups, seems plausible given findings that religious groups are less likely than other groups to dissolve after suffering a decapitation.

Johnston and Tominaga use especially rigorous methods designed to provide robust inferences about causality, but reach different conclusions about the impact of decapitation on attacks. Johnston's database covers 1975–2003, while Tominaga, relying on Price's database, examines 1980–2008. This could explain some of the difference, given substantial increases in US targeting after 2003.

Tominaga's two studies are notable for two reasons that may provide distinctive insights into the use of targeted strikes. First, his 2018 study focuses on the effects of targeting on groups not directly targeted. He argues that deterrence theory may explain why these groups engage in fewer attacks after such targeting. In particular, Tominaga suggests that capture may have a deterrent effect because it signals authorities' resolve, and because nontargeted groups perceive a risk that those who have been captured will provide information about them. Second, Tominaga's 2019 study on group survival relies on methodology designed to capture the impact of repeated targeting on groups, which single-shot analysis fails to incorporate. This approach could have great promise in analyzing the effects of ongoing targeting campaigns on terrorist groups.

Finally, the findings from studies that combine analysis of group survival and attacks suggest that targeting leaders of older and larger religiously oriented groups is especially unlikely to be effective in reducing attacks by the group as a whole, or in affecting its rate of survival.

The following chapter begins Part II of the book, which is an examination of the impacts of US targeted strikes on Al-Qaeda and associated groups. Chapter 5 provides an overview of US strikes, Chapter 6 describes and assesses quantitative empirical studies of the impacts of strikes, and Chapter 7 examines qualitative material on such impacts. Chapter 8 concludes Part II by discussing what the combination of quantitative and qualitative evidence suggests about the impacts of US strikes on the terrorist groups against which they has been used.

NOTES

1. Price, B. C. (2019). *Targeting top terrorists: Understanding leadership removal in counterterrorism strategy*. Columbia University Press.
2. Id. Kindle 858.
3. Id. 4455.
4. Id. 4588.
5. Id. 4629.
6. Id. 4821.

7. Id. 5405.
8. Id. 6823.
9. Id.
10. Id. 6820.
11. Tominaga, Y. (2019). Evaluating the impact of repeated leadership targeting on militant group durability. *International Interactions, 45*(5), 865–892. https://doi.org/10.1080/03050629.2019.1647836.
12. Id. 869.
13. Id.
14. Id. 866.
15. Id. 878.
16. Id. 882.
17. Id.
18. Id. 885.
19. Id.
20. Id. 886.
21. Id.
22. Id. 886.
23. Id.
24. Id.
25. Id. 872.
26. Id. 873.
27. Id. 888.
28. Cronin, A. K. (2011). *How terrorism ends: Understanding the decline and demise of terrorist campaigns*. Princeton University Press.
29. Id. 7.
30. Id.
31. Id. 16.
32. Id. 14.
33. Id.
34. Id. 32.
35. Langdon, L., Sarapu, A. J., & Wells, M. (2004). Targeting the leadership of terrorist and insurgent movements: Historical lessons for contemporary policy makers. *Journal of Public & International Affairs, 15*(Spring), 59–78. https://jpia.princeton.edu/sites/jpia/files/2004-4.pdf.
36. Id. 62.
37. Id. 69.
38. Tominaga, Y. (2018). Killing two birds with one stone? Examining the diffusion effect of militant leadership decapitation. *International Studies Quarterly, 62*(1), 54–68. https://doi.org/10.1093/isq/sqx055.
39. Id. 54.
40. Id. 64.
41. Id. 62.

42. Id. 64.
43. Id. 66.
44. Mannes, A. (2008). Testing the snake head strategy: Does killing or capturing its leaders reduce a terrorist group's activity? *Journal of International Policy Solutions, 9*(4), 40–49. https://dx.doi.org/10.2139/ssrn.2988670.
45. Id. 43.
46. Id. 43.
47. Id.
48. Id.
49. Id. 44.
50. Id.
51. Jordan, J. (2019). *Leadership decapitation: Strategic targeting of terrorist organizations* (pp. 62–92). Stanford University Press.
52. In 46 cases involving 29 groups, there was an attack in the first year but not the second. In 39 cases involving 22 groups, there were no attacks in the first year but were attacks in the second year.
53. Id. 77.
54. Id. 199–201.
55. Johnston, P. B. (2012). Does decapitation work? Assessing the effectiveness of leadership targeting in counterinsurgency campaigns. *International Security, 36*(4), 47–79. https://doi.org/10.1162/isec_a_00076.
56. Id. 49.
57. Id.
58. Id. 60.
59. Id. 65.
60. Id. 66.
61. Id. 67.
62. Id. 69.
63. Id. 77.
64. Id. 50.
65. Rowlands, D., & Kilberg, J. (2011). Organizational structure and the effects of targeting terrorist leadership. Centre for Security & Defence Studies, Paterson School of International Affairs, Carleton University. http://www3.carleton.ca/csds/docs/working_papers/RowlandsKilbergWP09.pdf.
66. Id. 8.
67. Id. 10.
68. Id. 19.
69. Id. 20.
70. Id. 20.

Impacts of US Strikes on Terrorist Groups

CHAPTER 5

Overview of US Targeted Strikes

This chapter provides an overview of US targeted strike operations outside theaters of active combat, or what I call war zones, through 2021. Both the Department of Defense (DOD) and the Central Intelligence Agency (CIA) conduct strikes, but the US has never officially acknowledged the latter because they generally are covert operations. Speculation has been that CIA strikes may occur in locations in which the host government does not want to publicly disclose that it has consented to strikes.

This has likely been the case for at least part of the time in Pakistan, Yemen, and Somalia, the three countries that are the focus of this book. As the *New York Times* reported in 2015, for instance, "[T]the Pentagon has long been banned from conducting drone strikes in Pakistan, part of a 2004 deal with Pakistan that all such attacks be carried out by the C.I.A. under its authority to take covert action — allowing Pakistan to publicly deny any knowledge of the strikes and American officials to remain silent."[1] DOD is presumed to conduct strikes in theaters of active combat such as Iraq, Afghanistan, Syria, and Libya, and perhaps during periods of active combat in Yemen and Somalia.

The US government began only in 2016 to provide reports that provide some information on strikes along with other types of operations. As Chapter 9 describes in more detail, nongovernmental organizations (NGOs) provide more detailed estimates of strikes, total fatalities, and

M. Regan, *Drone Strike–Analyzing the Impacts of Targeted Killing*, https://doi.org/10.1007/978-3-030-91119-5_5

civilian fatalities in Pakistan, Yemen, and Somalia. Some estimates are for drone strikes specifically, while others are for airstrikes generally. The detailed tables in the Appendix that follows Chapter 9 provide this information on an annual basis, along with estimates by the US government, and some estimates of civilian injuries.

US strikes evolved in different ways in Pakistan, Yemen, and Somalia. The discussion below describes the NGO estimates of the number of strikes, total fatalities, and civilian fatalities through 2010, and provides a short overview of the evolution of US targeted strikes in each country.

Pakistan

Estimates of the number of strikes in Pakistan through 2021 range from 404 to 588.[2] The most intense period of operations has been from 2008 to 2013. Strikes have focused on persons identified as Al-Qaeda Core (AQC) leaders, mid-level commanders, and specialized operatives, along with leaders and members of other "associated" groups working with Al-Qaeda. For periods of time, the US also conducted signature strikes against unidentified persons whose behavior was deemed to indicate that they were actively participating in hostilities on behalf of Al-Qaeda and associated groups. The vast majority of strikes have been in the Federally Administered Tribal Areas (FATA) in the northwest region of the country.

The FATA was a focus of attention because in late 2001, a substantial number of AQC leaders fled US and Pakistani military forces in Afghanistan and settled in that area. The FATA historically has been governed by colonial era regulations rather than ordinary Pakistani law. In practice, the Pakistani government has not established a significant presence in the region and has relied substantially upon tribal leaders to maintain order. The area is remote and mountainous, with few routes of ingress or egress.

After the migration of AQC into the FATA, Al-Qaeda recruited new members and developed relationships with Pakistani militant groups that provided protection, such as the Tehrik-i-Taliban Pakistan (TTP). By 2004, "al Qaida had rebuilt itself in the South and North Waziristan agencies of Pakistan's tribal areas, receiving support from young leaders."[3]

Khalid Sheikh Mohammed, who planned the 9/11 attacks, provided a steady supply of funds to Al-Qaeda from an entity in Karachi. As one person familiar with these operations described to scholar Asfandyar Mir, the group used these funds to "establish training centers, suicide bomb training, IED [improvised explosive device] production, weapons and explosive handling, material printing, and lodging facilities."[4] Bin Laden set up specialized units to conduct attacks in the US, and against US and other Western interests in Pakistan and in Afghanistan. At the same time, the TTP grew in size and influence, although it did not formally affiliate with Al-Qaeda. A 2011 study conducted by Paul Cruickshank concluded that of the 32 serious jihadist terrorist plots against the West between 2004 and 2011, 53% had "operational or training links to established jihadist groups in Pakistan."[5]

In June 2004, the US Central Intelligence Agency (CIA) and Pakistan's Inter-Services Intelligence (ISI) agency agreed to allow US drones to fly over "flight boxes" in two regions of FATA, the Waziristan and Bajaur Agencies. It also permitted CIA forward bases in the FATA and arranged for intelligence-sharing between the US and the ISI. The ISI did not, however, provide the CIA access to its infrastructure for intercepting domestic communication. The US needed to receive permission from the ISI and the Pakistani president before conducting a strike. In 2006, the US government added the requirement that a strike be approved by the CIA station chief in Islamabad, a US military commander, and the US ambassador to Pakistan.

From 2004 to 2007 the US government carried out only a few strikes in the FATA. It mostly provided information to Pakistani forces to undertake ground operations, which generally had only limited success. The US had a small number of drones available in the area and did not have substantial intelligence assets in the region. The combination of incomplete intelligence and a lengthy approval process meant that in many cases targets had disappeared by the time a strike had been authorized.

As Mir describes this period:

> In sum, the minimal pressure applied by the United States against al-Qaida and the Pakistan Taliban from 2004-2007 allowed both groups to recover from their losses relatively quickly and to avoid future losses while maintaining their growth trajectories. During this period, al-Qaida became more deeply institutionalized and attracted large numbers of specialized cadres. And by late 2007, the Baitullah Mehsud–led [TTP] had become a formidable and sizable armed group.[6]

In 2008, the US and Pakistan revised their agreement. Pakistan permitted the US to conduct strikes at times and locations of its choice.[7]

The two countries also deepened intelligence collaboration. The ISI increased US access to communication interception in the FATA; shared more information on the local population in North Waziristan; collaborated more extensively with US intelligence agencies; and coordinated human intelligence operations with the CIA's Islamabad station.[8] The US substantially increased intelligence collection and analysis resources for the campaign and brought online a significantly larger number of drones. The result was a sharp increase in the number of drone strikes in the FATA beginning in 2008, principally against Al-Qaeda and the TTP.

Estimates of the number of persons killed through 2020 are between 2957 and 4026. There is greater dispute about estimates of civilian casualties from these strikes. Pakistan Body Count estimates are between 1306 and 2544, while estimates by the most prominent other NGOs are between 274 and 969. There are various reasons why the Pakistan Body Count figures is so much higher than those of other organizations. Chapter 9 discusses these, as well as differences in methodology among the organizations that provide estimates, and estimates of annual strikes and casualties from them.

YEMEN

Estimates of the number of US strikes in Yemen through 2021 range from 328 to 346. The most intense period of strikes has been from 2012 to 2018. Strikes in Yemen have been mainly against members of Al-Qaeda in the Arabian Peninsula (AQAP), a group that is the 2009 merger of Al-Qaeda organizations in Yemen and Saudi Arabia. Each group was comprised of many persons who had traveled to Al-Qaeda training camps in Afghanistan and been dispatched back to their home country by bin Laden shortly before 9/11 to serve as the vanguard of Al-Qaeda's jihad in the Arab world. One such person was Yemeni Nasir al-Wuhayshi, who had served as bin Laden's personal secretary for four years, and would later become the head of AQAP.

Even before 9/11, the group in Yemen attacked the US destroyer *USS Cole* in Aden harbor in October 2000, killing 17 and wounding 39 Americans. The November 2002 US drone strike that killed the group's then-leader Qaed Salim Sinan al-Harithi described in Chapter 1, however, "destroyed the organization's infrastructure" in that country.[9] "Without Harithi," Gregory Johnsen says, "al-Qaeda in Yemen could not function."[10]

AQAP eventually reemerged as a significant group, however. Wuhayshi escaped from prison along with 23 others in the capital of Sana'a in 2006, and ultimately became AQAP leader. He began to rebuild Al-Qaeda "[u]sing the blueprint he had seen bin Laden perfect in Afghanistan."[11] He recruited locally, building on tribal and clan ties, laying the foundation "for a durable organization, appointing local amirs, or commanders, who would direct al-Qaeda's operations in their home districts."[12] AQAP also benefited from President Saleh's focus on conflicts with tribal groups and rivals, and his inconsistency in taking aggressive action against jihadists. In 2008, AQAP conducted an attack on the US Embassy in Sana'a, killing 12 people.

In announcing the formation of AQAP in January 2009, "[a]s bin Laden had years earlier, AQAP left no doubt. It was targeting the US."[13] "By God," the video said, "we are coming."[14] In December 2009, the group fell just short of successfully destroying a plane preparing to land in Detroit when a bomb sewn into the underwear of an operative on board failed to detonate. In October 2010 two bombs concealed in printers were intercepted that had been sent on separate cargo planes headed for the US, after AQAP had earlier conducted a dry run by sending several packages to different locations in the US. Both had been built by master bomb-maker Ibrahim al-Asiri in Yemen, who had also built the bomb carried by the operative on the plane to Detroit.

President Saleh gave the US consent to conduct drone strikes under certain conditions in Yemen, but publicly characterized any operations as carried out by Yemen. In 2012, new President Abed Rabbu Hadi substantially expanded US authority, giving the US "unfettered access to targets in Yemen."[15] Estimates of US airstrikes that year ranged between 41 and 56, whereas they were estimated at 1–13 in 2011. In 2012, President Obama also authorized signature strikes for the first time in Yemen.

AQAP has conducted many lethal terrorist attacks in Yemen, and periodically has captured and occupied significant territory in the south. The group took advantage of instability during the Yemen Arab Spring to increase its influence in 2011–2012, but a 2012 Yemeni military offensive in the south, assisted by US air support that included drone strikes, regained considerable territory.

Wuhayshi was killed by a drone strike in summer 2015, but AQAP remained resurgent and claimed considerable territory in 2015–2016 with the advent of Saudi Arabian intervention in the government's conflict with the Houthis in the north of the country. Military offensives by the

United Arab Emirates military from 2016 to 2018, however, accompanied by intensified US drone strikes in 2017, weakened the group. Wuhayshi's successor Qasim al-Raymi was killed in January 2020.

The data on strikes in Yemen do not contain detailed differentiation between strikes in support of combat operations and those that have targeted individuals. Total deaths from strikes in Yemen through 2020 are estimated at between 875 and 1537, with estimates of civilian deaths between 105 and 142.

SOMALIA

Strike estimates in Somalia through 2021 range from 141 to 249, although the latter figure also includes some ground operations. The most intense period of strikes has been 2017 to 2021, reflecting the perceived increase in the threat that Al-Qaeda affiliate Al-Shabaab poses to the US and to US persons in the region.

The roots of Al-Qaeda in Somalia lie in Al-Qaeda's denunciation of the deployment to Somalia of the US and other forces under the authority of the UN from 1992 to 1995 to help monitor a cease-fire and ensure delivery of humanitarian aid.[16] Bin Laden used a cell in Nairobi to send weapons and provide training to Somali warlords battling US forces. These were used in operations such as the "Black Hawk Down" incident in Mogadishu in 1993 that resulted in 19 dead and 73 wounded US forces. After forces withdrew in 1995, Sharia courts in the country merged to form the Islamic Courts Union (ICU) to unify the country under Islamic law.

In 2001 and 2002, more than a hundred Somalis traveled to Afghanistan to fight alongside Al-Qaeda and the Taliban, including several future Al-Shabaab leaders. Many returned to Somalia after the defeat of the Taliban and secured leadership positions in the ICU. In June 2006, the ICU took power in Somalia, and in August 2006 Al-Shabaab formally announced its establishment. At the time it comprised an increasing core of several hundred fighters and its leaders were influential in the ICU militias. At the end of 2006, however, Ethiopian forces invaded Somalia to fight the ICU and other militia, and quickly ousted the ICU from power.

Al-Shabaab focused on rebuilding itself and strengthening its presence in southern Somalia. It was aided by jihadists who came to oppose the occupation by Ethiopia and, later, occupation by forces from several countries under the authority of the African Union Mission to Somalia

(AMISOM). The group also received substantial donations by the Somalian diaspora, many of whom were in the US. In addition, the group's alignment with Al-Qaeda helped it obtain funding from wealthy Arab donors. When Ethiopia withdrew in 2009, Al-Shabaab quickly expanded its control of territory in Somalia, and began to conduct attacks in Kenya. It then conducted attacks that killed almost 200 civilians in Kampala, Uganda, and Mogadishu.

After losing ground to AMISOM and Kenyan forces from 2011 to 2013, Al-Shabaab nonetheless conducted a substantial number of high-profile suicide attacks in Somalia on government buildings, the international airport, and numerous hotels and restaurants. In 2013, it conducted an attack at Westgate Mall in Nairobi, Kenya that killed 67 people and wounded almost 200 others. As a report by RAND describes, "The attack was well planned and involved careful intelligence collection, surveillance, and reconnaissance of the mall."[17] In 2017, a truck bomb killed more than 500 people at a busy intersection in downtown Mogadishu, although later reports suggested that the truck had been delayed in reaching its ultimate target of a military installation. In 2019, UN experts said that Al-Shabaab's use of explosive devices to carry out attacks reached the "greatest extent in Somali history" in 2018 thanks to its expanding sophisticated bomb-making operations.[18]

In recent years, Al-Shabaab has issued threats against the US and US persons. In 2019, the leader of the group, Abu Ubaidah, issued a video declaring the US a legitimate target and urging attacks against Americans wherever they are located. Somalia's national security advisor Abdisaid Muse Ali said that such attacks represent an attempt by the group to broaden its global jihadist appeal. "Al Shabab tries to internationalize their aggression," he said, "by saying they are fighting America while seeking attention from Al Qaeda leaders."[19]

In September 2019, a suicide bomber detonated a car packed with explosives at the gate of a US military airfield in Somalia, and in January 2020 there was an attack at Manda Bay, Kenya that killed three Americans. In December 2020 a member of the group was charged in New York with planning to conduct a 9/11—style attack in the US.[20] In preparation for this, the defendant had completed training in the Philippines necessary to obtain his pilot's license. Philippine authorities arrested him but another Al-Shabaab member who was studying to be a pilot at a school in that country managed to flee.[21]

The US did not engage in many strikes in Somalia until 2017. Available estimates for US strikes are for airstrikes generally, although a significant number of these are believed to be drone strikes. From 2007 to 2016, estimates are between 36 and 50 total strikes. In 2017, the number jumped to 34–35 and in 2018 to 43–47. Total deaths from 2007 to 2020 are estimated at between 1156 and 2320, with civilian deaths between 70 and 143.

The next two sections describe the US legal and policy standards for designating targets, a description of the process that the Obama administration used to make such decisions, and available information about the process during the Trump administration.

Targeting Standards

The US regards itself as in an armed conflict with what it describes as "Al Qaeda and associated forces." As Department of Defense General Counsel Jeh Johnson explained in 2012, an associated force is: "(1) an organized, armed group that has entered the fight alongside al Qaeda, and (2) is a co-belligerent with al Qaeda in hostilities against the United States or its coalition partners."[22] Johnson elaborated, "In other words, the group must not only be aligned with al Qaeda. It must have also entered the fight against the United States or its coalition partners. Thus, an 'associated force' is not any terrorist group in the world that merely embraces the al Qaeda ideology."[23]

US characterization of its operations against Al-Qaeda and associated forces as occurring during an armed conflict means that the US regards its use of force as governed by the law of war, which is comprised principally of the Geneva Conventions and their two Additional Protocols. An important feature of this body of law is that it permits lethal force against all enemy combatants, regardless of their specific conduct at the time, without the requirement first to attempt to capture them. A second key provision is that unintended harm to civilians is permissible in attacks against combatants and objects being used for military purposes, as long as it is not "excessive" in comparison to the military advantage that is anticipated from the attack.

The armed conflict with Al-Qaeda and associated forces is what is known as a non-international armed conflict (NIAC) between a state and a nonstate organized armed group, rather than an international armed conflict (IAC) between states. Unlike combatants in state military forces, persons fighting on behalf of a nonstate group typically do not wear uniforms that distinguish them from civilians. Determining who is a nonstate combatant who may be killed without attempted capture therefore must rest upon intelligence about their behavior, specifically the extent to which they are regularly "directly participating in hostilities." Civilians who occasionally but not regularly directly participate in hostilities may be targeted without an attempt to capture them, but only while they are engaged in hostilities.

There is some disagreement about who falls into the category of nonstate combatant. The International Committee of the Red Cross (ICRC) says that it includes persons who perform a "continuous combat function," and not persons who provide other forms of support to a party to the conflict.[24] The US, however, rejects the distinction between combat and support functions. It says that "[b]eing part of a non-State armed group that is engaged in hostilities against a State is a form of engaging in hostilities" that makes persons combatants.[25] "An individual who is integrated into the group," says the US, "such that the group's hostile intent may be imputed to him or her may be deemed to be functionally (i.e., constructively) part of the group."[26] This distinguishes them from those "who are merely sympathetic to the group's goals."[27]

As Chapter 1 noted, the US takes the position that it may use lethal force under the law of war against persons it considers combatants wherever they are furthering hostilities against the US, even if there is no armed conflict in that location. As that chapter also has noted, others argue that the law of war applies only where there is an active armed conflict, that is, intense fighting between the two sides. Where this is not the case, they argue, force may be used only under more restrictive law enforcement standards that reflect human rights law.

In May 2013, President Obama announced standards for the use of "direct action," which includes strikes, outside "areas of active hostilities," that were responsive to the latter claim.[28] A 2016 report by the Director of National Intelligence said that the administration regarded Iraq, Afghanistan, and Syria as areas of active hostilities.[29] The 2013 Presidential Policy Guidance (PPG) provided that lethal force could only be used outside these areas against targets that posed "a continuing imminent threat to US persons."[30] In addition, the PPG said the following criteria must be satisfied:

(1) Near certainty that the terrorist target is present;

(2) Near certainty that non-combatants will not be injured or killed;

(3) An assessment that capture is not feasible at the time of the operation;

(4) An assessment that the relevant governmental authorities in the country where action is contemplated cannot or will not effectively address the threat to U.S. persons; and

(5) An assessment that no other reasonable alternatives exist to effectively address the threat to U.S. persons.[31]

These standards are very similar, although not identical, to law enforcement standards that are governed by human rights law. They reflect policy, not legal, standards, that may be overridden by the President in cases in which this is deemed necessary.

The Trump administration issued Principles, Standards, and Procedures (PSP) that superseded the PPG, but retained some of its provisions. They provided guidance "to all CT [counterterrorism] action wherever it is conducted abroad."[32] The PSP, in other words, abandoned the distinction between areas inside and outside of active hostilities. They also eliminated the PPG requirement that a target pose a "continuing imminent threat" to US persons, providing instead that direct action could be taken against targets "whose removal, either independently or as part of a broader campaign, is assessed to be reasonably necessary to US efforts to address the threat posed by the terrorist group."[33]

The PSP authorized direct action against groups "subject to the use of lawful force by the United States, that are engaged in ongoing hostilities against the United States, or pose a continuing imminent threat against the United States."[34] Finally, the PSP said that the US would continue "to take extraordinary measures to ensure with near certainty that noncombatants will not be injured or killed in the course of operations."[35] Reports indicated that while the PSP were being prepared, President Trump expanded locations that were regarded areas of active hostilities, to include parts of Somalia. The White House provided no information on this, and the PSP were not released until the Biden administration took office. Expectations are that the Biden administration will adopt targeting standards more stringent than those in the PSP.

TARGET DESIGNATION PROCESS

The White House issued a fact sheet in connection with President Obama's announcement of the PPG, but the full PPG was not disclosed until August 2016 in connection with a Freedom of Information Act lawsuit brought by the American Civil Liberties Union (ACLU). The full PPG described the process that must be followed in nominating a person as a target for a strike. This requires first that an agency formally nominate an individual as a high-value target (HVT) following confirmation by the agency's general counsel that such individual would be a lawful target. The agency was required to note any gaps in intelligence, as well as inconclusive and contradictory intelligence reports.

A nomination must then be submitted to a Restricted Counterterrorism Security Group (RCSG) chaired by the National Security Council (NSC) Senior Director for Counterterrorism, and including representatives of the Departments of State, Treasury, Defense (DOD), Justice (DOJ), and Homeland Security, and the Joint Chiefs of Staff (JCS) and National Counterterrorism Center (NCTC). For each nomination, the NCTC must conduct its own assessment prior to RCSG review if feasible prior to consideration of the nomination by the Deputies Committee. The NSC Legal Adviser and the General Counsel of the nominating agency shall also consult with other interagency lawyers depending on the particular nomination.

If the RCSG approves, the nomination must be sent to the Deputies of the Department of State, and the DOD, JCS, DOJ, DHS, Director of National Intelligence (DNI), CIA, and NCTC. In addition to other criteria, the deputies must consider whether "the threat posed by the individual to U.S. persons can be minimized through a response short of lethal action [and] the implications for the broader regional and international political interests of the United States."[36] The Deputies must then determine whether to recommend to the Principal of the nominating agency that lethal action be taken against the proposed individual. Following deliberation by the Deputies, "departments and agencies shall submit to the NSC the final positions of their Principals."[37]

The Principal of the nominating agency may approve lethal action against the proposed individual if: "(1) the relevant Principals unanimously agree that lethal action should be taken against the proposed individual and (2) the Principal of the nominating agency has notified the President...of his intention to approve lethal action and has received notice... that the President has been apprised of that intention."[38] A nomination is then presented to the President for decision, along with the views expressed by departments and agencies during the process, when: "(1) the proposed individual is a U.S. person, or (2) there is a lack of consensus among Principals regarding the nomination, but the Principal of the nominating agency continues to support approving the nomination."[39]

Finally, the department or agency conducting a strike must provide to the NSC in writing within 48 hours of the operation the following information:

(1) A description of the operation;
(2) A summary of the basis for determining that the operation satisfied the applicable criteria contained in the approved operational plan;
(3) An assessment of whether the operation achieved its objective;
(4) An assessment of the number of combatants killed or wounded;
(5) A description of any collateral damage that resulted from the operation; and
(6) A description of all munitions and assets used as part of the operation;

The Obama administration originally limited strikes to those against HVTs, but strikes increased over time against persons who were not in this category, such as mid-level commanders, persons with specialized skills, and other operatives. Brian Glyn Williams quotes a US official about this trend in Pakistan, who said, "This effort has evolved because our intelligence has improved greatly over the years, and we're able to identify not just senior terrorists, but also al-Qaeda foot soldiers who are planning attacks on our homeland and our troops in Afghanistan."[40] In addition, the PPG authorized strikes "when fleeting opportunities arise."[41] In those cases, an agency could submit a request to the NSC after clearance by its General Counsel. The PPG required that an appropriate NSC official "consult with other departments and agencies, as appropriate and as time permits, before submitting the proposal to the President for his decision."

John Brennan's memoirs contain a composite description of a strike based on a fleeting opportunity when he was Homeland Security Advisor to President Obama. Upon receiving a request from a department or agency, "When time allowed, the seriousness of the threat and the request to strike would be the topic of discussion in several interagency meetings held in the Situation Room, where the intelligence would be thoroughly scrubbed and challenged."[42] However, "when the threat appeared imminent, I would receive urgent secure-line calls heralding the imminent arrival of classified emails with attachments providing the nature of the threat and the proposal on how to neutralize it with a lethal strike, forcing me to decide quickly whether to bring it to the president's immediate attention."[43]

When Brennan did so, the vice-president, national security adviser, deputy national security adviser, the president's chief of staff, and the White House counsel would join the meeting if their schedules permitted. Brennan provides an illustration of a discussion, modified for security purposes, which is worth quoting at length:

> Mr. President, we have located one of the key operatives involved in a plot to blow up our embassy in Sana'a with a truck bomb. We have confirmation from human and technical sources that he is a member of AQAP. He has bedded down for the night at a compound about seventy-five miles outside the city. Earlier today, our drones observed a pickup truck at the same compound being loaded with a large amount of explosives. Based on previous terrorist attacks and plots we have uncovered, the analysts believe that the loading of the truck and its colocation with the operative make it likely that the truck will depart the compound tomorrow morning for the attack in Sana'a.[44]

Brennan then handed the president a map and photographs showing the specific location and configuration of the compound in question. He continued:

> Mr. President, there are at least fifteen individuals on the compound, eleven of whom are noncombatants, including some women and children, so we are unable to strike the truck at this time. The Yemeni government has no military or security forces in the area. We recommend against notifying the Yemenis at this point, as AQAP has many moles inside the intelligence services and would likely be alerted that we have located the truck and operative. Moreover, any attempt by Yemeni forces to try to avert the threat by raiding the compound themselves would likely result in the death of most, if not all, of the others on the compound.[45]

US special forces were not in position to conduct a raid against the compound that evening, Brennan said. Furthermore, "[e]ven if they were, the assessment is that the risk to our forces would be too great, as AQAP has numerous compounds with many heavily armed fighters in the area. The bottom line, sir, is that there is no available option to conduct an on-the-ground disruption or capture operation."[46]

Brennan continued:

> Mr. President, our drones are maintaining constant observation of the compound. The weather forecast calls for another twelve hours or so of clear skies before clouds start rolling in. If that holds, we should be able to see the truck and the operative depart. The analysts have mapped the most likely roads the truck will travel once it leaves the compound, and they have identified areas that would allow for a clean strike before the truck gets to the congested roads of Sana'a. Mr. President, all criteria for a strike have been met, and the lawyers have signed off on it. I recommend that you authorize a strike as long as it can be taken consistent with the standing guidance of near certainty of no civilian casualties. Our folks believe they can find a stretch of road that will allow them to take a clean shot.[47]

Brennan said that the US ambassador to Yemen concurred with the recommendation. The situation, he said, is virtually identical to a hypothetical scenario that Brennan had discussed with Yemeni President Abdrabbuh Mansur Hadi when he visited Yemen last month. "He told me that we could take such strikes when there is an imminent threat to American life. Our ambassador will inform Hadi as soon as we hit the truck. If the strike is successful and no civilians are injured or killed, I am confident that the Yemenis will not object, although they might criticize it publicly for their own domestic political purposes."[48]

The president then asked, "What if we see someone else get into the truck with the AQAP guy? And what happens if the clouds roll in early and obscure our view, and we lose sight of the truck and the terrorist?" Brennan responded, "If anyone else gets in the truck, there will need to be near certainty derived from intelligence that the individual is AQAP or aware of the truck's true purpose. The operators know that they would need to contact us for further guidance if they cannot make a near certainty assessment."[49] He said that if operators lost sight of the truck because of extended cloud cover, "the Yemenis will be immediately contacted and given details of the truck and the operative so that they can set up roadblocks on the edge of the city."[50]

The president concluded, "Okay. I approve the strike if there is near certainty there will be no civilian casualties. Keep me updated, including on the security situation around the embassy. Let me know when the truck leaves the compound and whether or not anyone other than the terrorist gets in it."[51] Brennan would immediately convey the president's decision to the US entity that had requested approval for the strike. He usually would limit the period of authorization: "'You have authorization to strike if the criteria are met within the next twenty-four hours,' I would say on the secure line call. 'After twenty-four hours, you will need to provide an update and request an extension.'"[52]

Brian Glyn Williams also described the process within the CIA for determining whether to conduct a strike against an authorized target:

> [T]he CIA's Covert Action Review Group leads a debate on the "kill"; then, the target is passed to the CIA's Counterterrorism Center. The CIA drones cannot fire unless their pilots receive final approval from the CIA director or his deputy. Describing former CIA chief Leon Panetta's direct involvement in the strikes, one senior intelligence official said, 'He asks a lot of questions about the target, the intelligence picture, potential collateral damage, women and children in the vicinity.'[53]

Williams says that "Other reports have said that the U.S. ambassador to Pakistan must approve drone hits to make sure there is no political fallout from a strike."[54]

The Trump Administration reportedly eliminated much of the inter-agency review required by the PPG, creating a process that was more streamlined and efficient, but that benefited less from a range of perspectives outside of the defense and intelligence communities. In addition, the Trump Administration no longer required presidential approval for most proposed operations. Instead, the decision about whether to conduct many lethal targeting operations likely rested with military combatant commanders and thus was not subject to interagency review by senior-level officials.[55]

In addition, the Trump administration conducted at least one notable strike against a target who was not a member of Al-Qaeda or an associated group. In January 2020, a US drone strike killed Iranian Major General Qasem Soleimani, the head of Iran's Quds Force, while he was in Iraq.[56] Although the US described General Soleimani as a terrorist, he was not affiliated or associated with Al-Qaeda.

CONCLUSION

The US has conducted hundreds of targeted strikes, typically using drones, over the last two decades or so in Pakistan, Yemen, and Somalia. The largest number of these strikes have occurred in the FATA in Pakistan. Since 2013 US policy has prescribed substantive and procedural standards for conducting strikes outside areas of active hostilities, which has included these three countries for the most part.

The next three chapters review evidence on the impact of these strikes on Al-Qaeda and associated forces. Chapter 6 describes and evaluates quantitative empirical studies, Chapter 7 discusses qualitative material, and Chapter 8 draws conclusions based on the combined insights of these sources of evidence.

NOTES

1. Mark Mazzetti & Eric Schmitt. (2015, April 12). Terrorism case renews debate over drone hits. *New York Times*. https://www.nytimes.com/2015/04/13/us/terrorism-case-renews-debate-over-drone-hits.html.
2. Chapter 9, Appendix, Table 1.
3. Mir, A. (2018). What explains counterterrorism effectiveness? Evidence from the U.S. drone war in Pakistan. *International Security, 43*(2), 45–83, 63. http://doi.org/10.1162/isec_a_00331.
4. Id. 64.
5. Cruickshank, P. (2011, July). *The militant pipeline between the Afghanistan–Pakistan border region and the west* (p. 1). New America Foundation. https://newamerica.org/documents/887/the-militant-pipeline.
6. Mir. 67.
7. Id. 62.
8. Id. 61.
9. Johnsen, G. D. (2012). *The last refuge: Yemen, al-Qaeda, and America's war in Arabia* (p. 132). W. W. Norton Company.
10. Id.

11. Id. 208.
12. Id.
13. Id. 235.
14. Id.
15. Id. 286.
16. Joseph, D., & Maruf, H. (2018). *Inside Al-Shabaab: The secret history of Al-Qaeda's most powerful Ally.* Indiana University Press.
17. Jones, S. G., Liepman, A., & Chandler, N. (2016). *Counterterrorism and counterinsurgency in Somalia: Assessing the campaign against Al Shabaab* (p. 31). RAND. https://doi.org/10.7249/RR1539.
18. United Nations Security Council. (2019, November 1). Letter dated 1 November 2019 from the Chair of the Security Council Committee pursuant to resolution 751 (1992) concerning Somalia addressed to the President of the Security Council, 3. https://www.securitycouncilreport. org/atf/cf/%7B65BFCF9B-6D27-4E9C-8CD3-CF6E4FF96FF9%7D/ S_2019_858_E.pdf.
19. Schmitt, E., & Dahir, A. (2020, March 21). Al Qaeda branch in Somalia threatens Americans in East Africa—And even the U.S. *The New York Times.* https://www.nytimes.com/2020/03/21/world/africa/al-qaeda-somalia-shabab.html.
20. Critical Threats, Africa File. (2020, December 18). *Africa File: Al Shabaab member charged with plotting 9/11-style attack.* https://www.cri ticalthreats.org/briefs/africa-file/africa-file-al-shabaab-member-charged-with-plotting-9-11-style-attack.
21. Schmitt & Dahir.
22. Johnson, J. (2012, November 30). *The conflict against Al Qaeda and its affiliates: How will it end?* https://www.lawfareblog.com/jeh-johnson-speech-oxford-union.
23. Id.
24. International Committee of the Red Cross. (2009). *Interpretive guidance on the notion of direct participation in hostilities under international humanitarian law* (p. 33). https://www.icrc.org/en/doc/assets/files/ other/icrc-002-0990.pdf.
25. US Department of Defense. (2016). *Law of war manual*, §4.18.4.1. https://tjaglcspublic.army.mil/documents/27431/61281/DoD+Law+ of+War+Manual+-+June+2015+Updated+Dec+2016/5a02f6f8-eff3-4e79-a46f-9cd7aac74a95.
26. Id. §5.7.3.2.
27. Id.
28. White House. (2013, May 22). *U.S. policy standards and procedures for the use of force in counterterrorism operations outside the United*

States and areas of active Hostilities (PPG). American Civil Liberties Union. https://www.aclu.org/sites/default/files/field_document/presidential_policy_guidance.pdf.

29. Office of the Director of National Intelligence. (2016). *Summary of information regarding U.S. counterterrorism strikes outside areas of active hostilities between January 20, 2009 and December 31, 2015.* https://www.dni.gov/files/documents/Newsroom/Press%20Releases/DNI+Release+on+CT+Strikes+Outside+Areas+of+Active+Hostilities.PDF.

30. White House. (2013, May 23a). *Fact sheet: U.S. policy standards and procedures for the use of force in counterterrorism operations outside the United States and areas of active hostilities.* https://obamawhitehouse.archives.gov/the-press-office/2013/05/23/fact-sheet-us-policy-standards-and-procedures-use-force-counterterrorism.

31. Id.

32. White House. (n.d.). *Principles, standards, and procedures for direct action against terrorist targets* (p. 1). American Civil Liberties Union. https://www.aclu.org/foia-document/psp-foia-document-april-30-2021.

33. Id. 4.

34. Id.

35. Id.

36. PPG 4.

37. Id. 10.

38. Id. 14.

39. Id.

40. Williams, B. G. (2013). *Predators: The CIA's Drone War on Al Qaeda.* Potomac Books, 93.

41. Id. 16.

42. Brennan, J. O. (2020). Undaunted. Adfo Books, 210.

43. Id. 210–211.

44. Id. 212.

45. Id.

46. Id.

47. Id. 212–213.

48. Id. 213.

49. Id.

50. Id. 213–214.

51. Id. 214.

52. Id. 214–215.

53. Williams, B.G. (2013), 101.

54. Id. 102.

55. Savage, C., & Schmitt, E. (2017, September 21). Trump poised to drop some limits on drone strikes and commando raids. *The New York Times*. https://www.nytimes.com/2017/09/21/us/politics/trump-drone-strikes-commando-raids-rules.html.
56. White House. (2020). *Notice on the legal and policy frameworks guiding the United States' use of military force and related national security operations*. Federation of American Scientists. https://fas.org/man/eprint/frameworks-soleimani.pdf.

CHAPTER 6

Quantitative Research

This chapter discusses quantitative studies on the impact of US targeted strikes outside war zones on members of Al-Qaeda (AQ) and associated groups in the Middle East, South Asia, and Africa over roughly the last two decades. I use the term "targeted strikes" to refer to all types of operations whose goal is to kill a member of a terrorist organization. Drone strikes have been a substantial portion of such operations, but not the only form that the operations take. Osama bin Laden, for instance, was killed in a ground operation by US Navy SEALS, and Al-Qaeda in Iraq leader Abul Musab al-Zarqawi was killed in a strike by an F-16 fighter jet.

By AQ, I refer both to what is regarded as Al-Qaeda Core (AQC), the group's upper echelon leadership, and to groups affiliated with AQ, such as Al-Shabaab. Associates are groups not affiliated with AQ, but that sometimes work in concert with it, such as the Afghan and Pakistani Taliban (TTP). I will use the term "AQ" in this chapter to refer to all these groups, except where it is necessary to differentiate among them.

While AQ and the Islamic State (commonly referred to as "ISIS") have been rivals in recent years, ISIS traces its origins to the formation of AQ in Iraq (AQI). The US regards this connection as sufficient to subject ISIS to targeting. With one exception, however, there have not been any quantitative studies on the effects of specifically targeting ISIS apart from AQ. Finally, some of the studies described in this chapter focus on the

M. Regan, *Drone Strike–Analyzing the Impacts of Targeted Killing*, https://doi.org/10.1007/978-3-030-91119-5_6

impacts of strikes on particular high-level individuals, while others do not differentiate among targets for the strikes that they analyze.

If effectiveness is defined as the elimination of a terrorist group, US targeted strikes have been ineffective. AQ continues to exist and to be active in various locations. It seems reasonable, however, to assume that the goals of US strikes have been, in order of priority, to weaken the ability of AQ to conduct attacks:

(1) in the United States;
(2) against US targets outside the US;
(3) in the West, where most close US allies are located;
(4) against Western targets outside the West;
(5) in allied countries outside the West, especially Pakistan because of the risk of instability to a country with nuclear weapons;
(6) that do not fall within the first four categories but are international in nature, that is, conducted by a group outside its region[1];
(7) in other countries, conducted by an AQ affiliate or associate in those countries.

We can think of goals one (reducing attacks in the US) and three (reducing attacks in the West) as related to attacks against what AQ regards as the "far enemy." This is in contrast to the "near enemy," which consists of regimes in the Muslim world that are deemed apostates. Even though it rank third in priority, attacks in the West likely are of particular concern to the US because they demonstrate the ability to conduct attacks outside areas where the bulk of AQ and associates are located, in countries with defensive measures similar to the US. They also are more complex to coordinate than attacks by AQ groups in their home regions, which reflects the potential to conduct an attack in the US.

Attacks against US targets outside the US (goal two) and against Western targets outside the West (goal four) are also against the far enemy, although they may be conducted in the Muslim world. Reducing attacks against US allies outside the West (goal five) is a goal because the US relies on these allies to weaken AQ through local initiatives. Reducing international attacks (goal six) outside the West that are not in allied countries is a goal because the ability to coordinate and conduct such attacks may reflect the potential to launch attacks in the West. Finally, we can think of goal seven as the desire to reduce "local" attacks where AQ groups operate that do not fall within the previous six categories.

Thus, while the US ideally would like to seriously weaken AQ as a whole and reduce the total number of attacks it conducts, it has priorities that reflect more modest goals. The total number of attacks by AQ could decline because of fewer attacks in all the categories, or because decreases in some categories and increases in others result in a net decrease. The total number of attacks also could increase because of increases in all categories, or because decreases in some categories and increases in others result in a net increase. In each case, the most significant figures for US decision-makers would be the change in attacks related to the priorities listed above.

Strikes against AQC have been regarded as especially important in achieving the most important US goal of reducing attacks in the US; goal three, reducing attacks in the West; and goal six, reducing international attacks. As Chapter 8 describes in more detail, AQC has persistently focused in particular on attacks against the far enemy in the US and the West. In addition, international attacks require extensive planning and coordination that top leadership can provide. The assumption is that reducing the ranks of top leaders and disrupting their operations will impair their ability to provide such planning and coordination, and will lessen their ability to coordinate attacks in the West. Strikes against AQC also are important in achieving goals two and four, reducing attacks against US targets outside the US and Western targets outside the West, respectively, since AQC also has encouraged and assisted groups to conduct attacks against US and Western targets in Muslim countries.

Strikes against AQ mid-level commanders, specialists, and operatives also are regarded as valuable because they can weaken the ability to carry out complex international attacks. Strikes against other groups such as the TTP, which are not affiliated with AQ but associated with it, can be seen as designed mainly to reduce the risk of attacks against US targets outside the US, Western targets outside the West, and allies outside the West.

The description and assessment of quantitative studies below is organized according to those studies that analyze strikes (1) against AQC (2) Taliban leaders and (3) members of these groups and other militants more generally.

Most of the quantitative research to date that is most relevant to strikes outside war zones focuses on strikes in the FATA and Pakistan, with one case study on Somalia. The US also has conducted several drone strikes in Yemen, but there have been no rigorous empirical studies on their impact on terrorist groups in that country. In addition, events there since the Arab Spring in 2011, Saudi Arabian intervention in a civil war with the Huthis in 2015, and United Arab Emirate military operations in 2016–2018 make it difficult to isolate the impact of strikes from other influences on terrorist strength and activity. Chapter 8, however, which weighs the quantitative and qualitative evidence together, discusses the rise of AQ in the Arabian Peninsula (AQAP) in that country and its significance in assessing the long-term impact of the US targeting campaign on AQC. Finally, two studies described below examine strikes in war zones, in Afghanistan and Iraq.

QUANTITATIVE STUDIES

An ideal study of whether targeting AQ achieved the most important US goals would use strikes on AQC as the independent variable because of AQC's distinctive focus on attacks in the US and the West, and against US targets outside the US. In order to assess the effect of strikes against AQC, it ideally would use attacks in these locations and against these targets as dependent variables. It might also include international attacks outside a group's region as a dependent variable because these may indicate AQC capacity to conduct an attack in the US and the West. A study also ideally would use an identification strategy that controls for other variables that might influence the dependent variables, and that permits robust inferences of causality.

Nine studies use independent variables that represent or can reasonably be construed to include strikes against AQC. These are, in declining order of their focus on AQC, strikes:

(1) against *specific individual members of AQC*;
(2) against *leaders of AQ generally*;
(3) against *militant leaders in the FATA and in Pakistan*, where AQC was concentrated;
(4) in the *FATA and Pakistan generally*, for the same reason as (3) above; and
(5) against *militant leaders in Yemen and Somalia*, many of whom are likely to be leaders of Al-Qaeda in the Arabian Peninsula (AQAP) and AQ affiliate Al-Shabaab, respectively.

Some of these studies use dependent variables that reflect AQ attacks outside the countries in which strikes occurred, which are potentially most relevant to the goals of reducing attacks in the US and the West, and international attacks. Others use dependent variables related to attacks in the countries in which strikes occurred, which, depending on the country, may be relevant to the goals of reducing AQ attacks in allied countries outside the West, against US and Western targets, and reducing AQ attacks generally.

Other studies use as independent variables strikes against targets that include leaders or members of AQ and/or the Afghan and/or Pakistani Taliban. These examine strikes:

(6) against *Taliban leaders*;
(7) against *militant leaders in countries other than Pakistan, Yemen, and Somalia*, which include AQ leaders along with leaders of other groups; and
(8) in Afghanistan or Iraq.

The discussion below describes the independent and dependent variables that all these studies use, their methodological approaches, and their most important findings.

STRIKES AGAINST AQC
Specific Individual Members of AQC

Carson (2017)
Jennifer Varriale Carson analyzes the effects of the targeted killing of ten AQ leaders, relying on data from the Global Terrorism Database (GTD) on attacks from 1994 to 2013 by what she calls "the global jihadist movement" and by AQ.[2] She includes what she calls AQC Core in the latter attack category along with the affiliates, but does not separately differentiate attacks by these nine groups. She controls for several variables in order to separate the effect of killing each leader from the effects of other strikes and other counterterrorism measures.

In addition to using an interrupted time-series approach based on specified time intervals after a targeting, Carson uses what is known as a series hazard approach to assess the variation in lethality of attacks and suicide attacks. This is designed to take account of the effect of any attack-specific variables on the lethality of subsequent attacks that is not captured in an interrupted time-series model.[3]

Carson's dependent variables are the frequency and "hazard," or lethality, of attacks and the frequency and hazard of suicide attacks. This reflects the view that the effectiveness of counterterrorism measures "cannot be measured solely through a decrease in the frequency in total incidents. Rather, the complexity of these incidents should be taken into consideration."[4] She also examines the frequency and lethality of attacks in the countries in which the killings occurred. In addition, Carson characterizes the ten leaders as either political or military leaders to determine if this made any difference.

Carson concludes that none of the leader deaths affected the total number of attacks committed by the global jihadist movement or by AQ. She finds that some deaths had no effect, some were associated with increases in certain dependent variables, and others were associated with decreases. Carson also finds that killings that involved civilian casualties were not more likely to lead to an increase in attacks than those that did not, and that the deaths of military leaders did not have a deterrent effect that led to decreases in attacks. She concludes that her analysis indicates that the targeting of the ten AQ leaders had "mostly negligible effects on terrorism."[5] She explains, "Although small effects consistent with the deterrence perspective were discovered, these become inconsequential when their backlash counterparts [i.e., increases in attacks and/or lethality] are taken into account."[6]

Carson's findings on the extent to which there were statistically significant effects of the deaths of the ten AQ leaders are as follows[7]:

Military or Military/Political Leaders
Atwah

Time Series: No effects
Series Hazard: No effects

Al-Zarqawi

Time Series: No effects
Series Hazard: No effects

Habib

Time Series: Increases frequency of suicide attacks
Series Hazard: No effects

Al-Rahman

Time Series: Increases frequency of suicide attacks
Series Hazard: Increases hazard of suicide attacks

Al-Umda

Time Series: Increases frequency of suicide attacks
Series Hazard: Increases hazard of highly lethal attacks and decreases
Al-Qaeda and suicide attacks and attacks in Yemen

Political Leaders
Al-Harethi

Time Series: No effects
Series Hazard: Decreases hazard of highly lethal attacks

Rabia

Time Series: No effects
Series Hazard: No effects

Bin Laden

Time Series: No effects
Series Hazard: Decreases hazard of suicide attacks

Al-Awlaki

Time Series: Increases frequency of suicide attacks
Series Hazard: Increases hazard of attacks in Yemen

Al-Libi

Time Series: No effects
Series Hazard: Decreases hazard of Al-Qaeda attacks

Carson acknowledges that, "given the complex nature of the many conflicts during this time period, there may be historical threats to validity that remain unaccounted for in the models."[8] These may limit the extent to which periods preceding the deaths of the leaders in the study can serve as genuine counterfactuals that permit robust inferences about causality. She also notes that "the aggregation of multiple groups as one outcome" in the database may affect her findings.[9] Additional research, she says, should be conducted "to narrow the mechanisms responsible for the effects found here and continue to replicate them in other contexts with other controls."[10]

Finally, Carson suggests that it may be premature to declare targeted killing a failed policy based on her study. She notes that there has been no significant attack on the US since 9/11, although she notes that this "is more likely a result of other targeted hardening in counterterrorism strategies".[11] She also says that the increase in attacks could have been even larger had these leaders not been killed, but it is difficult if not impossible to demonstrate this. In addition, she suggests that the long-term effects of targeted killing may still be unclear in light of the fact that "group mortality is a long-term process."[12]

While she acknowledges its limitations, Carson's study is a careful attempt to assess whether targeted strikes against AQ leaders affected the frequency and lethality of attacks by both the global jihadist movement in general and by AQ in particular. Taking into account the possibility of confounding variables, her findings tentatively suggest that targeting AQ leadership has had mixed results at best.

Hepworth (2014)

Daniel Hepworth examines the impact on terrorist attacks of the targeted killing of four top AQC leaders: Abu Musab al-Zarqawi (2006), Abu Ayub al-Masri (2010), Osama bin Laden (2011), and Anwar al-Awlaki (2011).[13] His goal is to determine whether after each death there was a significant increase in attacks that ostensibly indicated a desire to retaliate for the strike.[14] He draws on the Global Terrorism Database to focus on attacks by what he called the "AQ Network" (AQN) that occurred two months prior to and two months following the death of each of the four leaders. In previous work, he lists 19 groups as members of this network.[15]

Hepworth also identifies the specific terrorist group carrying out each attack, and whether it was a group led by the leader who had been killed. In addition, he focuses on whether the attack was on a government or civilian target, the number of fatalities for each attack, and whether the attack was a bombing or an armed assault.

Hepworth finds that the number of attacks in the two months before and after a leader's death was essentially identical. There was a slight increase in the number of attacks by groups whose leader had died but this was statistically insignificant. The average number of fatalities per overall attacks by AQN declined, however, from 4.16 to 3.01, and fatalities per attacks by groups whose leader had died decreased from 9.43 to 7.89. There was a slight increase in suicide attacks after a targeted killing, but only by groups other than those whose leader had been killed. There was no statistically significant change in terrorist attack success rates, the targeting of softer targets, or use of more difficult tactics. "In the end," Hepworth says, "this study produces some indication of a weakening of terrorist groups in regard to the decrease in fatalities per attack; however there appeared no other significant changes and certainly no evidence of retaliation on the part of the terrorist groups."[16]

The aim of this study is to determine if a targeted strike against a leader resulted in an increase in attacks prompted by a desire for retaliation. While Hepworth did not find this is the case, one might also characterize his overall results as indicating that targeted strikes at best are only mildly effective. There is no significant changes in the number of attacks or in their success rates, although there was some reduction in the number of fatalities.

AQ Leaders Generally

Jenna Jordan (2019 and 2014)
I discuss here Jordan's analysis of decapitation operations against AQ and ISIS contained in a portion of her book described in Chapter 3, as well as in a 2014 article.[17] Jordan rightly emphasizes that Al-Qaeda is not a single integrated organization but comprises a network that includes local affiliates that exercise considerable autonomy. Her analysis focuses on what she calls AQ Core (AQC), or top leadership, and leadership of several affiliates in the Middle East and South Asia.

Jordan examines annual data on 288 cases of successful targeting of leadership of these groups from 1995 through 2016, and on the number of attacks the groups conducted from 1992 through 2017. She notes that her targeting data are "by no means an exhaustive list," but are meant to convey "the frequency with which these groups have been targeted" and to "track changes in their activity."[18] Her basic approach is to determine whether the independent variable of changes in the number of annual decapitations is accompanied by increases or decreases in the dependent variable of the annual number of attacks.

The data on annual successful targeting and number of attacks over this period are set forth below. Jordan depicts her data in graph form rather than in figures, so the numbers are my estimates based on the graphs. I have not attempted to separately estimate figures for AQC and the various affiliates because the subtle shading for each group on the graph in the book makes this very difficult. She says that her data indicate, however, that AQC "has undergone a significant decline in activity, and while some affiliates have become less active, others have increased activity."[19]

Decapitations	Terrorist attacks
1995: 1	
1998: 3	1998: 2
	2000: 1
2001: 6	2001: 4
2002: 3	2002: 5
2003: 6	2003: 15
2004: 20	2004: 15
2005: 31	2005: 80
2006: 10	2006: 10
2007: 3	2007: 70
2008: 24	2008: 60
2009: 11	2009: 40
2010: 33	2010: 60
2011: 23	2011: 95
2012: 38	2012: 225
2013: 46	2013: 200
2014: 20	2014: 375
2015: 7	2015: 225
2016: 3	2016: 170

Jordan argues that, aside from some outliers, these data indicate that decapitations are associated with an increase in attacks and fatalities. Without reproducing the plot charts here, however, it seems more accurate to say that the data indicate considerable variation with no clear pattern.

Jordan's data do not include attacks carried out by AQ in Iraq (AQI) after 2006, because by then the group was operating as the Islamic State. Jordan includes a separate chart on attacks, but not annual decapitations, for AQI and for its Islamic State successor. This makes it difficult to assess her claims about the effect of decapitation on this group. She says that AQI suffered 36 decapitations from 2004 to 2007, and that it carried out six attacks in 2004, 68 in 2005, five in 2006, and 41 in 2007. AQI leader al-Zarqawi was killed on June 7, 2006, but Jordan argues that the significant decline in attacks in that year was due to a variety of factors beyond the decapitation. She might also have suggested that the significant increase in attacks in 2007 may indicate that the removal of al-Zarqawi did not significantly damage AQI.

Jordan also notes that ISIS suffered 17 decapitations in 2010, but carried out 26 attacks in that year, 31 in 2011, 304 in 2012, and 82 in 2013. She states that this indicates "a highly resilient organization that seemed to become even more active after sustained decapitation efforts."[20] Without annual data for both decapitations and attacks, however, it is difficult to assess this claim.

Finally, Jordan discusses activity by ISIS from 2013 to 2017 in another chapter of her book. She examines the number of attacks by the group between 2013 and 2017, and says, "Despite a large number of attacks against ISIS, the group is still active."[21] She does not, however, provide data on ISIS decapitations. Jordan notes a 40% decline in attack fatalities from 2016 to 2017, but says that the group is "still remarkably active despite the loss of a considerable amount of territory."[22]

It is difficult from these data to assess the impact of targeting on the group, given the absence of information on decapitations. In addition, it is not clear how many of the attacks by ISIS occurred during the intensive military operations by Iraq and the US that resulted in the group losing considerable territory over this period. Both attacks and decapitations may have occurred during the course of these operations, which would make it difficult to isolate a relationship between the two.

Jordan's work on targeting against AQ and its affiliates and against ISIS does not employ any identification strategy that would provide a basis for strong inferences about causality. The analysis of AQ and its affiliates plots annual decapitations, attacks, and fatalities over time and attempts to look for trends on an annual level. This does not permit analysis over briefer periods of time that might support more rigorous conclusions about causality. The discussion of ISIS does not provide enough detail to enable assessment of causal relationships.

On the other hand, Jordan's book provides a more rigorous theoretical framework for analyzing and explaining the data than do many who study this subject. This framework is based on studies of several groups, not simply AQ and ISIS. Based on this work, she spends considerable time in her book discussing the characteristics of AQ in particular that provide it with organizational resilience. These are their level of bureaucratic organization and community support, and their religious ideology.[23]

A bureaucratic structure, Jordan argues, "can provide groups with the organizational redundancy necessary to survive leadership attacks."[24] She describes AQ's structure as "quasi-bureaucratic" in the sense that it has a hierarchical command capable of coordinating and providing resources for terrorist attacks, combined with a decentralized network of affiliates that can initiate and carry out attacks.[25] AQC sets the ideological orientation and broad political goals and the strategy to reach them, while the affiliates have considerable organizational and operational autonomy. Each affiliate has its own goals, structure, political messages, and strategy.

AQC has been targeted more than any organization other than ISIS and the Islamic State in Iraq (ISI), and has been weakened with respect to the frequency of its attacks. It remains active, she says, in messaging and franchising efforts in extending affiliations into different regions. This is consistent with the research by Smith and Walsh on AQ propaganda activity described below. The significance of affiliates is reflected in the fact that the data on attacks from 1992 to 2017 include eight such entities involved in attacks in addition to AQC, and that affiliates have carried out the vast majority of attacks for the last several years.

Jordan says that her research indicates that groups with a religious ideology also are more resilient in responding to leadership decapitation. This is because their members are motivated by allegiance to a set of ideas rather than a charismatic individual. She describes bin Laden's formulation of Islamist doctrine as a basis for attracting individuals to AQ and its jihadist project. The animating power of this ideology, she argues, means that the deaths of particular individuals are unlikely to bring about the demise of the organization. Finally, Jordan says that popular support can allow a group to "recruit, raise money, and obtain critical resources."[26] It also can help it to avoid surveillance, detection, and attack by security forces. Jordan maintains that AQ has support on both the local and global level that helps it withstand operations against its leadership.

In sum, Jordan's claims about the effectiveness of targeting rest on a basic comparison of annual trends in decapitations, terrorist attacks, and deaths from such attacks, without any attempt to draw on more refined identification strategies. At the same time, her data provide a plausible basis for claiming at least that the number of successful strikes is not correlated with the overall number of AQ attacks and fatalities from them, and her conceptual framework offers plausible explanations for this. Finally, especially important with regard to the primary US goal of reducing the threat of attacks in the US, is her finding that several affiliates have become more active conducting attacks, while AQC "has undergone a significant decline in activity."[27]

Militant Leaders in the FATA and Pakistan

A large percentage of AQC were in the FATA after 9/11. It thus seems reasonable to assume that using strikes against leaders in the FATA as an independent variable could serve as a rough proxy for analyzing strikes against AQC. Strikes against militant leaders in Pakistan more generally also can serve as a rough proxy for strikes against AQC since most strikes in Pakistan were in the FATA.

Rigterink (2021)
Anouk Rigterink analyzes the impact of successful and unsuccessful targeting attempts against leaders of 13 terrorist groups in the FATA from 2004 to 2015.[28] She reviews 45 strikes, of which 15 succeeded in killing the target. As does the study by Johnston and Sarbahi described below, and Jaeger and Paserman's study of Israeli targeting described in Chapter 3, she uses an identification strategy that assumes that whether a strike is successful or unsuccessful is quasi-random. Her dependent variable is the number of attacks worldwide, excluding the US, Europe, and Australia, for each month after each successful or unsuccessful strike, for up to 15 months. Thus, months in which there was a successful attack against a group's leader are the treatment group, while months in which there was an unsuccessful attempt on a group's leader are the control group.

Rigterink succinctly summarizes her main finding: "[T]he number of attacks committed by a terrorist group increases in the 6 months after a drone strike hits one of its leaders, whereas no change in terrorist violence can be detected after a strike that targets but misses a leader."[29] Beginning with two months after a "hit," there is a statistically significant increase in three of six months after the hit, which ranges between 47.7% and 70.3%. There is no statistically significant association between hits and either increases or decreases in attacks beyond seven months.

The author finds that the number of terrorist attacks against civilian and nongovernmental targets is statistically higher after a successful strike than an unsuccessful one. Rigterink argues that this indicates that increases in attacks after successful leadership targeting are best explained as a loss of control over an organization by a leader who favors more discriminating attacks than do lower-level members. Research indicates, she says, that leaders discourage attacks against civilians and eschew claiming group responsibility for such attacks, because of concern that this will reduce public support for the group. This is reflected in the fact that the effect of a successful strike on an increase in attacks on civilian and nongovernmental targets is stronger for AQ and the Taliban than for other groups. At the same time, there is no significant decline in the number of attacks against military targets.

Finally, the author finds no relationship between strikes that harm civilians and increases in attacks, as one "backlash" theory suggests. "If anything," she says, the data indicate "a *decrease* in the number of terrorist attacks, by the terrorist group itself and by an aggregation of all terrorist groups in the study."[30]

In contrast to other studies that focus on overall strikes in the FATA, Rigterink focuses on strikes against top leaders. She examines changes in attacks worldwide rather than in particular locations within the FATA. Since a significant portion of AQC was located in the FATA during the period of her study, this could provide insight into whether decapitation impaired AQC leaders' ability to coordinate international attacks. She only examines 15 successful strikes, however, which is a small percentage of overall strikes. She does note that she did an analysis based on a database with a broader definition of leaders, which included 137 strikes, as a robustness check. She does not, however, indicate what portion of these strikes were successful.

In addition, Rigterink's dependent variable excludes attacks in the US, Europe, and Australia, but reducing such attacks was a crucial goal of

US strikes. Although it would be interesting to investigate the effect of a drone hit on terrorist attacks in "'the West,'" she says, "there have been only eight such attacks over the research period, making this impossible."[31] This in itself, however, could be significant in light of the most important US goals. Finally, Rigterink argues that the increase in attacks against civilian and nongovernmental targets reflects a reduction in control by terrorist group leaders, who tend to favor more discriminate attacks. If this is the case, it supports a claim that strikes in the FATA weakened AQC and decreased its ability to influence attack targets.

Johnston and Sarbahi (2016)

Patrick Johnston and Anoop Sarbahi examine the impact of targeted strikes in the FATA from January 2007 through September 2011.[32] They compare various measures of terrorist activity in the FATA during weeks in which there were and were not such strikes in each of seven agencies in the FATA, which are local districts. For each week and agency, their independent variables are the number of strikes and senior leaders killed, while dependent variables are the number of militant attacks, the number of dead or wounded from those attacks, and the number of militant attacks against tribal elders. The latter figure is relevant, they maintain, because "terrorist groups frequently see [these persons] as colluding with the enemy and impeding the pursuit of their agenda."[33] The discussion in this section focuses on their findings regarding the impact of strikes on senior leaders, while the section that follows discusses their findings concerning the impact of strikes in general.

Johnston and Sarbahi suggest that targeted strikes occur on a "quasi-random" basis because several factors unrelated to terrorist group activities can influence when they occur. These include weather, availability of an aircraft with a weapon, work schedules of those who must authorize strikes, and when a clear opportunity to strike arises.[34] This gives them some confidence that there are no systematic differences between groups that are targeted and those that are not.

They find that a strike in which a senior terrorist leader was killed is associated with a statistically significant decrease in the number of attacks. The direction of the relationship is also negative for the lethality of attacks, but is not statistically significant. "Overall," the authors conclude, "there is some evidence that key militant leaders do matter for a terrorist organization's ability to conduct kinetic attacks. The evidence that removing [senior leaders] reduces the lethality of militant violence is less conclusive."[35]

The authors' independent variable of senior leaders killed likely included AQC leaders, given the concentration of its senior leaders in the FATA at the time. Their dependent variables, however, are local, focusing on various measures of terrorist activity in the area. While instructive, this provides less insight into the effect of strikes on top leadership than studies that focus on attacks in the West and international attacks, whose complexity may require planning and coordination by such leaders. Finally, if strikes are not in fact quasi-random, but features of groups affect the likelihood of a successful strike, strikes will not be wholly exogenous. This could weaken any claim of causality.

Strikes in the FATA and Pakistan Generally

Studies that examine strikes in the FATA and Pakistan generally, rather than strikes against leaders in those areas, could still provide some insight because of the concentration of top AQC leaders there. Studies of strikes in Pakistan in general also shed some light on the impacts of strikes on AQC, since most targeting in Pakistan was in the FATA where AQC was concentrated.

With respect to dependent variables, attacks outside the FATA and Pakistan are most relevant to achievement of the most important US goals. Attacks within these locations are relevant to the goals of reducing attacks in Pakistan, against US and Western targets, and reducing attacks generally. Attacks by militants in the FATA and in Pakistan in general during the study periods were conducted mainly by the Pakistani Taliban (TTP) and other groups. A 2018 study by Jaeger and Siddique described below says, "Because Al-Qaeda has directly claimed responsibility for a very small number of terrorist attacks (nine incidents in Pakistan and none in Afghanistan)... we will refer to the 'Taliban' as the terrorist actor in the analysis."[36] AQC, however, provided some training and other forms of assistance to these groups. Changes in attacks in the FATA and in Pakistan as a whole thus may reflect the impacts of strikes on AQC as well as on groups associated with it.

The studies by Lehrke and Schomaker, Javier Jordan, and Smith and Walsh described below use militant activity outside Pakistan as independent variables, while Mir and Moore, Mahmood and Jetter, Jaeger and Siddique, Johnston and Sarbahi, and Carson use attacks in the FATA or

Pakistan. Finally, a study by Bauer, Reese, and Ruby examines the effects of terrorist group punishment of local collaborators with the US drone campaign in the FATA on the number of militant leaders, other militants, and civilians killed by drone strikes.

Lehrke and Schomaker (2016)
Jesse Lehrke and Rahel Schomaker analyze the effects of different US counterterrorism measures in the period from 2001 to 2011 in order to determine the relative effectiveness of killing, capture, and traditional defensive tactics in reducing the number or lethality of terrorist attacks.[37] These measures included decapitation (by which they mean killing) of top leaders of 96 terrorist groups, discussed later in this chapter; drone strikes in Pakistan and Yemen; troop levels in Afghanistan and Iraq; arrest; rendition; and more than 30 defensive counterterrorism measures. Since the period of their study is 2001–2011, the vast majority of drone strikes were in Pakistan, and most of these were in the FATA.

The discussion in this section examines their analysis of drone strikes, while discussion in another section below focuses on their analysis of the effects of targeting of leaders of the 96 groups. The authors rely on roughly two dozen regression models to identify the effects of different measures on several dependent variables. Those most relevant to US goals are annual attacks and deaths from them by AQ or the Taliban; total worldwide attacks by terrorist groups and jihadist terrorist groups; terrorist attacks in Western countries and against Western targets worldwide; jihadist attacks against Western targets worldwide; terrorist group attacks consisting of multiple simultaneous coordinated attacks; and deaths from terrorist attacks and coordinated attacks.

The authors find that drone strikes are correlated with a statistically significant increase in the number of *total terrorist attacks* worldwide. This is the case for both strikes in Pakistan and for all strikes. Strikes in Yemen have no statistically significant effect, which the authors suggest may be because of their small number prior to 2011. Strikes in Pakistan and total strikes also are correlated with a statistically significant, although lower, increase in *jihadist* attacks worldwide. In addition, strikes in Pakistan are significantly correlated with an increase in total attacks in Afghanistan and Iraq, although the effect is not as large as worldwide. The number of militant deaths from strikes is also associated with a statistically significant increase in total attacks worldwide and attacks in war zones.

Drone strikes are not significantly correlated one way or the other, however, with any attacks in Western states, nor are civilian deaths in drone strikes correlated with jihadist attacks worldwide, attacks in the West, or attacks on Western targets. Nor are there any statistically significant correlations between drone strikes and the number of fatalities from attacks by AQ or the Taliban.

The authors suggest that findings of increases in attacks provides support for a possible "backlash" effect of drone strikes, although this appears not to be in response to civilian casualties from such strikes.[38] This is consistent with some studies described later in this chapter. The authors also argue that drone strikes appear to have no effect on the organizational capability of terrorist groups, given findings that strikes are not correlated with deaths in coordinated attacks, deaths per coordinated attack, deaths worldwide, and "attacks in the West (which are more complex to organize)."[39]

The authors find that variables reflecting an array of defensive measures have the most significant effect in reducing attacks in the West, although they were associated with increases in jihadist attacks worldwide. They conclude, "Defenses make the West safer and also overall make it harder to conduct sophisticated multipronged attacks," with some indication that they also reduce fatalities from such attacks.[40] They speculate that the association with increase in worldwide attacks may mean that hardening Western defenses serves to redirect terrorist to more vulnerable targets in other parts of the world.

The fact that drone strikes during the authors' study period were mainly in Pakistan means that this independent variable might serve as a rough proxy for strikes against AQC. In addition, using defensive measures as a control variable holds the promise of isolating the impact of strikes. Their dependent variable for attacks in the West is total terrorist attacks, however, not attacks by AQ, and their dependent variable for AQ attacks is total attacks. This makes it difficult to make a claim about the impact of strikes on an outcome especially important to the US, which is AQ attacks in the US and West. Finally, their findings apply only through 2011, and do not reflect the possible cumulative effects of strikes. Some of the qualitative material discussed in the next chapter suggests that there may have been such effects.

Javier Jordan (2014)

Javier Jordan uses as his independent variable drone strikes in Pakistan beginning in 2008.[41] He says that the number of AQ members killed by strikes is "a very high percentage of its command cadres," but does not differentiate between strikes that target leaders and those that target other group members.[42]

As his dependent variables, Jordan examined the number and lethality of attacks attributable to AQC in the US and Western Europe from 2001 to 2012. This is an especially useful approach, since a major goal of strikes has been to reduce attacks in these locations. From 2001 to 2006, there were 20 attempts that included three successful attacks. The latter were the attacks on 9/11, the 2004 Madrid train bombings, and the 2005 London bombings, all of which in total resulted in 3220 deaths. From 2007 to 2012, there were 13 attempts, none of which were successful. Jordan argues that this indicates that strikes contributed to weakening AQC by undermining its ability to provide coordination that enabled the most ambitious types of attacks, thinning the ranks of leaders and persons who had valuable specialized skills, and reducing the material resources it had available to conduct its operations.

Jordan argues that the effectiveness of drone strikes is attributable to three impacts. The first is impairment of the hierarchical structure of AQC, as continuous targeting of leaders "forces them to devote substantial attention and energy to self-protection rather than to coordinate the organization."[43] Second, strikes have deprived AQC of several leaders responsible for military, financial, and religious operations. Jordan notes that recruitment and training activities have been substantially impaired due to the need for "frequent changes of location, splitting into small groups, hiding out for most of the day in small mountain huts, use of human couriers to avoid electronic communications, etc."[44] Finally, he argues that strikes have reduced the flow of key material resources from AQC to the larger group.

Jordan acknowledges that one cannot attribute the decline in attacks in the West solely to targeted strikes. "[T]he decline in the lethality of Al Qaeda in the United States and Europe," he says, "can be ascribed to tighter border controls, the adaptation of legislation to the operating methods of jihadist terrorism, increased international cooperation and the greater attention devoted to the threat by intelligence agencies and police forces."[45] He suggests, however, that the data provide reason to believe that the effects of targeted strikes complement these other measures.

"Were it not for the drone strikes in Pakistan," he says, "AQ recruits who managed to reach the tribal areas would enjoy greater possibilities to receive training and to act in a coordinated manner."[46]

While his study is suggestive, Jordan does not attempt to control for the effect of other variables that likely affected attacks in the West. Nor does he use an identification strategy that might illuminate what would've happened had there been no drone strikes but other measures were adopted, although the latter admittedly is difficult. He does draw on some qualitative evidence in support of his conclusion, which Chapter 7 discusses. Other qualitative studies described in that chapter also provide support for his conclusions.

Smith and Walsh (2013)

Megan Smith and James Walsh analyzed the impact of US targeted strikes in Pakistan on AQ's overall propaganda output.[47] The authors' independent variable is the number of US targeted strikes in Pakistan, while their dependent variable is the amount of annual AQ propaganda from January 2006 through November 2011. They are unable to disaggregate data on strikes to identify the target of each strike, which means that "the dataset includes all drone strikes, including those that may not have been targeted at AQ Central."[48] They measure daily propaganda output based on information from the database of AQ messages and propaganda maintained by IntelCenter. These data cover statements and other public or semi-public media communications issued by AQ through its as-Sahab Media, which is its formal outlet, and related dissemination channels.

Controlling for variables that might otherwise affect the rate of propaganda, the authors find no statistically significant evidence that targeted strikes either increase or decrease propaganda up to 31 weeks after a strike. They suggest, however, that the absence of any demonstrable effect one way or another is problematic for the claim of drone strike efficacy. "Creating sophisticated propaganda," they say, "requires a cadre of experienced producers, media workers, and 'stars' who are all vulnerable to drone strikes. Thus if drone strikes hinder AQ's ability to operate effectively, this should be reflected in changes in the organization's propaganda. We find little evidence that this is the case."[49]

Smith and Walsh rely on a metric for evaluating the impact of drone strikes that is distinctive from ones used in other studies. Its plausibility is suggested in Jenna Jordan's work described above, which observes that an important function of AQC is the dissemination of propaganda to decentralized affiliates that carry out many of the attacks. The study therefore uses a dependent variable that may provide insight into the impact of targeted strikes on an activity that is distinctive to AQC, even though what is necessary to conduct that operation is different from what is necessary to plan and coordinate attacks.

Mir and Moore (2019)

Asfandyar Mir and Dylan Moore analyze data on strikes and attacks in the North Waziristan agency in the FATA between January 2002 and November 2011.[50] Their independent variable is drone strikes and their dependent variables are the number of insurgent attacks and fatalities from attacks, both analyzed according to local areas in North Waziristan and the FATA known as tehsils. They compare militant violence before and after the 2008 escalation of US strikes in the FATA, most of which occurred in North Waziristan. They find that the escalation corresponds with a reduction of 9–13 attacks and 51–86 casualties per month in North Waziristan. They also find that this reduction was not offset by increases in neighboring areas, indicating that militants did not simply move their operations outside the "flight box" in which strikes were authorized.

Their causal claim in part relies on use of the difference-in-differences identification strategy described in Chapter 2. They assume that the post-2008 change in expected monthly attacks and casualties outside North Waziristan reflects what would have occurred in a counterfactual North Waziristan without targeted strikes. This purports to use the areas in the FATA outside North Waziristan as a control group. The authors acknowledge, however, that variation in violence prior to 2008 increased at a much faster rate in North Waziristan than in other districts, which undermines the parallel trends assumption on which the difference-in-differences approach is based.

Mir and Moore attempt to compensate for this by incorporating local unit trends within tehils, and by controlling for variables that may have affected attacks. They then use regression analysis to estimate the level of correlation between strikes and levels of violence in North Waziristan. They also rest their causal claim on other empirical data. They note, for instance, that post-2008 violence in North Waziristan was marked by an absence of large spikes in violence that occurred in that agency in 2006 and 2007. In addition, pre-2008 activity in North Waziristan involved sustained attacks against Pakistani state targets, which virtually ceased after strikes began. In contrast, Taliban attacks against such targets in a FATA agency outside North Waziristan were frequent prior to 2008 and continued at the same level afterward.

Mir and Moore suggest that their results reflect the potential of strikes to reduce militant violence through both kinetic and anticipatory effects. Kinetic effects consist of "damage to insurgent organizations directly caused by drone strikes, such as leadership decapitation, rank-and-file attrition, lost capabilities, and casualties of civilian supporters."[51] Anticipatory effects are changes in insurgent behavior based upon fear of being targeted in the future.

Although any threat of force by state forces may have anticipatory effects, "a drone program's sustained surveillance and swiftly executed strikes may produce especially high levels of perceived risk of targeting."[52] As a result, "[i]nsurgents may feel compelled to significantly adjust their organizational practices to mitigate the threat posed by a drone program, inducing changes in the way they move, communicate, and interact within their group in a bid to avoid targeting."[53] These changes, they argue, prevented groups like AQ and the Pakistan Taliban from successfully adapting to the drone program because they resulted in "three major changes in insurgent life: restricted movement, constrained communication, and compromised intragroup trust."[54]

Mir and Moore contend that these anticipatory effects can produce more enduring changes than those in the immediate aftermath of individual strikes. They find that most of the correlation they identify between the strike program from 2008 and afterward "cannot be explained as simply the aggregation of the impact of many individual drone strikes," which would reflect only kinetic effects.[55] Rather, it represents anticipatory changes in militant behavior that contributed to fewer attacks. Thus, "kinetic effects interacted with anticipatory effects in first damaging and then constraining the recovery" of AQ and the Pakistan Taliban.[56]

Mir and Moore note the importance of local partner capacity and cooperation, in this case from Pakistan. In a separate article, Mir argues that an effective counterterrorism campaign by a "counterterrorism state" outside its borders is marked by what he calls "legibility" and "speed of exploitation."[57] The first refers to the acquisition of detailed intelligence about the area of operations, which includes information on various characteristics of the population, their activities, and personal, social, economic, and political networks. A state can leverage legibility "to generate information – cues, leads and other details – on an armed group hiding within the population."[58] Because of its limited ground presence, the counterterrorism state must rely on technology and local partner cooperation in order to achieve legibility.[59] Speed of exploitation refers to the rate at which such intelligence can be utilized to conduct operations such as targeted strikes.

Not all campaigns are in a position to create these two conditions for success, but Mir argues that the US strike campaign in the FATA was. Support for Mir's framework also comes from the research on the Israeli targeting campaign described in Chapter 3, which relied on extensive intelligence on local conditions combined with the rapid pace of strikes. As that chapter describes, studies generally find that these operations reduced fatalities from suicide attacks, although they did not reduce the number of attacks.

Mir and Moore maintain that their finding of anticipatory effects beyond the immediate aftermath of a strike "challenges the popularly held notion that 'drones create more terrorists.'"[60] Either the program did not increase militant recruitment, they argue, or, if it did, "insurgent groups struggled to integrate these new recruits into their organizations... The crisis of in-group trust may have imposed constraints on the extent to which insurgents could benefit from the availability of recruits."[61] Chapter 11 examines more closely the claim that drone strikes increase terrorist recruitment, and finds that the most robust research provides reasons to doubt it. Finally, Mir and Moore warn that policymakers "should be very cautious in interpreting our results for design of future campaigns. We remain uncertain about the level of capabilities required in other weak state contexts like Afghanistan and Yemen."[62]

Mir and Moore acknowledge that the absence of exact parallel trends inside and outside of North Waziristan means that terrorist activity in areas outside of North Waziristan may be subject to some confounding variables that make these areas less than a perfect control group. The study nonetheless reflects a careful effort to conduct a study that provides a basis for more robust inferences about causality than traditional analysis of correlations.

Mahmood and Jetter (2019)
Rafat Mahmood and Michael Jetter analyze the effect of US drone strikes in Pakistan on terrorist activity in that country from January 1, 2006 to December 31, 2016.[63] The authors' use of attacks in Pakistan as their

dependent variable focuses on the important US goal of reducing attacks against allies in general and Pakistan in particular.

Mahmood and Jetter note that using conventional regression analysis to predict the number of attacks after a strike raises concerns about endogeneity, in that anticipated terrorist activity may cause strikes to be conducted. The authors address this concern by using an identification strategy based on the relationship between the strength of wind and drone strikes. Specifically, they find that wind is a negative and statistically significant predictor of strikes because drones are prone to crash at wind levels greater than just under 28 km/h (14 mph). They acknowledge that wind is only one factor the US military takes into account, but that it is a significant predictor when controlling for terrorist attacks and Pakistani military actions preceding a strike, as well as for time-specific characteristics such as Friday and Ramadan in the Islamic tradition.

Mahmood and Jetter first predict drone strikes on a given day based on an index of the maximum wind gusts on that day at Miran Shah, the capital of North Waziristan in the FATA. Wind gusts there are strongly correlated with those from Wana, the capital of South Waziristan. Drone strikes in these two agencies constitute 93% of all strikes in Pakistan, with 71% in North Waziristan. Wind levels are not correlated with any events that might affect the probability of a strike. The predicted drone strikes on that day are then used to predict terrorist attacks in Pakistan following each strike.

The authors find that drone strikes are "a positive and statistically precise predictor of subsequent terrorism."[64] Specifically, "one drone strike causes more than four terror attacks per day in the subsequent week,"[65] or 16% of the terror attacks per average day.[66] This effect remains constant for periods up to sixty days after the initial strike. The authors argue that the retaliatory nature of strikes is reflected in the fact that attacks that are easier to conduct, such as bombings and assaults, increase, but not those that require more complex planning. Finally, they find that 53% of the predicted attacks are on government targets, consistent with a "retaliatory narrative of terrorists who perceive the Pakistani government as a US collaborator in the Pakistani military and government as apostates."

Mahmood and Jetter use an ingenious identification strategy in an effort to address the risk of endogeneity. Its plausibility hinges on the degree to which wind levels influence drone strike decisions. Conversations with some experts, however, suggest that drones are often able to operate in strong winds, and that wind at ground level may not be indicative of conditions at the higher altitudes at which drones fly. More empirical information on the role of wind in decisions about drone operations would help clarify the strength of the authors' conclusions. Their work nonetheless reflects commendable acknowledgment of the importance of doing careful empirical research that seeks to provide robust inferences about causality.

Jaeger and Siddique (2018)
David Jaeger and Zahra Siddique examine the impact of US strikes on Taliban leaders in Afghanistan and Pakistan.[67] They analyze daily data from January 1, 2007 to September 30, 2011 to construct time-series model estimates. Their independent variable is daily strikes in each country, while the dependent variables are the number and probability of attacks in those countries up to 21 days after a strike. They conclude, "Our most important finding is that drone strikes matter, but primarily for Taliban violence in Pakistan. There is less of an effect of drone strikes on Taliban violence across the border in Afghanistan."[68] As with Mahmood and Jetter, the authors' analysis of the effect of strikes on attacks in Pakistan focuses on an important US goal.

In Pakistan, they find mixed impacts of strikes over a 21-day period. First, an attack by the Taliban is 9% more likely to occur five days after a drone strike and 7.4% more likely to occur six days after a strike. This indicates that strikes may trigger retaliatory Taliban attacks. There are, however, 0.11 fewer attacks twelve days after a strike, and a statistically significant decline in attacks after a month. Jaeger and Siddique say, "This suggests an intertemporal reallocation of terrorist attacks in Pakistan, which are pushed forward by the Taliban in response to drone strikes."[69] That is, strikes may not cause an overall increase in strikes, but simply affect their timing.

The authors then analyze whether there are different effects between successful and unsuccessful strikes in Pakistan. With respect to statistically significant changes in the *probability* of an attack following a successful strike, an attack is 17.7% less likely three days after a strike, and 13.5% less likely 14 days afterward. With regard to statistically significant changes in *number* of attacks following a successful strike, there are 0.121 fewer attacks 12 days after a strike, 0.283 fewer attacks 14 days after, and 0.25 fewer attacks 19 days afterward.

The statistically significant effects of unsuccessful strikes are mixed. An attack is 9.7% more likely five days after an unsuccessful strike attempt and 7.6% more likely six days afterward. Twelve days after an unsuccessful strike, however an attack is 7.5% less likely, and after thirteen days it is 8.7% less likely. With regard to the number of attacks after an unsuccessful strike, there is a 0.099 increase in attacks six days after a strike, but a decrease of 0.121 twelve days after strike.

The authors conclude that because all of the statistically significant changes associated with successful strikes indicate a decline in attacks "it appears that there is an incapacitation effect of the Taliban due to a lost militant leader."[70] In addition to incapacitation, they also refer to a "deterrent" effect of strikes.[71] These explanations are comparable to Mir and Moore's kinetic and anticipatory mechanisms.

Jaeger and Siddique suggest that the mixed results from unsuccessful strikes indicate that any retaliation "is in response to these kinds of drone strikes, rather than drone strikes which are able to take out a militant leader."[72] While there might also be a desire for vengeance in response to successful strikes, presumably this effect is outweighed by the incapacitation from the strike that makes it more difficult to conduct attacks afterward.

This study thus suggests that drone strikes in Pakistan had mixed effects. Successful strikes reduced the probability and number of attacks. Unsuccessful strikes prompted a short-term, perhaps retaliatory, increase in attacks but some long-term decline. It is difficult to determine without more detailed data the net effect of unsuccessful strikes. The study indicates, however, that it would be important to take this effect into account when assessing the overall effectiveness of a drone campaign in which there are both successful and unsuccessful strikes.

Johnston and Sarbahi (2016)

In addition to studying the impact of strikes against senior militant leaders, the research by Johnston and Sarbahi described above finds that weeks in which a strike is conducted in a district in the FATA are associated with a statistically significant five percentage point reduction in attacks on civilians in that district, from 0.88 per week to 0.68 per week, and that the lethality of attacks declines by an average of nearly 25 percentage points. The authors also find that strikes are associated with declines in targeting of tribal elders. Some evidence suggests that the effect of a strike may be as long as five weeks, but the authors regard this as mainly speculative.

Johnston and Sarbahi conclude that the decline in attacks in a district is not the result of militants leaving unsafe areas and conducting attacks elsewhere in the region. Instead, violence declines in areas within 50 miles of the strikes. Thus, the authors conclude, "there is no evidence that drone strikes have a 'whack-a-mole' effect in which militant violence is pushed to other areas."[73]

The authors offer two explanations for why strikes have these effects. One mechanism is "degradation," which removes "leaders and other 'high value individuals'" who have "valuable skills, resources, or connections." Another mechanism is "disruption." This reflects drone strikes' ability to "reduce militants' ability to operate in a cohesive, efficient manner and limit their ability to control local areas."[74] The interaction of the two effects thus is that a strike against a leader deprives an organization of someone with distinctive skills, while the threat of drone strikes can make it difficult to replace them because "recruiting and deploying their replacements... will be costly and difficult."[75] These are comparable to Mir and Moore's concepts of kinetic and anticipatory effects, respectively.

The authors acknowledge that achieving long-term effects may require a campaign of ongoing strikes: "Given drone strikes' disruptive short-term efficacy, using drones to counter terrorism effectively may require counterterrorists to apply continual pressure against terrorist networks."[76] While they assume that strikes are quasi-random, they also admit that strikes are not fully exogenous. They thus "urge caution in inferring causality."[77] Their study nonetheless represents use of an identification strategy that attempts to provide a more robust basis for causal inference than a study based on simple correlation.

Carson (2018)

Jennifer Varriale Carson conducted an analysis of the impacts of 31 targeted killings in Pakistan, Yemen, and Somalia from January 2006 to November 2014.[78] These include 13 strikes in Pakistan, 12 in Yemen, and six in Somalia. Strike targets are differentiated by whether they are high-value targets and/or military leaders, and whether they cause civilian casualties. The dependent variables are the number of fatalities and number of injuries resulting from global jihadist attacks in each country; and attack hazard rates, reflecting the number of days until the next attack, the next attack causing ten or more deaths, and the next suicide attack. Carson controls for counterterrorism measures that include the number of monthly drone strikes in each country, along with US defense spending. She also controls for predictors of terrorism in each country. This section discusses her findings regarding Pakistan, while the section that follows describes her findings for Yemen and Somalia.

Carson finds that eight strikes against high-value military leaders are related to a decrease in the hazard of future attacks in the country in which the strike occurred. These include four such targets in Pakistan. She says that, "these types of targets are more likely to be involved in the day-to-day activities of a terrorist group," so that strikes against them result in a group's "decreased ability to operate efficiently."[79] She finds, however, that strikes against terrorist military targets are correlated with a significant increase in attack fatalities in Pakistan. Finally, Carson finds that in two models strikes causing civilian casualties are associated with a decrease in the hazard of future attacks.

Carson emphasizes that her study analyzes correlations. "[T]his examination," she says, "cannot purport to claim causality when such a complex phenomenon is the focus." She notes that other studies have found short-term benefits of strikes, and suggests that "it is too early to designate targeted killings a failure," quoting Forst's assertion that "'failure to find is not at all the same as a finding of failure.'"[80] She notes the possibility that even increases in attacks after a strike might be at a lower rate than if the strike had not occurred. This possibility is what identification strategies that go beyond basic correlation analysis are designed to determine.

Bauer, Reese, and Ruby (2021)
Vincent Bauer, Michael Reese, and Keven Ruby analyze the effects of terrorist group punishment of collaborators with the drone program in the FATA on the impacts of strikes in that area.[81] They note that militant groups in the tribal areas created a special counterintelligence unit to identify and kill such collaborators, and to publicize their deaths, in order to discourage residents from providing information that enabled targeting of militants. They draw on a dataset with information on the deaths of 319 persons accused by militants of having spied for the US drone campaign in the tribal areas between 2004 and 2013. The unit of analysis is the drone strike event, with the main independent variable the

number of alleged collaborators killed within 10 km of and thirty days prior to each strike.

The authors define "drone strike tactical effectiveness as eliminating militant leaders and fighters while avoiding civilian fatalities."[82] Executing informers can decrease such effectiveness by reducing the quality of information available to conduct strikes. Dependent variables are the number of militants, high-value targets (HVTs), and civilians killed in a strike. The authors hypothesize that the larger the number of collaborators killed in temporal and geographical proximity prior to a strike, the fewer the militants and HVTs, and the more civilians, will be killed in the strike. They also distinguish between the effects of eliminating intelligence sources and deterring other local residents from providing information. They hypothesize that if *elimination* serves to reduce the effectiveness of strikes, killing collaborators will reduce effectiveness for a relatively long period in a small geographical area. If *deterrence* reduces effectiveness, collaborator deaths will reduce effectiveness for a relatively brief period in a large geographical area.

The authors rely on an identification strategy that involves controlling for potential confounding variables that could affect both collaborator deaths and drone strike outcomes. They argue that after controlling for these variables, "the number of collaborator killings occurring before a strike is plausibly random, depending idiosyncratically upon the ability of insurgents to identify likely collaborators connected to previous drone strikes."[83]

The authors' models find a strong association between recent proximate collaborator deaths and strikes that kill fewer militants and HVTs. Shifting from the minimum to maximum number of collaborator killings prior to a drone strike is associated with a decrease of more than 50% in the expected number of militants and HVTs killed by a strike. A drone strike with no prior collaborator killings is expected to kill nearly eight militants on average, while a similar strike with four previous killings is expected to kill fewer than five militants on average. The authors find no association, however, between collaborator killings and the number of civilian deaths. They also use as "placebo" tests cases of political violence by militant groups in Pakistan against civilians who spied for nations other than the US, and violence against civilians for reasons unrelated to spying. These indicate that the effect of militant violence against civilians "is limited to violence used selectively against alleged collaborators with the drone program."[84]

Finally, the authors conclude that deterrence, rather than the elimination of specific intelligence sources, is the mechanism that best explains the association between collaborator deaths and reductions in drone strike effectiveness. Collaborator killings occurring up to 50 km from the drone strike have a significant negative effect on the number of militants killed in a strike, and collaborator deaths anywhere in Pakistan have a significant negative effect on the number of HVTs killed in a strike. This effect, however, decreases quickly over time and largely disappears by 180 days after a collaborator death. The evidence, say the authors, reflects "the primary operation of a deterrence mechanism, where collaborator killings send a message about the strength and determination of the militants to punish spies throughout the tribal areas."[85]

Bauer, Reese, and Ruby suggest that their study indicates that signals intelligence cannot fully substitute for the important contribution of human intelligence in strike operations. The ability of militants to punish collaborators "continually increase[es] the costs entailed in maintaining a given level of [drone strike] effectiveness."[86] The longer a campaign relying on local informants operates, the more militant retribution could significantly reduce the availability of intelligence unless there is concerted attention to protecting informants. In addition, the authors note, collaborator deaths indicate that those who may be harmed by a drone campaign go beyond those who are killed in strikes. This study provides a valuable analysis of the complex dynamics involved in drone strikes, and directs attention to considerations that must be taken into account in evaluating their effectiveness.

Strikes Against Militant Leaders in Yemen and Somalia

Shire (2020)
Mohammed Shire examines the impact of a successful targeted strike on Ahmed Abdi Godane, leader and co-founder of AQ Somalia affiliate Al-Shabaab, on the number and type of suicide attacks carried out by the group.[87] He compares this with data on attacks after what he calls a "targeting error" in an attack by Al-Shabaab in October 2017 that killed more than 500 civilians in Mogadishu. Shire compiles data on attacks between August 2001 and Godane's death on September 4, 2014; from after his death until the attack in Mogadishu on October 14, 2017; and from after this attack through December 2019. The period most relevant to assessing the impact of the strike against Godane therefore is September

4, 2014–October 14, 2017, with the dependent variables the number and nature of Al-Shabaab attacks.

Shire organizes the data according to whether an attack involved a single suicide bomber or multiple bombers. The latter may include simultaneous or sequential explosions by two or more individuals, which requires more planning and coordination than a single bomber. Before the strike against Godane, Al-Shabaab conducted 56 suicide attacks, consisting of 38 single and 18 multiple attacks. The successful single attacks killed 111 military targets, which Shire calls "combatants," and 200 civilian targets. The successful multiple bomber attacks killed 38 combatants and 74 civilians. Thus, of the 423 total death prior to Godane's death, civilians constituted 64.3% of single attacks and 66.1% of multiple attacks.

After his death in September 2014 until September 2017, Al-Shabaab carried out 91 attacks that killed a total of 1284 people. Single attacks increased from 38 to 70, killing 901 persons, while multiple bomber attacks increased from 18 to 21, killing 383 persons. Civilian deaths dropped from 64% to 40.7% of single bomber fatalities, and from 66.1% to 58.7% of multiple bomber attacks. Shire says that the high number of combatant deaths from single suicide attacks resulted from "well-coordinated" attacks against African Union Mission in Somalia (AMISOM) bases. At the same time, civilians continued to be the primary targets of attacks, with attacks against civilians in single operations increasing by 200% and in multiple operations by 100%.

Finally, after the mass casualty attack in September 2017, single suicide bomber attacks dropped by 71.4% from the previous period, and multiple bomber attacks declined by 58%. Shire maintains that this reflects Al-Shabaab's response to widespread condemnation of the attack.

With respect to the three-year period after Godane's death, Shire argues that the increase in attacks represented "a vengeful response to the killing."[88] He suggests that the desire to "quickly exact vengeance and outwardly communicate the group's resilience" led to greater reliance on single suicide bomber operations that require less planning and fewer resources.[89] He notes that the increase in single bomber attacks on military targets, and the substantial increase in combatant fatalities from such attacks, contradicts the claim in other studies that decapitation "decreases a group's striking capability, meaning it is forced to settle for less difficult targets."[90] Shire claims that before his death, Godane had steered Al-Shabaab through challenges in its formative stage that resulted in eventual stability. Within five days after his death, Al-Shabaab's leadership Council had appointed a successor. This suggests that the group possessed the kind of quasi-bureaucratic features that Jenna Jordan argues enhances organizational resilience.

The data on attacks after Godane's death are striking, and the increase in attacks on military targets challenges the claim that decapitation diminishes groups' operational capabilities. At the same time, Shire does not control for other variables that may have produced these effects, and makes no attempt to devise a counterfactual that could better support a claim about causality. Conditions in Somalia have been quite volatile, and Al-Shabaab's strength has waxed and waned for various reasons, during the period he studies.

In addition, Shire acknowledges that the group shifted to emphasize single suicide bomber attacks because those require less planning and coordination. This suggests that Godane's death did in fact degrade Al-Shabaab's capabilities. The fact that large numbers of military fatalities nonetheless resulted from such attacks could suggest AMISOM vulnerabilities rather than the capabilities of the group. In any event, studies that control for more variables would be useful in explaining the changes after Godane's death that Shire describes.

Carson (2018)

Carson's study of strikes against ten AQ leaders described in the previous section finds that one strike against a high-value military leader in Yemen and three in Somalia were related to a decrease in the hazard of future attacks in each country. She finds, however, that one strike was correlated with an increase in the hazard of suicide attacks in Somalia, and that total monthly strikes were associated with small increases in attack fatalities in Yemen and Somalia. Overall, she concludes, results from the three countries in her study indicate that strikes are uncorrelated in either direction "with the especially noxious outcomes resulting from terrorism; namely, casualties, along with the more detrimental attacks involving high civilian deaths and suicide attackers."[91]

Strikes involving civilian casualties occurring in both Somalia and Yemen were correlated with an increase in attack casualties, in contrast to the finding that such strikes in Pakistan were associated with a decrease in the hazard of attacks. The fact that strikes causing civilian casualties were associated with both positive and negative outcomes, she says, may indicate that "whether an attack kills innocent bystanders is irrelevant to an already motivated terrorist and does not, for instance, increase recruiting efforts."[92]

Summary of Research on Targeting AQ Leaders

Javier Jordan uses independent and dependent variables that are most relevant to the important US goal of reducing AQ attack in the West, arguing that intensification of strikes in Pakistan beginning in 2008 contributed to the significant decline in such attacks. He does not, however, attempt to control for other variables that might account for this outcome. Nor does he use an identification strategy that might furnish a counterfactual that indicates what would have occurred had strikes not been conducted. His study thus does not provide strong quantitative evidence of the impact of strikes on AQC. As Chapters 7 and 8 discuss, however, qualitative evidence does provide reasonable support for his conclusion.

Other quantitative studies that to varying degrees can be treated as focusing on strikes against AQ leaders find that such strikes did not have an effect on various metrics relating to overall attacks by the group. Most of these studies do not, however, differentiate among attack locations. This makes it difficult to determine if strikes achieved the important US goals of reducing the threat of attacks in the US and the West. Focusing on the overall number of attacks does not necessarily provide insight into the effect of strikes on the attacks against the "far enemy" on which AQC focused, and which require the kind of guidance and coordination it could provide.

Studies that do include data on attacks in the West unfortunately use an independent variable that does not differentiate strikes against AQ leaders from those against others. Of these, Lehrke and Schomaker's study is most relevant because one independent variable they use is drone strikes, which occurred mainly in Pakistan during their study period. Because of the concentration of AQC in the FATA, this could serve as a rough proxy for strikes against AQC. In addition, they control for several defensive counterterrorism measures in addition to drone strikes that could affect the number of attacks. Their dependent variable for attacks in the West, however, is total terrorist attacks. Thus, while they find that drone strikes do not affect the number of overall terrorist attacks in the West, this does not provide evidence of the effect of strikes on AQ attacks in the West, which is an important concern of the US.

One finding from Jenna Jordan's research on targeting AQ top leaders could provide some support for a claim that the drop in attacks in the West since 2007 is due to the impact of strikes on AQC. Jordan finds that attacks attributable to AQC have substantially declined since 2007, while attacks by affiliates have significantly increased. While her intention is to demonstrate that strikes against AQ leaders have been ineffective because they have not reduced the total number of attacks by AQ, one could argue that the decline in attacks in the West reflects the decline in attacks by AQC. Jordan does not, however, control for any variables that might affect the number of attacks, nor does she disaggregate attacks by location. This suggests some caution in interpreting her data on AQC attacks in the way I have described.

Research on the impacts of strikes in the FATA and Pakistan is among the most methodologically sophisticated work that has been done on targeting. Four of these, by Mir and Moore, Jaeger and Siddique, Carson, and Johnston and Sarbahi, find that strikes are associated with a reduced rate or hazard of attacks in the FATA or Pakistan more generally, while one, Mahmood and Jetter, concludes that they are associated with an increase in attacks in Pakistan. Mahmood and Jetter use wind levels as their independent variable in an effort to avoid strike endogeneity. This means that the strength of their conclusions depends upon whether this is a better approach than using strikes as an independent variable while using other means to control for endogeneity.

To the extent that strikes are associated with a reduction in attacks in Pakistan, this would achieve the US goals of reducing attacks against Pakistan, and possibly against US and Western targets in that country. Jaeger and Siddique find a decrease in attacks in that country as long as a month after a strike, but longer-term effects may require an extended strike campaign.

Strikes Against AQ, the Taliban, and Other Groups

Lehrke and Schomaker (2016)

The study by Lehrke and Schomaker described above also uses the decapitation of top leaders of 96 different terrorist groups as an independent variable. Some of these presumably included AQ leaders, but the study does not disaggregate the data by group. The authors found mixed results. Decapitation was not significantly related to the total number of attacks worldwide, total jihadist attacks worldwide, total attacks in the West, and attacks in war zones. At the same time, the direction of any correlation varied but more often was negative (meaning fewer attacks), and was always negative for jihadist groups. "Thus, overall," the authors say, "we cannot reject or confirm" whether this tactic is effective.[93]

Abrahms and Mierau (2017)

The study by Abrahms and Mierau that analyzes the impact of Israeli targeted killing described in Chapter 3 also includes a section that analyzes the effects of strikes against terrorist group leaders in the Afghanistan–Pakistan theater from 2008 to 2011.[94] The focus is on the extent to which strikes change the tactical behavior of terrorist groups. Their independent variables are successful and unsuccessful strikes against leaders, while their dependent variable is the proportion of attacks against civilian and military targets following successful and unsuccessful decapitation strikes.

The authors find that "the ratio of attacks on military targets versus civilian ones is markedly lower in the two-week period immediately after an operationally successful strike, when tactical decision-making is presumably most affected."[95] By contrast, they found that unsuccessful strikes have no effect on attack targets.

As do Rigterink, as well as Johnston and Sarbahi, the authors adopt an identification strategy based on the assumption that whether a strike is successful depends on random factors unique to each strike attempt.[96] They find that in the wake of a successful strike, the likelihood of attacks on military targets drops in the two weeks following the strike by 30%. "[T]argeted killings," they conclude, thus "change the tactical behavior of the militant groups," causing them to redirect their violence toward civilians."[97] It is possible, they note, that over a longer period militant group violence may become more selective as groups regain capability and new leadership exerts discipline over lower-level members.[98]

The authors' explanation is based on the theory that, consistent with Rigterink, strikes deplete the ranks of experienced leaders who are more strategically discriminating. In support of this explanation, the authors point to research on the Taliban that indicates that leaders exhort members not to attack civilians, and that they take steps to discourage this from occurring, because such attacks cause local populations to become hostile toward the group. This is consistent with observations of a shift in

Taliban leadership to younger more doctrinaire leaders over the relevant period noted by van Linschoten and Kuehn in the next chapter.

The study appears to combine data on all strikes in Afghanistan, a theater of active combat, and Pakistan, which is not. The effects of strikes in the former are difficult to isolate from the effects of overall military operations designed to defeat the enemy. The strikes in Pakistan constitute a more paradigmatic leadership decapitation campaign intended to weaken AQC. Furthermore, there likely are significant time-varying differences between the two countries based on political dynamics that limit the ability to draw causal inferences from a combined data set of the two countries. It therefore would have been more useful to analyze separately the effects of strikes in each country.

Finally, authors find strikes are effective based on the shift from military to civilian militant attack targets. It is at least open to question, however, whether greater risk to civilians should be counted as a metric of effectiveness, even if it may reduce local population support for a group.

Lyall (2017)

Jason Lyall's study of US airstrikes in Afghanistan between 2006 and 2011 does not deal specifically with targeted strikes, although it does include some data on drone strikes.[99] The latter in Afghanistan likely targeted more mid- to low-level insurgents than top leaders. Lyall analyzed 23,000 airstrikes of all types, as well as nonlethal shows of force, to estimate the effect of air operations on insurgent attacks.

Lyall constructed treatment and control villages by matching villages based on information about the level of hostilities in them. This reflects a difference-in-differences approach that assumes that trends in the rate of insurgent attacks are comparable for treatment and control villages. These trends are then used to estimate the number of attacks that would occur without strikes in each location. A village suffering a strike thus serves as the independent variable. The difference between the number of attacks and the estimated number of attacks in villages suffering airstrikes and those not targeted is then assumed to reflect changes in behavior attributable to the strikes, serving as the dependent variable. Lyall also argues that the allocation of strikes among villages is quasi-random, in that the likelihood of a strike depends on many factors unrelated to the gravity of a threat.

The study finds that there are a larger number of insurgent attacks at seven, 45, and 90 days in villages suffering airstrikes compared to those that did not. Lyall suggests that increases in insurgent attacks are not responses to civilian casualties, but reflect the desire of the Taliban to maintain its reputation for resolve in the eyes of the local population. Drone strikes are associated with an increase in attacks, although this was substantially smaller than the increase associated with other types of strikes. It is unclear, however, what percentage of drone strikes in Afghanistan were targeted killing missions as opposed to support for conventional military operations. Finally, Johnston and Sarbahi note that Lyall studies an area in which there are many more opportunities for attacks on counterinsurgency forces than in an area outside of armed conflict such as the FATA.[100] These concerns limit the insights from Lyall's study regarding targeted strikes outside areas of active hostilities, although the study is a sophisticated effort to use an identification strategy to assess causal claims about airstrikes.

Rinehart (2016)

Christine Sixta Rinehart reviews the impact of drone strikes in Afghanistan, Iraq, Pakistan, Somalia, Syria, and Yemen.[101] The only empirical analysis, however, is of Afghanistan, Yemen, and Pakistan. Rinehart's independent variable is the number of drone strikes in each country. For Afghanistan and Yemen, Rinehart's dependent variable is the number of terrorist attacks over the periods January 2007–December 2013 and 2011–2015, respectively. She uses linear regression analysis to determine if there is any statistically significant correlation between drone strikes and attacks over these periods. She finds that there is not, which leads her to conclude that targeting has been ineffective in these countries.

For Pakistan, her dependent variable is the number of suicide bombings from January 2004 to September 2015. She finds a positive correlation between the number of drone strikes and the number of suicide bombings, which leads her to conclude that targeting has been counterproductive in that country. She concludes with respect to Afghanistan, Yemen, and Pakistan that, "whether the drone strikes are responsible for more terrorist attacks or not, drone strikes are definitely not decreasing terrorist attacks."[102]

The book is limited to examining broad trends, and reflects all the limits of relying on traditional correlation described in Chapter 2. In addition, there is no effort to control for other variables that might affect attacks at various times over the period, such as periods of considerable instability in Yemen, or for the possibility that drone strikes are endogenous. Nor is there any attempt to establish a counterfactual control group that would permit robust causal inferences. This limits the insights that the research can provide.

Long (2014)

Austin Long studied the impact of targeted killing operations in Iraq and Afghanistan from 2004 to 2013 in order to test his thesis that the vulnerability of a terrorist group to decapitation decreases with the degree to which it has institutionalized its operations.[103] By institutionalization, Long means that a group is organized around rational bureaucratic principles of authority based on organizational position rather than personal qualities. This establishes clear lines of succession after the death of a leader. Institutionalization also involves functional specialization and standard operating procedures that provide clear direction on how to conduct the organization's activities. These procedures mean that "[a]ll parts of the organization will therefore conduct operations, including the replacement of leadership, in an at least broadly similar manner," which "makes the movement of leaders and the training of replacement leaders easier."[104]

Long found substantial evidence based on captured material that both Al-Qaeda in Iraq (AQI) and the Taliban in Afghanistan exhibited characteristics of well-institutionalized organizations for much of his study period compared to other insurgent groups. The independent variable in Long's study is the number of targeted strikes against these groups, while the dependent variable is their ability "to generate and employ substantial force across a wide geographic area" despite losing top leaders and middle-level operatives.[105] Long drew most of his data from Anbar province in Iraq and Kandahar province in Afghanistan. He regards these provinces as similar in important ways, which enables him to control as much as possible for variation both within and between the two countries.

Long finds that despite successful targeting of "middle managers" in both Anbar province and nationally in 2005–2006, the monthly level of violent events in Anbar, most related to AQI, nearly doubled during that year, from just over 500 in February 2005 to almost 1000 in February 2006, peaking at more than 1500 in October 2005. Long says, "AQI, which quickly became well institutionalized, survived the largest and most sustained leadership targeting campaign ever launched against an insurgent or terrorist organization without losing cohesion."[106] By contrast, poorly institutionalized organizations in Iraq "proved remarkably frail when their leadership was targeted."[107]

In June 2006, an airstrike killed the top AQI leader Abu Musab al-Zarqawi. Yet violent events in Anbar went from just under 1000 in February 2006 to nearly 1500 in February 2006, peaking in October 2006 at more than 2000 events. Long says there was significant escalation of the counterinsurgency effort beginning in 2007, which enhanced the institutionalization of this campaign and finally enabled it to reduce attacks.

With respect to the Taliban in Afghanistan, Long finds that the loss of that group's leaders and officials did not appreciably curtail its ability to engage in violence against civilians, coalition forces, and local police. The Taliban continued its own leadership targeting campaign in 2010, with a particular focus on leaders of a new US and Afghan effort to build local defense forces, as well as on other government leaders. Long concludes, "The Taliban, well institutionalized by 2005, suffered no loss of cohesion through 2013 despite an effective and expanding [US] leadership targeting campaign."[108]

Long's analysis of targeting in Afghanistan is consistent with Wilner's finding described below that the number of attacks increased after the targeted killing of four Taliban leaders in 2007 and 2008. Long does not, however, assess the sophistication and lethality of attacks as does Wilner. His focus on the overall level of attacks, as opposed to their sophistication and lethality, thus makes him more skeptical than Wilner about the effectiveness of targeted strikes. He concludes that "dedicating massive resources to leadership targeting of well-institutionalized groups, while under-resourcing efforts to protect and institutionalize useful anti-insurgent organizations, appears suboptimal."[109]

Long's study is suggestive, but, as with Lyall, the targeting he studies occurred in theaters of armed conflict. This makes it extremely difficult to separate out the impact of targeted strikes from other operations. In addition, targeting operations in Iraq proceeded at a much higher tempo than in Afghanistan because of significant integration of intelligence and operations. Targeting therefore may have been an especially significant element of the escalation of the counterinsurgency campaign in that country. Long's model of institutionalization nonetheless is well-grounded, and offers a plausible account of terrorist groups' susceptibility to targeting.

Wilner (2010)

Alex Wilner studied the killing of four Taliban leaders in Afghanistan in 2007 and 2008 to determine their effects on the "professionalism" of the group, as measured by "success rates vs. failure rates vs. foiled rates [of attacks], along with changes in kill ratios."[110] He analyzed a two- or three-week period before and after the death of each leader. One set of dependent variables was the number of attacks, their success rate, and the number of persons killed in the attacks. A second set was designed to measure the sophistication of the attacks, and included attacks from suicide bombings, improvised explosive devices (IEDs), and small arms and rocket fire (SA/R). It also included whether attacks were on "hard" targets such as military and police, or "soft" targets such as civilians.

Wilner argues that his study is meant to move beyond general claims that targeted strikes result in an increase in retaliatory violence. He describes suicide attacks as both the most dangerous and the most complex to organize. IEDs are less dangerous but easier to coordinate. Finally, SA/R are the least preferred tactic. They require the least sophistication, but are less accurate and not very effective against "hard" targets.

Overall attacks increased following all of the targeted killings, but suicide bombings declined by over 30%. IED attacks increased by 6% and SA/R attacks by about 15% percent during the same periods. Wilner suggests that this indicates that "[a]s leaders and facilitators were eliminated, the Taliban began using less-sophisticated forms of violence that required less energy, expertise, and time to organize effectively."[111]

Wilner asserts that lower professionalism is also indicated by a rise in IED failure rates from 20% to roughly 35% after the leader deaths, and an increase in suicide bombing failure by five percentage points. In addition, while the number of suicide attacks on soft targets remained the same at six, attacks on hard targets declined from 24 to 13. Following the death of Mullah Dadullah, suicide bombings decreased from 13 to 10, but attacks on soft targets increased from two to six. The author explains, "As leaders were killed, remaining forces selected less formidable targets to attack, like Afghan government officials, civil-society actors, and off-duty police commanders, rather than hardened, military actors."[112]

Wilner concludes, "In sum, targeted killings in Afghanistan have resulted in a short-term change to the Taliban's effectiveness, professionalism, and motivation."[113] Declining professionalization, he says, reflects the damage to a group directly caused by a strike, while difficulty in recruiting skilled replacements reflects the deterrent impact of decreasing willingness to join a terrorist group. Wilner also draws on qualitative evidence on the impact of Dadullah's death on the Taliban that is described in the next chapter, which he says indicates the effects of targeting in decreasing Taliban morale and motivation, and in increasing mistrust within the organization.

A decline in suicide attacks after the targeted killings is certainly a benefit, given that such attacks are especially destructive. It is still the case, however, that overall levels of violence rose after each killing. In addition, Wilner focuses only on strikes for up to three weeks; it is unclear whether strikes have any effects beyond this. Finally, while a greater focus on soft targets may reflect a decline in professionalism, it also means that more civilians are in danger. This raises the potential concern described above in the discussion of the study by Abrahms and Mierau about whether this should be regarded as a metric of strike effectiveness.

CONCLUSION

The quantitative studies described in this section do not permit a definitive conclusion about whether US strikes against AQ and associated forces have furthered the important US goals of reducing attacks in the US and the West, and against US targets. The research on strikes against AQ leadership generally finds that such targeting did not affect the overall level of attacks conducted by AQ as a whole.

Attacks by AQ as a whole, however, may not capture the distinctive impact of strikes on AQC without more detailed information on the location and targets of attacks. As Chapter 8 discusses, AQ has grown considerably in recent years by focusing on issues of local concern to affiliates in various parts of the world. Overall attacks could reflect an increase in local attacks by such affiliates, but a decline in attacks in the US and the West. Existing studies thus unfortunately do not provide the detail that would enable a clearer indication of the extent to which strikes against AQC furthered the most important goals of the US. As the discussion above describes, Javier Jordan's study uses independent and dependent variables that focus most directly on this question, but he does not control for other variables that may be responsible for the decline in attacks in the West. Lehrke and Schomaker provide a more rigorous empirical analysis that includes some independent and dependent variables relevant to the question, but these variables do not squarely address it.

The research arguably most relevant to assessing the impact of strikes against AQC is Jenna Jordan's study of targeting AQ leaders that finds that attacks by AQC have significantly declined, while attacks by affiliates have substantially increased. Combined with Javier Jordan's finding that attempted attacks in the West have declined since 2007, one might argue that this decline is because strikes have weakened AQC's ability to plan and coordinate such attacks. Chapter 8 describes AQC's historical focus on attacks in the West, which lends some plausibility to this claim. No quantitative study to date, however, examines this claim and controls for other variables that may account for the drop in attacks in the West.

Other studies described in this chapter examine whether strikes against a set of targets beyond top AQ leaders have impacts on terrorist activity in specific locations. Some, although not all, such studies suggest successful local effects of strikes, with declining numbers of attacks, hazard of attacks, and attack fatalities for some period of time afterward. The explanation is that strikes weaken the ability of groups to operate, and that they also have a deterrent effect by prompting more cautious behavior in order to avoid future strikes. At the same time, the effects of strikes may be relatively short-term, which means that more enduring impacts would require persistent targeting over a longer period of time. In addition, these studies focus mainly on strikes in Pakistan, so we should be cautious in automatically assuming that their findings also apply to Yemen and Somalia.

While quantitative studies are helpful, it also can be valuable to complement them with qualitative evidence that provides insight into the social and individual dynamics behind the numbers. Claims of causality rely on the logic that an independent variable does or does not produce a change in a dependent variable through an intervening causal process:

Independent Variable $\rightarrow\rightarrow$ Causal Process $\rightarrow\rightarrow$ Dependent Variable

Quantitative studies focus on whether there are changes in dependent variables that can be attributed to an independent variable, controlling for other variables that might have produced the outcome. If there are such changes, researchers assume that they are a result of a causal process generated by the independent variable.

Quantitative research thus does not directly analyze causal processes, but infers them from changes in the independent and dependent variables. Researchers suggest what those processes might be by providing explanations that they regard as plausible, reflecting narratives about how human beings may have behaved to produce the outcomes in their studies. Thus, for instance, Mir and Moore suggest that declines in attacks following a strike reflect direct weakening of a terrorist group from loss of members and other resources (a "kinetic" effect), and the disruption of operations because of the desire to avoid strikes in the future ("anticipatory" effect). Johnston and Sarbahi use the terms "degradation" and "disruption" to make the same claim. Those who find no declines in attacks or other metrics infer that strikes failed to have such causal effects.

Qualitative research can provide more direct insight into causal processes by providing evidence of how people actually behaved in response to an independent variable such as strikes. They can indicate, for instance, whether strikes inflicted serious losses on terrorist groups and whether they caused them to change their operations because of the fear of future ones. The combination of quantitative and qualitative material thus may provide a richer account than either source of information alone.

The next chapter discusses a range of qualitative material that describes how members of AQ and the Taliban were affected by strikes in Pakistan, sometimes in their own words. This material includes interviews conducted by researchers who endeavor to avoid selection bias, reports by especially knowledgeable local journalists with networks of contacts within terrorist groups and local officials, an account provided by a *New York Times* reporter held hostage by the Taliban for seven months, and contemporaneous correspondence by terrorist leaders in documents seized during operations against AQ and the Taliban, particularly in the mission against Osama bin Laden. Together with the quantitative research, this qualitative material may enable a fuller assessment of the effect of strikes on AQ and groups associated with it.

Notes

1. A terrorist attack is categorized as "international" in the Global Terrorism Database if the nationality of the group and/or the location of the attacks is different from that of its victims, or the ideology is designated as international." Carson, 2018, 1286, note 32.
2. Carson, J. V. (2017). Assessing the effectiveness of high-profile targeted killings in the "War on Terror." *Criminology & Public Policy, 16*(1), 191–220. https://doi.org/10.1111/1745-9133.12274.
3. For a comparison of interrupted time-series and hazard series approaches, see Dugan, L. (2011). The series hazard model: An alternative to time series for event data. *Journal of Quantitative Criminology, 27*, 379–402.
4. Id. 198.
5. Id. 211.
6. Id. 213.
7. Id. 212.
8. Id. 214.
9. Id.
10. Id.
11. Id. 213.
12. Id.
13. Hepworth, D. P. (2014). Terrorist retaliation? An analysis of terrorist attacks following the targeted killing of top-tier Al Qaeda leadership. *Journal of Policing, Intelligence and Counter Terrorism, 9*(1), 1–18. https://doi.org/10.1080/18335330.2013.877374.
14. Id. 8.
15. Hepworth, D. (2013). Analysis of Al-Qaeda terrorist attacks to investigate rational action. *Perspectives on Terrorism, 7*(2), 23–38, 35. https://www.jstor.org/stable/26296922?seq=1#metadata_info_tab_contents.
16. Id. 14.
17. Jordan, J. (2019). *Leadership decapitation: Strategic targeting of terrorist organizations*. Stanford University Press, 151–180 (Al Qaeda), 186–191 (ISIS); Jordan, J. (2014). Attacking the leader, missing the mark: Why terrorist groups survive decapitation strikes. *International Security, 38*(4), 7–38. https://doi.org/10.1162/isec_a_00157.
18. Jordan, 2019, 159.
19. Id. 160.
20. Id. 161.
21. Id. 190.
22. Id. 190.
23. Id. 181.
24. Id. 182.
25. Id. 168.

26. Jordan, 2014, 16.
27. Jordan, 2019, 160–161.
28. Rigterink, A. (2021). The wane of command: Evidence on drone strikes and control within terrorist organizations. *American Political Science Review, 115*(1), 31–50. https://doi.org/10.1017/S00030554 20000908.
29. Id. 40.
30. Id. 47 (original emphasis).
31. Id. 47.
32. Johnston, P. B., & Sarbahi, A. K. (2016). The impact of US drone strikes on terrorism in Pakistan. *International Studies Quarterly, 60*(2), 203–219. https://doi.org/10.1093/isq/sqv004.
33. Id. 204.
34. Id. 208.
35. Id. 214.
36. Jaeger, D. A., & Siddique, Z. (2018). Are drone strikes effective in Afghanistan and Pakistan? On the dynamics of violence between the United States and the Taliban. *CESifo Economic Studies, 64*(4), 667–697, 673. http://www.djaeger.org/research/wp/Jaeger-Siddique.pdf.
37. Lehrke, J. P., & Schomaker, R. (2016). Kill, capture, or defend? The effectiveness of specific and general counterterrorism tactics against the global threats of the post-9/11 era. *Security Studies, 25*(4), 729–762. https://doi.org/10.1080/09636412.2016.1220199. Defensive measures include identity cards and biometrics; data-retention and data sharing; communication interception and data retention; visual surveillance; criminal penalties for material support for terrorism; exceptional procedures for terrorist suspects; denial of entry, stay and visa and biometrics; and exclusion/deportation clauses and limitation of movements. Epifanio, M. (n.d). Appendix A: "Codebook," Legislative Responses to International Terrorism dataset, Peace Research Institute of Oslo. http://www.polsci.org/epifanio/codebook.pdf.
38. Id. 755.
39. Id.
40. Id. 759.
41. Jordan, J. (2014). The effectiveness of the drone campaign against Al Qaeda Central: A case study. *Journal of Strategic Studies, 37*(1), 4–29. https://doi.org/10.1080/01402390.2013.850422.
42. Id. 17.
43. Id. 15.
44. Id. 18.
45. Id. 2.
46. Id. 25.

47. Smith, M., & Walsh, J. I. (2013). Do drone strikes degrade Al Qaeda? Evidence from propaganda output. *Terrorism and Political Violence, 25*(2), 311–327. https://doi.org/10.1080/09546553.2012.664011.
48. Id. 318.
49. Id. 325.
50. Mir, A., & Moore, D. (2019). Drones, surveillance, and violence: Theory and evidence from a US drone program. *International Studies Quarterly, 63*(4), 846–862. https://doi.org/10.1093/isq/sqz040.
51. Id. 2.
52. Id.
53. Id.
54. Id.
55. Id. 14.
56. Id.
57. Mir, A. (2018). What explains counterterrorism effectiveness? Evidence from the U.S. drone war in Pakistan. *International Security, 43*(2), 45–83. http://doi.org/10.1162/isec_a_00331.
58. Id. 52.
59. Id. 53.
60. Id. 15.
61. Id. 7.
62. Id. 15.
63. Mahmood, R., & Jetter, M. (2019, April). Military intervention via drone strikes: Discussion paper no. 12318. *IZA Institute of Labor Economics*. http://ftp.iza.org/dp12318.pdf.
64. Id. 17.
65. Id. 3.
66. Id. 19.
67. Jaeger, D. A., & Siddique, Z. (2018). Are drone strikes effective in Afghanistan and Pakistan? On the dynamics of violence between the United States and the Taliban. *CESifo Economic Studies, 64*(4), 667–697. http://www.djaeger.org/research/wp/Jaeger-Siddique.pdf.
68. Id. 669.
69. Id. 668.
70. Id. 695.
71. Id. 696.
72. Id. 696.
73. Johnston & Sarbahi, 215.
74. Id. 206.
75. Id. 207.
76. Id. 216.
77. Id.

78. Carson, J.V. (2018). Assessing the nuances of counterterrorism programs: A country-level investigation of targeted killings. *Crime & Delinquency*, *65*(9), 1262–1291. https://journals.sagepub.com/doi/abs/10.1177/0011128718784742.
79. Id. 1281.
80. Id. 1283.
81. Bauer, V., Reese, M., & Ruby, K. (2021, September 29). Does insurgent selective punishment deter collaboration? Evidence from the Drone War in Pakistan. *Journal of Conflict Resolution*, 1–30 (original manuscript) https://journals.sagepub.com/doi/abs/10.1177/00220027211041158.
82. Id. 10.
83. Id. 15.
84. Id. 19.
85. Id. 21.
86. Id. 23.
87. Shire, M. I. (2020). How do leadership decapitation and targeting error affect suicide bombings? The case of Al-Shabaab. *Studies in Conflict & Terrorism*. https://doi.org/10.1080/1057610X.2020.1780021.
88. Id. 12.
89. Id.
90. Id. 13.
91. Carson 1281.
92. Id. 1282.
93. Lehrke & Schomaker, 2016, 756.
94. Abrahms, M., & Mierau, J. (2015). Leadership matters: The effects of targeted killings on militant group tactics. *Terrorism and Political Violence*, *29*(5), 830–851. https://doi.org/10.1080/09546553.2015.1069671.
95. Id. 834.
96. Id. 835.
97. Id. 838.
98. Id.
99. Lyall, J. (2017, September 3). Bombing to lose? Airpower, civilian casualties, and the dynamics of violence in counterinsurgency wars. SSRN. http://dx.doi.org/10.2139/ssrn.2422170.
100. Johnston & Sarbahi, 2016, 211.
101. Rinehart, C. S. (2016). *Drones and targeted killing in the Middle East and Africa: An appraisal of American counterterrorism policies*. Lexington Books.
102. Id. 117.
103. Long, A. (2014). Whack-a-mole or coup de grace? Institutionalization and leadership targeting in Iraq and Afghanistan. *Security Studies*, *23*(3), 471–512. https://doi.org/10.1080/09636412.2014.935229.

104. Id. 478.
105. Id. 482.
106. Id. 500.
107. Id.
108. Id. 508.
109. Id. 511.
110. Wilner, A. S. (2010). Targeted killings in Afghanistan: Measuring coercion and deterrence in counterterrorism and counterinsurgency. *Studies in Conflict & Terrorism, 33*(4), 307–329, 318. https://doi.org/10.1080/10576100903582543.
111. Id. 319.
112. Id.
113. Id. 324.

CHAPTER 7

Qualitative Evidence

This chapter describes qualitative material that sheds light on the impacts of US targeted strikes on Al-Qaeda (AQ) and associated groups. The material does not meet social science standards designed to ensure that it is representative or is drawn from a random sample. Much of it, however, consists of private communications among terrorist group members, reports as events were occurring, and interviews with key participants. These provide unique insights into what, if any, impacts strikes had on terrorist groups.

The discussion below focuses on eleven studies or sources of qualitative material. Bryce Loidolt and Asfandyar Mir draw on especially rich sources of information in their research: Loidolt on correspondence among AQ members and Mir on 66 interviews in the FATA, many in Urdu, in which he is fluent. Other material varies in depth, but provides at least some insight into the impacts of strikes.

LOIDOLT (2022)

Loidolt reviews the correspondence among AQ leaders who generally constitute Al-Qaeda Core (AQC) in material captured in the May 2001 raid on Osama bin Laden's compound and organized by the Combating Terrorism Center (CTC) at West Point.[1] His goal is to assess the extent to which drone strikes in Pakistan: (1) degraded the quality and experience

© The Author(s), under exclusive license to Springer Nature Switzerland AG 2022
M. Regan, *Drone Strike–Analyzing the Impacts of Targeted Killing*,
https://doi.org/10.1007/978-3-030-91119-5_7

of AQC (2) reduced the group's organizational efficiency and control, and (3) prompted it to leave its safe haven in the FATA. The collection of documents consists of several hundred thousand files. Loidolt uses several steps to cull this down to a sample of over 400 documents, which he reviews in their original Arabic.

He then develops measurements of the three relevant outcomes. Regarding effects on personnel quality and experience, these include failure of AQC to nominate a replacement for someone killed in a strike, reservations expressed about persons proposed as replacements or the subsequent performance of replacements, and any concerns that AQC members expressed about the supply of capable leaders and skilled personnel.

Regarding organizational efficiency and control, indicators are reductions in the frequency of meetings, movement of personnel, resources, or communications; delays in decision-making and other procedures; and dissension within AQ related to reductions in the availability of capable senior leaders. Finally, with respect to use of FATA as a haven, Loidolt considers redirection of incoming recruits to other regions; efforts to permanently relocate personnel, families, or activities; and steps toward full evacuation of the region. Documents indicating the opposite of the indicators for each outcome would indicate that strikes failed to weaken the respective aspect of AQC operations.

Strikes in Pakistan began to increase significantly in 2008 and continued at especially high levels until 2012. Loidolt finds that in the early years of this period AQC had little difficulty finding qualified replacements for most persons killed in strikes. The exception, however, was AQ's external operations unit, which coordinated attacks outside the Afghanistan-Pakistan region. A leader who took over these operations in 2008, Saleh al-Somali, was candid in acknowledging his limited experience and competence. Persons in charge of AQ's operations in Afghanistan and Pakistan were killed in 2008–2010, and the organization faced challenges in replacing them. In April 2009, al-Somali lamented that he did not have the "required cadres" to fully staff external operations.

In August 2009, bin Laden requested that al-Somali be reassigned because of poor performance, but was informed that "we no longer have an appropriate individual to fill this position."[2] A replacement who took over in March 2010 was subject to considerable criticism of his work. In addition, in August 2010 bin Laden rejected two persons proposed to take over planning an attack on US soil, because of poor performance and lack of experience, respectively.

In early 2010, shortages became more significant in areas beyond external operations. By mid-2010 strikes had killed several middle managers and senior leaders, as well as persons with specialized skills. A person responsible for reviewing replacements for some of them reported that "the middle-level leadership and cadres are tormented by the killing...compensating [for the killing] is proceeding slowly...and the spy war does not provide a large opportunity."[3]

Senior leader Attiya Abd al-Rahman complained in summer 2010 that "spy planes...have killed many of the leadership, cadres, and others in the past two years," and noted AQ's "incomplete strength and power" in the border region.[4] In November of that year, he stated, "Our situation is difficult due to a severe deficiency in cadres."[5] Loidolt concludes, "Put simply, the evidence suggests that US drone strikes outpaced AQ's organizational processes for managing personnel turnover and mentoring new personnel."[6]

While not included in Loidolt's analysis, it is also worth mentioning another document from the CTC collection from around this time. Bin Laden expressed concern about the growing risk to senior leaders in a letter to Attiyah in October 2010: "It is important to have the leadership in a faraway location to gain expertise in all areas. When this experienced leadership dies, this would lead to the rise of lower leaders who are not as experienced as the former leaders and this would lead to the repeat of mistakes."[7]

Loidolt found that strikes caused restrictions and delays in AQ's operations, but that the evidence is mixed about how much this impaired leaders' ability to exercise control over subordinates and affiliates. AQ operated smoothly within the FATA through 2009, but strikes led it to limit and decrease communication and meetings beginning in 2010. In April 2010, Ayman al-Zawahiri ordered a halt to meetings due to "security concerns."[8] Two months later, bin Laden accepted Attiyah abd al-Rahman's proposal to stop much of the group's activity in the FATA in order to avoid strikes.

Loidolt says that "[b]y the fall of 2010, the fear of U.S. drone strikes led to prohibitions on Attiya and Abu Yahya's movements, with Attiya only on exceptional occasions allowing disguised cars to come near his location. Some al-Qaeda operatives were prohibited from traveling in cars at all."[9] In October 2010 bin Ladin instructed Ayman al-Zawahiri to limit his communications within AQ to two persons who would serve as a liaison to the rest of the organization, who should "not come to you frequently, even if that leads to the delay of some of the work during this phase."[10] After he narrowly avoided a drone strike in early 2011, Attiya told bin Laden, "Even motorcycles are getting bombed...any message and any movement is danger....the next correspondence is coming in two months...maybe three."[11]

That same month, bin Laden wrote to Attiya about the need to begin moving people out of the FATA. "As for you," he said, "if you think that it is dangerous to move by car, then you can stay in the area, but you need to do your work through two brothers, and only one of them should carry your messages to the brothers..."[12] Bin Laden acknowledged that this might cause delays in operations. He said, "The brother should visit you no more than once or twice a week. The other brother comes to you only for necessary issues only, even if this slows down the work. We pray to God for things to change. You should know the locations of the brothers, but they should not know your location, except for the carriers."[13]

Loidolt observes that such restrictions may have made it challenging for AQ leaders to maintain discipline over some subordinates, and that the organization became concerned about defections to other groups. At the same time, AQ had faced similar issues prior to the intensification of strikes. Loidolt notes that financial difficulties also may have prompted some dissension because of the inability to pay some subordinates, although this problem arguably arose because routine operations had become more laborious as a result of strikes. In 2010 and early 2011 senior leaders were still able to coordinate several activities by subordinates and affiliates. Loidolt concludes:

> Lethal targeting did force al-Qaeda's leaders to take measures that would reduce their exposure, which, in turn undermined organizational efficiency. And, there is some evidence that these reductions contributed to leaders' inability to assert control down the chain of command. Nevertheless, al-Qaeda's leaders were far from absent or silent during this period, and instead likely remained focused on the most immediate operational priorities.[14]

Thus, he concludes, "even as drone strikes reached their peak, al-Qaeda was still able to orchestrate rather complex organizational tasks.

This suggests at least a portion of its internal control remained intact even as the group faced significant operational challenges."[15]

Finally, while AQ-inspired militants exercised significant influence in all seven of the agencies in the FATA by 2008, the area became increasingly unsuitable as a safe haven beginning in 2010. In spring of that year, AQ leader Younis al-Mauritani leader wrote to bin Laden that "the field here [in Waziristan] has become like a trap, the killing has tormented the cadres and leaders...no step will be fruitful so long as this work is here."[16] Al-Qaeda leaders eventually told him and his cadres to train in Iran rather than Pakistan because of the persistent strikes in the latter.[17] Attiyah expressed concern in June over the safety of operatives "due to our security circumstances (the bombings that have exhausted us).!!".[18]

In July 2010 bin Ladin directed Attiya "to arrange safe places far from the reach of the airplanes' photography and bombing" for leaders and specialized cadres.[19] In describing his response to "bombings," in October 2010 Attiya described how he had begun relocating operatives to Kunar and Nuristan in Afghanistan, recommending to bin Ladin that Al-Qaeda operatives could also be sent to "liberated" areas in other provinces.[20] Bin Laden responded, "I am leaning toward getting most of the brothers out of the area... The brothers who can keep a low profile and take the necessary precautions should stay, but move to new houses on a cloudy day. A warning to the brothers: they should not meet on the road and move in their cars because many of them got targeted while they were meeting on the road."[21]

By January 2011, bin Laden authorized the complete evacuation of AQ from the FATA. He wrote to Attiyah:

It appears to me that the region has been very heavily revealed and that leaving the region completely is the best solution...once we disperse in Pakistan and Afghanistan, the enemy will lose the ability to focus the surveillance on our movements and place us under the photography and monitoring.[22]

Loidolt concludes that drone strikes in the FATA gradually depleted AQ's pool of qualified personnel, slowed its ability to operate, and steadily made the FATA a more dangerous location from which to operate. "Nowhere in any of al-Qaeda's documents," he says, "does the group reference the counterproductive effects many pessimistic accounts claimed the drone strikes produced."[23] Leaders were still, however, able to coordinate some complex tasks and exercise some internal control in the face of these challenges. While more difficulties may have emerged after the May 2011 correspondence that Loidolt reviewed, this evidence suggests that targeted killing campaigns "may only be able to imperfectly contain or limit the reach of a terrorist group, not eliminate it outright."[24] As Loidolt summarizes his findings:

> U.S. drone strikes did not yield an immediate, asymmetric effect on al-Qaeda's ability to operate; the payoff from U.S. drone strikes generally rose in tandem with their frequency. It took years of sustained pressure for al-Qaeda to begin reflecting on many of the detrimental effects drones were having on its organizational capabilities and processes.[25]

MIR (2018)

Asfandyar Mir, who co-authored the study Dylan Moore described in Chapter 6 and is fluent in Urdu, conducted 66 interviews in the FATA with members of AQ, the Pakistan Taliban (eventually known as Tehrik-i-Taliban, or TTP), members of the Pakistan military and Inter-Services Intelligence agency (ISI), the CIA and other US agencies, and Karachi police; as well as with residents of areas where drone strikes occurred, three individuals who had been kidnapped by AQ or the Pakistan Taliban, and journalists in contact with AQ and the TTP[26] (Mir 2018). The interviews were conducted between March 2016 and August 2017. They indicate that drone strikes caused considerable damage to AQ and the TTP, significantly impairing their ability to operate.

Mir reviews the US counterterrorism program in Pakistan from 2004 to 2014. The program was restricted in various ways from 2004 to 2007, which Mir says allowed both terrorist groups to rebuild and renew their activity after the 2001 invasion of Afghanistan. AQ established an especially strong presence in the North and South Waziristan agencies, and in 2005 the group's core leadership moved to North Waziristan. Mir describes the group during this period as establishing "a vast operational infrastructure" financed from a steady stream of funds.[27] As one ISI official described, this enabled AQ to "establish training centers, suicide bomb training, IED [improvised explosive device] production, weapons and explosive handling, material printing, and lodging facilities."[28] AQ also established specialized units to conduct attacks in Afghanistan and against US and other Western interests in Pakistan.

By 2007, Mir says, AQ "became more deeply institutionalized and attracted large numbers of specialized cadres," was actively training and planning attacks against targets inside and outside of Pakistan, and, according to a TTP operative, had "global ambitions."[29] In addition, the TTP "had become a formidable and sizable armed group."[30]

Beginning in 2008, there was a substantial escalation of counterterrorism operations in the FATA, most notably marked by a significant increase in the number of targeted strikes. According to an AQ operative, by 2009, AQ was struggling to conduct its activities and had scrapped "a dozen" plans for attacks.[31] A TTP operative said that by late 2009 AQ had pulled out most of its master trainers and mid-level commanders who had been helping Taliban forces.[32] In their detailed account of AQ's operations from 9/11 until the death of bin Laden in May 2011, Adrian Levy and Catherine Scott-Clark state that "[i]n the face of the omnipresent drones, AQ Central shuttered safe houses, closed down communications, and relocated families in a scramble to regroup. Couriers went into hiding. The network went dark."[33]

AQ also began to suffer substantial personnel shortages because of desertions. A Pakistani official monitoring Waziristan during this time reported, "I read intercepts of al-Qaida and Taliban for around three years [2008 to 2011]. There was chaos in these groups by 2010 due to drone strikes. I heard al-Qaida's leadership, known for its cool and strong discipline, regularly lose its composure. So much of the chatter was about 'my men have left me!'"[34] A member of AQ who was in North Waziristan from 2009 to 2010 said, "Drone strikes became a major concern for all jihadi organizations, including al-Qaida... the majority of the members were not as committed ideologically. I noticed that many left."[35] In November 2010, al-Qaida leader Sheikh Attiya wrote to bin Laden, "We are facing difficulties due to the grave shortages in personnel in some cadres."[36] A Karachi-based journalist who followed terrorist group activity observed that by 2010, many jihadis from Waziristan were returning home "because of drone strikes."[37]

Between 2008 and 2011 AQ lost twenty-five major leaders to drone strikes and the TTP lost ten. Interviewees commented on the effect of these losses on the groups' capabilities. Senior AQ leader Abu Laith al Libi, for instance, was killed in a drone strike in January 2008. One TTP operative said, "Libi... was one of the most important persons of al-Qaida... His death was a big loss."[38] Another operative commented, "[In 2008] an al-Qaida leader who was responsible for jihadi activities in Pakistan was killed in a drone strike. After his death, many plans came to a halt."[39]

Mir reported that multiple interviewees also said that increasing exposure of the TTP to drone strikes beginning in 2009 substantially disrupted operations. As one TPP operative reported: "When drones started flying [in 2008], we became very careful about our movement. They surely made many of us anxious."[40] Another operative said, "We had to close so many important centers after drone strikes. So many plans fell through."[41]

The impact of strikes was especially damaging to plans for transnational attacks. One TTP operative told Mir, "During Sheikh Libi's time, al-Qaida had global ambitions."[42] By 2009, however, "it was struggling to maintain its global and local operational activities, scrapping 'a dozen plans' for attacks in this period.[43] Still another noted that the 2009 killings of Qari Tahir Jan of the Islamic Movement of Uzbekistan and his field commanders in an air strike set back both AQ and the TTP: "[It was] a great loss, as they were commanding many Uzbek, Turkmen, and other foreign fighters who would fight alongside both al-Qaida and the Pakistan Taliban."[44]

Other TTP operatives noted the disruption of plans to attack Europe resulting from the targeted killing of Qari Hussain Mehsud. One said, "Qari Hussain was considered the 'nuclear power' of TTP. Many great plans remained incomplete due to his killing."[45] Another stated:

Under [Qari Hussain's] leadership, a number of tasks were completed successfully until drones came in our way. I remember one drone attack in Mir Ali, in which seven Germans were killed. They were soon to undertake suicide attacks in Germany and France . . . A few days later Qari Sahib was martyred . . Due to drone strikes, the plan of sending the German suicide bombers to France and Germany was never realized.[46]

Targeting also deprived AQ of persons with valuable specialized expertise. Sheikh Abu Khabab ran an explosives project for the group in North Waziristan that provided training in explosives. He prepared instruction materials, gave lectures, and guided TTP leaders. He was killed in a 2008 drone strike, as were persons in 2009–2011 whom he had trained to build dirty bombs, land mines, and other explosives, and who served as instructors and examiners for his explosives training course.[47] A TTP operative said that the explosives project was first transferred to a Pakistani faction and later to Khabab's teenage son. The Pakistani group tried to continue the project by translating Khabab's manuals from Arabic to Urdu for mass circulation. Without reliable trainers, however, this was insufficient to compensate for the loss of Khabab and his team. By late 2011, the quantity and quality of AQ's and TTP's explosives expertise had significantly declined.

In 2011, an AQ leader writing under the pseudonym Hikmatullah Lodhi summarized the overall impact of strikes on AQ and the TTP from 2008 to 2011:

> We need to do our utmost to recover from the losses due to drone strikes . . . if leaders continue to be killed, the jihadi movement's entire direction and pace can suffer; if field commanders continue to die, training will be poorer and the operational capabilities of mujahideen will suffer, and the next generation of mujahideen will not be of high quality. In short, drone strikes can overwhelm the strength of the mujahideen.[468]

Interviewees described continuing impairment of operations by the two groups resulting from strikes from 2011 to 2014. Mir observes:

> As they had from 2008 to 2011, the anticipatory effects of U.S. drone strikes caused enormous harm to both al-Qaida and the Pakistan Taliban from 2012 to 2014; multiple interviewees highlighted challenges to conducting operations, maintaining bases, and finding new recruits. By 2012, said an ISI official, AQ was struggling to train and produce fighters.[49]

Mir reports, AQ "closed most of its training centers, explosives production facilities, and lodging in and around the town of Mir Ali, which had once powered both global and local operations."[50] Much of TTP's capability, said an ISI official, also was "a shadow of the past."[51] In addition, a TTP operative reported that "senior leaders struggled to contact their subordinate commanders due to frequent flying of drones over the area," and "avoided interacting and travelling with drones flying."[52]

Mir notes that other operations that accompanied drone strikes contributed to weakening the TTP and AQ. These made it difficult for the groups to find new safe havens in other areas of the FATA or in

Afghanistan. A 2009 Pakistani military operation prevented the Pakistan Taliban from relocating training centers, housing, and IED factories to South Waziristan. The surge of US forces in Afghanistan prevented AQ from its desired move to eastern Afghanistan.[53]

At the same time, interviewees emphasized the particularly substantial impact of drone strikes. As one Taliban leader summarized:

> Drone strikes had a major impact . . . it was not Zarb-e-Azb [Pakistan's military operation to clear North Waziristan starting June 2014] that shattered Talibanization but drone strikes. They are the real cause of our downfall. Although jihad can never be eliminated as it will continue till the day of judgment, but the drone strikes greatly weakened the Taliban [and al-Qaida].[54]

Mir concludes from his interviews that drone strikes played a key role in "largely enabl[ing]" the US to achieve its goals of "scaling back al-Qaida's capability to execute plots against the U.S. homeland and reducing the threat of al-Qaida and the Pakistan Taliban to a nuclear-armed Pakistani state."[55]

Mir and Moore (2019)

Mir and Moore's quantitative study described in Chapter 6 also includes a discussion of qualitative material, including Mir's interviews and correspondence between Osama bin Laden and his subordinate commanders in the North Waziristan Agency that were captured during the US raid on the bin Laden compound in Abbottabad.[56] This material is consistent with Mir's research indicating that the escalation of drone operations in 2008 significantly disrupted AQ and TTP operations.

Interviewees said that the surge in drone activity made surveillance "inescapable," seriously constraining operations based on fear of strikes.[57] As one TTP operative said, "Drones were an absolute headache for us and other jihadi groups [in the region] because there is no solution for them."[58] Concern about detection limited movement, and resulted in an internal prohibition on moving in four-wheel vehicles. Even moving on foot or motorbikes "became very high risk."[59] One TTP leader said this reduced the operational capability of units in Waziristan by 2009. In a document seized in the Abbottabad raid, AQ leader Sheikh Attiya complained to bin Laden, "We really worry because of our present security situation and the airstrikes really wore us down."[60]

Mir and Moore also note that the surge in strikes created significant distrust among Al-Qaeda and Taliban leaders because of fear that the US relied on local spies, and because of concern that lower-level members were less cautious about security. One AQ operative said, "We knew that targeting by drones was not possible without a high-quality spying network on the ground."[61] In a letter to bin Laden, Attiya noted, "We bought some quantities of ammunition and devised some simple plans. We are facing difficulties due to... the abundance of spies operating in our areas."[62]

This distrust and concern about constant surveillance also led the groups to limit the use of means of communication that could be intercepted. Attiya wrote to bin Laden that "we [have] put a ban on communications except with a special permission."[63] Several TTP interviewees described serious challenges in using messengers and other forms of communication from 2009 to 2014. One said, for instance, "We were told to avoid communication devices, including wireless sets."[64]

CRUICKSHANK (2011)

Paul Cruickshank's *The Militant Pipeline*, also discussed in the next chapter, examines the extent to which intensification of drone strikes in 2008 affected AQ's ability to direct and provide training for terrorist attacks against the West as of June 2011.[65] It found that these measures reduced but did not eliminate the organization's ability to operate in the FATA, as AQ had "shown a significant ability to adapt its operations to the threat from the missile strikes."[66] Cruickshank observed that between January 2009 and June 2011 there were seven plots foiled against the West that had the capability of killing ten or more persons in which plotters were trained or directed by jihadist groups in Pakistan. Four of these occurred in 2010, the most in any year since AQ began to consolidate operations in the FATA.

Examination of five plots between 2008 and 2010 indicated that AQ was being forced to adapt to increasing pressure from strikes. One recruit said that while in the FATA they were moved frequently because strikes were "very effective."[67] AQ shifted to training recruits indoors in small mountain shacks, and limited housing to groups of ten or fewer.[68] Some recruits described feeling isolated and unclear about where they would be moved and what their next orders would be. One group also expressed displeasure at having to pay about $18,000 each for training and equipment, possibly reflecting AQ's financial problems.[69]

In addition, the threat of drones may have led AQ to decentralize operations, such as training recruits from different militant groups in temporary training camps set up by those groups, and delegating some coordination responsibilities to persons outside the tribal areas. A 2010 article in *Foreign Policy* provides support for this: "Today, Al Qaeda outsources most of its training to Pakistani outfits... The camps these groups run are often small, just one or two buildings, and temporary – such groups stay on the move to avoid detection by satellite or intelligence agents."[70]

Cruickshank says that recruits limited their time outdoors. As one recalled, "There was the fear of a missile attack coming from the unmanned drones that were overhead. These drones could be heard overhead and sometimes seen flying in the skies overhead."[71] This risk is reflected in the fact, described above, that five German militants plotting an attack in Europe were killed by a drone strike in North Waziristan, and two others narrowly missed being killed in the attack, once intelligence about the plot emerged. "There were many areas where we once had freedom, but now they have been lost," an AQ spokesperson in Pakistan stated in an audiotape in Urdu in January 2011. "We are the ones that are losing people, we are the ones facing shortages of resources. Our land is shrinking and drones are flying in the sky."[72]

Cruickshank found that, notwithstanding these difficulties, recruits in the five cases he studied were able to obtain training and maintain communication with contacts in Pakistan once they returned to prepare attacks in the West. The recruit who attempted to detonate a bomb in Times Square, for instance, was able to exchange information about the bomb he was building and the vehicle he would be using with members of the TTP, and informed them when the attack failed.[73] The experience of another recruit reflected "AQ's leaders' continuing ability to communicate with and recruit operatives in Pakistan outside their safe haven in North Waziristan."[74] This appeared to be enhanced by new encryption methods that enabled use of the Internet to direct plots in the West.[75]

Cruickshank acknowledged that further intensification of counterterrorism efforts in Pakistan could eventually reduce the number of terrorist plots linked to that area. As of June 2011, however, he said, "These metrics do not yet bear out Obama administration claims that the terrorist threat from Pakistan's tribal areas has been reduced."[76] This is consistent with Loidolt's conclusion that as of 2011 AQ leaders were still able to coordinate some external operations despite disruption.

WILNER (2010)

Alex Wilner's quantitative study of strikes against four Taliban leaders in Afghanistan, described in Chapter 6, also includes a description of the Taliban response to the killing of Mullah Dadullah in Afghanistan in May 2007.[77] Wilner's discussion highlights the effects of targeting on terrorist group morale, motivation, and internal dynamics apart from whatever kinetic or deterrent effects it may have. His account is drawn from the reporting of Syed Saleem Shahzad, an *Asia Times* correspondent who was exceptionally knowledgeable about the Taliban and its relationship with AQ. In August 2007, Shahzad wrote that the loss of Dadullah "was a huge blow" for the Taliban in southwestern Afghanistan because "there was no one of his stature to replace him."[78] "Amid the demoralization," said Shahzad, "the entire Taliban leadership left Helmand, Uruzgan, Zabul and Kandahar and sat idle in Quetta, Pakistan, for several weeks."[79]

Finally, in June Taliban leader Mullah Omar issued guidelines in response to Dadullah's death. These prescribed that: (1) no members of the Taliban central military command would work in southwest Afghanistan; (2) group commanders would be given control of specific districts and allowed to develop their own strategy; (3) the strategy would be communicated only to the Taliban–appointed "governor" of the area, who would then transmit it to the Taliban central command council; (4) the Taliban would discourage personality cults like Dadullah's, because the death of a "hero" demoralizes followers; and (5) four spokesman were appointed to decentralize information operations, so that in case of arrest of any of them only information about that zone could be obtained.[80]

Dadullah's death also apparently fostered dissension within Taliban ranks. According to Rahimullah Yusufzai, a Pakistani journalist, after Dadullah's death, "suspicion [was] falling even on trusted men and [was] creating tension in Taliban ranks."[81] Yusufzai has also reported that a lack of trust among the Taliban forced some leaders to become "extra careful in selecting fighters to serve as their bodyguards."[82]

Wilner suggests that the Taliban found it difficult to identify a suitable successor to Dadullah. Mullah Omar appointed Mullah Mansoor

Dadullah to replace his brother after Dadullah's death. When Mansoor was captured in Pakistan in February 2008, however, reports indicated that Mullah Omer had removed him from his top commander post.[83] Taliban statements suggest that Mansoor had "not obey[ed] the rules of the Islamic emirate [of Afghanistan] and violate[d] it. Therefore it was decided not to appoint any post in the emirate to him."[84] Wilner argues that Mansoor's demotion "speaks volumes." This is because:

> It signaled, first and foremost, that the Taliban was having difficulty finding a suitable replacement for Dadullah, as the theory on targeted killings suggests. It also reveals a potential lack of morale (Mansoor was not willing to lead as his brother had); a lack of strategic depth in the Taliban's leadership pool (elite positions were offered on the basis of familial ties rather than merit and ability); and general difficulty in attracting and retaining the best quality leaders. (Mansoor, although a weak leader, was nonetheless the best available option)[85]

VAN LINSCHOTEN AND KUEHN (2011 AND 2012)

Work by Alex van Linschoten and Felix Kuehn, writers and researchers who began working in Afghanistan in 2006, is broadly consistent with the claim by Abrahams and Mireau described in Chapter 6 that targeted strikes served to thin the ranks of experienced Taliban leaders. The authors express concern, however, that this resulted in the emergence of a more rigidly ideological group of younger leaders. Van Linschoten and Kuehn's work is based on their fieldwork in Afghanistan, and is contained in a 2011 report and a 2012 book.[86]

The authors note that in July 2010, NATO statistics indicated that in the previous six months 130 important insurgent figures had been captured or killed in Afghanistan. Later in the year, NATO reported that in the ninety days prior to November 11, 2010, Special Operations forces had conducted 1572 operations that resulted in 368 insurgent leaders killed or captured, and 968 lower-level insurgents killed and 2477 captured.

As van Linschoten and Kuehn observe, "The campaign to target the mid- and high-ranking leadership appears to be a key part of the U.S. strategy against the Taliban...Its impact has been felt."[87] The result, they say, is that "the older generation of Taliban leadership is struggling to maintain its hold over the insurgency," as "[y]ounger Taliban members have moved into the command structures and leadership positions."[88] They describe the implications of this trend:

> With little or no memory of Afghan society prior to the Soviet war in the 1980s, this new generation of commanders is more ideologically motivated and less nationalistic than previous generations, and therefore less pragmatic. Members of the youngest generation, often raised solely in refugee camps and madrasas in Pakistan, have no experience of traditional communities, productive economic activity, or citizenship in any state; they are citizens of jihad.[89]

Van Linschoten and Kuehn conclude, "The U.S. military appears to hope that aggressive targeting of the insurgency leadership leaves local networks more open to reconciling with the government, thus avoiding the need to deal politically with the movement... The more likely outcome, however, is potentially very different: a still growing and ever more radical but largely leaderless insurgency."[90] In other words, targeting appears to be successful on the tactical level in eliminating Taliban leaders, but the longer-term strategic effect may be counterproductive.

JAVIER JORDAN (2014)

Javier Jordan's study described in Chapter 6 notes that there was a delay of a month and a half in AQ's announcement of Ayman al-Zawahiri as the replacement for bin Laden after the latter's death. He says that bin Laden's letters recommended extensive security measures to protect against drone strikes, which made management of the organization more difficult. These measures included "frequent changes of location, splitting into small groups, hiding out for most of the day in small mountain huts, [and] use of human couriers to avoid electronic communications."[91] Jordan also notes reports that the drone campaign appeared to reduce the duration of AQ training courses from at least a month to a few days, and therefore the sophistication of operations.[92]

INTERNATIONAL CRISIS GROUP (2013)

The International Crisis Group published a 2013 review of US drone operations in the FATA "based primarily on interviews in Pakistan with stakeholders in the legal, political and NGO communities, as well as activists, journalists and researchers working on FATA."[93] The report was skeptical about the long-term effectiveness of drone strikes, but said, "The threat of drone attacks, and in particular reported signature strikes, has led militants to avoid regrouping or using cell phones and forced a number of their leaders away from FATA and into the urban areas—thus undermining communication and command."[94] The group also reported a conversation with a "senior Pakistani journalist who has extensively covered militancy in FATA," who stated that "drones are the only thing militants fear."[95]

PLAW AND FRICKER (2012)

Avery Plaw and Matthew Fricker note that when a 2009 drone strike killed Baitullah Mehsud in South Waziristan, the TTP was cast into immediate confusion, and soon into a succession struggle.[96] While Hakimullah Mehsud was able to win the internal struggle within a few weeks, the infighting appears to have weakened the organization. Moreover, Hakimullah was not deemed the rightful successor by all of the TTP, resulting in further weakening of the movement. With the TTP in disarray, Pakistan seized this opportunity to launch a South Waziristan offensive, which began on October 17, 2009. Baitullah's targeting thus appears to have contributed significantly to throwing the movement onto the defensive at least for awhile.

JOHNSTON AND SARBAHI (2016)

Patrick Johnston and Anoop Sarbahi note in their study described in Chapter 6 that in a document obtained from Abbottabad bin Laden offered suggestions for securing protection from drones.[97] He advised Al-Qaeda members to move from Pakistan to Afghanistan's Kunar province because "Kunar is more fortified due to its rougher terrain and many mountains, rivers and trees, and it can accommodate hundreds of the brothers without being spotted by the enemy. This will defend the brothers from the aircraft."[98]

ROHDE (2009)

New York Times reporter David Rohde was held captive by the Afghan Taliban from November 2008 to June 2009 in North and South Waziristan. There were 22 drone strikes in the area during this period as reported in the press. "During my time in the tribal areas," Rohde says, "it was clear that drone strikes disrupted militant operations. Taliban commanders frequently changed vehicles and moved with few bodyguards to mask their identities. Afghan, Pakistani, and foreign Taliban avoided gathering in large numbers."[99] Rohde also reports that because of drone strikes, "[t]he training of suicide bombers and roadside bomb makers was carried out in small groups to avoid detection."[100] Rohde says that strikes:

> have taken out top militants, such as the Pakistani Taliban commander Baitullah Mehsud, who was responsible for the killing of thousands of Pakistani civilians in suicide bombings. And they have slowed the training of suicide bombers and roadside bomb makers, most of whose victims are innocent Afghan and Pakistani bystanders, not American troops.[101]

Rhode maintains that drones are not a long-term solution to the problem of terrorism. In particular, he says, the failure of US to be transparent about them and to give Pakistan greater influence over their use can create public resentment that hinders counterterrorism efforts. Nonetheless, his first-hand report provides support for research findings that strikes can impose damage by disrupting terrorist group operations.

CONCLUSION

The qualitative material described above indicates that targeted strikes in the FATA, and to some extent in Afghanistan, deprived AQ and the Afghan and Pakistani Taliban of several important leaders; made it more difficult, although not impossible, for leadership to coordinate operations; disrupted the ability of these groups to conduct attacks; and eventually led to abandonment of the FATA as a safe haven. These reflect both immediate kinetic effects and long-term anticipatory effects as suggested by Mir and Moore, or what Johnston and Sabahi call degradation and disruption, respectively. The impacts on AQC appear especially substantial.

Relevant to the most important US goals, the material indicates that the weakening of leadership in the FATA caused the abandonment of some attacks that were planned in the West, a conclusion reinforced by Loidolt's finding that AQ's external operations were the first to feel a shortage of experienced leaders. Loidolt concludes that as of 2011 leaders were still able to coordinate at least some complex operations. Similarly, Cruickshank suggests that as of 2011 AQ had the ability to organize attacks against the West. Mir's interviews, however, indicate continued weakening from 2012 to 2014, into the period when evacuation of the FATA was relatively complete. This is consistent with Loidolt's observation that the effects of targeting were not immediate but were cumulative and became more significant over time. There is thus some reason to believe that whatever ability AQC still had in 2011 to coordinate attacks outside the region had declined further by 2014.

Finally, while reducing the ranks of experienced leaders in AQ and the Taliban created challenges for those groups' operations, van Linschoten and Kuehn sound a cautionary note by suggesting that this resulted in the emergence of a more radical leadership group within the Taliban. This could be relevant to the extent that the US held out the possibility of a negotiated settlement in Afghanistan that included the Taliban. The same impact on Al-Qaeda, however, likely would be regarded as less relevant because of that group's ideology.

The evidence in this chapter is not, of course, the product of a strict random sample that would ensure that the sources on which authors rely are representative. Such a sample would be extraordinarily hard to obtain, however, in the relevant locations. Mir does use a nonprobability sampling approach that he regards as suitable for his project.[102] He thus does not rely for interviewees on contacts by organizations that may have an interest in propagating a certain point of view, or who are likely to be in contact mainly with persons who subscribe to a particular perspective. AQ and Taliban members would have no reason in interviews to exaggerate the impact of drone strikes on their operations, and it is reasonable to regard contemporaneous communications by members of these groups to one another as accurately expressing the views of those who transmitted them.

In addition, Mir consulted other sources such as documents obtained during the mission against bin Laden and internal AQ documents to corroborate interview information. Loidolt drew extensively on these sources as well. Articles by local journalists are likely to be based on cultivation of knowledgeable sources both within terrorist groups and local governments. Finally, David Rohde's account of his time in captivity obviously is a first-hand report. It thus seems reasonable to regard the sources that I have described here as quite probative, if not definitive, about the impacts of targeted strikes. As such, they provide support for the claim that targeting disrupted terrorist group operations for at least some period of time, and AQC's efforts to plan attacks in the US and the West in particular.

The next chapter considers what conclusions we may be able to draw from assessment of the combined quantitative and qualitative evidence about the impacts of US strikes on AQ and associated forces. It focuses in particular on whether the weakening of AQC leadership in the FATA had only short-term effects, or whether it resulted in a more enduring reduction in the risk of attacks in the US and in the West. Answering this question requires a close examination of the relationship between AQC and AQ affiliates.

NOTES

1. Loidolt, B. (2022). Were drone strikes effective? Evaluating the drone campaign in Pakistan through captured al-Qaeda documents. *Texas National Security Review*, 5(2), 53–79. https://tnsr.org/2022/01/were-drone-strikes-effective-evaluating-the-drone-campaign-in-pakistan-through-captured-al-qaeda-documents/.
2. Id. 66 (online PDF version).
3. Id. 67.
4. Id. 69.
5. Id.
6. Id. 70.
7. Combating Terrorism Center (CTC), West Point, Harmony Project Documents, Letter from UBL to Letter from UBL to 'Attiyatullah Al-Libi 3 Reference Number: SOCOM-2012-0000015-HT, 3.
8. Loidolt 71.
9. Id. 72.
10. Id.
11. Id.
12. Combating Terrorism Center (CTC), West Point, Harmony Project Documents, Letter from UBL to 'Attiyatullah Al-Libi 3 Reference Number: SOCOM-2012-0000015, 2.
13. Id. 3.
14. Loidolt 75.
15. Id. 78.

16. Id. 76.
17. Id.
18. Id.
19. Id. 77.
20. Id.
21. Combating Terrorism Center (CTC), Reference Number: SOCOM-2012-0000015, 2.
22. Loidolt 77.
23. Id. 79.
24. Id.
25. Id.
26. Mir, A. (2018). What explains counterterrorism effectiveness? Evidence from the U.S. drone war in Pakistan. *International Security, 43*(2), 45–83. http://doi.org/10.1162/isec_a_00331.
27. Id. 63.
28. Id.
29. Id. 67.
30. Id.
31. Id. 68.
32. Id.
33. Levy, A., & Scott-Clark, C. (2017). The exile: The stunning inside story of Osama bin Laden and Al Qaeda in flight. Bloomsbury.
34. Id. 69.
35. Id. 69–70.
36. Id. 69.
37. Id. 70.
38. Id. 71.
39. Id.
40. Id. 73.
41. Id. 72.
42. Id. 68.
43. Id.
44. Id. 71.
45. Id. 72.
46. Id. 72.
47. Id. 71.
48. Id. 74.
49. Id. 75.
50. Id.
51. Id. 75.
52. Id. 77.
53. Id. 78.
54. Id. 81.

55. Id. 82.
56. Mir, A., & Moore, D. (2019). Drones, surveillance, and violence: Theory and evidence from a US drone program. *International Studies Quarterly, 63*(4), 846–862. https://doi.org/10.1093/isq/sqz040.
57. Id. 14.
58. Id.
59. Id.
60. Us Department of Justice. (2015a). "Motion in Limine to Admit Bin Laden Docs, Government Exhibit 421 10-CR-019(S-4)(RJD)." http://kronosadvisory.com/Abid.Naseer.Trial_Abbottabad.Documents_Exhibits.403.404.405.420thru433.pdf.
61. Mir & Moore, 2019, 14.
62. US Department of Justice. (2015b). "Motion in Limine to Admit Bin Laden Docs, Government Exhibit 429 10-CR-019(S-4)(RJD)." http://kronosadvisory.com/Abid.Naseer.Trial_Abbottabad.Documents_Exhibits.403.404.405.420thru433.pdf.
63. Department of Justice, 2015b.
64. Id. 15.
65. Cruickshank, P. (2011, July). *The militant pipeline between the Afghanistan-Pakistan Border Region and the West.* New America Foundation. https://newamerica.org/documents/887/the-militant-pipeline.
66. Id. 2.
67. Id. 31.
68. Id.
69. Id.
70. Keating, J. (2020, May 10). What Do You Learn at a Terrorist Training Camp? *Foreign Policy.* https://foreignpolicy.com/2010/05/10/what-do-you-learn-at-terrorist-training-camp/.
71. Cruickshank, 37.
72. Id. 34.
73. Id. 42–43.
74. Id. 39.
75. Id. 50.
76. Id. 2.
77. Wilner, A. S. (2010). Targeted killings in Afghanistan: Measuring coercion and deterrence in counterterrorism and counterinsurgency. *Studies in Conflict & Terrorism, 33*(4), 307–329. https://doi.org/10.1080/10576100903582543.
78. Shahzad, S. S. (2007, August 11). Taliban a step ahead of US Assault. *Asia Times.* https://web.archive.org/web/20070818133337/http://www.atimes.com/atimes/South_Asia/IH11Df01.html.
79. Id.
80. Id.

81. Yusufzai, R. (2007, May 18). Spies in Their Ranks Worry Taliban. *The News International.*
82. Id.
83. BBC, "Taliban Sack Military Commander," 29 December 2007; Bill Roggio, "Mullah Omar Confirms Firing of Mullah Mansoor Dadullah," The Long War Journal, 2 January 2008; Bill Roggio, "Taliban Dismisses Senior Afghan Commander [Update]," *The Long War Journal,* 29 December 2007.
84. BBC, "Taliban Sack Military Commander," 2007.
85. Wilner, 2010, 323.
86. van Linschoten, A. S., & Kuehn, F. (2011). Separating the Taliban from al-Qaeda: The core of success in Afghanistan. *New York University Center on International Cooperation.* https://cic.es.its.nyu.edu/sites/default/files/gregg_sep_tal_alqaeda.pdf; van Linschoten, A. S., & Kuehn, F. (2012). *An enemy we created: The myth of the Taliban-al-Qaeda merger in Afghanistan.* Oxford University Press.
87. van Linschoten, A. S., & Kuehn, F., 2011, 11.
88. Id. 9.
89. Id.
90. Id. 10.
91. Javier Jordan, 2014, 18.
92. Id. 22.
93. International Crisis Group. (2013, May 21). Drones: Myths and reality in Pakistan. https://d2071andvip0wj.cloudfront.net/drones-myths-and-reality-in-pakistan.pdf, 2.
94. Id. 22–23.
95. Id. 23.
96. Plaw, A., Fricker, M. S. (2012). Tracking the predators: Evaluating the US drone campaign in Pakistan. *International Studies Perspectives, 13,* 344–365. https://academic.oup.com/isp/article-abstract/13/4/344/1786989.
97. Johnston, P. B., & Sarbahi, A. K. (2016). The impact of US drone strikes on terrorism in Pakistan. *International Studies Quarterly, 60*(2), 203–219. https://doi.org/10.1093/isq/sqv004.
98. Id. 207.
99. Rohde, D. (2012, January 26). The drone wars. *Reuters Magazine.* https://www.reuters.com/article/us-david-rohde-drone-wars/reuters-magazine-the-drone-wars-idUSTRE80P11I20120126.
100. Id.
101. Id.
102. Mir, 2018, Appendix 2.

CHAPTER 8

Weighing the Evidence

What conclusions can we draw from the quantitative research and qualitative material about whether US targeted strikes against Al-Qaeda (AQ)
and associated groups have furthered US counterterrorism goals? By AQ,
I refer both to what is regarded as Al-Qaeda Core (AQC), the group's
top leadership, and to groups affiliated with AQ, such as Al-Shabaab.
Associates are groups not affiliated with AQ, but that sometimes work
in concert with it, such as the Pakistani Taliban (TTP).

As Chapter 5 describes, US goals in order of priority have been to
weaken the ability of AQ and associates to conduct attacks:

1. in the United States;
2. against US targets outside the US;
3. in the West, where most close US allies are located;
4. against Western targets outside the West;
5. in allied countries outside the West, especially Pakistan because of
   the risk of instability to a country with nuclear weapons;
6. that do not fall within the first four categories but are international
   in nature, that is, conducted by a group outside its region[1];
7. in other countries, conducted by an AQ affiliate or associate in those
   countries.

© The Author(s), under exclusive license to Springer Nature   185
Switzerland AG 2022
M. Regan, *Drone Strike–Analyzing the Impacts of Targeted Killing*,
https://doi.org/10.1007/978-3-030-91119-5_8

As Chapter 5 also indicates, we can characterize attacks in categories one and three as "external" attacks conducted against the "far enemy" outside the Muslim world, which are of particular importance to the US.

Targeted strikes are theorized to weaken the ability of AQ and associates to conduct attacks for two reasons. First is what Mir and Moore call their direct "kinetic" impact, and Johnston and Sarbahi describe as "degrading" a terrorist group. Killing leaders and important operatives deprives a group of experienced and capable personnel who are involved in planning, coordinating, and conducting attacks. Their replacements may not be as effective in carrying out these tasks. Second are "anticipatory" impacts that disrupt a group. These are changes that a group makes in how it operates in an effort to avoid future targeting of its members. They can make group operations more cumbersome and less efficient in conducting attacks. Strikes thus are assumed to have both direct immediate impacts and indirect longer-term impacts that weaken a group, resulting in fewer attacks. What does the evidence suggest about (1) whether targeted strikes had these impacts, and, if so, (2) whether these impacts helped achieve US goals?

Impacts on AQ and TTP

As Chapter 7 describes, most qualitative evidence relates to the impacts of strikes on AQC and the TTP. It provides strong support for the conclusion that strikes in Pakistan, and the FATA in particular, had both kinetic and anticipatory impacts. They diminished AQC and TTP capabilities by killing several experienced and capable leaders, and by eliminating the FATA as a safe haven. Second, they had anticipatory impacts, in that both groups, especially AQC, imposed significant restrictions on leader mobility and on communication between leaders and other members. These effects disrupted, although they may not have eliminated, the ability to plan and coordinate group operations. To what extent did these impacts further US goals?

Attacks in the FATA and Pakistan

Most attacks in the FATA, and in Pakistan more generally, were conducted by the TTP and other local groups, but Al-Qaeda provided some assistance for such attacks. The strongest quantitative evidence indicates that strikes in the FATA were associated with declines in militant attacks in areas that suffered strikes. Johnston and Sarbahi find that attacks and deaths from them declined in weeks in which strikes occurred, while Mir and Moore find that intensification of strikes beginning in 2008 is associated with monthly reductions in attacks and casualties compared to previous levels.

Second, the two studies that use identification strategies to focus on strikes in Pakistan more generally come to different conclusions. Jaeger and Siddique find some short-term increase, but longer-term decrease, in attacks after a strike, and find that both the probability and number of attacks decline after a successful strike. Mahmood and Jetter, however, find that strikes are associated with an increase in attacks, using wind levels as their independent variable. Carson's study of correlation finds a decrease in the probability of an attack after a strike, but one model finds an increase in fatalities from attacks.

Mahmood and Jetter's finding suggests the possibility of retaliatory attacks and/or diversion of attacks from the FATA, where most strikes occurred, to other parts of Pakistan. The first possibility is consistent with Jager and Siddique's finding of a short-term increase in attacks, but Jaeger and Siddique suggest that a longer-term decline may indicate a change in the timing of attacks, not an increase in their number. In addition, they differentiate between successful and unsuccessful strikes and find a uniform decline in attacks after a successful strike. Mahmood and Jetter do not make such a distinction. With regard to displacement of attacks to areas beyond strike locations, Johnston and Sarbahi found that declines in attacks in the FATA were not accompanied by increases in neighboring areas.

While the evidence is not uniform, there is at least some reason to believe that strikes in Pakistan were associated with a decline in attacks in that country. Quantitative studies on Pakistan in general, and particularly on the FATA, thus provide substantial, although not uniform, support for the conclusion that the direct and indirect impact of strikes on AQ and TTP contributed to declines in attacks in Pakistan, which is the fifth US goal listed above.

AQ ATTACKS BEYOND PAKISTAN

Studies that focus specifically on targeting AQ leadership find no association with the frequency or lethality of worldwide attacks by AQ as a whole. Not all these studies use identification strategies or control for all relevant variables, but they come to the same conclusion. This finding is consistent with studies of terrorist databases that find that decapitation of top leaders does not reduce attacks by older, well-established, religiously motivated groups. It also reflects the fact, discussed in more detail below, that AQ has grown substantially in recent years through increased affiliation by groups in several parts of the globe. One result of this is that AQC faces greater challenges in influencing the activities of groups that have a range of priorities that may not fully align with those of AQC.

What about the effects of strikes in furthering the important US goals of reducing attacks in the US, on US targets outside the US, and in the West? Javier Jordan's study of strikes in Pakistan concludes that the decline in attempted and successful AQC attacks in the West since 2007 is attributable to the loss of many AQC members from strikes. Jordan does not, however, control for the significant increase in defensive and counterterrorism measures in the West that may account for this decline.

Unfortunately, no quantitative study that focuses specifically on targeting AQC and controls for such measures uses dependent variables that reflect attack location. Lehrke and Schomaker come the closest, using drone strikes as their independent variable. Most strikes during their study period were in Pakistan, so one might argue that this serves as a rough proxy for strikes against AQC. They find that strikes were not associated with attacks in the West, but their dependent variable is total terrorist, not AQ, attacks in the West. Their study also is the only one that also examines attacks against Western targets, which would include attacks on US targets outside the US. These are attacks by terrorist groups and jihadist groups, however, not AQ specifically.

Jenna Jordan's research finds that attacks by AQC have dropped dramatically beginning in 2007, while attacks by affiliates have significantly increased. Since attacks in the West have declined over that same period, one might argue that this decrease is because of the decline in AQC attacks, and that the latter decline is because strikes have weakened AQC. Therefore, the argument goes, strikes against AQC have been successful in achieving the most important US goals. The absence of research on strikes against AQC that controls for other variables that could be responsible for the drop in attacks in the West, however, still suggests some caution in making this claim.

The available evidence does not enable a determination of the impact of strikes against AQC on AQ attacks against US targets outside the US. Is it plausible, however, to claim that strikes that weakened AQC have achieved the important goals of helping reduce attacks in the US and the West, despite evidence that they have had no effect on global attacks by AQ as a whole? As the next two sections describe, there is a reasonable basis for this claim if we appreciate the relationship between AQC and the larger AQ entity, how this relationship has evolved in the last two decades, and the distinctive role of AQC within AQ of focusing on attacks in the US and the West.

With respect to attacks by AQ as a whole, AQC has never attempted to control the ability of affiliates to conduct attacks when and where they see fit as long as they are consistent with the broad goals articulated by AQC. Furthermore, AQ has grown substantially in recent years through affiliation by a variety of groups, not all of whose priorities necessarily are perfectly aligned with those of AQC. As Bruce Hoffman and Fernando Reinares have described, Al-Qaeda has become a geographically and organizationally diverse entity that Hoffman and Reinares call "polymorphous."[2] The result is that it is "no longer possible to equate the global terrorism threat solely with the threat posed by Al-Qaeda central."[3]

With respect to attacks in the US and the West, which I will refer to as attacks in the West for the sake of brevity, AQC historically has played the distinctive role of persistently focusing on encouraging, planning, and coordinating large-scale attacks in these locations. After 9/11, AQC provided assistance such as propaganda, information campaigns, and training to groups for local attacks as a way to expand the AQ network. At the same time, it never wavered in its belief that defeating the "far enemy" in the West was the precondition for imposing its version of Islam in the Muslim world.[4] As detailed case studies of attacks in the edited volume by Hoffman and Reinares describe, AQC provided various forms of assistance to almost every major plot to conduct attacks in the West after 9/11.[5]

Hoffman and Reinares observe that throughout its history AQC "has depended more than anything on its possession of or access to physical sanctuary and safe haven."[6] The overthrow of the Taliban in 2001 deprived it of its haven in Afghanistan and, as we have seen, targeted strikes in the FATA eventually resulted in the loss of that haven as well. It is therefore reasonable to believe that, in combination with other counterterrorism measures, as well as AQC's shift in emphasis to some extent after 9/11, strikes against AQC contributed to reducing the threat of major AQ attacks in the West.

The next two sections elaborate on these explanations for the effects of strikes against AQC on AQ attacks as a whole, and on AQ attacks in the West. The chapter then closes with a discussion of the nature of the current threat posed by AQ as a whole and the implications for the future use of targeted strikes against it.

Total AQ Attacks

The exact nature of AQ is a subject of considerable debate, reflecting the difficulty of clearly identifying the features of a clandestine organization. To the extent that it is a hierarchical entity in which operational units rely upon instruction from top leadership in order to conduct attacks, the loss of major leaders would seriously impair its ability to carry out attacks. There are few if any experts who hold this view of AQ, however. The major point of contention is whether AQ is now a "leaderless" movement that is united only by a general commitment to the cause of violent jihad, or whether it is a loosely organized network that combines some general direction from leadership with considerable local group autonomy.[7]

While it is not possible to make a definitive pronouncement about the structure of AQ, there is considerable evidence for the second view. As Daveed Gartenstein-Ross and Nathaniel Barr observe, "From the outset, Al-Qaeda adopted a unique organizational design, whereby its senior leadership outlined a strategic course for the organization a whole, but empowered mid-level commanders to execute this strategy as they saw fit."[8] This is captured in the principle "[c]entralization of decision and decentralization of execution."[9] As Abu Obaida Yusuf al-Anabi, the head of Al-Qaeda in the Islamic Maghreb (AQIM) described it, Al-Qaeda "identifies the overall goals and sets the broad outlines of the jihadist strategy, but leaves the details of the operational tactics on the ground to the branches to determine."[10] As long as attacks further the broad strategic objectives of the organization as articulated by AQC, group leaders draw on their knowledge of local conditions to determine when and where to conduct them.

This organizational structure reflects the idea that the goal of AQ is to mobilize the *ummah*, or Islamic community, in a global jihadist revolution, but that AQC must serve as the vanguard of this movement. In this role, its primary responsibilities are to "provide strategic guidance to affiliates and to advise them on major personnel and operational decisions, including the appointment of local leaders."[11] Thus, for example, bin

Laden and Zawahiri chastised Al-Qaeda in Iraq (AQI) leader Zarqawi for using brutal methods that included attacks on fellow Muslims he regarded as heretics. Similarly, bin Laden rejected AQAP leader Wuhayshi's suggestion that Anwar al-Awlaki replace him as head of that affiliate. AQC correspondence is replete with discussion of the strategic impact of decisions such as when to declare an emirate in a country, whether it was advisable for the group to affiliate with Al-Qaeda, and what kinds of targets a group should attack.

The idea that the goal of AQC is to mobilize the *ummah* is reflected in the fact that AQ has grown by developing relationships with a variety of groups, which vary in their formality. Thomas Joscelyn notes that "AQ has always sought to push forward its agenda by working with, co-opting, or otherwise directing like-minded jihadist groups. The principal AQ organization – its general command – is itself a joint venture, which bin Laden's organization and Ayman al Zawahiri's Egyptian Islamic Jihad (EIJ) forged through a merger."[12]

Hoffman and Reinares, as well as Seth Jones, thus suggest that by the time of bin Laden's death AQ was comprised of four separate but interconnected components: (1) AQC (2) AQ affiliates (3) groups associated with AQ that have benefited from periodic collaboration and (4) cells and individuals inspired by AQ but that are not part of any terrorist organization.[13] AQ therefore is better conceptualized as a network than as either an integrated organization or a social movement without any organizational structure at all.

The weakening of AQC resulting from the invasion of Afghanistan and strikes in the FATA, combined with the continuing growth of the network, has led AQ over the last two decades to adapt through even greater decentralization of capabilities and authority. Groups began to work among themselves to compensate for less material AQC assistance by developing their own sources of financing, acquiring territory that can serve as safe havens for training and indoctrination, and collaborating with each other to assemble resources that enable them to conduct attacks outside their own regions. Groups still look to a more dispersed AQC in Pakistan and Afghanistan for strategic guidance, but now are less dependent on it for resources to conduct their operations. The 9/11 Monograph on Terrorist Financing presciently suggested even as early as 2004:

As AQ becomes more diffuse—or becomes essentially indistinguishable from a larger global jihadist movement—the very concept of AQ financing may have to be reconsidered. Rather than the AQ model of a single organization raising money that is then funneled through a central source, we may find we are contending with an array of loosely affiliated groups, each raising funds on its own initiative.[14]

These developments have enabled some affiliates and associates to launch international attacks without much assistance from AQC. Even as targeted strikes began to intensify in Pakistan in 2008, for instance, AQAP was able to organize a nearly successful attack in December 2009 on an airliner landing in Detroit, which failed only when the operative was unable to detonate a bomb sewn into his underwear. In 2010 AQAP was able to install explosives in printers on flights to cargo planes bound for the US and the UK, a plot that was foiled with assistance from Saudi Arabian intelligence.[15] In 2010, the TTP, which previously had conducted attacks only in Pakistan, organized and attempted a car bomb attack in Times Square in New York, in which the bomb ignited but failed to explode.[16]

Another thwarted AQAP plot in 2012 involved an attempted attack on a US airliner with a modified version of the underwear bomb used in the 2009 airliner operation.[17] In 2013, intercepted communication between bin Laden's successor Zawahiri and AQAP leader Wuhayshi referred to an expansive plot to target US facilities in multiple locations, which resulted in the closure of 19 US embassies across the world. In December 2019, an attack at Naval Air Station Pensacola in Florida that killed three US sailors and wounded eight other people on December 6, 2019 was the "culmination of years of planning and preparation by a longtime AQAP associate."[18]

In December 2020, a member of Al-Shabaab was indicted who was planning an attack on the US. The defendant was arrested in the Philippines after already completing training necessary to obtain his pilot's license at the time of the indictment, with the goal of hijacking and crashing an aircraft into a building in the US.[19] Another individual who had taken lessons with him and was wanted by Kenyan authorities escaped to Somalia in March 2021.[20] These incidents all reflect growth in the capabilities of AQ network members.

AQAP played an important role in this evolution of AQ. It was able to compensate to some extent for the loss of experienced leaders in

AQC because many of its own leaders had worked with bin Laden in Afghanistan in the conflict with Russia and in planning attacks up to the time of 9/11. AQAP leader Wuhayshi served as bin Laden's personal secretary in Afghanistan, and after bin Laden's death was appointed by Zawahiri as the general manager of AQ, a position second only to Zawahiri.

The group used this experience to provide some of the types of advice and guidance to other groups that previously had been furnished exclusively by AQC. As one observer noted in 2015, "AQAP ... looks after other groups in the franchise by providing tactical and strategic training, and sharing resources in a manner characteristic of bin Laden's group in the 1990s and early 2000s."[21] It has a close relationship with Al-Shabaab, and reportedly assisted it with the purchase of a large amount of weapons including explosives, possibly PETN (Pentaerythritol tetranitrate), and provided training for the group's operations between 2010 and 2011. AQAP also appears to have arranged for hand-carried communication of messages between Al-Shabaab and AQC.

In addition, AQAP helped establish the Muhammad Jamal Network (MJN) in Egypt, likely at the request of Zawahiri. The head of that group said in his letters to Zawahiri that he received financial support from AQAP, which also helped fighters reach the MJN's camps in Egypt and Libya, and assisted the group in building its own training camps. Wuhayshi also offered written strategic guidance to the head of AQIM on how best to manage the group and cautioned him about prematurely proclaiming an emirate. AQAP also was the leader in the move toward horizontal collaboration among groups in the network in order to enhance their capabilities. David Knoll reports that "[s]ince 2009, AQAP has pioneered a 'new model' for Al-Qaeda's franchises, in which affiliates plan their own external operations and cultivate horizontal relationships with one another."[22]

Katherine Zimmerman notes that other affiliates "adapted to AQAP's model and cultivated inter-group connections spanning the region. These connections facilitate broader coordination and cooperation within the AQ network, and have increased its overall resiliency."[23] The Senate Intelligence Committee report on the attacks on the US consulate in Benghazi, Libya in 2012 concluded that the embassy was attacked by "[i]ndividuals affiliated with terrorist groups, including AQIM, Ansar al-Sharia, AQAP, and the Mohammad Jamal Network."[24] The report found that:

Al-Qa'ida-affiliated groups and associates are exploiting the permissive security environment in Libya to enhance their capabilities and expand their operational reach. This year, Muhammad Jamal's Egypt-based network, al-Qa'ida in the Arabian Peninsula (AQAP), and al-Qa'ida in the Lands of the Islamic Maghreb (AQIM) have conducted training, built communication networks, and facilitated extremist travel across North Africa from their safe haven in parts of eastern Libya.[25]

AQ's geographic expansion through a widening group of affiliates and associated groups has helped secure territory for at least some training and indoctrination that compensate to some extent for the AQC loss of a safe haven in the FATA. Occupation of a larger amount of territory also creates opportunities for groups to develop their own sources of financing.

The expansion of the AQ network has been assisted by the instability created by the Arab Spring in 2011, and by a decision to deemphasize international attacks to some extent. Zimmerman says that a greater local focus "better enabled al-Qaeda to extend its relationships into various communities, preying on their vulnerabilities, and broaden its reach into the Muslim world."[26] As she observes, Al-Qaeda "has strengthened without raising alarms in Western capitals, building a popular base through its 'localization' effort while still pursuing capabilities to conduct international terror attacks."[27] As a result, Al-Qaeda affiliates have emerged in Afghanistan, Pakistan, the Indian Subcontinent, Syria, Yemen, East Africa, the Maghreb, and the Sahel.[28]

In sum, as Zimmerman as put it with respect to AQ, "There is no group at the heart of the network. The core group in Pakistan maintains a mediatory or advisory role, but it no longer issues directives. Therefore, operations specifically targeting a single group, including AQAP, would have a limited overall effect on the network."[29] "The heart of the network," she says, "is now its latticed structure, which is composed of the interconnections among AQ core, the affiliates, and the associates. The relationships among AQ groups facilitate inter-group cooperation and the sharing of resources."[30] This, she says, is the source of AQ's "strength and resilience."[31]

Once we understand that AQ is a network in which members are not dependent on either permission or resources from AQC to conduct attacks, we can see why strikes weakening AQC would have minimal if any effect on the goal of reducing attacks by the network as a whole. AQC's role has been to provide strategic guidance to the groups that comprise the network, but there have been several instances in which a group has ignored such guidance and pursued its own agenda.[32] For these reasons, if the goal of US strikes is to cripple the ability of AQ as a whole to operate, strikes against AQC are unlikely to accomplish it.

Crucial US goals, however, have been to reduce attacks in the US and the West. Understanding why weakening AQC may have furthered these goals requires appreciating the distinctive historical role of AQ leadership in focusing on attacks in the West. The next section discusses this role in more detail.

Attacks in the West

AQC has played a distinctive role throughout AQ's history in persistently focusing on attacks on the "far enemy" in the US and the West. As Gartenstein-Ross and Barr explain, this has been "motivated by a strategic belief that al-Qaeda could only topple local regimes and establish Islamic emirates if it first crippled the West, because Western military and economic support would prevent 'near enemy' regimes from falling."[33] AQ thus historically has grown through the strategy of, as Daniel Byman puts it, "transforming preexisting Salafi-jihadist groups with a local agenda into Al-Qaeda affiliates with a more global perspective."[34] Seth Jones notes that this global perspective regards the US as the main target. "For al-Qaida," he says, "the United States was the most significant far enemy. Al-Qaida's leaders argued that the United States was a corrupting influence due to its Christian roots, aid to Arab regimes, support to Israel, and predilection toward democratic governance rather than Islamic law. To reestablish a caliphate, al-Qaida had to target the supporters of Muslim regimes."[35]

Aside from strategic reasons, AQC historically has played this role because affiliates generally, although not exclusively, tend to focus on local concerns in places like Syria, Iraq, Yemen, and the African Maghreb and Sahel. Furthermore, compared to AQC in Afghanistan and the FATA, the safe havens that affiliates have been able to acquire generally are in countries where groups' occupation of territory is contested to varying degrees by the local government. This means that affiliates must devote time and resources to defending local territory. As a result, few of them thus far have attempted attacks in the US or the West, although they have conducted operations against Western interests in their areas.

Bin Laden elaborated on the importance of attacking the West in a May 2010 letter appointing Attiyah Abd al-Rahman to a senior leadership position, in a passage that is worth quoting at length:

> Thus, the plague that exists in the nations of Muslims has two causes: The first is the presence of American hegemony and the second is the presence of rulers that have abandoned Islamic law and who identify with the hegemony, serving its interests in exchange for securing their own interests.

> The only way for us to establish the religion and alleviate the plague which has befallen Muslims is to remove this hegemony which has beset upon the nations and worshippers and which transforms them, such that no regime that rules on the basis of Islamic law remains. The way to remove this hegemony is to continue our direct attrition against the American enemy until it is broken and is too weak to interfere in the matters of the Islamic world.[36]

Bin Laden formulated guidance to AQ affiliates that declared that the organization's focus was the "bigger external enemy before the internal [enemy]."[37] He told his lieutenants, "The most important activities the [al-Qaeda] Organization can carry out are operations that directly affect the security and economy of all of the American people... Operations inside America and targeting oil abroad...are among the strongest and fastest ways to affect the [American] people..."[38]

Thus, for instance, documents obtained at Abbottabad indicate that bin Laden advised AQAP not to target the Yemeni army and police force. "The Americans are our desired goal," he said.[39] He used the metaphor of a tree to make his point. The enemies of Muslims, he said, "are like a malignant tree: it has a 50 cm American trunk and branches that differ in sizes... Thus, the sound and effective way to bring the tree down would be to focus our saw on its American root."[40] Focusing instead on the branches, he said, "would disrupt our efforts and energy."[41]

Similarly, he wrote in his appointment letter to Attiyah that AQ's priority should be attacks in the US. "Given that the difference of the impact of attacks against the foes inside or outside of America is substantial" he said, "we need to confirm to the brothers that every effort that could be spent on attacks in America would not be spent outside of it."[42] To the extent that AQ had capacity to do more than this, the next priorities should be attacks on American interests in non-Islamic countries, and then attacks on such interests in Islamic countries where AQ had no affiliates or allied groups that would be put in danger.[43]

The historical ability of AQC to operate in a safe haven largely free from threats enabled it to concentrate its efforts on planning and coordinating attacks in the West. The report on AQ financing to the 9/11 Commission estimated that AQ paid the Taliban in Afghanistan between $10 and $20 million a year for protection, securing its agreement to resist international pressure to expel the group or turn bin Laden over to a third country.[44]

As the 9/11 Commission described, "The alliance with the Taliban provided AQ a sanctuary in which to train and indoctrinate fighters and terrorists, import weapons, forge ties with other jihad groups and leaders, and plot and staff terrorist schemes."[45] Estimates are that from 1996 to September 11, 2001, "between 10,000 and 20,000 fighters underwent instruction in AQ camps in Afghanistan."[46] The Commission observed, "In addition to training fighters and special operators, this larger network of guesthouses in camps provided a mechanism by which al Qaeda could screen and vet candidates for induction into its own organization."[47]

The 9/11 Commission Monograph on Terrorist Financing noted that the CIA estimated that AQ spent about $30 million a year at the time of 9/11 to sustain its operations. The report said, "Contrary to popular myth, Usama Bin Ladin does not support AQ through a personal fortune or a network of businesses. Rather, AQ financial facilitators raise money from witting and unwitting donors, mosques and sympathetic imams, and nongovernment organizations such as charities."[48] Such fundraising drew on the emphasis on funding charitable work in Saudi Arabia's culture. AQ used this money "to create alliances with other Islamic terrorist organizations. AQ's cash contributions helped establish connections with these groups and encouraged them to share members, contacts, and facilities."[49] They also helped fund the attacks on the US embassies in Kenya and Tanzania in 1998, and the attack on the US destroyer USS Cole in 2000 in Yemen.

The 9/11 attacks reflected AQC's ability to draw on all these distinctive contributions, even though there had been a difference of opinion within leadership about the wisdom and feasibility of the operation. The attacks were conceived by Khalid Sheikh Mohammed, who first presented it to bin Laden in 1996. In late 1998 or early 1999, bin Laden gave him approval to proceed. The two met with bin Laden's deputy Mohammed Atef in early 1999. In late 1999, a group of men arrived from Hamburg,

Germany. Bin Laden selected them for the operation because they were educated, could speak English, and had lived in the West. Another arrival was recruited because he already had a commercial pilot's license. Atef provided operational support that included selecting targets and helping arrange travel for the hijackers.

The 9/11 Commission Monograph on Terrorist Financing concluded that the total cost of the 9/11 attacks was between $400,000 and $500,000. This included travel expenses and expenses in the US for "tuition for flight training, living expenses (room, board and meals, vehicles, insurance, etc.), and travel (for casing flights, meetings, and the September 11 flights themselves)."[50] This did not include "the cost of running training camps in Afghanistan where the hijackers were recruited and trained or the marginal cost of the training itself."[51]

The invasion of Afghanistan and the overthrow of the Taliban eliminated AQ's safe haven in that country. A large number of top leadership generally fled to Northwest Pakistan, with many in the FATA and the Northwest Frontier Province. The Pakistani government devoted minimal attention to the remote, mountainous tribal areas, and what eventually became the TTP pledged to offer protection. While this did not offer as secure a haven as Afghanistan, it nonetheless gave AQ considerable opportunity to operate relatively freely. As Gartenstein-Ross and Barr describe:

> The tribal areas of Pakistan offered an ideal location to rebuild the organization and reestablish structured decision-making processes. In the immediate post-9/11 period, the Pakistani army was reluctant to intervene in the tribal areas, and proved to be largely ineffective when it conducted military operations there. The ability of the United States to collect and act on intelligence in the tribal areas was also limited.
>
> Moreover, some of the local Pakistani population was sympathetic to the Arabic-speaking foreigners who sought shelter and protection there after the United States invasion of Afghanistan. In the tribal areas, therefore, al-Qaeda found a permissive environment in which to operate. Al-Qaeda commanders could conduct in-person meetings, reinitiate training exercises, and plan military operations without attracting the attention of counterterrorism forces.[52]

Asfandyar Mir's report of his interviews indicates that AQ used its safe haven to "establish training centers, suicide bomb training, IED [improvised explosive device] production, weapons and explosive handling, material printing, and lodging facilities."[53] Mir reports, "From 2006 to 2007, al-Qaida established elaborate bases in areas of Data Khel, Dosali, Mir Ali, and Miramshah—all in the North Waziristan Agency. By 2006, its leadership had begun referring to the Agency as the Islamic State of Waziristan."[54] Daniel Byman notes that training camps provide an especially valuable opportunity to further AQC's focus on attacks in the West: "Many individuals who enter the camps without a strong anti-American agenda leave with virulent anti-American views."[55]

While AQ supported efforts by local groups to engage in attacks in their areas, it devoted considerable attention to planning attacks in the West. Bruce Hoffman and Fernando Reinares note that "core leadership was progressively weakened as a result of the US drone campaign and the number of its members decreased considerably ... [but] [i]t remained active in the ideation, planning, and preparation of major terrorist attacks in and outside the West."[56] As the previous chapter describes, Paul Cruickshank documents the role of Pakistan as a source of training for a significant portion of plots against the West from 9/11 to 2011. Of the 32 "serious" jihadist terrorist plots against the West between 2004 and 2011, 53% had operational or training links to established jihadist groups in Pakistan.[57]

Among these were an October 2002 bombing of sites in Bali frequented by Western tourists that killed 202 people and injured 209 more. The attack was financed by AQ and carried out by Jemaah Islamiyah, not an AQ affiliate but a group that collaborated with it. A week after the attack Al-Jazeera aired an audio-cassette purportedly carrying a recorded voice message from Osama Bin Laden saying that the Bali bombings were in retaliation for the US war on terror and Australia's role in the liberation of East Timor.

AQC also financed and help direct the series of July 7, 2005 bombings on the London public transport system that killed 52 and injured more than 700, and four follow-up bombings two weeks later in which only the detonators exploded, which caused one minor injury. In addition, it coordinated a 2006 plot to simultaneously detonate liquid explosives in nine commercial airplanes departing Heathrow airport for North America.[58] Operatives in this plot received training from AQ in Pakistan. They also received assistance there from Rashid Rauf, and a person believed to be Abu Ubaidah al Masri, in determining the best solution to use for explosions, how to construct an explosive device, and testing whether the explosive solution could be detected by airport security. Rauf was in continuous contact with the operatives from Pakistan until the plot was discovered two weeks before the planned attacks.

Peter Bergen notes that:

> as the tenth anniversary of 9/11 approached, bin Laden was angry that his central goal of attacking the United States again had failed, as had other operations to attack key European targets. In a report on "external operations," an al-Qaeda official explained to bin Laden that a plot to attack the U.S. embassy in Russia had fizzled and that despite sending al-Qaeda members to the U.K. to hit "several targets," these operations had also come to nothing. Al-Qaeda had also sent "three brothers" on a terrorist mission to Denmark... but those agents had disappeared.[59]

Daniel Byman also observes that Algeria's GSPC "first declared loyalty to bin Ladin in 2003 but then took over a year to designate France, rather than the Algerian government, as its primary target—a more 'Western' orientation in keeping with al Qaeda priorities."[60] Furthermore, "To the disappointment of al Qaeda's core leadership, even after its 2007 name change to AQIM, the affiliate has not tried hard to mobilize supporters in Europe on behalf of global jihad and has not brought the 'war' to the Continent."[61]

Chapter 7 describes how intensification of strikes by the FATA in 2008 began to thin the ranks of experienced AQ leaders and disrupt their ability to communicate efficiently with members. Loidolt's research indicates that AQ's external operations were the first to be significantly affected by the strikes. The group found it increasingly difficult to replace leaders of those operations and to coordinate them as easily as before, although Loidolt suggests that they were able at least as of 2011 to maintain some oversight.

One example of an important loss was the death by drone strike in November 2008 of Rashid Rauf, the British AQ operative in Pakistan who was the contact for operatives in the UK who planned to use liquid explosives to blow up nine airliners departing from Heathrow to North America in 2006. Rauf also was the handler for the attackers in the July 7, 2005 and July 21, 2005 attacks in London. At the time of his death, Rauf was planning an April 2009 attack in Manchester, a September

2009 attack in New York, and a July 2010 attack in Scandinavia. A US counterterrorism official said his death was a major blow to AQ's ability to plan attacks against the West, "as the terror network had no other operative able to coordinate plots overseas with his level of operational tradecraft."[62] As interviews described in Chapter 7 indicate, after the deaths of others involved in planning external attacks, many of those plots were abandoned.

Aside from the loss of leaders and key operatives, the pressure from strikes caused AQ to significantly curtail its training activities in the FATA, and eventually to move them elsewhere. AQC thus lost a safe haven in which it could provide training under the supervision of top leaders, as well as focus on planning international attacks rather than ones against hostile local government forces.

The result, as Jenna Jordan's data indicate, is that attacks attributed to AQC have substantially declined even as attacks by affiliates have increased. Jordan argues that the overall increase in attacks indicates that targeting top AQ leaders has been ineffective, but this does not focus on the key US goals of reducing attacks in the US and the West.

Finally, Clarke and Mir suggest some lingering deterrent effects of US targeted strikes that may induce some caution even if AQC is able to regain strength. While some in leadership desire another major attack against the US, others:

> appear aware of the costs of a large-scale terrorist operation. One lesson Zawahiri seems to have internalized is that U.S. counterterrorism capabilities remain powerful, a fact that can limit al Qaida's freedom of movement while making it costly for some affiliates and allies to support the group. They also seem to assess that rapid turnover of leadership—as in the period from 2008 to 2015—could potentially lead to al Qaida's collapse.[63]

There is thus a reasonable basis for concluding that strikes weakening AQC helped reduce the risk of AQ attack in the US and the West, even if they did not reduce overall attacks by AQ, because they weakened the element of AQ that focused on planning and coordinating such attacks. This did not occur because of strikes alone. We must acknowledge the contribution of extensive defensive counterterrorism measures in the US and the West to this reduction, as well as AQC's greater emphasis on local concerns after 9/11 as a means of expanding the AQ network. At the same time, it is plausible to claim that weakening AQC's ability to plan, coordinate, finance, and provide training for attacks in the West helped reduce the number of attacks there by making it more difficult to organize and execute them.

Finally, there is much less evidence that would enable a determination of whether weakening AQC furthered the important US goal of reducing attacks on US targets outside the US. AQ affiliates with significant local concerns sometimes attempt to satisfy AQC's emphasis on attacking the far enemy by attacking US and Western targets in their own theater. As Daniel Byman describes, "Striking Western targets in a local region enables the group to straddle the line between local and global missions and thus please multiple constituents."[64] Weakening AQC could reduce the degree to which affiliates feel compelled to engage in such attacks, since these attacks can divert resources from local struggles and attract the attention of Western states. At the same time, however, such attacks generally are not reliant on assistance from AQC, so weakening leadership does not deprive affiliates of resources they need to conduct them.

What implications do the conclusions in this chapter have for the role, if any, that targeted strikes should play in future US counterterrorism operations against AQ and associated groups? The next section addresses this question.

Looking Ahead

Targeting AQC

In assessing the potential future use of US targeted strikes it is useful to distinguish between strikes against AQC and those against groups in the AQ network. With respect to strikes against AQC, the empirical evidence suggests that strikes are unlikely to have much effect on the number of attacks by the AQ network as a whole. As the discussion above describes, that network grew substantially even as strikes significantly weakened AQC, affiliates are not dependent on AQC to conduct attacks, and AQC's role has evolved even more than before toward providing general guidance.

The main US goal, however, has been to reduce the threat of attacks in the US and, to some extent, in the West. While there is room for argument, it is not clear that strikes against AQC at this point would appreciably further this goal. On the one hand, AQC continues to regard attacking the US as its main objective. It has not abandoned this priority even as it has been more supportive in recent years of groups focusing on local concerns. AQC leader Ayman Zawahiri reiterated that "America is the First Enemy of Muslims."[65] Therefore, he has said, "our message is very brief to our Ummah: undertake jihad against America, the head of the snake and the Hubal of the era, undertake it for the glory of this world and the victory of the Hereafter."[66] As Daniel Byman and Asfandyar Mir note, the deep commitment to this goal is reflected in the fact that leaders "know that their avowed anti-U.S. platform is the reason for their relentless targeting — yet they continue."[67]

On the other hand, there is some question about whether AQC has the capabilities to pursue this objective. A paper by Byman and Mir provides a valuable discussion of differing views on this issue. One view is that the absence of attacks in the US and the West in recent years does not necessarily reflect the inability of AQC to organize such attacks. Rather, it has been a strategic temporary retreat in order to provide safe spaces for the network to grow and strengthen by incorporating groups whose local focus does not make them targets of the US. During this time, the Islamic State has borne the brunt of US targeting activity. This has allowed AQ to expand in the Middle East, Africa, and South Asia, adding thousands of members to its network while maintaining impressive cohesion within it.

Those who believe that AQ poses a serious threat to the US maintain that this growth and geographical expansion provides a valuable pool of resources on which AQC can draw to mount attacks in the US and the West. These resources include "cash, training centers, weapons and ammunition, bomb-making facilities, and specialized personnel like plotting experts," as well as "fundraising sources; infrastructure to move funds; and full-time local, regional, and Western foreign fighters."[68] Regional groups appear to be consolidating, providing more organizational cohesion for the network. Some groups also appear to be enhancing their capability to conduct external operations. Thus, "Zawahiri appears to have limited plotting terrorist attacks in the West to the affiliates in Syria, Somalia, and Yemen, even if that means fewer and more modest plots."[69] In addition, Iran provides shelter for some members of AQC, as well as enabling the group to move resources around the network.

By contrast, others are more skeptical that AQC has the capability to mobilize groups in the network to further the goal of conducting attacks in the US and the West. These groups overwhelmingly focus on local campaigns, and must devote most of their resources to waging them and to avoiding local counterterrorism operations. Skeptics note that "local al-Qaeda forces are caught up in civil wars, with their energies focused on local enemies. They are often on the run or at least under pressure and thus find it harder (though not impossible) to plan sophisticated terrorist attacks that take years to bear fruit."[70] Carrying out attacks in the US and the West would only increase the pressures they face, impairing their ability to achieve their local objectives.

A prominent example of this was the decision of then-Syrian affiliate Jabhat al-Nusra to leave AQ in 2015.[71] The group "publicly articulated a trade-off between local success against the regime of Bashar al-Assad and al-Qaeda's anti-West platform."[72] Al-Nusra leader Abu Mohammed al-Jolani publicly distanced himself from AQC's focus on the far enemy: "Nusra Front doesn't have any plans or directives to target the West. We received clear orders not to use Syria as a launching pad to attack the US or Europe in order to not sabotage the true mission against the regime. Maybe al-Qaeda does that but not here in Syria."[73] He reiterated this in April 2021 when he said in an interview with PBS's *Frontline*, "First and foremost, this region does not represent a threat to the security of Europe and America. This region is not a staging ground for executing foreign jihad."[74]

In addition, AQC is unable to provide the kinds of resources such as funding and training camps that made it so influential in earlier years. More intensive measures against terrorist financing have reduced the funding available to it, and the loss of a safe haven free from counterterrorism pressure has prevented it from establishing training camps under its direction. AQ has not been able thus far to attract a significant number of Western foreign fighters who are important for conducting attacks in the West. Furthermore, the diffusion of AQC members to different locations to limit the effects of targeted strikes means that "[b]ecause Al Qaeda cannot regularly communicate and otherwise exercise command, by necessity, affiliates enjoy a high degree of autonomy," which means that they "regularly go their own ways."[75] As a result, "[w]ith its leaders on the run and communication difficulty and risky, top-down terrorist plots in far-away lands are more difficult."[76] For all these reasons, the argument goes, AQC may emphasize the importance of attacks in the US and the West as a rhetorical matter, but does not have robust capability to realize this aim.

Without attempting to resolve disagreement about AQC's capabilities, it seems reasonable at a minimum to believe that targeting AQC at this point would not have nearly the effect that earlier strikes had in northwest Pakistan. Those strikes helped reduce the threat of attacks in the US and the West because (1) AQC was concentrated in northwest Pakistan, especially the FATA; (2) the safe haven in that area enabled AQC to focus on planning and coordinating external attacks, and conducting training for them, without concern for local threats; (3) AQC's resources at the time gave it more influence over affiliates in encouraging and assisting such attacks than it does now; and (4) affiliates then were more reliant on AQC to conduct external attacks.

These conditions have changed as AQC has lost resources and its safe haven, AQC is more dispersed to limit the impact of strikes, the larger organization has adapted to and compensated to some extent for these losses, and AQC now mainly plays the role of providing general guidance. As Byman and Mir describe, "Many scholars, analysts, and policymakers evaluate al-Qaeda by focusing on the strength and size of the 'core' group of al-Qaeda senior leaders. However, al-Qaeda has steadily branched out for over a decade."[77] Thus, "al-Qaeda has intentionally reduced its central node and delegated most operational activities to affiliated organizations. The group's central leadership has given its regional nodes more strategic autonomy, specialized responsibilities, and decision-making authority."[78]

Strikes against AQC helped achieve crucial US goals because they occurred at a particular stage of AQ's evolution. The group has continued to evolve since then, however, in a direction that could make such strikes less likely to have an appreciable effect on the main US goals. This suggests that strikes against AQC now may achieve modest if any benefits.

It is conceivable that strikes could further the goal of making it more difficult for AQC to operate, even if it does not cripple the core. The dispersal of AQC members, and the adoption of precautions that make communication more difficult within AQC and between it and the network, reflect ongoing concern about the risk of targeted strikes. As Matthew Levitt and Aaron Zelin suggest, "communications among senior leaders [of AQ] have been less efficient for years due to security concerns stemming from drone campaigns."[79] In addition, the decentralization of AQ and the greater focus on local issues appears to have been a strategic decision based on, in large measure, the desire to reduce the risk of US strikes. Strikes thus may have had significant impacts on AQC even if it has been able to readily replace leaders killed by them. In this sense, to use Mir and Moore's framework, the anticipatory impact of strikes may be more important than their kinetic impact. To the extent that these responses to strikes have lowered the threat of attacks in the US and the West, one might argue that strikes should continue in combination with other counterterrorism measures.

This claim about the ongoing impact of targeting is more speculative than the claim about its impact in the FATA. In contrast to the latter, we do not have extensive contemporaneous Al-Qaeda correspondence or other sources of information that provide valuable empirical evidence of the effects of targeting in recent years. There have been no major attacks in the US or the West for many years, but it is difficult to determine how much current strikes are responsible for this compared to other factors. The fact that there appear to be only two attacks in the West even plotted by AQC since 2010 is more suggestive, although it is difficult to know if this reflects recognition of the greater difficulty of conducting such attacks rather than the pressure of strikes on leadership.[80]

Continuing strikes against AQC to maintain pressure on it would reflect an approach designed not to eliminate core leadership, nor respond to an immediate threat from it, but to manage the threat it poses by persistently weakening its capabilities. The US would be using strikes to engage in what some in Israel coldly call "mowing the grass"—periodically cutting back terrorist capability rather than attempting to destroy it.[81] Instead of seeking a decisive victory, the US would settle for what Byman calls "good enough."[82] This is the view that "although jihadi terrorism may be impossible to fully and permanently eradicate—or the costs of trying to do so are simply too high—the threat can be reduced to the point where it kills relatively few Americans and no longer shapes daily life in the United States."[83]

Strikes against AQC could have this impact, but research by Mir and Moore and by Mir on the effect of strikes on local attacks finds that strikes can reduce attacks especially if they are part of an intensive campaign that involves detailed local intelligence collection and its rapid exploitation to conduct strikes. This suggests that periodic strikes against AQC members in diverse locations may not do much to reduce the risk of attacks in the US and the West. Uncertainty about this should be taken into account when weighing the putative benefits of using strikes in this way against the potential costs of civilian casualties, and the effects on local population attitudes, described in the chapters that follow. Decision-makers also would need to consider whether strikes would complement or undermine other counterterrorism measures, as well as whether such measures could be as or more effective than strikes without imposing their costs.

While this chapter focuses on the effectiveness of US strikes against AQ and associated groups, it is worth briefly noting that using strikes in this way also would raise legal and ethical issues. The legal issue is the authority under which the US would conduct strikes. One legal justification could be that the US continues to be engaged in an armed conflict against AQ and associated groups, and that members of AQC are enemy combatants. There is disagreement in the international community, however, about whether strikes against combatants in locations outside war zones are permissible under the laws of war.

If the US concludes that this conflict has ended, it could claim that a strike reflects the exercise of self-defense against an imminent threat of attack. As described earlier in this book, under the Obama administration the standard for a strike outside a war zone was that the target posed a "continuing imminent threat" to the US or US persons. This requirement was eliminated during the Trump administration, although it may be revived by President Biden. The US conception of imminence has been controversial, however, because some claim that it is too permissive. This controversy is likely to continue if the US engages in periodic strikes not to prevent attacks likely to occur in the near future, but to prevent AQC from becoming capable enough to plan and coordinate such attacks. The former is regarded as legally permissible "preemptive" use of force, while some may claim that the latter is impermissible "preventive" violence.

One important ethical issue is how much the US should be able to use strikes to keep the risk of attacks in the US as low as possible by keeping AQC weak, while imposing the cost of such strikes on populations where strikes occur. Is using strikes to attempt to reduce the risk of attacks below a certain level ethically unjustified if it increases the risk of harm to others? If so, what is that level? In addition, what would be the ethical implications of a country engaging in ongoing targeted killing operations for the indefinite future? Fully analyzing these issues would easily require another book, but identifying them here underscores how understanding the impacts of strikes on terrorist groups can help frame legal and ethical questions and inform deliberation on them.

A scenario that could change assessment of the need for strikes against AQC if this leadership group is once again able to find a safe haven in which it is relatively free to plan and coordinate attacks in the West. As Elizabeth Arsenault and Tricia Bacon have observed, "Terrorist organizations that have posed the greatest threat to their adversaries over the longest period of time share one characteristic that has little to do with their ideology, size, or goals: they possessed a safe haven."[84] Havens are "places in which terrorist groups can operate without fear of counterterror retaliation or pressure," in which they can conduct support activities such as "training, recruitment, fundraising, and communications."[85]

Reacquiring a safe haven could enable AQC to replicate conditions in Afghanistan and the FATA to some extent, when it was able to gather resources and attract recruits to undergo training for attacks in the West. In this case, AQC would not need to rely as much on affiliates to conduct attacks against the "far enemy," and could be in a position to offer more resources to them for this purpose. Protection by a friendly government would provide the most freedom of action. This would obviate the need for AQC to defend itself from local threats and to concentrate on planning and coordinating attacks against the far enemy.

It is possible that the return of the Taliban to power in Afghanistan could present this scenario. The UN Analytical Support and Sanctions Monitoring Team report to the Security Council in April 2021 noted that "[a] significant part of the leadership of Al-Qaida... resides in the Afghanistan and Pakistan border region."[86] It stated that the main Taliban liaison with Al-Qaeda is the Haqqani Network, and that "[t]ies between the two groups remain close, based on ideological alignment, relationships forged through common struggle and intermarriage."[87] The Taliban has rejected demands that it denounces AQ. In addition, since the UN report, Sirajuddin Haqqani, designated as a terrorist by the US, has been appointed to the powerful position of Minister of the Interior in Afghanistan. Furthermore, even if the Taliban were inclined to constrain the use of Afghanistan as a haven for AQ to plot attacks in the West, there likely would be practical difficulties in monitoring and enforcing any such restriction. The UN report concluded, "it is impossible to assess with confidence that the Taliban will live up to its commitment to suppress any future international threat emanating from Al-Qaida in Afghanistan."[88] Opinions differ, but the return of the Taliban presents an opportunity for creation of an AQC safe haven that it has not had for almost a decade.[89]

If this occurs, could strikes achieve the same effects on AQC as they did in northwest Pakistan? Not necessarily. Bryce Loidolt observes that "many of the conditions that likely contributed to US success in Pakistan will not be present in Afghanistan."[90] As Chapter 7 describes, his research indicates that strikes in Pakistan took quite some time to have an impact and did not completely eliminate AQC's ability to operate. The US would not be able to rely in Afghanistan on the local government for intelligence and security assistance, access, and bases, nor on its consent to conduct strikes. Loidolt concludes, "U.S. policymakers should not be under any illusion that solely killing terrorist operatives will keep al-Qaeda's external operations at bay. Instead, they should be sure to supplement lethal strikes with complementary multi- and bilateral efforts designed to make the financing of external terrorist operations more difficult and the movement of terrorist operatives into and out of Afghanistan more treacherous."[91] Loidolt appears not to rule out strikes as one instrument, but underscores the need not to place too much reliance on them.

The absence of significant US assets in Afghanistan, and the availability of fewer local intelligence sources, also likely would increase the risk that drone strikes in that country will cause civilian casualties. This was illustrated vividly by the US drone strike in Afghanistan in August 2021 that mistakenly killed ten civilians during US withdrawal from the country, which is discussed in more detail in Chapter 10. The Department of Defense said that the strike was based upon faulty intelligence, combined with a sense of urgency because there was an imminent threat of additional attacks three days after a suicide bomber killed 183 people at Kabul airport.[92] Even under less demanding circumstances, however, the likely scarcity of US intelligence assets in Afghanistan and the inability to rely on cooperation from the Taliban will create challenges in avoiding civilian casualties from strikes.

Targeting Local Groups

While AQC may now play a less significant role than before in orchestrating attacks in the West, the potential ability of groups within the network to draw on resources from one another means that any group may unexpectedly emerge with the capacity to conduct such an attack. How effective might targeted strikes be against particular AQ affiliates deemed to pose a serious threat of attacks in the US and the West?

AQAP was regarded for several years as the main threat to the US. It recently has declined, however, because of UAE military operations against it complemented by US strikes. One might think that this has reduced the threat of attacks in the US by AQ. Al-Shabaab, however, now could be emerging as a more of a threat to the US. The December 2021 indictment against the individual planning to conduct a 9/11-style attack indicates that he received assistance from a senior Al-Shabaab commander, and that he conducted research on the Internet on security on commercial airliners and how to breach a cockpit.

A recent report by the DoD Inspector General (IG), which serves as the Lead IG for the East Africa Counterterrorism Operation and the North and West Africa Counterterrorism Operation, noted US Africa Command's (USAFRICOM) assessment that there has been a "definite shift" in the focus of Al-Shabaab, AQ's affiliate in East Africa, to target US interests in Somalia and East Africa.[93] The Lead IG report stated that USAFRICOM indicated that Al-Shabaab has the intent, but not the current ability, to attack the US itself.

This may underestimate the potential of a group, however, to expand its capabilities by combining its local resources with those drawn from the larger AQ network. As Bruce Hoffman noted in early 2020 before the Al-Shabaab aviation plot against the US was discovered, "[T]here is alarming evidence that [AQAP bomb-maker] al-Assiri's ordnance crafts-manship has already migrated to other al-Qaeda partners — including groups that have never hitherto targeted commercial aviation. In this respect, the comparatively technologically unsophisticated al-Shabaab nearly succeeded in downing a Daallo Air passenger jet departing Mogadishu in February 2016 with an improvised explosive device concealed in a laptop computer."[94]

General Dagvin Anderson, Commander, US Special Operations Command Africa, commented in September 2020 about the al-Shabaab plot that was the basis of the indictment. "[W]hat I would say is the concerning part for me," he said, "is that that was a significant invest-ment in time and money and resources and recruitment to make that happen. And we didn't know about that. We weren't aware of it. And we stumbled upon some information that alerted us to that. And so then, the question is what else are they doing, what else are they planning that we aren't aware of."[95]

Furthermore, said Anderson, he sees AQIM as potentially an even more dangerous threat. They have established safe havens, and are deriving income from kidnapping, gold mining, and trade routes from the Gulf of Guinea to the Mediterranean whose value is "in the billions of dollars."[96] As a result, Anderson said "as we look at this, it's not a matter of if they'll become a threat; it's a matter of when they become a threat to the West, if they're left unchecked and the trajectory continues the way it is."[97] The intelligence community does not presently share this view,[98] but it reflects the possibility that other groups may emerge with capability to launch international attacks.

At the same time, one should not assume that the network is a collection of like-minded groups that can seamlessly provide assistance to one another. It is made up of groups in different parts of the world with a variety of aims that are not necessarily congruent with one another or with the main goals of AQC. Audrey Kurth Cronin suggests that it is a mistake to regard Al-Qaeda as a monolithic entity. Even though groups that comprise it may be loosely aligned, she argues, "many groups are far more interested in local political aims than they are in the rhetoric of Al-Qaeda."[99] Similarly, Daniel Byman maintains, "In the case of al Qaeda, affiliations often create new vulnerabilities and difficulties and should not always be seen as a net gain by the organization. Without understanding these costs, it is too easy to overstate the danger."[100]

We can infer from much, although not all, of the quantitative research described in Chapter 6 that strikes can weaken the ability of a group to conduct attacks, based on findings of declines in local attacks following strikes. This could mean that the ability to conduct attacks in the West also is weakened, although it is possible that local and external attacks draw on different resources.

As described in Chapter 6, Asfandyar Mir argues that strikes can achieve short- to medium-term decreases in attacks if they are part of a "legibility and exploitation" effort that involves extensive intelligence operations providing detailed information on an area, combined with rapid exploitation of this information for targeting purposes.[101] The ability to combine these activities will not necessarily exist in all cases, but Mir argues that a persistent ongoing campaign that has these features "can severely damage resilient armed groups and constrain their recovery."[102] His study with Moore on strikes in Pakistan described in Chapter 6 presents empirical evidence for this claim. Decision-makers contemplating the use of strikes against a local group would need to determine if conditions would enable a legibility and exploitation campaign. This requires considerable assistance from a local partner, which may not always be available.

How much enduring long-term effect could such a campaign have? This is a crucial question because a group that is weakened by strikes may be able to draw on resources from other groups, or take advantage of opportunities in their own region, to regain their ability to attack in the West. Or, as the case of Al-Shabaab in the wake of AQAP's decline indicates, other groups may be able to acquire this ability. The US thus could use strikes to reduce the threat from a group temporarily but not permanently, or might need to confront a new threat from one or more others. Under what conditions might strikes against a group result in a permanent decline in the threat that it poses to the US and the West, rather than achieve a temporary respite?

The experience with targeting AQAP leadership over the last twenty years may offer some lessons. As described in Chapter 5, the death of what was then AQ in Yemen leader al-Harithi in 2002, combined with Yemen's aggressive pursuit and arrest of other leaders, decimated the group and left it moribund. This reflected the fact that the group in Yemen was still relatively new and not organizationally mature, although it had conducted the attack on the *USS Cole* in 2000. It is consistent with research by Jenna Jordan and by Long indicating that terrorist groups without well-established organizational structures are especially vulnerable to leadership decapitation, and research by Tominaga and by Price that groups in the early stage of their lives are as well. The effect of the strike also illustrates that strikes are likely to be most effective in combination with other measures, such as the crackdown by the Yemeni government in this case.

Not long after the strike against al-Harithi, however, Yemen became embroiled in disputes with Houthis in the north, which turned into armed conflict in 2004. The conflict weakened the military and distracted the government from dealing fully with AQ. In addition, as Gregory Johnsen describes, "In time, the fighting that started in the north would grow into a contest between Yemen's powerful Zaydis and its more numerous Sunnis, weakening [President] Salih and his military while encouraging groups like al-Qaeda."[103]

In 2006, Nasir al-Wuhayshi, who had served as bin Laden's personal secretary in Afghanistan, escaped from prison in Sana'a in a break that freed 23 Al-Qaeda members. Many of these members had experience in Afghanistan and had moved to Yemen after the fall of the Taliban in 2001 before being swept up in arrests.[104] Wuhayshi began rebuilding a more durable AQ in Yemen by establishing relationships with powerful tribes and local populations.

By 2009 and 2010, what was by then AQAP was able to plan and coordinate attacks in the US. The 2009 attack almost succeeded, while the 2010 plot was thwarted with the assistance of Saudi intelligence. In 2011–2102, AQAP capitalized on instability following Yemen's Arab spring to establish Islamic emirates in parts of the South. Although its territory shrank after a Yemeni military offensive assisted by US air support in 2012, instability resulting from large-scale conflict between a Saudi-led military coalition and the Houthis beginning in 2015 led to another resurgence.

Wuhayshi was killed in a drone strike in summer 2015. A US spokesman said that his death "removes from the battlefield an experienced terrorist leader and brings us closer to degrading and ultimately defeating these groups."[105] AQAP named Qassim al-Raymi as his successor within three days, however. In August it staged an assault on a prison in Mullakah that freed 300 jihadists. It also seized military equipment, robbed the central bank of US$100 million, and established another emirate in parts of the south.[106]

AQAP operated as a de facto state in those areas in 2015–2016, which was the zenith of its power. The strike against Wuhayshi thus did not slow APAP's ascent after his death. AQAP was well-established and had considerable tribal support in the south by then, and the strike was not part of a larger counterterrorism campaign because the government was preoccupied with hostilities with Houthis in northern Yemen.

Elizabeth Kendall notes that the group has suffered severe losses from the UAE-led military offensive against it from 2018 to 2019, and from escalation of US drone strikes in 2017 (although strikes substantially declined after that). The latter have killed key commanders, which has "put a large dent" in the pool of people available to replace those who have been killed.[107] Al-Raymi was killed in a drone strike in late January 2020, but, unlike with the death of Wuhayshi in 2015, AQAP did not name a successor for almost a month. "Incessant strikes," says Kendall, "have convinced the group that it has been infiltrated by informers, leading it to severely limit communications and essentially paralyze itself."[108] As a result, AQAP's activities have declined sharply.

Kendall cautions that Yemen and the US should not, however, assume that the group has now been permanently defeated. It retains considerable appeal, continues to urge attacks against the US, and has demonstrated resilience in the past. She argues that the group's current disarray provides "a short-term window of opportunity for preventive measures" that could be more durable in weakening AQAP. This opportunity, she says, should be used to "address the underlying reasons behind the persistent phenomenon of militant jihad in Yemen."[109] This requires "careful, thoughtful, and nonmilitary strategies that are locally led" to respond to the desire of young males in particular for material subsistence and commitment to a higher purpose, and to the grievances of tribes that believe they have been marginalized by years of government neglect.[110] This may be unlikely, however, if the Houthis come to power.

The experience with strikes against AQAP leadership thus suggests that the impact of strikes depends upon the extent to which a group has become well-established, the existence of political and military circumstances that provide opportunities for it to expand, and whether strikes are used in combination with other extensive counterterrorism measures. If Kendall is right, however, the most that strikes can accomplish under such circumstances is to buy time—to help inflict losses that create a window of opportunity to neutralize a group more thoroughly. The measures that can achieve this larger goal are political, social, and economic, not simply military. In order to be effective with AQAP, they must be carried out ultimately by Yemen, not by outsiders, even if that country may need assistance to help it do so.

This is what Kendall argues is necessary to weaken one group in the network. Achieving the goal of seriously weakening the larger network would require a similar counterterrorism strategy that aims to neutralize the underlying appeal of the AQ call to jihad in the Middle East, Africa, and South Asia. This task would be enormously difficult, given uncertainty about the roots of that appeal, and the formidable challenges to building democratically responsive nation-states in regions without a robust tradition of such institutions. The paucity of resources in many countries compounds the difficulty and suggests the need for outside assistance. States providing such assistance, however, must provide it without purporting to assume primary responsibility for nation-building in countries that they do not fully understand.

If Kendall is right that meaningful local political reform is necessary to achieve long-term reduction of the threat posed by terrorist groups, the daunting nature of that task suggests that achieving such a reduction is unlikely to happen any time in the near future. The most that targeted strikes might achieve therefore is to temporarily reduce a serious threat from a particular group, while recognizing that it may be periodically necessary to reduce other such threats as they arise—another version of "mowing the grass."

A more modest US long-term goal than permanently crippling a group might be to inflict enough damage on it that it eschews attacks in the US and the West and focuses instead on local concerns. As the discussion above describes, concern about being the target of strikes appears to have convinced Syrian affiliate al-Nusra to leave Al-Qaeda and renounce the intention to conduct attacks in the West. More generally, as Byman and Mir observe, the "political calculus" of other groups indicates that they "may have been deterred by the possibility of being targeted by proximate US presence."[111] Attempting to redirect the focus of jihadist groups away from the US would reflect abandonment of the aim of defeating terrorist groups in a "war on terror," and would seek simply to limit the threat they pose to the US.

The US could still attempt to achieve long-term reduction of the threat to the US and the West by relying on other counterterrorism measures. This would include intelligence-sharing, building local counterterrorism capacity, and restricting terrorist financing and travel. Some analysts also suggest that using a variety of non-kinetic means to exploit the differences among groups in the AQ network and drive a wedge among them may be a promising approach.[112] Decision-makers would need to consider whether strikes would complement or impair the effectiveness of such measures. In addition, they would need to assess whether strikes would enhance or inhibit the local political reform efforts that Kendall prescribes, based on the anticipated impacts of strikes on civilians and local population attitudes.

Decision-makers also would need to address the legal and ethical dimensions of using strikes in this way. The legal issues would be those that are described above. One ethical issue is whether strikes that induce a group to abandon efforts to attack the US and focus exclusively on local aims would reduce the risk of violence in the US by unfairly increasing that risk to the local population. Militant groups already focus predominantly on local issues, so strikes would not direct their attention to a new objective. At the same time, is there any limit to how low the US can seek to reduce risk to itself if doing so appreciably increases the risk to populations where terrorist groups are operating? The US as a practical matter likely would want to continue assistance to states to strengthen their counterterrorism capabilities in order to reduce this risk. Might it in fact have an ethical obligation to do so? There is no space here to fully analyze such questions, but it is important to recognize that using strikes to redirect the focus of terrorist groups away from the US raises them.

CONCLUSION

Quantitative research does not squarely address the issue, but qualitative evidence suggests that there is reason to believe that targeted strikes in northwest Pakistan that weakened AQC helped reduced the risk of AQ attacks in the US and the West. This is because AQC has persistently focused on such attacks, and it was able to assemble resources in Pakistan that enabled it to plan, coordinate, and execute them. While AQC did not enjoy the protection of a national government as it had in Afghanistan, the FATA offered considerable opportunity to operate because of the area's traditional peripheral status in Pakistan, the historical tendency for the Pakistani government not to attempt to exercise control over it, and protection from a number of terrorist groups, some of whom may have had relationships with Pakistan's Inter-Services Intelligence S-Wing.[113] The adoption of several defensive counterterrorism measures played a significant role in reducing attacks in the US and the West, but it is reasonable to believe that strikes complemented these by weakening the element of AQ most focused on such attacks.

AQC continues to emphasize the importance of attacks in the US and the West. AQ has grown considerably in recent years, however, through the affiliation of diverse groups whose focus is largely, although not exclusively, local. AQC now has fewer material resources to offer these groups to induce them to attack the West. It also faces some challenges in communicating with the network because leadership is more dispersed and takes precautions that make communication less efficient. The result is considerable autonomy for local AQ groups that may prefer to focus on local issues rather than risk being targeted by the US.

The combined effect of these conditions is that targeting AQC now may have modest if any impact in further reducing the risk of attacks in the US and the West. It is conceivable that continuing to target AQC could ensure that it does not regain strength and influence. The case for this is more speculative, however, than it was for strikes against AQC in the FATA. As this chapter has briefly discussed, this strategy also potentially raises legal and ethical issues. Were AQC to reacquire a safe haven, as could be the case in Afghanistan with the Taliban back in power, this calculus could change.

Research suggests that strikes against a local AQ group that poses a serious threat to the US could reduce the risk of attacks for a period of time if it is part of a campaign that involves detailed intelligence collection and rapid exploitation of it for targeting purposes. A long-term reduction in the threat that a group poses likely is more difficult to achieve. Ideally, meaningful local political reforms would accomplish this by reducing the appeal of extremist groups. This is enormously challenging in most areas in which such groups operate, however, and the US is not in a position to make it happen. A more modest goal therefore might be to use strikes to reduce long-term risk to the US by convincing a group to focus only on local concerns, which also could raise ethical questions.

This and preceding chapters for the most part do not discuss strikes against the Islamic State, or ISIS. Although the US has conducted many strikes against ISIS, there is not rigorous empirical research on the impacts of these strikes that is comparable to the body of scholarship on strikes against AQ. In addition, a large percentage of strikes against ISIS have been in war zones, while the focus of this book is on strikes outside such zones.

Nonetheless, there is reason to believe that conclusions about the impacts of strikes on AQ likely apply at least in broad terms to strikes against ISIS. This group is similar to Al-Qaeda in its relatively decentralized structure, with relationships between leaderships and local groups varying in strength. It also harbors the aspiration to conduct attacks in the US, but has mainly sought to accomplish this by encouraging individuals to conduct such attacks on their own. As with AQC, it is not clear that targeting ISIS core leadership at this point would have an effect on the risk of attacks in the US, but this calculation could change if ISIS reacquires territory that can serve as a safe haven to plan such attacks. Finally, research on the impacts of persistent targeting based on Mir's legibility and exploitation model are applicable to any terrorist group, not just AQ and associated groups.

Whatever the impact of strikes on terrorist groups, a full assessment of them must consider their impacts on civilians. This is the focus of Part III, comprised of the following three chapters. The next two chapters examine evidence on the role of strikes in causing civilian deaths and injuries, while Chapter 11 discusses their other impacts on local populations.

NOTES

1. A terrorist attack is categorized as international in the Global Terrorism Database if the nationality of the group and/or the location of the

attacks is different from that of its victims, or the ideology is designated as international." Carson, 2018, 1286, note 32.

2. Hoffman, B., & Reinares, F. (Eds.). (2014). Conclusion. In *The evolution of the global terrorist threat: From 9/11 to Osama bin Laden's death*. Columbia University Press, 618–640, 624.

3. Id. 622.

4. Id. 638.

5. Hoffman & Reinares, 2–372.

6. Id. 636.

7. Marc Sageman has proposed that AQ now effectively is a "leaderless jihad." Marc Sageman, Leaderless Jihad (2008). For a critique of Sageman's view, see Hoffman, B. (2008, May/June). The myth of grassroots terrorism: Why Osama Bin Laden still matters. *Foreign Affairs*. For Sageman's response, see Sageman, M. (2008, July/August). Does Osama still call the shots? Debating the containment of Al Qaeda's leadership. *Foreign Affairs*.

8. Gartenstein-Ross, D., & Barr, N. (2018, June 1). *How Al-Qaeda works: The Jihadist group's evolving organizational design*. Current Trends in Islamist Ideology. https://www.hudson.org/research/14365-how-al-qaeda-works-the-jihadist-group-s-evolving-organizational-design.

9. Id.

10. Nasr, W. (2019, May 30). Exclusive: FRANCE 24 questions AQIM Jihadist leader. *France 24*. https://www.france24.com/en/20190530-aqmi-jihadist-leader-maghreb-france-terrorism-al-qaeda-islamic-youssef-al-Aanabi.

11. Id.

12. Joscelyn, T. (2013, July 18). Global al Qaeda: Affiliates, objectives, and future challenges, *Long War Journal*. https://www.longwarjournal.org/archives/2013/07/global_al_qaeda_affi.php.

13. Hoffman & Reinares, 620–622; Jones, S. (2021). The evolution of Al-Qaida: 1988 to present day. In M. Sheehan, E. Marquardt, & L. Collins (Eds.), *Routledge handbook of U.S. counterterrorism and irregular warfare operations* (pp. 41–53, 50–51). Routledge.

14. National Commission on Terrorist Attacks upon the United States. (2004). *Monograph on terrorist financing* (p. 28). https://govinfo.library.unt.edu/911/staff_statements/911_TerrFin_Monograph.pdf.

15. CNN Wire Staff. (2010, November 5). Yemen-based al Qaeda group claims responsibility for parcel bomb plot. *CNN*. http://edition.cnn.com/2010/WORLD/meast/11/05/yemen.security.concern/index.html.

16. Joscelyn, T. (2010, June 23). Times Square bomber discusses Taliban ties at plea hearing. *FDD's Long War Journal*. https://www.longwarjournal.org/archives/2010/06/times_square_bomber.php.

17. Knickmeyer, E., & Gorman, S. (2012, May 10). Behind foiled jet plot, stronger Saudi ties. *The Wall Street Journal*.

18. Shortell, D., & Perez, E. (2020, May 19). FBI finds al Qaeda link after breaking encryption on Pensacola attacker's iPhone. *CNN*. https://edi tion.cnn.com/2020/05/18/politics/pensacola-shooting-al-qaeda/.

19. https://www.nytimes.com/2020/03/21/world/africa/al-qaeda-som alia-shabab.html?action=click&module=RelatedLinks&pgtype=Article.

20. Shahidi News Team. (2021, March 30). Wanted Kenyan pilot linked to Al-Shabaab escapes to Somalia. *Shahidi News*. https://shahidinews.co. ke/2021/03/30/wanted-kenyan-pilot-linked-to-al-shabaab-escapes-to-somalia/.

21. Lee, 44.

22. Knoll, D. (2017, October). Al-Qaeda in the Arabian Peninsula (AQAP): An Al-Qaeda affiliate case study. *CNA* (p. 5). https://www.cna.org/cna_files/pdf/DIM-2017-U-016116-2Rev.pdf.

23. Zimmerman, K. (2013, September 18). Statement before the House Committee on Homeland Security Subcommittee on Counterterrorism and Intelligence on "Understanding the Threat to the Homeland from AQAP", AQAP's Role in the al Qaeda Network (p. 2). https://docs.house.gov/meetings/HM/HM05/20130918/101 315/HHRG-113-HM05-Wstate-ZimmermanK-20130918.pdf.

24. Senate Select Committee on Intelligence. (2014, January 15). *Review of the terrorist attacks on US facilities in Benghazi, Libya*, September 11–12, 2012 (p. 40). https://www.intelligence.senate.gov/sites/default/files/press/benghazi.pdf.

25. Id.

26. Zimmerman, 2021, 12.

27. Id.

28. Mir, A., & Clarke, C. (2020, September 9). AQ's franchise reboot. *Foreign Affairs*; Clarke, C., & Lister, C. (2019, September 4). AQ is ready to attack you again. *Foreign Policy*.

29. Zimmerman, 2013, 5.

30. Id. 6.

31. Zimmerman, 2013, 2.

32. Byman, D. (2014). Buddies or burdens? Understanding the Al Qaeda relationship with its affiliate organizations. *Security Studies, 23*(3), 431–470. https://www.tandfonline.com/doi/abs/10.1080/09636412. 2014.935228.

33. Gartenstein-Ross & Barr.

34. Byman, 2014, 454.

35. Jones, 2021, 43.

36. West Point, Combating Terrorism Center (CTC), Harmony Project, Reference Number: SOCOM-2012–0000019, 22.

37. Id.
38. Id.
39. Id. 33.
40. Id.
41. Id.
42. CTC, Reference Number: SOCOM-2012-0000019, 8.
43. Id.
44. National Commission on Terrorist Attacks upon the United States. (2004). *Monograph on terrorist financing* (p. 28). https://govinfo.lib rary.unt.edu/911/staff_statements/911_TerrFin_Monograph.pdf.
45. National Commission on Terrorist Attacks upon the United States. (2004). *The 9/11 Commission Report* (p. 66). https://www.govinfo. gov/content/pkg/GPO-911REPORT/pdf/GPO-911REPORT.pdf.
46. Id. 67.
47. Id.
48. Monograph, 17.
49. Id.
50. Monograph, 133.
51. Id. 143–144.
52. Gartenstein-Ross & Barr.
53. Mir, A. (2018). What explains counterterrorism effectiveness? Evidence from the U.S. drone war in Pakistan. *International Security, 43*(2), 45–83, 63. http://doi.org/10.1162/isec_a_00331.
54. Id. For a detailed account of AQ activities in the FATA as of 2008, see Gunaratna, R., & Nielsen, A. (2008). Al Qaeda in the tribal areas of Pakistan and beyond. *Studies in Conflict & Terrorism, 31*(9), 775–807. https://www.tandfonline.com/doi/full/10.1080/105761008022 91568.
55. Byman, 2014, 450.
56. Hoffman & Reinares, 620.
57. Cruickshank, P. (2011, July). *The militant pipeline between the Afghanistan–Pakistan border region and the west* (p. 1). New America Foundation. https://newamerica.org/documents/887/the-militant-pip eline.
58. Robertson, N., Cruickshank, P., & Lister, T. (2012, April 30). Document shows origins of 2006 plot for liquid bombs on planes. *CNN*. https://www.cnn.com/2012/04/30/world/al-qaeda-documents/index.html.
59. Bergen, P. (2021). *The rise and fall of Osama bin Laden* (p. xxiv). Simon & Schuster.
60. Byman, 2014, 456.
61. Id.
62. Robertson et al.

63. Clarke & Mir.
64. Daniel Byman, 2014, 449.
65. Zawahiri, A. (2018). *America is the first enemy of Muslims.* English translation. https://www.longwarjournal.org/wp-content/uploads/2018/03/18-03-20-Zawahiri-22America-is-the-First-Enemy-of-Muslims22-translation.pdf.
66. Id.
67. Byman, D., & Mir, A. (Working Draft May 2021). Assessing Al-Qaeda: A Debate.
68. Id. 14.
69. Id. 15.
70. Id. 33.
71. Lister, C. (2018, February). How Al-Qa'ida lost control of its Syrian affiliate: The inside story. *CTC Sentinel, 11*(2), 1–9. https://ctc.usma.edu/wp-content/uploads/2018/02/CTC-Sentinel_Vol11Iss2-2.pdf.
72. Byman & Mir, 8.
73. Al Jazeera. (2015, May 28). *Nusra leader: Our mission is to defeat Syrian regime.* https://www.aljazeera.com/news/2015/5/28/nusra-leader-our-mission-is-to-defeat-syrian-regime.
74. Boghani, P. (2021, April 2). Syrian militant and former Al Qaeda leader seeks wider acceptance in first interview with U.S. journalist. *Frontline.* https://www.pbs.org/wgbh/frontline/article/abu-mohammad-al-jolani-interview-hayat-tahrir-al-sham-syria-al-qaeda/.
75. Id. 30.
76. Id. 34.
77. Id. 9.
78. Id.
79. Levitt, M., & Zelin, A. (2020, December 11). Al-Qaeda's External operations one year after the Pensacola attack. *The Washington Institute.* https://www.washingtoninstitute.org/policy-analysis/al-qaedas-external-operations-one-year-after-pensacola-attack.
80. Byman & Mir. (2021). *Table 1: Major attacks and plots by Al Qaeda.*
81. Taylor, A. (2021, May 21). With strikes targeting rockets and tunnels, the Israeli tactic of 'mowing the grass' returns to Gaza. *Washington Post.* https://www.washingtonpost.com/world/2021/05/14/israel-gaza-history/.
82. Byman, D. (2021). The good enough doctrine: Learning to live with terrorism. *Foreign Affairs, 100*(5), 32–43. https://www.foreignaffairs.com/articles/middle-east/2021-08-24/good-enough-doctrine.
83. Id. 32.
84. Arsenault, E., & Bacon, T. (2015). Disaggregating and defeating terrorist safe havens. *Studies in Conflict & Terrorism, 38*(2), 85–112, 86. https://www.tandfonline.com/doi/abs/10.1080/1057610X.2014.977605?journalCode=uter20.

85. Id. 87.
86. United Nations. (2021, April 28). Letter dated 28 April 2021 from the Analytical Support and Sanctions Monitoring Team addressed to the Chair of the Security Council Committee established pursuant to resolution 1988 (2011), 3/22. https://undocs.org/pdf?symbol=en/s/2021/486.
87. Id.
88. Id.
89. See Mir, A. (2021, September). Twenty years after 9/11: The terror threat from Afghanistan post the Taliban takeover. *CTC Sentinel*, *14*(7), 29–43. https://ctc.usma.edu/twenty-years-after-9-11-the-terror-threat-from-afghanistan-post-the-taliban-takeover/; Bacon, T. (2018, September 11). Deadly cooperation: The shifting ties between Al-Qaeda and the Taliban. *War on the Rocks*. https://warontherocks.com/2018/09/deadly-cooperation-the-shifting-ties-between-al-qaeda-and-the-taliban/.
90. Loidolt, B. (2012, May 18). Managed risks, managed expectations: How far will targeted killing get the united states in Afghanistan? *War on the Rocks*. https://warontherocks.com/2021/05/managed-risks-managed-expectations-how-far-will-targeted-killing-get-us-in-afghanistan/.
91. Id.
92. United States Department of Defense. (2021, November 3). *Investigation into 29 Aug CIVCAS in Afghanistan*. https://www.washingtonpost.com/context/air-force-inspector-general-s-findings-of-errant-drone-strike-in-kabul-on-aug-29-2021/a7d9edaf-b8d3-497b-9be1-8db427ca7cf6/?itid=lk_interstitial_manual_5.
93. United States Department of Defense. (2020, July 1–September 30). *Lead Inspector General Report to the United States Congress, East Africa Counterterrorism Operation; North and West Africa Counterterrorism Operation* (p. 8). https://media.defense.gov/2020/Dec/04/2002546287/-1/-1/1/LEAD%20IG%20EAST%20AFRICA%20AND%20NORTH%20AND%20WEST%20AFRICA%20COUNTERTERRORISM%20OPERATIONS.PDF.
94. Hoffman, B. (2020, March 12). *Al-Qaeda: Threat or anachronism?* https://hoffmangroup.global/terrorist-threats/al-qaeda-threat-or-anachronism/.
95. American Enterprise Institute, 4.
96. Id.
97. Id.
98. Office of the Director of National Intelligence. (2021, April 9). *Annual threat assessment of the US intelligence community*. https://www.dni.gov/files/ODNI/documents/assessments/ATA-2021-Unclassified-Report.pdf.

99. Cronin, A. K. (2011). *How terrorism ends: Understanding the decline and demise of terrorist campaigns* (p. 188). Princeton University Press.

100. Byman, 2014, 468.

101. Mir, 2018, 47.

102. Id. 49.

103. Johnsen, G. D. (2012). *The last refuge: Yemen, al-Qaeda, and America's war in Arabia* (p. 159). W. W. Norton.

104. Zimmerman, 2013, 3.

105. Mazzetti, M., & Schmitt, E. (2015, June 16). For U.S., killing terrorists is a means to an elusive end. *New Yok Times.* https://www.nytimes.com/2015/06/17/world/middleeast/al-qaeda-arabian-peninsula-yemen-nasser-al-wuhayshi-killed.html.

106. Kendall, E. (2018, July). *Contemporary jihadi militancy in Yemen: How is the threat evolving?* (p. 4). Middle East Institute. https://www.mei.edu/sites/default/files/publications/MEI%20Policy%20Paper_Kendall_7.pdf.

107. Kendall, E. (2020, February 14). *Death of AQAP leader shows the group's fragmentation—And durability* (p. 2). The Washington Institute for Near East Policy. https://www.washingtoninstitute.org/policy-analysis/death-aqap-leader-shows-groups-fragmentation-and-durability.

108. Id.

109. Id.

110. Id.

111. Byman & Mir, 2021, 23.

112. Cronin, 2011, 186–196; Byman, 2014, 466–469.

113. For a detailed account of these ties, see Coll. S. (2018). *Directorate S: The C.I.A. and America's secret wars in Afghanistan and Pakistan.* Penguin Books.

PART III

Impacts of US Strikes on Civilians

CHAPTER 9

Civilian Casualties from US Targeted Strikes

One important reason for US reliance on targeted strikes as a counterterrorist measure has been belief that such strikes can weaken terrorist groups while causing less harm to civilians than conventional military operations, when law enforcement measures are not feasible. The US has consistently claimed that targeted strikes outside active war zones rarely cause civilian casualties because drones are more precise than other weapon platforms. The vast majority of these strikes have occurred in Pakistan, Yemen, and Somalia. Officials have characterized strikes in these areas as "surgical," maintaining that they can kill terrorist targets without harming innocent civilians.

The US generally has not, however, provided the kind of detailed data about strikes that enable meaningful assessment of its claim of surgical precision. Indeed, the history of US strikes involves several years in which the US refused even to admit engaging in them. This was followed by acknowledgment of them, accompanied by the claim that they rarely if ever cause civilian deaths.

Investigations by nongovernmental organizations (NGOs) have challenged this claim over the years by identifying several strikes in which such casualties occurred. These investigations have drawn on several sources of information, which may include interviews with residents, community groups, and officials in areas of drone strikes; visits to strike sites; examination and analysis of weapons remnants; and use of satellite imagery. In

© The Author(s), under exclusive license to Springer Nature Switzerland AG 2022
M. Regan, *Drone Strike–Analyzing the Impacts of Targeted Killing*,
https://doi.org/10.1007/978-3-030-91119-5_9

response to consistent discrepancies between US and NGO estimates, the US has provided more information in recent years, although there is still room for improvement.

This chapter first describes challenges in compiling accurate information about casualties from strikes. It then discusses how attention to claims about civilian casualties has evolved since the first US strike outside a theater of combat, which was in Yemen in 2002. Finally, the chapter will review estimates by organizations outside the US government of civilian casualties from targeted strikes in Pakistan, Yemen, and Somalia. By "targeted strikes," I mean airstrikes against persons in operations away from areas of active combat. For the most part, with the exception of some periods in Yemen and Somalia, these countries have not been theaters of such combat. The end of the chapter contains an Appendix that presents tables of estimates of annual civilian deaths and injuries in Pakistan, Yemen, and Somalia. While estimates are not uniform, they provide a useful sense of the order of magnitude of civilian casualties.

CIVILIAN CASUALTIES

Discussion of civilian casualties in this chapter focuses mainly on deaths rather than injuries. While determining accurate figure for deaths can be challenging, determining the number of injuries is even more difficult. As a result, there are more sources of estimates of deaths than injuries. As Tables 9.4 and 9.5 in the Appendix indicate, the only estimates of injuries are for total injuries, without characterization of victims as civilians or militants.

Taking the average of the ranges of estimates of total persons killed and total persons injured from 2004 to 2018, the Bureau of Investigative Journalism (BIJ) estimates are 0.44 injuries for every death in Pakistan, 0.17 injuries for every death in Yemen, and 0.05 injuries for every death in Somalia. For Pakistan, the figure for Pakistan Body Count is 0.31 injuries for every death. These figures are lower than for conventional armed conflicts, in which the number of injuries is usually greater than the number of deaths "by a factor of anything from 3:1 to 9:1."[1] This may reflect the suggestion in one NGO report that "[d]ue to the precision of drones when striking a particular target, a missile is far more likely to kill than to injure."[2]

Aside from the intrinsic harm that they cause, injuries can create significant challenges for victims and their families in the areas in which drone strikes have been most frequent. In the Federally Administered Tribal Areas (FATA) in Pakistan, for instance, there are only 13 doctors per 100,000 people, a ratio that is among the lowest in the world.[3] People from this area who need sophisticated care must travel to Peshawar, "a journey that can take anywhere from hours to several days due to rough terrain and poor security."[4] In addition, difficulties in traveling through conflict areas may mean that some victims arrive weeks or months after their injuries.[5] Victims also may incur substantial financial burdens in order to receive care.[6]

In addition, families must care for those who are unable to work or contribute to the household in other ways because of their injuries. Some families remove their children from school so that they can help take care of injured relatives.[7] Disabled persons can find it difficult to obtain prosthetics and wheelchairs that could make their lives and those of their family members easier. Interviewees in refugee camps also note the lack of facilities for the disabled.[8]

Because men are the breadwinners in Pakistan, Yemen, and Somalia, sons may have to drop out of school to provide for their families when men are unable to work because of injuries.[9] In addition, many breadwinners provide for more than one family, which means that a significant number of people may encounter hardship when a breadwinner becomes disabled. When women's injuries prevent them from caregiving, cleaning, fetching water, and cooking, "the heavy burdens of household and child-rearing duties are placed on other relatives, including elderly grandparents or younger siblings who might otherwise be in school."[10]

Thus, while the discussion of civilian casualties in this chapter and the next focuses primarily on deaths, it is important to keep in mind that strikes also may cause injuries that harm individuals and can cause hardship.

Determining how many civilians have been killed in targeted strikes by the US outside of war zones can be challenging. One reason is the nature of the locations in which strikes occur. Another is secrecy by the US government surrounding the program, which has led to an ongoing debate about the ability of the US to precisely strike intended targets without harm to others. The next two sections discuss these points in more detail.

COUNTING CIVILIAN DEATHS

In the FATA, Afghanistan, and parts of Yemen and Somalia, strikes may occur in remote areas to which access is difficult. The Pakistani government, for instance, generally has prohibited travel by outsiders to the FATA. In many cases it also has restricted access by foreigners to areas outside conflict zones in which displaced civilians are located.

In addition, militants have exercised control over some areas in which strikes have occurred. Those who attempt to enter incur the risk of being kidnapped or killed by these groups. The risk increases as troops who can provide protection are reduced or withdrawn. Militants also cordon off areas where strikes have occurred, and may quickly move the bodies of victims to conceal the identity of those who have been killed.

Those who are interested in identifying civilian casualties therefore may not have access to many areas where strikes occur. While some NGOs have conducted thorough investigations, outsiders sometimes must rely on local "stringers" for information. These persons typically will not have the capacity and resources to conduct extensive investigation. They also may not be able to visit the site where a drone strike has occurred because of restrictions imposed by the government or militant groups. This means that they must rely on statements by local officials or residents, who may have their own agendas. Amnesty International has said in a report on Pakistan, "Misinformation and politically driven propaganda about drone strike deaths is abundant, making it especially difficult for observers to determine the veracity of any claims about the identity of those killed."[11]

Some residents also may have limited understanding of what happens beyond their compound or village. In some areas, it is improper to ask questions of a male about female family members, or to photograph females. As a result, "male community members may not know details about one another's families or households, including the exact number of people who live there, and so may not be able to say how many people were inside a home before it was hit by a drone strike."[12]

In addition, bodies of victims may be in pieces, or religious beliefs may require that victims be buried quickly. It also can be unclear whether a particular attack was carried out by a drone or involved an explosion caused by another source. As one analyst noted, "The problem is that when something goes bang here, it's a very confused place, so sometimes it's not even clear if something was dropped from the sky or if it's an

IED."[13] Finally, local residents may fear retaliation from militants if they provide information or even speak to persons attempting to investigate what has occurred.

Another complication is that identifying who is a legitimate target is challenging in any armed conflict between a state and a nonstate group, since this requires an assessment of individuals' conduct and associations. With the general exception of women, children, and named militants, there is rarely enough information in media reports to enable an independent definitive assessment of whether victims are militants or civilians. BIJ reported that officials in the FATA eventually concluded after 2008 that it was too difficult to determine which victims were civilians, so they began to characterize them as "local" or "nonlocal."[14] The general assumption, one official said, is that nonlocals are militants.[15]

Getting an accurate count also is challenging because different observers may use different criteria to identify militants and civilians. The US says that militants are persons who are "part of a non-State armed group," which "may involve formally joining the group or simply participating sufficiently in its activities to be deemed part of it."[16] By contrast, the International Committee of the Red Cross (ICRC) takes the position that persons may be attacked as nonstate combatants only if they perform a continuous combat function on behalf of a nonstate armed group.[17]

A 2012 article in the *New York Times* reported that the US had adopted a standard that "counts all military-age males in a strike zone as combatants, according to several administration officials, unless there is explicit intelligence posthumously proving them innocent."[18] The description of US targeting criteria accompanying President Obama's 2013 National Defense University speech, however, stated, "Males of military age may be non-combatants; it is not the case that all military-aged males in the vicinity of a target are deemed to be combatants."[19]

Finally, determining civilian casualties can be especially difficult for signature strikes that target unidentified individuals based on their pattern of behavior. "Since their identity is unknown even during the strike, these targeted individuals may be confused with civilians," so "confirming their identity post-strike is a significant challenge without personnel to investigate."[20]

US government secrecy about targeted strikes outside war zones also makes it difficult to arrive at accurate civilian casualty figures, and to adequately assess US claims of strike precision. The history of US strike operations generally has been marked by government claims of no or few civilian casualties, with NGOs challenging these claims based on investigations that identify more casualties than the government acknowledges. As the next section describes, the result has been an ongoing debate about the precision of targeted strikes outside war zones.

GOVERNMENT SECRECY
AND THE DEBATE OVER PRECISION
2002–2013

The first US strike outside a war zone occurred in 2002, killing Qaed Salim Sinan al-Harithi, the leader of Al-Qaeda in Yemen, who had helped organize the attack on the *USS Cole* in Aden Harbor in 200 that killed 17 people and injured 37. For several years afterward, however, the US refused to acknowledge engaging in targeted strikes. This likely is because many of these operations, which occurred mainly in Pakistan, were conducted as covert activities by the CIA.[21] It was not until 2010 that officials of the Obama administration began to admit that the US engaged in strikes. The administration provided limited information about them, however, and rarely included information on individual strikes.

Indeed, it is unclear whether the US was even compiling information about civilian casualties, since the post-operation battle damage assessment (BDA) conducted by the military traditionally has focused on whether an operation successfully accomplished the goal of damaging an adversary. Furthermore, it is not clear what if any kind of process exists for reporting civilian casualties from covert operations conducted by the CIA.

The debate over strike precision began in earnest in 2010 when NGOs began to identify civilian casualties caused by drone strikes based on their own investigations. The first of these reports was by the Center for Civilians in Conflict (CIVIC) in 2010, which investigated casualties from operations in the FATA and adjoining Khyber Pakhtunkhwa (KPK) province. The report was based on interviews conducted from October 2009 to August 2010 with policymakers, nongovernmental and international organizations, and over 160 Pakistani civilians who had suffered direct losses since 2007 from the conflict.[22] CIVIC noted that the Pakistani government did not appear to systematically compile information on civilian casualties. District coordination officers in KPK, however, collected such information within their districts for compensation purposes, and several shared their estimates.

CIVIC estimated that since 2009, 124 strikes had killed between 788 and 1344 people. The US claimed that there were about 20 civilian deaths over this period. CIVIC stated, however, that its investigation of just nine individual strikes indicated more than 30 alleged civilian deaths, with one strike in June 2009 killing up to 18 civilians. The organization thus concluded that "it is certain that the number of civilians killed in drone strikes exceeds the low figure put forward by US officials."[23]

In February 2011, however, US officials disputed these figures. It claimed that a total of 30 civilians had been killed since the targeting program was expanded in 2008.[24] The US contested assertions that the toll was much higher, "arguing that interviews are not a reliable indicator because relatives of the dead often refuse to acknowledge the suspects were involved with militant groups."[25]

Similarly, in June 2011 White House US counterterrorism advisor John Brennan said that the US is "exceptionally precise and surgical in terms of addressing the terrorist threat. [I]f there are terrorists who are within an area where there are women and children or others … we do not take such action that might put those innocent men, women and children in danger." He added that within the last year, "there hasn't been a single collateral death because of the exceptional proficiency [and] precision of the capabilities that we've been able to develop."[26]

In July 2011, however, BIJ reported on its analysis of 116 US drone strikes in Pakistan from August 23, 2010 to June 29, 2011.[27] While hundreds of militants had been killed by strikes, there were 25 strikes in which civilian deaths had or were highly likely to have occurred. In ten cases, the evidence indicated that at least 45 civilians had died. In the additional fifteen, "at least 65 deaths have also been reported but are contested, or are reported by a single source only."[28]

In August 2011, however, the *New York Times* reported that officials still believed that Brennan's claim about the precision of drone strikes was accurate. "[S]ince May 2010, C.I.A. officers believe, the drones have killed more than 600 militants — including at least 20 in a strike reported Wednesday — and not a single noncombatant."[29] In May 2012, the *Times* noted that "in a recent interview, a senior administration official said that the number of civilians killed in drone strikes in Pakistan under Mr. Obama was in the 'single digits' — and that independent counts of scores or hundreds of civilian deaths unwittingly draw on false propaganda claims by militants."[30]

The period from 2002 to 2013 thus was characterized by US government claims that the precision of targeted strikes resulted in virtually no civilian casualties, with NGOs contesting these claims based on casualties they identified in their own investigations.

2013–2016

In May 2013, President Obama delivered a speech at National Defense University in which he acknowledged controversy about US claims regarding civilian casualties from targeted strikes, and admitted that strikes had caused some casualties. "[M]uch of the criticism about drone strikes," he said, "– at home and abroad – understandably centers on reports of civilian casualties. There is a wide gap between U.S. assessments of such casualties, and non-governmental reports. Nevertheless, it is a hard fact that U.S. strikes have resulted in civilian casualties, a risk that exists in all wars."[31] The President announced Presidential Policy Guidance (PPG) for lethal strikes "outside areas of active hostilities."[32] As described earlier, the Guidance said that such strikes could occur only if there is "near certainty that noncombatants will not be injured or killed."[33] This standard, the President said, is "the highest standard we can set."[34]

Reports by outside parties continued to document the civilian toll from targeted strikes. A 2013 report by UN Special Rapporteur Ben Emmerson stated that during his visit to Pakistan in March 2013 he was given statistics from the Ministry of Foreign Affairs indicating that at least 330 drone strikes had occurred in the FATA since 2004.[35] Some 2200 deaths had been caused by such strikes, with estimates of at least 400 civilian deaths. An additional 200 individuals "were regarded as probable noncombatants."[36] Emmerson said that officials indicated that, "owing to underreporting and obstacles to effective investigation, those figures are likely to be an underestimate."[37]

In a 2013 article, Larry Lewis and Sarah Holewinski noted three examples of strikes in Pakistan in March and May 2011 in which third parties claimed civilian deaths occurred, during the period in which the US said that there were no civilian casualties from drone strikes.[38] Lewis had earlier worked with Sarah Sewall and military command in Afghanistan to analyze and make recommendations for minimizing civilian casualties, and Holewinski was Executive Director of CIVIC.

The three strikes they analyzed included a follow-up strike that reportedly killed rescuers; a strike on a gathering at a suspected militant compound that turned out to be a tribal assembly of elders attempting to resolve a dispute at a local mine; and civilians killed at a religious school and restaurant during a strike on a vehicle. Local estimates of the civilian deaths from the strike on the assembly ranged from 13 to 44. While the US claimed that no civilians had been harmed, Pakistan provided compensation to the families of 39 persons killed during that strike.

In 2013, Human Rights Watch reported that it had investigated six air strikes, of which at least four were by drones, during two trips to Yemen in 2012 and 2013.[39] It said that these strikes, one from 2009 and the others from 2012 to 2013, killed 82 people, of whom at least 57 were civilians. Also in 2013, Amnesty International published a report on its investigation into nine of the 45 reported US drone strikes in Pakistan from January 2012 to August 2013.[40] Amnesty concluded that there had been between 81 and 89 deaths in the nine strikes, of which 50–60 were militants and 29–31 were civilians.

In 2013, BIJ announced that it had obtained information on civilian casualties from 75 drone strikes in Pakistan from 2006 to late 2009, drawn from reports by local political agents in the FATA filed with the FATA Secretariat.[41] Of the 746 deaths recorded in the document, at least 147 were explicitly characterized as civilians. By contrast, said BIJ, the US said "that no more than 50 to 60 'non-combatants' have been killed by the CIA across the entire nine years of Pakistan bombings."[42] In response, the US stated that leaked document was "'far from authoritative" because it was based on "erroneous media reporting" and "indirect input from a loose network of Pakistani government and tribal contacts," and that there was "no credible information whatsoever to substantiate the report's distorted figures."[43]

BIJ followed up in January 2014 by disclosing a Pakistani government document containing additional local official reports, which, it said, "records details of over 300 drone strikes, including their locations and an assessment of how many people died in each incident."[44] It provided information on attacks from 2006 to late September 2013, but did not include information for 2007. Reports through the end of 2008 specifically indicated whether victims were civilians, while those from 2009 onward used the terms "local" and "non-local."[45]

The document reported that 294 attacks occurred between 2009 and September 2013. In total, BIJ said, reports indicated about 200 civilian deaths, which included incidents "where ambiguous language such as 'local tribesmen' is used."[46] BIJ noted that the document omitted several incidents in which "multiple credible sources record civilian casualties - - and when local officials have acknowledged [them]."[47] It expressed concern that reports after 2009 did not include specific assessments of whether civilians were harmed in attacks.

In a 2014 report, UN Special Rapporteur Emmerson described the results of his review of 37 US drone strikes alleged to have caused civilian casualties to determine if investigations should be conducted in response to the allegations. Based on a review of the evidence, Emmerson found that in 30 of the 37 cases there was a "plausible and credible allegation of civilian casualties, from apparently reliable sources, so as to trigger the duties of investigation and transparency."[48]

In 2015, Open Society issued a report providing evidence of civilian casualties caused by nine US airstrikes that it investigated, "all apparently conducted by unmanned aerial vehicles (drones)" between May 2012 and April 2014 in Yemen.[49] These consisted of 26 deaths and 13 injuries. It asserted that its investigation "casts doubt on the U.S. and Yemeni governments' statements about the precision of drone strikes."[50]

In April 2016, Micah Zenko and Amelia Wolf published an article in *Foreign Policy* contesting the US claim of drone precision based on a comparison of casualties from drone strikes with those from strikes by manned aircraft in war zones. They argued that the claim that drones caused fewer civilian casualties than other weapons "is simply untrue."[51] Drone strikes outside of combat, such as in Pakistan, Yemen, and Somalia, they said, "result in thirty-five times more civilian fatalities than airstrikes by manned weapons systems in conventional battlefields, such as Iraq, Syria, and Afghanistan."[52]

The authors said that coalition airstrikes in battlefield operations against the Islamic State beginning in August 2014 had killed one civilian per 72 bombs. While some of these strikes were conducted by drones, in Iraq and Syria 93% of all bombs were dropped by manned aircraft. Zenko and Wolf said airstrikes in Afghanistan through the end of 2015 had killed one civilian per 21 bombs.

They noted that Air Force data indicated that drone strikes had increased from 7% of airstrikes in Afghanistan in 2013 to 56% in 2015. They argued that the imprecision of drones was reflected in the fact that in 2015 airstrikes had killed one civilian for every nine bombs, although data differentiating manned and unmanned weapons platforms were not available.

The authors said there had been 462 drone strikes outside theaters of active conflict in Pakistan, Yemen, and Somalia since Obama took office. These killed an estimated 289 civilians, or one civilian per 1.6 strikes. "In short," Zenko and Wolf stated, "drones are far less precise than airstrikes conducted by piloted aircraft," and "result in far more civilian fatalities per each bomb dropped."[53] The authors said that there are sound arguments in favor of drone strikes, "but their supposed precision should not be one of them."[54]

On July 1, 2016, President Obama issued Executive Order 13732 directing "all relevant agencies" to review or investigate incidents involving civilian casualties; to consider information from all credible sources, including NGOs; and to take steps to mitigate casualties.[55] It also required the Director of National Intelligence (DNI) to obtain and release by May 1, 2017 "information about the number of strikes undertaken by the U.S. Government against terrorist targets outside areas of active hostilities from January 1, 2016, through December 31, 2016," including "combatant and non-combatant deaths resulting from those strikes," and thereafter to release such information on an annual basis.[56] In addition, it required the DNI to address reasons for discrepancies between US and credible NGO estimates of civilian casualties. The discussion of civilian casualty estimates in the following section describes estimates in these US reports.

In August 2016, Steven Barela and Avery Plaw assessed the claim by Zenko and Wolf that drone strikes outside war zones are much less precise than manned aircraft strikes in such zones. They incorporated into their analysis data from DNI that had been released after the latter article.[57] While Barela and Plaw acknowledged the legitimacy of concerns about drone strikes, they argued that Zenko and Wolf's analysis was problematic in several ways.

First, they observed, neither Iraq and Syria on the one hand and Pakistan, Yemen, and Somalia on the other are perfect proxies for strikes by manned platforms and drones. Campaigns in both sets of countries, they said, involved both platforms, and most data sources failed to distinguish between which platforms carried out which operations. Several of

the strikes causing the most civilian casualties in the three latter countries during the period analyzed by Zenko and Wolff were carried out not
by drones but by other platforms. The strike that produced the highest
number of casualties in this set of countries, for instance, was a cruise
missile strike in Yemen that killed as many as 41 civilians. These accounted
for over two-thirds of the minimum civilian deaths reported by the DNI
in Pakistan, Yemen, and Somalia from January 20, 2009 to December
31, 2015. Distinguishing between drones and other platforms therefore
would result in a much lower civilian casualty figure for drones.

Similarly, regarding the increase in risk of civilian casualties in
Afghanistan in 2015, 42 of the casualties that year, or more than 40%,
were caused by one strike by a manned aircraft. BIJ data indicated that
although less than a third of strikes were carried out by manned aircraft
in Afghanistan, these accounted for almost 70% of civilian casualties.

Barela and Plaw also observed that data could not be disaggregated by
time or region, which obscured important differences. They noted that
civilian casualties from drone strikes had declined substantially since 2011,
reflecting significant improvement in US targeting standards, procedures,
and performance. Taking the aggregate data on Pakistan, Yemen, and
Somalia for more than seven years and comparing it with the relative
precision of strikes in Iraq and Syria over the last two, they said, thus
did not provide an appropriate comparison.

They suggested that a more apt comparison between the relevant areas
would be since August 2014, when airstrikes began in Iraq and Syria.
Based on an average of the main NGO estimates, the number of civilian
casualties per drone strike fell from 1.7 in 2009 to 0.052 in 2015, to
0.036 through June 9 of 2016, reflecting a decline by a factor of about
47. Using the same estimates that Zenko and Wolf used, Barela and Plaw
found that from 2014 to 2016 strikes in Iraq and Syria resulted in 0.099
civilian deaths per strike, compared with 0.067 civilian deaths per strike
in Pakistan, Yemen, and Somalia. Thus, the rate of civilian casualties was
33% higher in countries in which most strikes were by manned platforms.

The authors emphasized that they did not regard their article as vindi-
cating US claims of drone precision, nor were they dismissing legitimate
concerns about civilian casualties caused by drone strikes. They stressed
the need for more detailed data in order to conduct meaningful analysis,
the lack of which made it impossible to offer definitive pronouncements
about the precision of drones compared to other platforms.

The period from 2013 to 2016 thus featured more explicit US acknowledgment of civilian casualties from target strikes, adoption of a targeting standard intended to avoid such casualties, and the first government estimates of civilian casualties from targeted strikes outside war zones. As the discussion of casualty estimates below describes, however, criticism has continued that the US still fails to provide enough information to enable an accurate determination of civilian casualties and an assessment of the precision of targeted strikes.

2017–2021

President Trump took office on January 20, 2017. In March 2017, US officials said that the Trump administration was planning to "make it easier for the CIA and the military to target terrorists with drone strikes, even if it means tolerating more civilian casualties."[58] Reports were that parts of Yemen and Somalia had been declared "areas of active hostilities," and thus not subject to the PPG. More generally, officials said that the administration planned to grant the CIA and the military more autonomy to target militants without presidential sign-off in countries such as Yemen, Somalia, Iraq, Syria, Libya, and Afghanistan.

Later that year, the *New York Times* reported that the administration planned to replace the Obama PPG with Principles, Standards, and Procedures (PSP) that would loosen restrictions on targeting.[59] "But," the article stated, "administration officials have also agreed that they should keep in place one important constraint for such attacks: a requirement of 'near certainty' that no civilian bystanders will be killed."[60]

The Trump administration would not comment on its standards, but the PSP finally were disclosed in May 2021 as a result of a lawsuit under the Freedom of Information Act. They provided guidance "to all CT [counterterrorism] action wherever it is conducted abroad," and said that that they superseded the PPG.[61] The PSP, in other words, abandoned the distinction between areas inside and outside of active hostilities. They also eliminated the PPG requirement that a target poses a "continuing imminent threat" to US persons, providing instead that direct action could be taken against targets "whose removal, either independently or as part of a broader campaign, is assessed to be reasonably necessary to US efforts to address the threat posed by the terrorist group."[62] Direct action was authorized against groups "subject to the use of lawful force by the United States, that are engaged in ongoing hostilities against the

United States, or pose a continuing imminent threat against the United States."[63]

Finally, the PSP said that the US would continue "to take extraordinary measures to ensure with near certainty that noncombatants will not be injured or killed in the course of operations."[64] The *New York Times*, however, reported that Biden administration officials conducting a review of drone policy "discovered that Trump-era principles to govern strikes in certain countries often made an exception to the requirement of 'near certainty' that there would be no civilian casualties. While it kept that rule for women and children, it permitted a lower standard of merely 'reasonable certainty' when it came to civilian adult men."[65]

In 2017 Congress required the Secretary of Defense to issue an annual report "on civilian casualties caused as a result of United States military operations during the preceding year."[66] The report must list all military operations "that were confirmed, or reasonably suspected, to have resulted in civilian casualties,"[67] and list "civilian and enemy combatant casualties."[68]

Congress also provided that the Secretary "shall take into account relevant and credible all-source reporting, including information from public reports and nongovernmental sources."[69] The report must also describe how the Department investigates allegations of civilian casualties and steps it takes to mitigate such casualties.[70] The report is to be in unclassified form, but may include a classified annex. The section below on civilian casualty estimates discusses the figures that have been provided through 2020 operations. The reporting requirement applies only to strikes conducted by the military, unlike the DNI report, which includes all operations outside areas of active hostilities by any US entity.

In November 2017, the *New York Times* published an article detailing the results of its investigations between April 2016 and June 2017 of almost 150 airstrikes in northern Iraq shortly after ISIS was pushed out of the area.[71] The investigations involved inspections of strike locations, interviews with a wide range of individuals, review of local news sources, and use of satellite imagery. Reporters also visited the Combined Air Operations Center (CAOC) in Qatar that coordinates the coalition air campaign to learn about the strike approval and prosecution process.

The strikes that were investigated occurred within an area of active hostilities, and thus were not subject to the requirement that there be near certainty of no civilian casualties. The article, however, illuminated how civilian casualties could occur despite extensive efforts to avoid them, and why the US likely does not have full appreciation of the civilian casualties that it causes.

The article did not distinguish between drone strikes and other aerial strikes, but said with respect to its observations of the COAC targeting process that "if all goes well — the process concludes with a strike so precise that it can, in some cases, destroy a room full of enemy fighters and leave the rest of the house intact."[72] It reported that at the CAOC several officials walked reporters through the steps to avoid civilian casualties:

> Intelligence streams in from partner forces, informants on the ground, electronic surveillance and drone footage. Once the coalition decides a target is ISIS, analysts study the probability that striking it will kill civilians in the vicinity, often by poring over drone footage of patterns of civilian activity. The greater the likelihood of civilian harm, the more mitigating measures the coalition takes. If the target is near an office building, the attack might be rescheduled for nighttime. If the area is crowded, the coalition might adjust its weaponry to limit the blast radius.

> Sometimes aircraft will even fire a warning shot, allowing people to escape targeted facilities before the strike. An official showed us grainy night-vision footage of this technique in action: Warning shots hit the ground near a shed in Deir al-Zour, Syria, prompting a pair of white silhouettes to flee, one tripping and picking himself back up, as the cross hairs follow.[73]

After a strike, there is an assessment of its impact. If there is an allegation of civilian casualties, this triggers an internal assessment to determine if the report is credible. "If so, the coalition makes refinements to avoid future civilian casualties, they told us."[74]

Notwithstanding these efforts, the report found that one in five coalition strikes it investigated resulted in civilian deaths, a rate much higher than reported by the US. One reason for this was that the coalition did not routinely send investigators to strike sites because of security concerns or problems with access. The report suggested that another reason is that coalition records sometimes are incomplete or inaccurate. It cited examples in which GPS coordinates of damage locations initially were not confirmed by the coalition, but the coalition ultimately acknowledged strikes when presented with further evidence, such as the coalition's own video of a strike at that location.

The article also included an in-depth account of a man whose wife, daughter, brother, sister-in-law, and nephew all died in a strike on two adjoining houses in September 2015. Until the *Times* raised the issue, none of these victims were included in coalition civilian casualty figures. The man, who himself was seriously injured and required extensive surgery, had repeatedly contacted coalition representatives without any response.

The incident also illustrates how intelligence failures can cause civilian casualties. The coalition eventually acknowledged that it had conducted an airstrike on the two houses based on intelligence indicating they were an ISIS command center. Investigation concluded that this was based on full-motion video of an hour and thirty-five minutes over the course of three days in increments of 15–30 minutes.[75] Video showed adult males opening and closing the gate for arriving vehicles, but no women or children "or other evidence of domestic activities."[76]

The report said that "no overtly nefarious activity was observed," but that the observations "fit with the target characterization due to evidence of access control and the expectation that groups of ADM [adult males] would be observed at the target."[77] In hindsight, said the report, "It appears that some of the intelligence attributed to the target may have actually indicated an adjacent compound. Moreover, additional observation of the target may have revealed a pattern of activity consistent with a non-ISIL civilian presence."[78]

Nonetheless, the report concluded that it found "no evidence indicating carelessness or bad faith," and that the "targeting process remains sound."[79] As the incident indicates, however, "the margin for error is slim, and the result of potential mistake may be tragic, despite our best efforts to avoid them."[80] The *Times* suggested, "Such intelligence failures suggest that not all civilian casualties are unavoidable tragedies; some deaths could be prevented if the coalition recognizes its past failures and changes its operating assumptions accordingly. But in the course of our investigation, we found that it seldom did either."[81]

In the FY 2019 National Defense Authorization Act (NDAA), Congress required designation of a senior civilian official within the Department of Defense to develop and oversee compliance with a policy regarding civilian casualties resulting from military operations.[82] The policy must provide for uniform standards for recording military strikes, development and dissemination of best practices for reducing civilian casualties, channels to submit allegations of casualties, and uniform standards for investigating allegations. Preparation of the policy is still in progress.

Amnesty International issued a report in 2019 on five US airstrikes in Somalia from October 2017 to December 2018.[83] Since April 2017, Amnesty said, the US had tripled its annual rate of strikes, but claimed "that it has not killed any civilians in Somalia during this period."[84] Amnesty said fourteen civilians were killed and eight injured in the strikes. There was "credible evidence," declared the report, "that US airstrikes were responsible for four of these incidents and that the fifth was most plausibly caused by a US airstrike."[85]

US Africa Command (AFRICOM) contested the findings, stating, "Our assessments found that no AFRICOM airstrike resulted in any civilian casualty or injury. Our assessments are based on post-strike analysis using intelligence methods not available to non-military organizations."[86] It said that, "AFRICOM airstrikes are primarily conducted in secluded, low-populated areas," and that Al-Shabaab sometimes coerces residents to make false claims.[87]

The following month, however, AFRICOM acknowledged that a strike on Al-Shabaab in April 2018 had resulted in the deaths of two civilians.[88] The strike had not been included in the Amnesty International report, but discovery of the casualties occurred after the AFRICOM Commander ordered an internal review of strikes in Somalia since 2017. The statement said that there had been "credible evidence" of the deaths shortly after the strike, but the deaths had not been reported to senior officials until the previous week.[89] A news report noted that officials said that because of Al-Shabaab presence in strike locations, the US "often relied on overhead surveillance and communication intercepts to verify what happened on the ground."[90]

In March 2020, AFRICOM announced that it would begin to issue quarterly reports of allegations of civilian casualties resulting from its operations, along with the status of assessments of such claims.[91] Dan Mahanty of CIVIC noted the continued need for more expansive military outreach to local communities in conducting investigations, but said that AFRICOM's decision to issue reports "should be welcomed as a small but important step toward greater transparency."[92]

There has been substantial criticism of the Trump administration for reducing transparency about drone strikes and relaxing practices designed to minimize civilian casualties from them. While it did not deal specifically with drone strikes, Airwars issued a report in October 2020 on alleged and declared US kinetic actions in Yemen during the Trump administration.[93] About 60% of these involved air operations. The report said that 41 of the 230 actions allegedly caused civilian harm, and that Airwars concluded that 25 of these likely did so, resulting in the deaths of between 86 and 154 civilians.

Airwars said that CENTCOM acknowledged only between 4 and 12 deaths from actions in Yemen during the Trump administration, all from a single event in January 2017. The report noted that senior officials informed Airwars that CENTCOM has no unit to assess allegations of civilian casualties from outside sources. Airwars also noted that while the last action declared by CENTCOM was in June 2019, 30 US strikes reportedly had taken place in Yemen since then, suggesting an increase in covert operations. The report thus indicated continuing discrepancies between civilian casualty estimates by the US and outside organizations, the absence of systematic efforts to gain accurate estimates, and a decline in transparency about US operations.

In March 2021 Yemeni human rights organization Mwatana reported on its investigation of twelve operations carried out by the US in Yemen between January 2017 and January 2019, which included ten drone strikes.[94] The group found that these operations caused at least 38 Yemeni civilian deaths. The report said that the US had acknowledged civilian harm in only one incident, which is the January 2017 one mentioned in the Airwars report described above. Mwatana criticized the US for failing to thoroughly investigate possible civilian casualties, noting that its own investigation had involved visits to and collection of evidence from strike sites and local interviews.

In response to the Mwatana report, in April 2021 CENTCOM concluded that civilian casualties had occurred in two of the operations that Mwatana had identified.[95] It also conceded one additional civilian fatality from a Yemen strike in 2019. It said that with respect to a US ground raid in 2017, it had "previously assessed that this raid resulted in twelve civilians killed," and that the Mwatana information "is broadly consistent" with this assessment.[96]

Two sets of articles by the New York Times in late 2021 raised questions about the claimed precision of US airstrikes in the campaign against ISIS from 2014 to 2019. One set of articles by Azmat Khan were based on Department of Defense confidential assessments of 1,311 external reports of civilian casualties in Iraq and Syria between September 2014 and January 2018 obtained in a Freedom of Information request.[97] As with Khan's 2017 article with Gopal described above, these strikes differ from those that are the subject of this book in that they were conducted in war zones, and in that dynamic strikes were "an overwhelming majority" of the air campaign.[98] As with that earlier article and the August 2021 strike in Kabul, however, these incidents raise questions about the accuracy of US military estimates of civilian casualties more generally. In addition, one of the articles suggests that there are recurring types of problems that tend to result in such casualties, but that the military investigative process does not attempt to identify them.

External reports are assessed by the Department as "credible" if it was more likely than not that civilian casualties occurred, and "non-credible" if it was not. Of the 1,311 reports reviewed by the Times, 216 were deemed credible. Khan visited the sites of sixty incidents for which reports were deemed credible and thirty-six others either deemed non-credible or that had not yet been assessed. She also visited "dozens" of strike sites in Afghanistan. On such visits she viewed strike wreckage at the site, collected photo and video evidence, verified casualties through reliance on several documentary sources, and interviewed residents and current and former US officials.

Khan said that review of external claims of civilian casualties indicated that many allegations were dismissed as non-credible without thorough evaluation. In addition, her site visits led her to conclude that "hundreds of deaths" were not counted by the Pentagon, and that details obtained from site visits "were often in stark contrast to what had been assessed from the air."[99]

A second set of Times articles described a US Special Operations task force strike cell, known as Talon Anvil, that took a lead role in conducting airstrikes in the campaign against ISIS from 2014 to 2019.[100] The Times reported that the cell alarmed partners in both the military and the CIA by conducting strikes without sufficient regard for civilian casualties and "killing people who had no role in the conflict."[101] The cell was required to engage in a process of intelligence gathering and risk mitigation to minimize harm to civilians from offensive strikes, but "were under enormous pressure to protect allied troops and move the offensive forward."[102] As a result, the cell began to characterize most of its strikes as those conducted in defense of ground forces from imminent attack, which were subject to considerably fewer restrictions.[103] This sometimes led to strikes without thorough intelligence establishing that a person was hostile. Another article said that investigation of a strike that killed 70 civilians was thwarted by unresponsive superiors, falsification of strike records, and retaliation against personnel pushing for thorough assessment of the incident, even though a legal advisor had referred the case for consideration as a possible war crime.[104]

The task force had a second cell, which conducted only a "fraction" of the strikes, that worked with the CIA to target ISIS leaders, which often tracked them for days or weeks and appeared to operate with more deliberation.[105] These strikes more closely resemble those that occur outside war zones, compared to dynamic strikes conducted in the course of major combat operations that were the focus of the Times articles. In this respect, strikes that are the focus of this book generally do not occur under the kind of pressure that led to the conduct of the Talon Anvil task force. To the extent that strikes outside war zones are conducted under conditions of perceived urgency, however, the actions of the task force illustrate ways in which concern for civilian casualties can diminish.

Targeted strikes therefore have become a greater focus of public concern in the roughly two decades in which the US has conducted them. Estimates of casualties by the US and by outside organizations have consistently diverged over this period. Critics claim that the US is not fully accounting for civilian casualties from strikes because of the limited scope of its investigations and its failure to consider all potential sources of information, and thus has no clear understanding of the full impacts of its operations. The US contends that it has access to information that outside organizations do not, and that its reliance on precise technology means that civilian casualties are rare. With this as background, the next section describes estimates of civilian casualties caused by targeted strikes, with the main focus on Pakistan, Yemen, and Somalia.

CASUALTY ESTIMATES

NGO Estimates

The major organizations that have attempted to estimate deaths from US strikes in Pakistan, Yemen, and Somalia are the New America Foundation (NAF) and the Long War Journal (LWJ) in Washington, DC and the Bureau of Investigative Journalism (BIJ) and Airwars based in

London. Airwars took over BIJ's drones project in April 2019. As Table 9.1 in the Appendix at the end of the chapter reflects, Airwars has figures for Somalia that reflect updates and revisions of BIJ estimates for that country. Pakistan Body Count also has provided estimates of civilian deaths from strikes in Pakistan.

A 2012 study by the Columbia Law School Human Rights Clinic compared and evaluated the methodologies of each of these sources based on its own analysis of data on drone strikes in Pakistan in 2011.[106] The report concluded that it regarded the BIJ estimates as the most accurate, based on that organization's reliance on a larger number of media sources than NSF or the LWJ, as well as BIJ's reliance on its own occasional investigations. These factors, said the report, account for the fact that the BIJ estimates of civilian casualties generally were higher than those of the other two organizations. For 2011, the Columbia report estimated between 456 and 661 individuals killed in strikes in Pakistan, of whom alleged militants numbered between 330 and 575, and alleged civilians numbered between 72 and 155. As the figures below indicate, these estimates were closest to those of BIJ at the time:

BIJ: 473–669 total; 68–157 civilians
NA: 366–599 total; 331–524 militants; 3–9 civilians; 32–66 unknown
LWJ: 438–478 total; 421–475 militants; 3–38 civilians

Ritika Singh conducted a careful analysis of these four sources of information in October 2013 and concluded that BIJ and the Columbia Law School approaches were the most comprehensive and included the widest range of publicly available information.[107] "Although some of this information may not be independently verifiable," she said, "these databases are undoubtedly more dynamic – which is crucial in a debate as opaque as this one."[108]

While estimates involve a range rather than precise numbers, Singh noted that high-end estimates of NA and LWJ at the time of her analysis were roughly consistent with the low-end estimates of BIJ and Columbia. One might therefore treat the overlap as representing some common ground. For instance, NA's high-end estimate for Pakistan from 2004 to the time of her study was 15%, while BIJ's low-range estimate for the same period was 11%. Similarly, in Pakistan in 2011, BIJ and Columbia estimated as low as 8% and 11% civilian casualties, respectively, while NA estimated as high as 17%. Dropping the outlier for that period, which is the LWJ estimate, results in a civilian casualty rate for that period of between 8% and 17%. Note that these figures for 2011 do not precisely correspond to those in the tables at the end of this chapter, since organizations continually reassess estimates based on new information.

The organization Pakistan Body Count (PBC) also provided estimates of civilian casualties from drone strikes in that country from 2004 to 2017.[109] As the tables at the end of this chapter indicate, its estimates are substantially higher than those of the three organizations described above, as well as estimates of the Columbia Human Rights Clinic. Zeeshan-ul-hassan Usmani, the founder of PBC, and Hira Bashir, its head of data analysis, have said that "if no evidence of a particular group affiliation is found, the dead or injured are counted as civilians."[110] They note that confirmation of the number of dead and injured often is a lengthy process involving communication with local officials, hospital staff, and neighbors, and that "the records of people who died later in hospital or home, after being counted injured, should be and are included in our database."[111] This is the main reason, they say, "why the account in this database is larger than any other."[112]

It is difficult to evaluate this explanation for why PBC estimates are so much higher than estimates of any other organizations. Persons at groups that rely on extensive local sources such as BIJ have expressed support for PBC's efforts, but say they have not been able to find sufficiently credible evidence to support PBC's estimates.

It is true that international law requires that parties to a conflict adopt the presumption that a person is a civilian who may not be attacked unless evidence establishes otherwise. It is possible that PBC required a higher level of evidence to rebut this presumption than other organizations. In addition, requiring definitive evidence of combatant status makes sense with respect to targeting, but it may not be realistic for purposes of accurately determining the status of victims in an area in which there is a substantial concentration of militants who are not wearing uniforms, such as in the FATA for many years. As BIJ and NA have emphasized, it may be appropriate in some cases to eschew binary classification and to acknowledge the uncertain status of some victims in order to accurately report events on the ground.

It also is worth noting that the uncertainty surrounding targeted strikes affords an opportunity for estimates to reflect parties' views about the legal and ethical justification for such strikes. As the discussion below describes, for instance, US government estimates tend to be substantially lower than estimates by other organizations. By contrast, Usmani and Bashir of PBC say, "Drone attacks are rejected by a variety of legal entities because they kill without a declaration of war and without trial. Covert operations are also condemned because affected civilians are left with nowhere to turn to for justice and compensation."[113] PBC's high estimates may be subtly influenced by this view of the legality and legitimacy of drone strikes.

As the charts at the end of the chapter indicate, the most targeted strikes from 2004 to 2020 occurred in Pakistan, mainly in the FATA. NA, BIJ, and PBC have estimates for drone strikes, while LWJ's estimates are for airstrikes generally. Figures range from 404 to 430 by the three major organizations described above, and 588 by PBC. All sources report that strikes were in the single digits through 2007. The number of strikes jumped to the mid-thirties in 2008 according to NA, LWJ, and BIJ, and to 55 according to PBC. They peaked in 2010, with estimates between LWJ's 117 and PBC's 123. They then gradually declined by 2014 to the twenties according to NA, LWJ, and BIJ, although PBC estimated 52 strikes in that year. They have been even lower in recent years, with no strikes recorded by NA, LWJ, and BIJ in 2019–2020. No figures from PBC appear to be available after 2017.

The largest number of civilian deaths also was in Pakistan, ranging from LWJ's estimate of 159 to BIJ's range of 424–969, and PBC's estimate of between 1306 and 2544. During the most significant period of strikes from 2008 to 2014, the percentage of casualties that were civilians declined from the estimate of 36% in 2008 by BIJ to an estimate of 1% by BIJ in 2014, with NA and LWJ reporting no civilian casualties in 2014. The most significant decline for BIJ did not occur until 2013–2014. The figures for PBC also declined from 71% in 2008 to 3% in 2014. During the most intensive strike years from 2010 to 2012, NA and LWJ estimates of the percentage of casualties who were civilians ranged from 2% to 11%, while BIJ estimates were 15%, 20%, and 12%, respectively. PBC's were much higher, at 51%, 75%, and 65%. NA estimates of the number of civilian casualties are in the single digits from 2012 to 2020, as are BIJ estimates from 2013 to 2020, and LWJ estimates from 2012 to 2016, with the exception of an estimate of 14% in 2013.

Examining the NA and BIJ spreadsheets with information on each strike enables calculation of the number and percentage of strikes causing civilian deaths. This provides an especially useful indication of strike accuracy. The highest figure in Pakistan for NA was 14% of strikes resulting in civilian deaths in 2008, but the highest for BIJ was more than three times as high, at 48% for 2009. Indeed, the lowest figure for BIJ through 2012, which was 22%, was half again as high as the highest figure for NA for that period, which was 14%. In the intensive strike years of 2010–2012, NA's estimates of the percentage of strikes resulting in civilian deaths were 2%, 7%, and 4%, respectively, while BIJ's were 31%, 25%, and 22%. While both NA and BIJ show declines in this percentage from 2008 to 2014, BIJ's figures indicate a fairly high degree of inaccuracy in the early years of this period. There was significant improvement in 2013 and 2014, however, when the rates were 7% and 4%, respectively.

The second largest number of strikes among the three countries has been in Yemen. NA's estimates are for drone or airstrikes and LWJ's are for airstrikes. BIJ has figures for "confirmed airstrikes, including drone strikes," for 2002–2019, between 326 and 346. Reviewing BIJ original spreadsheet data on individual strikes also indicates eight "possible" additional US airstrikes, but the Bureau did not find sufficient evidence to attribute them to the US. The spreadsheet also contains an estimated 124 confirmed drone strikes for 2002–2016, which are part of the total confirmed airstrikes. Figures after 2016 are for confirmed air or drone strikes, but do not differentiate between the two. The most intensive periods of strikes in Yemen were in 2012 and 2017. This reflects US strikes in support of a Yemeni government military offensive against AQAP in 2012, and in support of a UAE military offensive against the group in 2017. Estimates of the number of strikes in 2012 are from 41 to 56, while for 2012 are much higher, from 127 to 131.

Estimates of civilian deaths from airstrikes in Yemen are from 91 to 142 from 2002 to 2020, with BIJ estimating between 71 and 100 such deaths from drone strikes from 2002 to 2016. For the two most intensive years of strikes in 2012 and 2017, NA estimates that 3% of deaths, or 16 persons, were civilians in 2012; LWJ estimates 16%, or 35 persons; and BIJ estimates 9%, or between 19 and 24 civilians. For 2017, NA estimates 12%, or 28 civilian deaths, while BIJ estimates 4%, or between 3 and 10 people (LWJ has no estimate for that year).

Focusing on the percentage of strikes causing civilian casualties in those two years, NA estimates that in 2012, four of 56 strikes, or 7%, resulted in civilian deaths, while BIJ estimates that seven of between 41 and 55, or

15%, did so.[114] For 2017, NA estimates that four of 130 strikes, or 3%, resulted in civilian deaths. BIJ estimates that two of 127, or 2%, did so. Thus, while strikes in 2017 were more than twice as high than in 2012, the percentage causing civilian deaths was much lower. The percentage jumped in 2018, however, with NA estimating six of 41 strikes, or 14%, causing civilian deaths, while BIJ's estimate was seven of 36, or 19%.

Finally, BIJ spreadsheet data contains estimates of deaths from confirmed drone strikes, a subset of airstrikes in Yemen, for 2012–2016. BIJ estimates that 31 of the 41–55 airstrikes in 2012, the second-highest year of strikes, were drone strikes. These caused 6–8 estimated civilian deaths, or 3% of all deaths, but, taking the high end of this estimate, eight of the 31 strikes, or 26%, caused at least one civilian death. Confirmed drone strikes constituted all of the confirmed 22 airstrikes in 2013, 15 of the 17–19 strikes in 2014, 21 of estimated 21–22 strikes in 2015, and 25 of 37 in 2016. These resulted in an estimated 31–58 civilian deaths in those years, or 12% of all deaths, with the percentage declining from 27% in 2013, to 10% in 2014, to 7% in 2015 to 0% in 2016. The percentage of strikes causing civilian deaths from drone strikes also declined over this period from 35% in 2013, to 27% in 2014, to 14% in 2015, to 0% in 2016.

Estimates of airstrikes in deaths in Somalia from 2007 to 2020 range from NA's estimate of 262 strikes to BIJ's estimate of 203 confirmed strikes. It should be noted that BIJ spreadsheets indicate an additional 110 "possible" US airstrikes, but there was not sufficient evidence to attribute them to the US. Estimates of civilian deaths over this period range from 7 to 77.5, with the percentage of deaths that were civilians estimated at 5% by NA and 3% by BIJ.

It also should be noted that when Airwars took over providing estimates from BIJ, it reviewed and revised BIJ data for Somalia. It has published the results of this process for 2007–2020, although its estimates are for *both* air and ground strikes that are declared, which total 249. Airwars notes, however, "While AFRICOM now declares almost all military airstrikes in Somalia it rarely reports ground actions."[115] It is thus reasonable to assume that most of the estimated 249 strikes are airstrikes. Airwars estimates that there were 2340 deaths from strikes over this period, of which 70–143, or 4.5%, were civilians. Airwars says that the civilian figure reflects "[l]ocally reported civilian deaths from declared or likely US Forces actions in Somalia for which the reporting was assessed by Airwars as Fair, or have been Confirmed by US Forces."[116] It estimated that 30 of 249 strikes, or 12%, resulted in civilian deaths.

The most intensive period of strikes in Somalia has been from 2017 to 2020, with NA estimating 262 strikes, BIJ 155, and LWJ 141 during that time. LWJ does not have estimates of civilian deaths, but NA estimates that 15 of 1061 deaths, or 1.4%, were civilians during this period, while BIJ estimates that civilian deaths ranged from 2 to 52 of total estimated deaths between 891 and 931. The average of these estimates results in 27 civilian deaths out of 881 total deaths, or 3%. NA estimated that eight of 192 strikes, or 4%, resulted in civilian deaths, while BIJ estimated that 12 of 155 strikes, or 8%, did so. Airwars' revision of BIJ estimates is not broken out by year.

The inability to differentiate drone strikes from other airstrikes in some datasets complicates analysis. Stepping back to review all strikes in the three countries from 2002 to 2020, however, indicates that since 2013 there has been a significant decline in the percentage of strike casualties who are civilians. From 2002 to 2012, NA estimates that 11.2% of deaths were of civilians, while BIJ's estimate is 23.3%.[117] By contrast, NA estimates that from 2013 to 2020, 3.5% of deaths were of civilians, and BIJ's estimate is 4.4%. This suggests that the standard of near certainty of no civilian casualties for strikes outside war zones in the 2013 PPG has made at least some difference, along with the improvements in US targeting practices as Barela and Plaw maintain.

The somewhat higher rates of civilian deaths from 2017 to 2020 during the Trump administration compared to 2013–2016 also suggest that the importance that an administration places on minimizing civilian casualties may make a difference. NA and BIJ provided estimates of civilian deaths for 2013–2020, while LWJ provided them only through 2016. From 2013 through the end of the Obama administration, NA estimated that 2.9% of deaths were civilians, and BIJ estimated 4.1%. For 2017 through 2020, NA's estimate increased to 4.2% and BIJ's slightly increased to 4.2%.

It is important to keep some caveats in mind when considering all these estimates. First, they are *estimates*. As this chapter has described, there are many challenges in attempting to gather accurate detailed information about targeted strikes, including the very fact that they have occurred. This is especially the case for strikes conducted by the CIA, which will virtually never be confirmed by the US. Second, organizations some-times use slightly different categories for their estimates, which can make comparisons difficult. Third, strikes in Yemen and Somalia sometimes have been used in support of major military offenses on active battle-fields, which can make it difficult to know exactly how many strikes in those countries have been targeting operations outside of war zones. All this means that we should not assume that these figures provide a precise count of civilian deaths. It may be more useful instead to focus on their orders of magnitude. Nonetheless, these estimates by NGOs are the best and most complete information we have about targeted strikes outside war zones over the last two decades.

It is also important to underscore that this chapter discusses estimates of civilian deaths from strikes only in Pakistan, Yemen, and Somalia, since the focus of the book is on targeted strikes as a counterterrorism measure outside active war zones. It therefore does not include figures, nor does it offer conclusions, on civilian deaths from strikes that have been conducted in areas of intense hostilities such as Afghanistan, Iraq, Syria, and Libya. Airwars is an especially thorough source of information on such operations.[118]

As the discussion below describes, official US estimates of civilian deaths from strikes outside war zones are consistently lower than estimates by these organizations. The US on occasion has had to acknowledge civilian deaths that it previously denied because of evidence presented by such organizations. The US does not provide information that enables rigorous analysis of the reasons for discrepancies. All this makes it diffi-cult to know how accurately *any* estimates capture the number of civilian casualties from targeted strikes. It also raises questions about whether the US is conducting strikes in a way that enables it to realize its claim of precision, and its standard of near certainty of no civilian casualties.

US Government Estimates

On July 1, 2016, the same day as President Obama's Executive Order on civilian casualties, the DNI issued a report on operations outside areas of active hostilities that covered January 20, 2009–December 31, 2015.[119] Relevant figures in this report are set forth in Table 9.2 in the Appendix at the end of this chapter. Areas outside of active hostilities were deemed those other than Afghanistan, Iraq, Syria, and Libya.[120] The report indi-cated that 473 strikes against terrorist targets had occurred during this period, resulting in a range of combatant deaths from 2372 to 2581. Noncombatant deaths were estimated at between 64 and 116.[121] The report stated that the latter figure included deaths "for which there is an insufficient basis for assessing that the deceased is a combatant."[122] Taking the averages of the figures, this reflected an estimate that civilian deaths were 7.2% of total deaths during this period.

The report acknowledged differences between its estimates and those by NGOs. The tables at the end of the chapter indicate that NA estimated 249 civilian deaths during this period, while BIJ estimated between 317 and 757. The LWJ estimate of a 6.9% civilian casualty rate was closest to the DNI estimate, while NA's was 8% and BIJ was considerably higher at 28.5%.

The DNI report suggested reasons for the discrepancies. First, it said, the US uses methodologies that have been refined over the years in "non-permissive environments" and relies on information generally unavailable to NGOs.[123] Second, US post-strike review involves "collection and analysis of multiple sources of intelligence before, during, and after a strike," which provides a unique combination of sources also unavailable to NGOs. Finally, it suggested, some allegations may reflect deliberate misinformation by terrorist groups and others in local media reports on which some NGOs rely.[124]

Sarah Knuckey of the Columbia Law School Human Rights Clinic welcomed the report as an important step that could permit a meaningful discussion of civilian casualties, and as noteworthy because the US explicitly acknowledged civilian deaths caused by its operations.[125] She noted, however, that the figures were not disaggregated by year or location, nor did the report include any information on specific cases that would permit comparison with estimates by other organizations. As a result, said Knuckey, "we have no way to know which strikes the US agrees entailed civilian deaths, or which they dispute, and why."[126]

The DNI issued a second report in January 2017 that indicated 53 strikes between January 1, 2016 and December 31, 2016.[127] It reported combatant deaths as between 431 and 441, and only one noncombatant death, reflecting a 0.2% civilian death rate. The report said, "No discrepancies were identified between post-strike assessments from the US government and credible reporting from nongovernmental organizations regarding noncombatant deaths resulting from the strikes."[128] NA estimated 2.5 civilian deaths during this period, while BIJ estimated from 3 to 6.

The US Deprtment of Defense (DOD) has also provided information on civilian casualties in recent years in accordance with Congressional direction. It thus far has issued annual reports on operations occurring from 2017 to 2020, relevant figures from which are set forth in Table 9.3 at the end of this chapter. These cover activities in Iraq, Syria, Afghanistan, Yemen, Somalia, and Libya. The reports for 2018–2020 provide information on the date and location of incidents, and whether air or ground operations were involved. Reports do not identify which casualties occurred from targeted strikes. It seems reasonable, however, to assume that many air operations in Yemen and Somalia include targeted strikes outside of active combat, although the US used strikes to support a United Arab Emirates military offensive in Yemen in 2017 and 2018.

In addition, the report on activities in 2017 mentioned four airstrikes in Afghanistan that killed leaders of either the Taliban or ISIS. It is conceivable that additional targeted strikes occurred there or in other countries during the years covered by the reports, but the reports do not provide such information.

Some have criticized the DOD for consistently understating the amount of civilian casualties compared to outside estimates.[129] Regarding the report on 2020 operations, for instance, Annie Shiel of CIVIC and Chris Woods of Airwars observe that the most conservative non-US estimate of civilian fatalities across five countries in 2020 was 102, but DOD reported only 23.[130] DOD figures for Afghanistan also are much lower than those of the United Nations Assistance Mission for Afghanistan (UNAMA). UNAMA estimated that pro-government airstrikes by international coalition forces in Afghanistan resulted in 393 civilian deaths in 2018, compared to 76 in the 2018 DOD report; 546 in 2019, compared to the DOD estimate of 108; and 83 through September 2020, compared to the DOD estimate for 2020 of 20.[131]

Some of the discrepancies could be because DOD distinguishes between US and other coalition partner operations, although US strikes are understood to represent the great majority of operations. With respect to Iraq and Syria, for instance, the reports on operations in 2017 and 2018 say that the US considered all civilian casualties to be the combined result of coalition action, and jointly attributable to coalition members.[132] The reports on operations for 2019 and 2020, however, say that they list only "civilian casualties attributed to the use of US weapons."[133] There is no discussion of this issue, however, with regard to operations in Afghanistan.

DOD reports explain discrepancies between estimates by DOD and other organizations. Concerning UNAMA specifically, the report on 2017 operations mentions an April 2018 report by the NATO Resolute Support Mission that addressed differences between DOD and UNAMA figures. That report said that investigation determined that "in several of the cases where casualties were alleged to be from airstrikes, no aerial platforms were nearby at the time, and reported explosions may have resulted from concealed IEDs or insurgents firing rockets and mortars."[134] In other instances, military investigators "have access to surveillance information that gives them confidence that civilians were not present at the scene of the strike."[135]

More generally, the report on 2020 operations says, "NGOs and media outlets often use different types of information and methodologies than DOD to assess whether civilian casualties have occurred. Some organizations conduct on-the-ground assessments and interviews, while others rely heavily on media reporting. Although such information can be valuable, this information alone can be incomplete, and it is important to ensure its validity."[136] The report said that DOD attempts to incorporate all information from outside sources, "as well as additional information and tools that are not available to other organizations – such as operational planning data and intelligence sources."[137]

Some argue that DoD's standard for evaluating the credibility of external allegations places an unduly onerous burden on those making allegations.[138] Other note that DOD often does not conduct site visits or interview local residents, as do many outside groups.[139] There is also reason to believe that initial DOD estimates may not take into account all available information. The report on operations in 2020, for instance, confirmed an additional 65 civilian deaths and 22 injuries for the years 2017–2019 based on review of external casualty allegations. This may reflect residual DOD resistance to fully collaborating with NGOs, given that its relationship with outside organizations was seen as adversarial for several years.

US estimates of civilian casualties from strikes outside war zones thus are consistently lower than those of other organizations, and the information that the US provides makes it difficult to assess reasons for these discrepancies. There is also reason to believe that the US does not draw as extensively as it could on all sources of information. The result has been skepticism about the accuracy of US figures, and continuing frustration about the difficulty of arriving at accurate casualty estimates.

CONCLUSION

Gaining a complete understanding of the number of civilian casualties from US targeted strikes outside war zones is no easy matter. The best data available suggest that there were significant casualties during the first several years in which the US conducted targeted strikes, which occurred mainly in Pakistan. Civilian casualties, generally have declined since 2013, when the US adopted the standard of near certainty of no civilian casualties, and as it has refined its targeting process.

Keeping in mind caveats about the complete accuracy of any figures, estimates by the major NGOs of civilian deaths from strikes outside war zones do not support claims that such strikes kill massive amounts of civilians, or that they kill more civilians than militants. The only exception to this is Pakistan Body Count (PBC), whose estimates for Pakistan are dramatically higher than those of other organizations. As I have described above, while PBC's figures underscore that estimates are based on different sources of data and assumptions, there is reason to be cautious about their accuracy. BIJ, for instance, has never been able to replicate casualty figures anywhere near as high as those of PBC, despite the fact that BIJ relies heavily on local sources in all strike locations, sometimes conducts its own investigations, and has many years of experience.

Some observers claim that strikes outside war zones are disproportionate based on a comparison of the number of leaders who are killed with the number of civilian deaths.[140] This is misleading, however, because strikes target not only leaders but mid-level commanders, persons with specialized skills, and other operatives. As the tables in the Appendix indicate, this means that there are many fewer civilians than militants who have been killed by strikes, with the percentage decreasing in the last several years. NA, for instance, estimates that strikes in Pakistan from 2004 to 2018 killed 95 leaders; strikes in Yemen from 2009 to 2020 killed 89 leaders; and strikes in Somalia from 2007 to October 2021 killed 33 leaders.[141] NA also estimates, however, that 3.5% of deaths since 2013 have been civilians. BIJ's estimate is 4.4%.

At the same time, the NA and BIJ estimates of civilian deaths are not zero, investigations have documented deaths in cases in which the US has been unaware of them, and US casualty estimates regularly are lower than those of other organizations. All this suggests that the US is not consistently complying with its own requirement of near certainty of no civilian casualties for strikes outside war zones. It also suggests that the US may not be fully informed about the impacts of strikes on civilians, which is a crucial requirement for avoiding and minimizing harm to civilians. This raises questions about the credibility of the claim of drone strike precision outside war zones. It also raises questions about the magnitude of civilian casualties from strikes inside war zones, although that is not the focus of this book.

The next chapter examines the claim of strike precision in more detail. It describes the various components of a drone strike that can affect both its precision in hitting a target and its risk of causing civilian casualties. It then discusses the broader targeting, investigation, analysis, and reporting system within which these components are embedded, which influences the likelihood that a strike will cause casualties. As the chapter describes, the US periodically has sought to refine this system to reduce civilian casualties, and has accomplished this goal in some cases. These efforts largely have been self-contained, however, and have not been institutionalized across all kinetic operations. The chapter concludes by discussing what would be necessary to minimize civilian casualties by fully capitalizing on this system's potential for precision.

Appendix

Civilian Casualty Data

NA: New America
LWJ: Long War Journal
BIJ: Bureau of Investigative Journalism
Methodology

NA's description of its methodology is at https://www.newamerica.org/international-security/reports/americas-counterterrorism-wars/methodology/#counting-the-strikes. With respect to the three countries that are the focus of this book, it tracks casualties from drone strikes in Pakistan, and from air and ground operations in Yemen and Somalia. It does not itself collect data on deaths, but counts those reported in media sources that it considers credible, which include major international wire services, leading Pakistani newspapers, prominent South Asian and

Middle Eastern TV networks, and Western media outlets with extensive reporting capabilities in Pakistan. The organization says, "There must be at least two credible media sources verifying a strike in order for it to be added to our databases. In Yemen, where reporting on strikes is often more sparse, we include strikes with one major news outlet reporting that it occurred."

NA separates casualties into three categories: "militant," "civilian," and "unknown." It characterizes persons as militants when "two or more news reports label the dead as 'militants,' while others call them 'people' or some other neutral term." It considers them civilians when "two or more media outlets explicitly refer to the dead as 'civilians,' 'women,' or 'children'." Finally, it characterizes casualties as unknowns when "a majority of reports do not refer to the dead as 'civilians,' 'women,' or 'children,' but one media outlet does" or when "the various media reports are [too] contradictory" to make a judgment. NA says that it resolves any conflicts that it encounters in the following way. When "a media report cites some 'civilians/women/children' but does not specify how many, and no other media sources provide a specific total, [it] report[s] one third of the total victims referenced in that source as 'civilians' or 'unknowns'."

LWJ tracked casualties from airstrikes in Pakistan, Yemen, and Somalia through 2016. It has continued to count strikes in those countries since then, but has discontinued casualty estimates. LWJ does not provide detailed information on its methodology. The organization says that "it is possible to get a rough estimate of civilian casualties by adding up the number of civilians reported killed from the media accounts of each attack." https://www.longwarjournal.org/archives/2010/01/analysis_us_air_camp.php.

BIJ initially compiled data on drone strike casualties in Pakistan from 2004 onward, and casualties from drone strikes, "airstrikes, missile attacks and ground operations" in Yemen and in Somalia. The organization says that its data reflect reliance on a larger number of international and local media sources than NA or LWJ uses. It also says that it also relies on information from field investigations, from WikiLeaks, and from "publicly available documents such as lawsuits." It says:

> Where the reporting is vague but appears to indicate civilian casualties, we will include the line "Possible reported civilian casualties" in that strike's casualty figures in the Timeline . . .Where the reporting is more specific, but conflicts with other reports or is from a single source, we use the

formula 0-X in our count of civilian deaths, with X referring to the highest reported number of civilian casualties. . . .This ensures that the minimum total number of reported civilian deaths is unchanged but the maximum total incorporates these possible civilian deaths. https://www.thebureauinv estigates.com/stories/2017-01-01/drone-wars-the-full-data

In April 2019, Airwars took over from BIJ the task of monitoring US strikes in Pakistan, Somalia, and Yemen. Drawing on multiple sources with a significant emphasis on local language reporting, Airwars "track[s] and assess[es] claims of civilian non-combatant casualties and 'friendly fire' deaths from international military actions – primarily air and artillery strikes." (Airwars, https://airwars.org/) It classifies possible civilian casualties based on the number of reports, credibility of sources, and quality of supporting evidence as those that are (1) confirmed; those for which evidence is (2) fair, (3) weak, or (4) contested; (5) reports that are discounted; and (6) events in which there were no civilian casualties.

Pakistan Body Count describes its methodology in this way: "Our unique database, Pakistan Drone Count (PDC), combines data from Pakistan Body Count with information from newspapers, media reports, think tank analyses, and personal contacts in media and law enforcement agencies. We provide a count of the number of people killed and injured in drone strikes, including those who died later in hospitals or homes due to injuries caused or aggravated by the strikes."[142] "If no evidence of a particular group affiliation is found, the dead or injured are counted as civilians."[143]

See Tables 9.1, 9.2, 9.3, 9.4, and 9.5.

Table 9.1 Estimates of US strikes and fatalities

Pakistan

NA	Number of drone strikes[144]	Total deaths	Civilian deaths	% Deaths that are civilians[145]	Strikes with civilian deaths[146]	% Strikes with civilian deaths
Total	414	3034	274	9	29	7
2004	1	7	1[147]	14	1	100
2005	3	15	4[148]	27	1[149]	33
2006	2	94	93	99	2	100
2007	4	62.5	0[150]	0	0	0
2008	36	285	28.5[151]	10	5	14
2009	54	542	61.5[152]	11	6	11
2010	122	830.5	16.5[153]	2	3	2
2011	70	503.5	55.5[154]	11	5	7
2012	48	294.5	6[155]	2	2	4
2013	26	142.5	4	3	1	4
2014	22	142.5	0	0	0	0
2015	10	55	2	4	1	10
2016	3	9.5	0	0	0	0
2017	8	39.5	2[156]	5	2	25
2018	5	11	0	0	0	0
2019	0	0	0	0	0	0
2020	0	0	0	0	0	0

LWJ	Number of air strikes	Total deaths	Civilian deaths	% Deaths that are civilians[157]	Strikes with civilian deaths[158]	% Strikes with civilian deaths
Total	404	2957	159	5	–	–
2004[159]	1	0	0	0		
2005	2	1	0	0		

(continued)

Table 9.1 (continued)

Pakistan

	Number of drone strikes[161]	Total deaths	Civilian deaths	% Deaths that are civilians[162]	Strikes with civilian deaths[163]	% Strikes with civilian deaths[164]
2006	3	142	20	14		
2007	5	73	0	0		
2008	35	317	31	10		
2009	53	506	43	8		
2010	117	815	14	2		
2011	64	435	30	7		
2012	46	304	4	1		
2013	28	137	14	10		
2014	24	152	0	0		
2015	11	65	3	5		
2016	3	10	0	0		
2017[160]	8	–	–	–		
2018	4	–	–	–		
2019	0	–	–	–		
2020	0	–	–	–		
2021	0	–	–	–		
BIJ	Number of drone strikes[161]	Total deaths	Civilian deaths	% Deaths that are civilians[162]	Strikes with civilian deaths[163]	% Strikes with civilian deaths[164]
Total	430	2515–4026	424–969	21	127	30[164]
2004	1	6–8	2	29	1	100
2005	3	16	5–11	50	2	67
2006	2	94–105	90–100	95	2	100
2007	5	36–56	11–46	62	4	80
2008	38	252–401	59–173	36	15	39
2009	54	471–753	100–210	25	26	48
2010	128	755–1108	89–197	15	40	31

(continued)

Table 9.1 (continued)

Pakistan

2011	75	362–666	20	52–152	19	25
2012	50	212–410	12	13–63	11	22
2013	27	109–195	1	0–4	2	7
2014	25	115–186	1	0–2	1	4
2015	13	60–85	5	2–5	2	15
2016	3	11–12	9	1	1	33
2017	5	15–22	8	0–3	1	20
2018	1	1–3	0	0	0	0
2019	0	0	0	0	0	0
2020	0	0	0	0^{165}	0	0

Pakistan Body Count

Year	Number of drone strikes	Total deaths	Civilian deaths	% Strikes with civilian deaths
Total	588	1946–3661	1306–2544	69
2004	1	5	0–4	20
2005	2	7	0–2	21
2006	3	0–100	0–100	100
2007	6	25–46	25–42	97
2008	55	214–368	149–264	71
2009	57	335–633	256–531	43
2010	123	561–993	458–849	51
2011	80	347–578	254–440	75
2012	104	155–345	94–233	65
2013	56	108–154	42–59	39
2014	52	119–230	0–9	3
2015	28	36–136	13–14	16
2016	6	2–10	1	17

(continued)

Table 9.1 (continued)

Pakistan Body Count

2017	15		44–53	5	10	

Yemen

NA	Number of air strikes[166]	Total deaths[167]	Civilian deaths	% Deaths that are civilian	Strikes with civilians deaths[168]	% Strikes with civilian deaths
Total	374	1537	137	9	25	7
2002	1	6	0	0	0	0
2009	2	95	41	43	1	50
2010	2	7	4.5	64	1	50
2011	12	111.5	4[169]	4	1	8
2012	56	475	16[170]	3	4	7
2013	25	126	19[171]	15	5	20
2014	18	144.5	10	7	2	10
2015	24	91	0[172]	0	0	0
2016	43	193	0[173]	0	0	0
2017	130[174]	230	27.5[175]	12	4	3
2018	41	77	14[176]	18	6	14
2019	11	21	1[177]	5	1	9
2020	4	4.5	0	0	0	0

LWJ	Number of air strikes	Total deaths	Civilian deaths	% Deaths that are civilian	Strikes with civilians killed[178]	% Strikes with civilian deaths
Total	328	875	105	12	–	–
2002[179]	1	6	0	0		
2009	2	55	41	75		
2010	4	16	6	38		

(continued)

Table 9.1 (continued)

Yemen

Yemen	Confirmed air strikes[181]	Total deaths	Civilian deaths	% Deaths that are civilian	Strikes with civilians killed[182]	% Strikes with civilians killed
2011	10	81	0	0		
2012	41	225	35	16		
2013	26	116	17	15		
2014	23	144	6	4		
2015	15	76	0	0		
2016	31	156	0	0		
2017[180]	131	—	—	—		
2018	36	—	—	—		
2019	8	—	—	—		
2020	0	—	—	—		
BIJ	**Confirmed air strikes[181]**	**Total deaths**	**Civilian deaths**	**% Deaths that are civilian**	**Strikes with civilians killed[182]**	**% Strikes with civilians killed**
Total	326–346	898–1258	91–142	11	34	10
2002	1	6	0	0	0	0
2009	2	30–34	0	0	0	50
2010	2	5–7	3–4	58	1	50
2011	13–16	76–132	36	35	3	21
2012	41–55	217–279	19–24	9	7	15
2013	22	79–129	17–37	26	8	36
2014	17–19	90–127	4–9	6	3	17
2015	21–22	75–103	1–7	4	3	14
2016	37	153–209	0	0	0	0
2017	127	135–184	3–10	4	2	2
2018	36	31–42	8–15	32	7	19
2019	8	1–6	0	0	0	0
2020	0	0	0	0	0	0

(continued)

Table 9.1 (continued)

Yemen

BIJ	Confirmed drone strikes[183]	Total deaths	Civilian deaths	% Deaths that are civilian	Strikes with civilian deaths	% Strikes with civilian deaths
Total	**124**	**547–801**	**71–100**	**13**	**25**	**20**
2002	1	6	0	0	0	0
2011	8	46–102	34	23	2	25
2012	31	204–262	6–8	3	8	26
2013	22	74–124	17–37	27	8	35
2014	15	93–127	9–14	10	4	27
2015	21	69–99	5–7	7	3	14
2016[184]	25	55–81	0	0	0	0

Somalia

NA	Number of air strikes[185]	Total deaths	Civilian deaths	% Deaths that are civilian	Strikes with civilian deaths[186]	% Strikes with civilian deaths
Total	**262**	**1682.5**	**77.5**	**5**	**16**	**6**
2007	5	71.5	44[187]	50	2	50
2008	2	22	3[188]	14	1	0
2009	1	7.5	0	0	0	
2011	11	28.5	7.5	26	1	50
2012	2	7	0.5	7	1	0
2013	2	11.5	0[189]	0	0	33
2014	3	15	1	7	1	0
2015	8	85.5	0	0	0	
2016	16	279	2.5[190]	1	2	

(continued)

Table 9.1 (continued)

Somalia

	Number of air strikes[196]	Total deaths	Civilian deaths	% Deaths that are civilian	Strikes with civilian deaths[197]	% Strikes with civilian deaths
2017	34	247.5	5[191]	2	1	3
2018	43	371.5	4[192]	1	3	7
2019	64	359.5	1[193]	0	0	0
2020	51	82.5	5[194]	9	4	8
2021	11[195]	23.5	0.5	2	1	9

LWJ	Number of air strikes[196]	Total deaths	Civilian deaths	% Deaths that are civilian	Strikes with civilian deaths[197]	% Strikes with civilian deaths
Total	141	[198]	—	—	—	—
2017[199]	35	—	—	—	—	
2018	47	—	—	—	—	
2019	59	—	—	—	—	
2020	0	—	—	—	—	

BIJ	Confirmed air strikes[200]	Total deaths	Civilian deaths	% Deaths that are civilian	Strikes with civilian deaths[201]	% Strikes with civilian deaths
Total	203	1170–1336	7–68	3	17	8
2007	3	21–28	2	8	0	0
2008	0	0	0	0	0	0
2009	1	2–6	0	0	0	0
2010	0	0	0	0	0	0
2011	1	2	0	0	1	50
2012	2	4–8	0–1	8	0	0
2013	1	2–3	0	0	1	33
2014	3	10–18	0–2	7	1	9
2015	11	20–33	0–4	8	1	9
2016	14	204–292	3–5	2	2	14
2017	35	216–242	0–15	3	3	9

(continued)

Table 9.1 (continued)

Somalia

	Confirmed drone strikes[202]	Total deaths	Civilian deaths	% Deaths that are civilian	Strikes with civilian deaths	% Strikes with civilian deaths
2018	45	335–336	2–8	1	4	9
2019	63	326–338	0–29	4	5	8
2020	12	14–15	0–2	10	2	17
BIJ	Confirmed drone strikes[202]	Total deaths	Civilian deaths	% Deaths that are civilian	Strikes with civilian deaths	% Strikes with civilian deaths
Total	29	77–135	5–13	8	4	14
2011	1	2	0	0	0	0
2012	2	4–8	0–1	8	1	50
2013	1	2–3	0	0	0	0
2014	3	10–20	2–5	23	1	33
2015	11	20–37	0–4	7	1	9
2016[203]	11	39–65	3	3	1	9

Airwars	Declared air and ground strikes	Total killed	Civilian deaths	% Deaths that are civilian	Strikes with civilian deaths	% Strikes with civilian deaths
2007–2020	249[204]	2320[205]	70–143	4.5	30	12

Table 9.2 US Director of National Intelligence Report on US counterterrorism strikes outside areas of active hostilities

Period	Strikes	Combatant deaths	Noncombatant deaths
Jan. 20, 2009–Dec. 31, 2015	473	2372–2581	64–116
Jan. 1, 2016–Dec. 31, 2016	53	431–441	1

Table 9.3 US Department of Defense Reports on civilian casualties in connection with US military operations

Year	Countries	Civilian deaths	Civilian injuries
2017	Iraq, Syria, Afghanistan, Yemen[206]	499	169

Year	Civilian deaths	Civilian injuries
Iraq and Syria[207]		
2018	42	7
2019	22	13
2020	1	0
Afghanistan[208]		
2018	76	58
2019	108	75
2020	20	3
Somalia[209]		
2018	2	0
2019	2	3
2020	1	5
Yemen		
2020	1	0

Table 9.4 BIJ estimates of injuries[210]

Year	Number of strikes[211]	Estimated injuries
Afghanistan		
2015	235–236	142–147
2016	1071	196–252
2017	2609–2611	162–298
2018	1985–1986	106–166
2019	7167	47–846
2020	1012	0–32
Total	14,079–14,083	653–1741
Pakistan		
2004	1	1
2005	3	1
2006	2	3
2007	5	20–37
2008	38	146–228
2009	54	266–404
2010	128	351–428
2011	75	158–236
2012	50	100–212
2013	27	43–89
2014	25	44–67
2015	13	25–32
2016	3	3–6
2017	5	1–5
2018	1	0
Total	**430**	**1161–1749**
Somalia		
2007	3	5–8
2008	0	0
2009	1	2
2010	0	0
2011	1	2–3
2012	2	0
2013	1	0
2014	3	0–1
2015	11	0–4
2016	14	3–16
2017	35	11–19
2018	45	21–11
2019	63	0–2
2020	12	2–4

(continued)

Table 9.4 (continued)

Year	Number of strikes[211]	Estimated injuries
Total	**191**	**46–81**
Yemen		
2002	1	0
2003	0	0
2004	0	0
2005	0	0
2006	0	0
2007	0	0
2008	0	0
2009	1	0
2010	2	2–3
2011	13	14–41
2012	41	55–125
2013	22	12–40
2014	17	9–20
2015	21	8
2016	37	6–11
2017	127	0
2018	36	0–3
2019	8	0
2020	0	0
Total	**326–346**	**106–251**

Table 9.5 Pakistan body count estimates of injuries in Pakistan[212]

Year	Estimated injuries
2004	0
2005	2
2006	4
2007	30
2008	58–154
2009	103–331
2010	115–413
2011	22–154
2012	22–98
2013	40–68
2014	27–47
2015	6–17
2016	1
2017	2
Total	**432–1321**

NOTES

1. Medact. (2012). *Drones: The physical and psychological implications of a global theatre of war*, 6. https://www.medact.org/wp-content/uploads/2012/10/report-drones-2012.pdf.
2. Center for Civilians in Conflict (CIVIC) & Columbia Law School Human Rights Clinic. (2012). *The civilian impact of drones: Unexamined costs, unanswered questions*, 21. https://web.law.columbia.edu/sites/default/files/microsites/human-rights-institute/files/The%20Civilian%20Impact%20of%20Drones.pdf.
3. Center for Civilians in Conflict. (2010). *Civilian harm and conflict in Northwest Pakistan*, 41. https://civiliansinconflict.org/wp-content/uploads/2017/09/Pakistan_Report_2010_2013.pdf.
4. Cavallero, J., Sonnenberg, S., & Knuckey, S. (2012, September 25). *Living under drones: Death, injury and trauma to civilians from US drone practices in Pakistan*. International Human Rights and Conflict Resolution Clinic, Stanford Law School, NYU School of Law, & Global Justice Clinic, 78. https://law.stanford.edu/wp-content/uploads/sites/default/files/publication/313671/doc/slspublic/Stanford_NYU_LIVING_UNDER_DRONES.pdf.
5. CIVIC, 2010, 43.
6. Shinwari, N. A. (2011). *Understanding FATA: Attitudes towards governance, religion and society in Pakistan's Federally Administered Tribal Areas* (Vol. V). Community Appraisal & Motivation Programme. http://crossasia-repository.ub.uni-heidelberg.de/2715/1/Understanding_FATA_Vol_V_11.pdf.
7. Cavallero, et al., 89.
8. CIVIC, 2010, 44.
9. Shinwari.
10. CIVIC, 2010, 38.
11. Amnesty International, 2013, 36.
12. Cavarello, et al., 40.
13. Ross, A. K., Serle, J., & Wills, T. (2014). *Tracking drone strikes in Afghanistan: A scoping study*. Bureau of Investigative Journalism, 6. https://v1.thebureauinvestigates.com/wp-content/uploads/2014/07/TBIJ-Afghanistan-Report.pdf.
14. Ross, 2014.
15. Id.
16. United States Department of Defense. (2016). Law of War Manual, ¶4.18.4.1. https://tjaglcspublic.army.mil/documents/27431/61281/DoD+Law+of+War+Manual+-+June+2015+Updated+Dec+2016/5a0 2f6f8-eff3-4e79-a46f-9cd7aac74a95.

17. International Committee of the Red Cross. (2009). *Interpretive guidance on the notion of direct participation in hostilities under international humanitarian law*, 33–34. https://www.icrc.org/en/doc/assets/files/other/icrc-002-0990.pdf.
18. Becker & Shane.
19. White House. (2013b). Fact Sheet, U.S. policy standards and procedures for the use of force in counterterrorism operations outside the United States and areas of active hostilities, May 23, 2013, Fact Sheet, p. 2, note 1.
20. CIVIC & Columbia, 33.
21. A covert operation is one in which a country seeks to avoid having an activity attributed to it, while a clandestine operation is one in which a country seeks to keep the operation secret.
22. CIVIC, 2010.
23. Id. 31.
24. Dilanian, K. (2011, February 22). CIA drones may be avoiding Pakistani civilians. *Los Angeles Times*. https://www.latimes.com/world/la-xpm-2011-feb-22-la-fg-drone-strikes-20110222-story.html.
25. Id.
26. Dilanian, K. (2011, June 29). U.S. counter-terrorism strategy to rely on surgical strikes, unmanned drones. *Los Angeles Times*. https://www.latimes.com/politics/la-xpm-2011-jun-29-la-pn-al-qaeda-strategy-201 10629-story.html.
27. Greenwald, G. (2011, July 19). *New study proves falsity of John Brennan's drone claims*. Salon. https://www.salon.com/2011/07/19/drones/.
28. Id.
29. Shane, S. (2011, August 11). C.I.A. is disputed on civilian toll in drone strikes. *The New York Times*. https://www.nytimes.com/2011/08/12/world/asia/12drones.html.
30. Becker, J., & Shane, S. (2012, May 29). Secret 'kill list' tests Obama's principles. *The New York Times*. https://www.nytimes.com/2012/05/29/world/obamas-leadership-in-war-on-al-qaeda.html.
31. White House. (2013, May 23b).
32. White House. (2013, May 23b). *Remarks by the President at the National Defense University*. https://obamawhitehouse.archives.gov/the-press-office/2013/05/23/remarks-president-national-defense-uni versity.
33. White House. (2013, May 23a), *Fact sheet: U.S. policy standards and procedures for the use of force in counterterrorism operations outside the United States and areas of active hostilities*. https://obamawhitehouse.archives.gov/the-press-office/2013/05/23/fact-sheet-us-policy-standa rds-and-procedures-use-force-counterterrorism.

34. White House. (2013, May 23b). *Remarks by the President at the National Defense University*. https://obamawhitehouse.archives.gov/the-press-office/2013/05/23/remarks-president-national-defense-uni versity.

35. Emmerson, B. (2013). *Report of the Special Rapporteur on the promotion and protection of human rights and fundamental freedoms while countering terrorism*. U.N. Human Rights Council. https://digitallibrary.un.org/record/751002?ln=en.

36. Id. 8.

37. Id.

38. Lewis, L., & Holewinski, S. (2013). Changing of the guard: Civilian protection for an evolving military. *Prism, 4*(2), 57–66. https://cco.ndu.edu/Portals/96/Documents/prism/prism_4-2/prism57-66_Lewis_and_Holewinski.pdf.

39. Human Rights Watch. (2013, October 22). *"Between a drone and Al-Qaeda:" The civilian cost of US targeted killings in Yemen*. https://www.hrw.org/report/2013/10/22/between-drone-and-al-qaeda/civ ilian-cost-us-targeted-killings-yemen.

40. Amnesty International. (2013, October). *"Will I be next?": US drone strikes in Pakistan*. https://www.amnestyusa.org/files/asa330132 013en.pdf.

41. Woods, C. (2013, July 22). *Leaked Pakistani report confirms high civilian death toll in CIA drone strikes*. Bureau of Investigative Journalism. https://www.thebureauinvestigates.com/stories/2013-07-22/leaked-pakistani-report-confirms-high-civilian-death-toll-in-cia-drone-str ikes.

42. Id.

43. BIJ noted this response in its 2014 follow-up report based on additional documentary reports on strikes in Pakistan. Ross, A. (2014, January 29). *Leaked official document records 330 drone strikes in Pakistan*. Bureau of Investigative Journalism. https://www.thebureauinvestigates. com/stories/2014-01-29/leaked-official-document-records-330-drone-strikes-in-pakistan.

44. Ross. The Pakistani document was entitled "Details of Attacks by NATO Forces/Predators in FATA." A copy is on file with the author.

45. Ross.

46. Id.

47. Id.

48. Emmerson, B. (2014). *Report of the Special Rapporteur on the promotion and protection of human rights and fundamental freedoms while countering terrorism* (¶33). https://digitallibrary.un.org/record/766937? ln=en.

49. Open Society Justice Initiative. (2015). *Death by drone: Civilian harm caused by US targeted killings in Yemen*, 6. https://www.justiceinitiative. org/uploads/1284eb37-f380-4400-9242-936a15e4de6c/death-drones-report-eng-20150413.pdf.
50. Id.
51. Zenko, M., & Wolf, A. M. (2016, April 25). Drones kill more civilians than pilots do. *Foreign Policy*. https://foreignpolicy.com/2016/04/25/ drones-kill-more-civilians-than-pilots-do/.
52. Id.
53. Id.
54. Id.
55. White House. (2016, July 1). *Executive order—United States policy on pre- and post-strike measures to address civilian casualties in U.S. operations involving the use of force*. https://obamawhitehouse.archives. gov/the-press-office/2016/07/01/executive-order-united-states-pol icy-pre-and-post-strike-measures.
56. Id.
57. Barela, S. J., & Plaw, A. (2016, August). *The precision of drones: Problems with the new data and new claims*. https://www.e-ir.info/2016/08/ 23/the-precision-of-drones-problems-with-the-new-data-and-new-cla ims/.
58. Dilanian, K., Nichols, H., & Kube, C. (2017, March 14). Trump admin ups drone strikes, tolerates more civilian deaths: U.S. officials. *NBC News*. https://www.nbcnews.com/news/us-news/trump-admin-ups-drone-strikes-tolerates-more-civilian-deaths-n733336.
59. Savage, C., & Schmitt, E. (2017, March 12). Trump administration is said to be working to loosen counterterrorism rules. *The New York Times*. https://www.nytimes.com/2017/03/12/us/politics/trump-loo sen-counterterrorism-rules.html.
60. Id.
61. White House. (n.d.). *Principles, standards, and procedures for direct action against terrorist targets*. American Civil Liberties Union, 2. https://www.aclu.org/foia-document/psp-foia-document-april-30-2021.
62. Id. 4.
63. Id.
64. Id.
65. Savage, C. (2021, May 6). Trump's secret rules for drone strikes outside war zones are disclosed. *New York Times*. https://www.nytimes.com/ 2021/05/01/us/politics/trump-drone-strike-rules.html.
66. National Defense Authorization Act Fiscal Year 2018, § 1057(a). Pub. L. No. 115-91, 131 Stat. 1283. (2017). https://www.congress.gov/115/ plaws/publ91/PLAW-115publ91.pdf.

67. Id. §1057(b)(1).
68. Id. §1057 (b)(2)(E).
69. Id. §1057(c)(1).
70. Id. §1057(b)(4).
71. Khan, A., & Gopal, A. (2017, November 16). The uncounted. *New York Times.* https://www.nytimes.com/interactive/2017/11/16/mag azine/uncounted-civilian-casualties-iraq-airstrikes.html.
72. Id.
73. Id.
74. Id.
75. United States Department of Defense. (2017, February 13). *Combined joint task force, operation inherent resolve.* CIVCAS allegation closure report.
76. Id. 6.
77. Id.
78. Id. 3.
79. Id.
80. Id.
81. Khan & Ghopal.
82. National Defense Authorization Act Fiscal Year 2019, § 936. Pub. L. No. 115-232, 132 Stat. 1636. (2018). https://www.congress.gov/115/plaws/publ232/PLAW-115publ232.pdf.
83. Amnesty International. (2019). *The hidden US war in Somalia: Civilian casualties from airstrikes in Lower Shabelle.* https://www.amnesty.org/download/Documents/AFR5299522019ENGLISH.PDF.
84. Id. 6.
85. Id.
86. United States Africa Command. (2019, March 20). *Statement on the Amnesty International report.* Joint Chiefs of Staff. https://www.jcs.mil/Media/News/News-Display/Article/1790860/us-africa-com mand-statement-on-the-amnesty-international-report/.
87. Id.
88. Gibbons-Neff, T. (2019, April 5). U.S. acknowledges airstrike in Somalia caused civilian deaths. *The New York Times.* https://www.nytimes.com/2019/04/05/us/politics/us-civilians-somalia-airstrikes.html.
89. Id.
90. Id.
91. Szuba, J. (2020, March 31). Promising transparency, US Africa Command to begin reporting civilian casualty claims. *Defense Post.* https://www.thedefensepost.com/2020/03/31/us-africom-report-civ ilian-casualties/.

92. Mahanty, D. (2020, April 21). *Great expectations: AFRICOM's new quarterly report on civilian casualties.* Just security. https://www.justse curity.org/69785/great-expectations-africom-new-quarterly-report-on-civilian-casualties/.
93. Airwars. (2020, October). *Eroding transparency: US counterterrorism actions in Yemen under President Donald Trump.* https://airwars.org/wp-content/uploads/2020/10/Eroding-Transparency-Trump-in-Yemen.-Airwars-October-2020.pdf.
94. Mtwana for Human Rights. (2021, March). *Death falling from the sky: Civilian harm from the United States' use of lethal force in Yemen January 2017–January 2019.* https://mwatana.org/wp-content/uploads/2021/03/Death-Falling-from-the-Sky-22.pdf.
95. United States Central Command. (2021, April 20). *Letter to Ms. Radhya A-Mutawakel & Ms. Priyanka Motaparthy.* Mwtana for Human Rights. https://mwatana.org/wp-content/uploads/2021/06/CENTCOM-Mwatana-Response-4-20-2021.pdf.
96. Id. 1.
97. Khan, A. (2021, December 18). Hidden pentagon records reveal patterns of failure in deadly airstrikes. *New York Times.* https://www.nytimes.com/interactive/2021/12/18/us/airstrikes-pentagon-records-civilian-deaths.html; Khan, A. (2021, December 19). The human toll of America's air wars. *New York Times.* https://www.nytimes.com/2021/12/19/magazine/victims-airstrikes-middle-east-civilians.html.
98. Khan, December 18.
99. Id.
100. Phillips, D., Schmitt, E., & Mazzetti, M. (2021, December 12). Civilian deaths mounted as secret unit pounded ISIS. *New York Times.* https://www.nytimes.com/2021/12/12/us/civilian-deaths-war-isis.html; Phillips, D., & Schmitt, E. (2021, November 15). How the US hid an airstrike that killed dozens of civilians in Syria. *New York Times.* https://www.nytimes.com/2021/11/13/us/us-airstrikes-civilian-deaths.html.
101. Phillips, Schmitt, & Mazzetti.
102. Id.
103. Id.
104. Phillips & Schmitt.
105. Phillips, Schmitt, & Mazzetti.
106. Columbia Law School Human Rights Clinic. (2012, October). *Counting drone strike deaths.* https://web.law.columbia.edu/sites/default/files/microsites/human-rights-institute/files/COLUMBIACountingDronesFinal.pdf.
107. Singh, R. (2013, October 25). *Drone strikes kill innocent people. Why is it so hard to know how any?* New Republic. https://newrepublic.com/article/115353/civilian-casualties-drone-strikes-why-we-know-so-little.

108. Id.
109. Pakistan Body Count, Drone Strikes, Pakistan. https://www.kaggle.com/zusmani/pakistandroneattacks?select=PakistanDroneAttacksWith Temp+Ver+11+%28November+30+2017%29.csv.
110. Usmani, Z., & Bashir, H. (2014, December 4). *The impact of drone strikes in Pakistan. Costs of war*, 3. https://watson.brown.edu/costso fwar/files/cow/imce/papers/2015/The%20Impact%20of%20Drone%20Strikes%20in%20Pakistan.pdf.
111. Id.
112. Id.
113. Id. 1.
114. Based on the midpoint of the 41-55 BIJ range estimate.
115. Airwars, US Forces in Somalia. https://airwars.org/conflict/us-forces-in-somalia/.
116. Id.
117. LWJ provided estimates of civilian deaths only through 2016, so its estimates are not included in the comparison.
118. For Afghanistan, see Airwars: https://www.thebureauinvestigates.com/projects/drone-war/afghanistan. For the US-led coalition in Iraq and Syria, see Airwars: https://airwars.org/conflict/coalition-in-iraq-and-syria/. For all belligerents in Libya in 2011, see Airwars: https://airwars.org/conflict/all-belligerents-in-libya-2011/. For all belligerents in Libya for 2012–present, see Airwars: https://airwars.org/conflict/all-belligerents-in-libya/.
119. Office of the Director of National Intelligence. (2016). *Summary of information regarding U.S. counterterrorism strikes outside areas of active hostilities between January 20, 2009 and December 31, 2015*. https://www.dni.gov/files/documents/Newsroom/Press%20Releases/DNI+Release+on+CT+Strikes+Outside+Areas+of+Active+Hostilities.PDF.
120. Id. 1.
121. Id.
122. Id.
123. Id. 2.
124. Id. 2–3.
125. Knuckey, S. (2016, October 24). *The good and bad in the US government's civilian casualties announcement*. Just Security. https://www.justsecurity.org/31785/good-bad-governments-civilian-casualties-announcement/.
126. Id.
127. Office of the Director of National Intelligence. (2017). *Summary of 2016 information regarding U.S. counterterrorism strikes outside areas of active hostilities between January 1, 2016 and December 31, 2016*. https://www.dni.gov/files/documents/Newsroom/Summary-of-2016-

Information-Regarding-United-States-Counterterrorism-Strikes-Out
side-Areas-of-Active-Hostilities.pdf.
128. Id. 2.
129. Mahanty, D., & Siemion R. (2020, May 7). *Grading DOD's annual
civilian casualties report: "Incomplete."* Just Security. https://www.jus
tsecurity.org/70063/grading-dods-annual-civilian-casualties-report-inc
omplete/.
130. Shiel, A., & Woods, C. (2021, June 7). *A legacy of unrecognized harm:
DoD's 2020 civilian casualties report.* Just Security. https://www.justse
curity.org/76788/a-legacy-of-unrecognized-harm-dods-2020-civilian-
casualties-report/.
131. United Nations Assistance Mission in Afghanistan. (2019, February).
*Afghanistan: Protection of civilians in armed conflict: 2018 annual
report.* https://unama.unmissions.org/sites/default/files/unama_ann
ual_protection_of_civilians_report_2018_-_23_feb_2019_-_english.pdf;
United Nations Assistance Mission in Afghanistan. (2020, February).
*Afghanistan: Protection of civilians in armed conflict: 2019 annual
report.* https://unama.unmissions.org/sites/default/files/afghanistan_
protection_of_civilians_annual_report_2019.pdf; United Nations Assistance Mission in Afghanistan. (2021, February). *Afghanistan: Protection
of civilians in armed conflict: 2020 annual report.* https://unama.unm
issions.org/sites/default/files/afghanistan_protection_of_civilians_rep
ort_2020_revs3.pdf.
132. DOD 2017 Report, 5-6; DOD 2018 Report, 11.
133. DOD 2019 Report, 9; DOD 2020 Report, 8.
134. DOD 2018 Report, 10.
135. Id.
136. DOD 2021 Report, 17.
137. Id.
138. Mahanty and Siemion.
139. Eviatar, D. (2020, May 14). *The fatal flaw in DOD's latest civilian
casualties report.* Just Security. https://www.justsecurity.org/70139/
the-fatal-flaw-in-dods-latest-civilian-casualties-report/.
140. See, e.g., Kilcullen & Exum; Spencer Ackerman. (2014, November
24). 41 men targeted but 1,147 people killed: US drone strikes—The
facts on the ground. *The Guardian.* https://www.theguardian.com/us-
news/2014/nov/24/-sp-us-drone-strikes-kill-1147. .
141. Pakistan: New America, https://docs.google.com/spreadsheets/d/
1nHZopMQpvDO1ETpMVP6ZJ22wk3fHRgB00sekIvqXB_c/pub
html?gid=1682788061#; Yemen: New America, https://docs.google.
com/spreadsheets/d/1FfDiYexanNftBXipPorJhgRDo_L34lrqoyVhVF
Rc5pk/pubhtml?gid=478247173#; Somalia: New America, https://
docs.google.com/spreadsheets/d/1Z4cue3_nMMTQMY18Zz8-Frz-

02jfyKPgq-ioJMOujeU/pubhtml?gid=1174069682#. Figures are based on reports in media sources on which New America relies.

142. Usmani, Z., & Bashir, H. (2014, December 4). The impact of drone strikes in Pakistan. Costs of war. https://watson.brown.edu/costso fwar/files/cow/imce/papers/2015/The%20Impact%20of%20Drone% 20Strikes%20in%20Pakistan.pdf.

143. Id.

144. Data are taken from Counterterrorism Wars—Pakistan, https://docs. google.com/spreadsheets/d/1nHZopMQpvDO1ETpMVP6ZJ22wk3 fHRgB00sekIvqXB_c/pubhtml?gid=478247173 (last visited June 17, 2021) (under Yearly strikes, by administration and Yearly Deaths, by combatant status).

145. Where estimates are in the form of a range, % civilians killed = (average of the range of estimates of civilians killed/average of the range of estimates of total killed).

146. Calculated from data in spreadsheet on individual strikes at https:// docs.google.com/spreadsheets/d/1nHZopMQpvDO1ETpMVP6ZJ22 wk3fHRgB00sekIvqXB_c/pubhtml?gid=478247173&urp=gmail_link#.

147. Status of five victims unknown.

148. Status of six victims unknown.

149. One additional strike with status of victims unknown.

150. Status of 11.5 victims unknown.

151. Status of 48.5 victims unknown.

152. Status of 110 victims unknown.

153. Status of 35.5 victims unknown.

154. Status of 32.5 victims unknown.

155. Status of 19.5 victims unknown.

156. Status of one victim unknown.

157. Where estimates are in the form of a range, % civilians killed = (average of the range of estimates of civilians killed/average of the range of estimates of total killed).

158. Detailed LWJ strike data not available to calculate number and percentage of strikes with civilian casualties.

159. Data from 2004 to 2016 are taken from Micah Zenko, *Obama's final drone strike data*. Council on Foreign Relations, January 20, 2017. https://www.cfr.org/blog/obamas-final-drone-strike-data

160. Data for 2017–2020 are taken from *US Airstrikes in the Long War*, Long War J., https://www.longwarjournal.org/us-airstrikes-in-the-lon g-war (last visited May 20, 2021). LWJ does not provide estimates of casualties for 2017–2020.

161. Data are taken from *Summary Tables and Casualty Rates*, CIA and US Military Drone Strikes in Pakistan, 2004 to Present, https://docs.goo gle.com/spreadsheets/d/1NAjFonM-Tn7fziqiv33HlGt09wgLZDSCP-

BQaux51w/edit#gid=694046452 (last visited May 20, 2021). Note that BIJ stopped tracking strikes in February 2020.

162. Where estimates are in the form of a range, % civilians killed = (average of the range of estimates of civilians killed/average of the range of estimates of total killed).

163. Drawn from spreadsheet on individual strikes at https://docs.google.com/spreadsheets/d/1NAjFonM-Tn7fziqiv33HlGt09wgLZDSCP-BQaux51w/edit#gid=1436874561.

164. Calculations based on average of the low and high casualty estimates.

165. BIJ stopped tracking strikes in February 2020.

166. Drone strikes. https://www.kaggle.com/zusmani/pakistandroneattacks?select=PakistanDroneAttacksWithTemp+Ver+11+%28November+30+2017%29.csv.

167. From New America, Yemen, Yearly Strikes by Type: https://docs.google.com/spreadsheets/d/1FfDiYexanNftBXipPorJhgRDo_L34lrqoyVhVFRc5pk/pubhtml?gid=1174069682#.

168. From New America, Yemen, Yearly Deaths by Combatant Status: https://docs.google.com/spreadsheets/d/1FfDiYexanNftBXipPorJhgRDo_L34lrqoyVhVFRc5pk/pubhtml?gid=1174069682.

169. Calculated from data in spreadsheet on individual strikes at https://docs.google.com/spreadsheets/d/1FfDiYexanNftBXipPorJhgRDo_L34lrqoyVhVFRc5pk/pubhtml?gid=1174069682#.

170. Status of 16.5 victims unknown.

171. Status of 18 victims unknown.

172. Status of four victims unknown.

173. Status of one victim unknown.

174. Status of three victims unknown.

175. Of the 131 strikes under the Trump administration, New America was unable to locate sufficient data for 82 of those strikes. Additionally, two 2014 strikes and two 2017 strikes were ground operation strikes as opposed to drone or air strikes. Data are taken from New America Data taken from Wars—Yemen, https://docs.google.com/spreadsheets/d/1FfDiYexanNftBXipPorJhgRDo_L34lrqoyVhVFRc5pk/pubhtml?gid=478247173 (last visited June 17, 2021) (under Yearly strikes, by administration and Yearly deaths, by combatant status).

176. Status of 12 victims unknown.

177. Status of 16 victims unknown.

178. Status of five victims unknown.

179. Detailed LWJ strike data not available to calculate number and percentage of strikes with civilian casualties.

180. Data from 2002 to 2016 are taken from Micah Zenko, *Obama's final drone strike data*. Council on Foreign Relations, January 20, 2017. https://www.cfr.org/blog/obamas-final-drone-strike-data

181. Data for 2017–2020 are taken from *US airstrikes in the Long War*. Long War J., https://www.longwarjournal.org/us-airstrikes-in-the-lon g-war (last visited May 20, 2021). LWJ does not provide estimates of casualties for 2017–2020.
182. Includes drone strikes, but not 110 "possible" strikes. "The Bureau records strikes as confirmed US operations when they have been reported as such by a named or unnamed US official, by a named senior Yemeni official, or by three or more unnamed official Yemeni officials in different published sources. All other operations are recorded as possible US attacks until new evidence comes to light which demonstrates they are US operations" https://docs.google.com/spreadsheets/d/1lb1hEYJ_ omI8lSe33izwS2a2lbiygs0hTp2Al_Kz5KQ/edit#gid=977256262. Data are taken from https://docs.google.com/spreadsheets/d/1lb1hEYJ_ omI8lSe33izwS2a2lbiygs0hTp2Al_Kz5KQ/edit#gid=492674230. Note that BIJ stopped tracking strikes in February 2020. Note that BIJ stopped tracking airstrikes in February 2020.
183. Calculated from data in spreadsheet on individual strikes at https:// docs.google.com/spreadsheets/d/1lb1hEYJ_omI8lSe33izwS2a2lbiyg s0hTp2Al_Kz5KQ/edit#gid=492674230.
184. "The Bureau records strikes as confirmed US operations when they have been reported as such by a named or unnamed US offi- cial, by a named senior Yemeni official, or by three or more unnamed official Yemeni officials in different published sources. All other operations are recorded as possible US attacks until new evidence comes to light which demonstrates they are US operations." https://docs.google.com/spreadsheets/d/1lb1hEYJ_omI 8lSe33izwS2a2lbiygs0hTp2Al_Kz5KQ/edit#gid=977256262. This does not include confirmed airstrikes that possibly were drone strikes. Data are taken from https://docs.google.com/spreadsheets/d/1lb1hEYJ_ omI8lSe33izwS2a2lbiygs0hTp2Al_Kz5KQ/edit#gid=492674230. Note that BIJ stopped tracking strikes in February 2020.
185. No data available from 2017 to 2020 for confirmed drone strikes, only for confirmed air strikes that may include drone strikes.
186. From New America, Somalia, Yearly Strikes by Type: https://docs.goo gle.com/spreadsheets/d/1Z4cue3_nMMTQMY18Zz8-Frz-02jfyKPgq- ioJMOujeU/pubhtml?gid=478247173#.
187. Calculated from data in spreadsheet of individual operations at New America, Somalia, Full Data: https://docs.google.com/spreadsheets/ d/1Z4cue3_nMMTQMY18Zz8-Frz-02jfyKPgq-ioJMOujeU/pubhtml? gid=478247173#.
188. Status of 7.5 victims unknown. Two strikes were ground operations, but no separate casualty figures available.
189. Status of 9.5 victims unknown.

190. One strike was a ground operation, but no separate casualty figures available.
191. Status of 10 victims unknown. Three strikes were ground operations, but no separate casualty figures available.
192. Status of 14 victims unknown. Four strikes were ground operations, but no separate casualty figures available.
193. Status of 9 victims unknown. Two strikes were ground operations, but no separate casualty figures available.
194. Status of 6.5 victims unknown. Three strikes were ground operations, but no separate casualty figures available.
195. Status of 5.5 victims unknown. Two strikes were ground operations, but no separate casualty figures available.
196. Through October 2021. https://docs.google.com/spreadsheets/d/1Z4cue3_nMMTQMY18Zz8-Frz-02jfyKPgq-ioJMOujeU/pubhtml?gid=1174069682. Last visited October 31, 2021.
197. Data for 2017–2020 are taken from *US Airstrikes in the Long War*. Long War J., https://www.longwarjournal.org/us-airstrikes-in-the-long-war (last visited May 20, 2021). LWJ does not provide estimates of casualties for 2017–2020.
198. Detailed LWJ strike data not available to calculate number and percentage of strikes with civilian casualties.
199. LWJ does not provide estimates of casualties for 2017–2020.
200. Data for 2017-2020 are taken from *US Airstrikes in the Long War*, Long War J., https://www.longwarjournal.org/us-airstrikes-in-the-long-war (last visited May 20, 2021). LWJ does not provide estimates of casualties for 2017–2020.
201. Includes drone strikes. Note that BIJ stopped tracking strikes in February 2020. In addition to "confirmed" strikes, BIJ found eight "possible" strikes through February 2020. The Bureau considers strikes that have been reported as US by a US official, a named senior Somalia government official, or three independent unnamed official Somali sources [as confirmed strikes]. All other operations are possible US attacks." https://docs.google.com/spreadsheets/d/1-LT5TVBMy1Rj2WH30xQG9nqr8-RXFVvzJE_47NlpeSY/edit#gid=1110953463. Data is from BIJ, US Strikes in Somalia: https://docs.google.com/spreadsheets/d/1-LT5TVBMy1Rj2WH30xQG9nqr8-RXFVvzJE_47NlpeSY/edit#gid=0.
202. From spreadsheet of individual operations at BIJ, US Strikes in Somalia: https://docs.google.com/spreadsheets/d/1-LT5TVBMy1Rj2WH30xQG9nqr8-RXFVvzJE_47NlpeSY/edit#gid=859698683.
203. "The Bureau considers strikes that have been reported as US by a US official, a named senior Somalia government official, or three independent unnamed official Somali sources [as confirmed strikes]. All

other operations are possible US attacks." https://docs.google.com/ spreadsheets/d/1-LT5TVBMy1Rj2WH30xQG9nqr8-RXFVvzJE_47N lpeSY/edit#gid=1110953463. Note that BIJ stopped tracking strikes in February 2020.

204. No data available from 2017–2020 for confirmed drone strikes, only for confirmed air strikes that may include drone strikes.

205. Airwars, *US Operations in Somalia*. https://airwars.org/conflict/us-for ces-in-somalia/.

206. Airwars, *New Somalia resource shines light on US counterterrorism campaign*. https://airwars.org/news-and-investigations/new-somalia-resource-shines-light-on-us-counterterrorism-campaign/.

207. Report did not differentiate among countries. Operation Inherent Resolve in Iraq and Syria against ISIS, and in Syria against Al Qaeda; Operation Freedom Sentinel and support to NATO Resolute Support Mission in Afghanistan against Al Qaeda, Taliban, and ISIS; operations in Yemen against AQAP and ISIS.

208. Operation Inherent Resolve against ISIS 2018-2020.

209. Operation Freedom Sentinel and support to NATO Resolute Support Mission in Afghanistan against Al Qaeda, Taliban, and ISIS 2018–2020.

210. Operations against ISIS and al-Shabaab 2018–2020.

211. Drawn from https://www.thebureauinvestigates.com/stories/2017-01-01/drone-wars-the-full-data.

212. Airstrikes, including drone strikes.

213. https://www.kaggle.com/zusmani/pakistandroneattacks?select=Pakist anDroneAttacksWithTemp+Ver+11+%28November+30+2017%29.csv. Does not distinguish between militant and civilian injuries.

CHAPTER 10

Civilian Casualties: Beyond the Numbers

As the previous chapter describes, the US claims that civilian casualties from targeted strikes are rare because strikes outside war zones are exceptionally precise, and that the US therefore consistently meets its own requirement that there be near certainty of no civilian casualties in such operations. This claim is contested, however, because US estimates of casualties are much lower than those by outside organizations. This chapter scrutinizes the US claim of precision by closely examining how a drone strike is conducted, and by considering the broader organizational processes that affect the risk of civilian casualties. As this analysis indicates, fully realizing the potential for precision requires structuring these processes in order to minimize the risk of such casualties.

DRONES, PRECISION, AND RISK

This section describes how targeted strikes are conducted and the mechanisms designed to ensure their accuracy.[1] Strikes have been carried out by drones known as the MQ-1 Predator and its successor the MQ-9 Reaper. The US began using the Reaper in 2007 and retired the Predator in 2018. The fullest available information on conducting a strike is on the steps followed by the military, but informed sources indicate that the process is comparable for operations conducted by the CIA.[2]

© The Author(s), under exclusive license to Springer Nature Switzerland AG 2022
M. Regan, *Drone Strike–Analyzing the Impacts of Targeted Killing*, https://doi.org/10.1007/978-3-030-91119-5_10

The Predator can fly at altitudes of up to 25,000 feet, at a cruising speed of 87 mph. It can fly up to 460 miles (740 km) to a target, loiter overhead for 14 hours, then return to its base. The Reaper, almost twice as heavy, can fly up to 50,000 feet (15,000 km), with a range of 1150 miles (1850 km). It has a cruising speed of 170–200 miles an hour and maximum speed of 300 mph. The basic model can remain aloft for 30 hours conducting intelligence, surveillance, and reconnaissance (ISR) missions, which declines to 14 hours if carrying a full weapons load.[3] Chris Woods of Airwars describes the technology contained in the Reaper's sensor ball, which includes "full-motion video cameras; infrared capabilities; tracking technologies and a laser targeting designator," as well as electronic pods on the wings designed to capture intelligence from the ground "from cellphones, Wi-Fi signals, or tiny hidden tracking devices."[4]

The Predator is equipped with two weapon stations and can carry a combination of two supersonic Hellfire missiles, four small Stinger missiles, and six Griffin air-to-air missiles. The Reaper has a much bigger payload. It can carry four 100-pound supersonic Hellfire missiles or two missiles and two Guided Bomb Unit (GBU)-12 Paveway II laser-guided bombs or two 500-pound GBU-38 Joint Direct Attack Munitions (JDAMs). A JDAM is a guidance kit that converts unguided bombs into precision munitions that rely on a global positioning system (GPS) guidance control unit.[5]

Hellfire missiles were originally designed as antitank missiles and have a maximum effective range of just under five miles (eight meters).[6] The circular error probable (CEP) of a Hellfire is 16 feet (five meters) or less.[7] This means that 50% of the time the Hellfire will strike within this distance and 50% of the time outside this range. Its blast and fragmentation radius can kill people within 50 feet (15 m) of impact and injure them within 65 feet (20 m).[8]

The bombs guided by the JDAM GPS have a range of 19.6 miles (31.3 km).[9] The GBU-12 Paveway II has a CEP of 29.5 feet (nine meters).[10] It has a radius of between 200 and 300 feet (61–91 m) within which 50% of people can be killed. The GBU-38 has a range of 15 miles (24.1 m).[11] It has a CEP of 16.4 feet (five meters), which increases to 98.4 feet (30 m) if GPS is denied, such as by jamming.[12] With a 500-pound bomb it has a blast and fragmentation radius that can kill people within 242 feet (80 m).

Drone video is based on a technology known as a "Wide Area Airborne Surveillance System," colloquially called Gorgon Stare, which is a spherical array of multiple cameras that provides full-motion video (FMV) surveillance capable of capturing motion imagery of an entire city. "This allows operators to zoom in on any one part of the imagery with a decent amount of detail."[13] There is a slight time lag before imagery is transmitted, however, which means that the technology is not used to conduct the strike itself.

The aircraft is operated from a ground control station (GCS) whose crew includes:

1. a pilot, who controls the flight of the aircraft and fires weapons;
2. a sensor operator, who gathers information from sensors on the aircraft and video surveillance reports to guide the flight, track ground objects, mark targets with lasers, and guide the weapon once released to the target;
3. a mission intelligence coordinator, who monitors intelligence sources outside the GCS and serves as liaison between the cockpit and the outside; and
4. a safety observer, who enters a GCS when the possibility of firing a weapon arises.

A launch and recovery element (LRE) team near the location of the aircraft uses line-of-sight control to launch it, and then turns control over to the GCS. The GCS controls the drone via satellite link, with its commands taking 1.2 seconds to reach the drone. The GCS controls the aircraft when airborne, including during a strike, and then transfers control to the LRE to return it to base. Each mission may be supported by up to 200 people. There are people outside the GCS involved in monitoring the flight, multiple sources of airborne and ground intelligence for each mission, and scores of intelligence analysts, as well as maintenance personnel.

Target identification relies on intelligence to direct the aircraft to the target. There must be positive identification (PID) of the target by at least two sources, and an unbroken view of the target at all times or the PID process must start over. Authorization to conduct a strike specifies coordinates of the target, location of any friendly forces, and intent of the ground commander.

The US military has refined several measures over the last couple of decades to minimize civilian casualties. A collateral damage assessment (CDE) must be conducted before any strike is authorized, generally based on a prescribed detailed collateral damage methodology (CDM). A CDE must be conducted in all cases, but the CDM is not required in unusual cases such as "fleeting and time-sensitive targets."[14] The CDM is designed to "mitigate unintended or incidental damage or injury to civilian or noncombatant persons or property or the environment."[15] Analysis is based on "empirical data gathered in field tests, probability, historical observations from weapons employed on the battlefield, and physics-based computerized models."[16]

This includes consideration of, for instance, the physical attributes of buildings, the blast and fragmentation radius of different weapons, weapon accuracy, population density, and other variables that are likely to affect the probability of civilian harm. The analysis considers ways to reduce estimated casualties, such as use of "delayed fuses, changes in ordnance, [and] angle of attack or delivery."[17] The CDE was developed by the military to meet its obligation under the Law of Armed Conflict (LOAC) to avoid excessive unintended civilian harm. As Chapter 1 describes, the US regards itself as engaged in an armed conflict against Al-Qaeda and associated forces governed by the laws of war. Since 2013, however, as a matter of policy strikes outside areas of active hostilities must meet the stricter standard of "near certainty" of no civilian harm. The CDE is used to as a means to help meet this standard.

Another way of avoiding civilian casualties is to delay strikes until a target is no longer in an area populated by civilians, such as on an open road or in a remote location. One expert observes, "It is very common ... for an operations center to monitor a targeted individual in a populated area for many hours, waiting to attack until he or she is no longer near civilians or civilian objects."[18] A third measure to reduce casualties is a "pattern of life" analysis. Defined in broad terms, this involves understanding the "complex... contexts within which people... move about and interact, normally with a type of recognizable regularity."[19]

While pattern of life analysis is used in targeting to identify and track targets, it also involves extended viewing and analysis of population movement and social activities at different times of day on different days of the week to determine when and how many civilians are likely to be present at a given time. Such understanding also enables operators "to establish a baseline of what [is] 'normal,' improving situational awareness and reducing the chances of mistaking regular activity as nefarious."[20]

Once a target has been positively identified and a CDE conducted, a pilot may be cleared to fire, from an optimal launch altitude generally of 10,000 feet. The weapon leaves the aircraft and seeks the lasered target, guided to it by the sensor operator, who keeps the guidance system crosshairs on the target to ensure that the missile hits it. If civilians unexpectedly appear, the sensor operator has about 30 seconds to shift the laser pointer to a pre-designated area that will avoid civilian casualties. This capability is not available, however, with bombs guided by a JDAM.

After the strike, there is a battle damage assessment (BDA). This is designed to answer the following questions:

Did the weapons impact the target as planned?

Did the weapons achieve the desired results and fulfill the objectives, and therefore purpose, of the attack?

How long will it take enemy forces to repair damage and regain functionality?

Can and will the enemy compensate for the actual damage through substitution?

Are restrikes necessary to inflict additional damage, to delay recovery efforts, or attack targets not successfully struck?

What are the collateral effects on the target system as a whole, or on other target systems?[21]

There is a detailed video and computer audit record of every mission, which is used for a debriefing of what went well and what did not. Lessons from debriefings are incorporated into training, and a Remedial Action Report identifies errors, which can result in persons being removed from missions while they undergo retraining.[22]

Larry Lewis and Diane Varichek, two authors who have extensively studied drone operations and civilian casualties, observe, "Although drones offer desirable capabilities, such as precision weapons, persistence, and full-motion capabilities for targeting and screening of collateral damage, these technical elements alone do not necessarily translate to surgical precision and the minimization of civilian casualties."[23] Focusing only on drone features "mistakes platform precision for a comprehensive process that minimizes civilian casualties."[24]

Thus, for instance, Lewis has reported that, based on research that he and Sarah Sewall did in Afghanistan in 2010, drone strikes in that country were ten times more likely to cause civilian casualties than manned aircraft.[25] He reports that in Yemen from 2009 to 2014, drone strikes had almost twice the number of civilian deaths per incident as other operations and were almost four times more likely to cause civilian casualties.[26]

This underscores that it is crucial to appreciate the ways in which various features of drone strike operations can create the risk of causing civilian casualties. First, a strike relies on a complex system of processing, exploiting, and disseminating information among multiple participants in different locations. Up to 50 aircrew may be involved in remotely flying the aircraft, with 80 or more intelligence analysts and staff offering real-time analysis of the drone's video feeds.[27]

A mission intelligence coordinator (MIC) communicates with multiple remote intelligence sources through text-only chat rooms, and by chat and voice with the GCS crew. The MIC is the only person in both direct contact with the GCS and with outside intelligence sources, while the GCS is in contact with the MIC and anyone on the ground. Intelligence analysts can directly communicate only with the MIC, and not with the GCS nor persons on the ground. This segmentation of communication is meant to enable effective management of what otherwise could be an overwhelming amount of information. It can create the risk, however, of fragmented information that results in incomplete situational awareness.

A report from the Center for Army Lessons Learned (CALL) on civilian casualties in Afghanistan notes regarding aerial operations that "important details are often known in one part of the air-ground team but are not shared with the rest of that team."[28] In addition, video can't identify individuals in a crowd, so operators must rely on other sources of intelligence for PID. Continuous PID can be challenging as individuals go into buildings or otherwise disappear from the video feed. When they do, confirming PID based on two independent sources must be reinitiated. This means reliance in many cases on sources of intelligence other than the video feed, if they are available.

The CALL report describes the risk of failing to rigorously follow this process: "[T]wo individuals who were positively identified as enemy ran into a building," the report says. "Moments later, two individuals ran out of the building and were engaged by air-to-ground fire. The two engaged individuals were a mother and her child fleeing the compound after being forced out by the two Taliban."[29]

Video feeds also can't see into buildings, which means that they may not show civilians in them. Reliance on pattern of life information compiled over an extended period of time can help compensate for this, but operators may need to exercise patience in waiting long enough to determine with confidence that civilians are not present. The CALL report notes that it is important for air-ground teams to ensure that there are no civilians present, rather than assuming that they are not. It emphasized, "Observing the outside of a building for minutes or even hours and not seeing activity does not give assurance that there are no civilians inside the building."[30]

Identifying civilians even when they are in view also can be challenging. Intelligence might not be available on persons in the target area who are not the target. Analysts must presume that any such persons are civilians. Observing certain behavior may be sufficient to rebut this presumption, but this is subject to interpretation and may not always be definitive. Larry Lewis notes that in his analysis of civilian casualties in Afghanistan, "the misidentification of civilians as the enemy was the basis for the majority of civilian casualty incidents and contributed to a lack of recognition of actual civilian tolls from operations."[31] This occurred when behavior or appearance was mistakenly regarded as threatening, or when persons in close proximity to hostile forces were believed to be associated with them. Drone strikes that are signature strikes can pose this risk more acutely than strikes against identified individuals, but either one can involve such misinterpretation.

The CALL report says that several incidents also illustrate how the use of "leading language" or communication of selective facts can unintentionally suggest that a person has hostile intent. One commonly used term to describe individuals, for instance, is "military-age males," which can imply "that the individuals are armed forces and therefore legitimate targets."[32] Another common practice, said the report, is to characterize people engaged in digging as emplacing an improvised explosive device, which can result in the deaths of persons involved in farming or irrigation.[33]

While a CDE must be done prior to any strike, it is based not on historical experience with similar operations, but on models that include data on population density, weapon and building characteristics, and terrain features.[34] This can limit CDE sensitivity to the social environment. Information on patterns of life in the area can enhance awareness, but compiling such information can be time-consuming and must be continually updated to account for changing conditions. As Larry Lewis and Ryan Goodman note, "The formal collateral damage estimation process, as rigorous as it is, has never been calibrated with real world data to test its accuracy in predicting operational outcomes. This could be remedied through a study that examines how well estimates match up with actual operational data."[35]

Executing a strike begins with a wide video focus and then zooms in right before a strike. This can create a "soda straw" effect that limits awareness of last-minute entry of civilians into the target area. Ideally, this perspective would be complemented by video with a wider view, or by zooming out one last time before a strike. Gorgon Stare provides expansive detailed video awareness, but the slight delay in its feed means that it can't be used in real time for weapon release. The sensor operator in the GCS is able to redirect a missile within 30 seconds after release if civilians move into the area, but this may not be sufficient to avoid casualties in some cases. In addition, this capability is not available when environmental conditions make reliance on laser targeting infeasible and a JDAM guided by GPS is used instead.

Another complication is that the desire to use low-damage ordnance to reduce risk of civilian casualties may mean that a first strike does not eliminate the target. A BDA may indicate that a follow-up strike is necessary to accomplish the mission. A new CDE may not be conducted, however, to redetermine if civilians are present for the second strike. This accounts for some reports that civilians attempting to provide assistance to victims of the first strike have been killed in a follow-up strike.

A post-strike BDA is used to verify the number of casualties and to determine if any are civilians. There are challenges, however, in relying on a BDA for this information. First, the traditional purpose of a BDA has not been to identify civilian casualties, but to determine if targets were successfully destroyed. Expanding the BDA to serve other purposes requires not only a change in procedure but a change in perspective.

In addition, a drone is used in some cases because the target is in a remote area where the US has no ground forces and few if any sources of human intelligence. In these cases, a BDA will be based solely on assessment by aerial assets. There are limits, however, to information that these assets can provide. Video of building rubble, for instance, will not necessarily indicate if there are bodies underneath it. In addition, determining if victims are civilians may require local sources of information unavailable from the air. The US has not consistently drawn on these sources, however, in its estimate of civilian casualties.

Amnesty International pointed out in a 2019 report on civilian casualties from airstrikes in Somalia:

> While Joint US Doctrine says that a battle damage assessment, as a best practice, should include 'aircraft cockpit video (ACV), weapon system video (WSV), visual/verbal reports from ground spotters or combat troops, controllers and observers, artillery target surveillance reports, SIGINT [signals intelligence], HUMINT [human intelligence], IMINT [imagery intelligence], MASINT [measurement and signals intelligence], and open-source intelligence (OSINT),' in practice intelligence assets are limited, and often rely on a single source.[36]

The organization noted that former AFRICOM and US Special Forces AFRICOM Commander General Bolduc stated in an interview with *The Daily Beast*, "The only assessment we [AFRICOM] have is we continue to fly over the objective post-strike to get a sense of the environment from the air."[37] As the commander of US Air Force Central Command in Qatar said to the *New York Times*, however: "Ground truth, that's what you're asking for. We see what we see from altitude and pulling from other reports. Your [*Times* reporters'] perspective is talking to people on the ground. It's got to be a combination of both."[38] Ideally, determining civilian casualties would involve collaboration between the US and these groups in order to arrive at the most accurate estimates possible.

The fact that drone strikes are especially likely to occur in remote areas in which there is little if any US ground presence thus creates a challenge both in minimizing civilian casualties and determining when they occur. As a result, Lewis suggests that "[i]t is likely that the United States does not have a true picture of the actual scale of civilian harm from its drone campaign."[39]

Two incidents offer insight into how operations using drones can result in civilian casualties. The first is the drone strike in Kabul, Afghanistan in August 2021 that mistakenly killed aid worker Zemari Ahmadi and nine family members, including seven children.[40] This occurred three days after a suicide bomber had killed 183 people at the Kabul airport. Marine Corps General Frank McKenzie told reporters that 36 hours before the strike, the strike cell commander had been notified that "ISIS-K would utilize a white Toyota Corolla as a key element in the next attack."[41] The US assigned several MQ-9 Reapers to surveil an "area of interest" connected to ISIS, and identified a white Corolla in the area. After it left this location, drones tracked it to six other locations. One of these was a site that the US learned only afterward was Nutrition and Education International, where Ahmadi was employed. As the civilians in the Corolla were unloading supplies at this site, US forces received additional intelligence that an ISIS cell leader was receiving supplies at the same time.

When the vehicle finally stopped at the Ahmadi home near the airport, "the vehicle was observed being approached by a single adult male assessed at the time to be a co-conspirator."[42] McKenzie said:

> When the vehicle came up to the final point [this was] actually, as I've noted..., the closest to the airfield it had been all day. We were very concerned about a white Corolla being involved in an attack, so the cumulative force of all those, all those, the intelligence that we gathered throughout the day, the position of the vehicle, it's newness to the airport, the imminence of the threat and the other [signals intelligence] that we're getting throughout the day, all led us to the moment of deciding to take the strike.[43]

The summary of the classified investigative report on the incident said, "Execution errors combined with confirmation bias and communication breakdowns led to regrettable civilian casualties."[44] A statement regarding the investigation said that it "made several recommendations for refinement of processes and procedures leading up to strikes in time-constrained scenarios and urban terrain, including:

- Implementing procedures to mitigate risks of confirmation bias
- Enhancing sharing of overall mission situational awareness during execution
- Review of pre-strike procedures used to assess presence of civilians."[45]

Luke Hartig, a former counterterrorism official in the Obama administration with experience in drone strikes, noted that the recommendations related "only to self-defense strikes against imminent threats to forces," when reasonable, rather than near, certainty of no civilian casualties was required.[46] He suggested, however, that the strike revealed underlying concerns about drone strikes in general, since they are "complex analytic and operational undertakings that rely on techniques and procedures developed and refined over many years."[47]

The first was confirmation bias. Hartig noted that once operators had identified Ahmadi as a suspect on the basis of driving a Toyota Corolla at a certain location, they "massively misread a number of totally innocent and commonplace facts and events."[48] Ahmadi was driving the most common vehicle in Afghanistan, he handed off a bag, and filled water bottles, all of which was interpreted in ways that reinforced the initial suspicion that he was a militant. Second, a man standing in the courtyard where the strike occurred was assumed to be a combatant because of his association with Ahmadi. Third, surveillance missed the presence of children in the courtyard, even though one of the most common criticisms of strikes over the past two decades has been that they have killed children. Fourth, although CIA analysts apparently did have information indicating that children were present, they were not located with the targeting cell and this information did not get to the cell in time. In addition, the cell was unaware that one of the places that Ahmadi visited before the strike was the office of a US NGO, a serious failure of situational awareness. Finally, with respect to the claim that there were secondary explosions that likely indicated that Ahmadi's car was carrying explosives, Hartig said that it was "incomprehensible that an organization that looks at explosions day in and day out would make such a mistake."[49] He concluded that the military focus on missteps in this individual strike reflected the failure to derive broader lessons based on systematic analysis of the drone program as a whole.

A publicly available full military investigative report of an airstrike that killed more than twenty civilians in Uruzgan province, Afghanistan in February 2010 offers even more detailed insights into how drone operations can result in civilian casualties.[50] The incident involved a strike not by a drone but by helicopters, with a drone providing intelligence, surveillance, and reconnaissance (ISR) support to ground forces. It illustrates, however, how the potential risks associated with elements of drone operations can materialize.

Early on February 21, 2010, a U.S. Special Forces team, Operational Detachment Alpha (ODA), accompanied by Afghan Army and Police, arrived by air in Uruzgan province for a daytime cordon and search operation. The Special Forces team was supported by an AC-130 helicopter gunship and a MQ-1 Predator drone providing ISR with the use of full-motion video (FMV), controlled by a ground control station (GCS) crew at Creech Air Force Base, Nevada. During this period, imagery analysts ("screeners" in the investigative report) at Hurlburt Air Force Base, Florida who were trained to interpret FMV from the Predator provided their assessment of the situation to the Predator crew, as text on computers via Internet Relay Chat (mIRC).

These texts were not available to ODA on the ground, but the Predator crew orally transmitted to ODA evaluations of the situation based on them. The crew in the GCS thus was the link between imagery analysts in Florida and ODA forces on the ground in Afghanistan. Command posts at Special Operations Task Force (SOTF) and Combined Joint Special Operations Task Force-Afghanistan (CJSOTF-A) had access throughout this time both to FMV and to the screener chat communications with the Predator crew. They thus had the fullest situational awareness of anyone in the operation.

While waiting for daylight, ODA received intelligence that enemy forces were preparing to attack. The Predator screeners and ground crew observed two special utility vehicles (SUVs) driving toward the location of US forces, and suspected that these were enemy forces. The SUVs drove around the area for about three and a half hours, changing directions several times, stopping to allow the occupants of the vehicles to pray, and moving to a position about 12 km from US forces. A pickup truck then joined the two SUVs.

ODA then received additional intelligence that the enemy might be planning an ambush. This information, and assessment of the situation based on reports from the Predator crew, led the ODA commander (CDR) to believe the unit was facing an imminent threat. He called for an airstrike on the three vehicles. Two OH-58 helicopters responded to the call and arrived within about 15 minutes, armed with Hellfire missiles. In the handoff from the Predator to the OH-58s, the Predator crew reported that they had positively identified at least three weapons and 21 "military-age-males," that the vehicles were engaged in "tactical maneuvering," that the crew had continuous PID, and that it was continuing to observe the vehicles.[51]

The helicopters fired their missiles on the vehicles. The first missile struck the first vehicle in the convoy. The second missile struck the third vehicle as the occupants were leaving it. A pilot from each of the helicopters confirmed that these persons "looked like they exited holding weapons and were crouching in a defensive firing position before the second missile struck."[52] The third missile struck immediately in front of the middle vehicle, disabling it. After the occupants of the second vehicle got out, the helicopters fired rockets at the people running from the scene, but none hit them. As they were coming around to fire again, the pilots observed that those running "had brightly colored clothing and looked like females," and "appeared to be waving a scarf or a part of the burqas."[53] The helicopters immediately stopped firing and reported the possible presence of civilians to the ODA.

An investigation into the incident concluded that "[t]he catastrophic nature of the strike makes an exact determination of the number killed impossible." Although the BDA at the strike site indicated 15–16 killed, "the village elders identified 23 men who were killed and claims were paid to the families of all 23."[54] No women or children were killed in the strike.

The investigative report described the reasons for the strike as follows:

> The strike occurred because the ground force commander lacked a clear understanding of who was in the vehicles, the location, direction of travel and the likely course of action of the vehicles. This lack of understanding resulted from poorly functioning command posts at SOTF and CJSOTF-A which failed to provide the ground force commander with the evidence and analysis that the vehicles were not a hostile threat and the inaccurate and unprofessional reporting of the Predator crew operating out of Creech, AFB Nevada which deprived the ground force commander of vital information.[55]

The report noted in particular that the descriptions of the situation that the Predator crew provided to the ODA CDR on the ground differed at times from the descriptions that imagery analysts had provided to the crew. As the report stated, "The Predator crew made or changed key assessments to the ODA CDR that influenced the decision to destroy the vehicles. The Predator crew has neither the training nor the tactical expertise to make these assessments."[56] Some of this reflected ambiguity in terminology, but the report also said, "The Predator crew possessed a desire to engage inconsistent with evolving target actions. The pervasive theme throughout several interviews with the Predator team, and seen throughout the internal crew dialogue was the desire to go kinetic."[57]

The report provided several examples of differences in assessments reported by the imagery analysts and the crew. First, at 0517 hours, early in the observation process, the screeners described the movement of the passengers in the vehicles as adult males standing or sitting. The crew, however, described passenger actions to ODA as "tactical maneuvering." The report noted that the term "tactical maneuver" is one of the elements that make vehicles a proper target.[58]

Second, at 0710 the screeners assessed that the vehicles might be leaving the area, but the crew disagreed, saying they "might be flanking as well."[59] The screener assessment that the vehicles might be leaving was never communicated to ODA. Instead, the crew reported to ODA, "convoy possibly flanking to the west." Third, the Predator pilot characterized what the report describes as "a scuffle near one of the vehicles" as the "potential use of human shields."[60] No screener had provided this interpretation, and the report said there was no basis for it. Next, despite several queries from ODA about the demographics of the passengers, the crew "never informed ODA they have not observed the occupants of the third vehicle joining the convoy and thus had never positively identified the age and gender of the occupants."[61]

In addition, on several occasions the Predator crew identified weapons on its own, independent of the screener's assessment, or appeared to prompt screeners to do so. At 0511 the crew asked screeners in the chat if they had identified any weapons. At 0518, the screeners reported that they could not confirm any. At 0529 the Predator pilot stated to the crew, "Does it look like he is [holding] something across his chest. It's what they've been doing here lately, they [wrap] their *expletive* up in their man dresses so you can't PID it."[62] He then says that a dismounted person on one of the trucks is carrying something that they can't identify. "After the Predator crew prompted them twice in mIRC," the screeners said that there was a possible weapon and asked the crew to go "white hot" to get a better look.[63] The crew sensor operator replied, "White hot is not going to give us anything better, that truck would make a beautiful target."[64]

The Predator pilot then made a radio call at 0534: "All players, all Players from our DGS the [military-age male] that just mounted the back of the hilux [truck] had a possible weapon, read back possible rifle."[65] During their post-strike review, the screeners determined that this was not a weapon. At 0624 the screeners called out a weapon, which "was the only time that the Screeners called out a weapon without being prompted by the Predator crew."[66] At 0655, the Predator pilot said on a radio call that the screeners had called out two weapons, although they had not made any such call. At 0741 the Predator pilot called, "Riding in the back of the hilux, so they don't have a lot of room. Potentially could carry a personal weapon on themselves."[67] The investigative report says, "Again, no call out from the screeners, this is his own opinion."[68]

Next, and "most importantly," the screeners initially identified children as passengers but later changed that assessment to "adolescents."[69] The crew reported to ODA that some passengers were "teenagers."[70] When handing off to the helicopters, the crew simply reported military-age males, with "no mention of children, adolescents, or teenagers."[71]

Communications about this subject also reflected different understandings of terminology by screeners and the crew. Three times early in the process a screener identified one or two children near a truck. ODA asked the crew about two hours later about earlier reports of children and asked, "whether we are talking 'teenagers' or toddlers."[72] The crew then asked for clarification from screeners, who changed the assessment to "adolescents."[73] The screener involved stated during the investigation that she regarded this term as applying to persons from 7 to 12 years old. The crew, however, assumed that it meant teenagers, and reported to ODA, "We're thinking early teens.... adolescents."[74] The report noted that when the screener was asked during the investigation, "Is adolescent a different call out than child or children?" she responded, "I think it varies from Screener to Screener. One Screener may be more comfortable with calling out adolescent. It is very difficult to tell."[75]

Both command posts were aware from the outset that the screeners had identified children, and had access to the communications between screeners and the crew and between the crew and ODA. The report said, "[L]eaders at both operations centers, with the ability to focus on the target and review chat logs, should have reexamined the PID determination prior to engaging the target. At a minimum, the presence of children required a proportionality analysis to determine the lawfulness of the target."[76]

The report said that initial determination of an imminent threat by the ODA CDR was reasonable, but that further information should have led to reassessment by the command posts monitoring the operation. The vehicles began about five kilometers north of the ground forces in Khod, moved west and south over the course of three-and-a-half hours, and ended up about twelve kilometers away. At the time they were struck, the vehicles had passed the most likely routes back to Khod. "Additionally," said the report, "the presence of children, while not ruling out that the force represented an imminent threat, was evidence that the force was most likely not in fact, moving to reinforce insurgents."[77]

The report concluded that the ODA CDR call for a strike was reasonable given the information he had, but that the problems described above prevented him from having accurate situational awareness. It said, "The movement away from the [ground forces], the bypassing of the most likely routes back to the objective, and the low number of weapons positively identified should have led to a reevaluation of the imminence of the threat."[78] Both command operations centers, the report said, "possessed all the information necessary to make that reevaluation but failed to piece the information together in a timely manner... [L]eaders at both operations centers, with the ability to focus on the target and review chat logs, should have reexamined the determination of hostile intent prior to engaging the target. Unfortunately, in this situation neither Ops Center was actively engaged in the operation."[79]

It is tempting to place blame for the incident on particular individuals, but the point is that we need to focus on the overall system. Several elements beyond the platform itself affect the risk that an aerial strike will harm civilians. Larry Lewis observes that a thorough analysis of the factors that contributed to the civilian casualties in this case include:

- The team on the ground that called in the airstrike received intelligence indicating the presence of hostile forces but not their location;
- Information among all components of the operation was not fully shared, which resulted in deficient situational awareness;
- Predator crew communications to ground forces were assumed to reflect the judgment of all members of the intelligence team;
- One vehicle was assumed to be hostile solely on the basis that it joined the convoy, without any analysis of its occupants;
- Civilian casualty guidance at the time focused on strikes on compounds rather than other types of targets;
- The Predator crew was eager to strike and did not exhibit tactical patience; and
- The convoy was deemed to pose an imminent threat even though it was "miles and hours from Coalition forces."[80]

We thus can regard the platform as the center of a set of concentric circles, all of which influence what ultimately happens at the time of a strike. The following section discusses an even larger circle within which all others are embedded, which is what Lewis calls a "civilian harm mitigation lifecycle."[81] Research indicates that the extent to which there is sustained focus on this lifecycle can have a significant effect on civilian casualties from military operations in general and from drone strikes in particular. While this research deals with military operations, it is equally relevant to kinetic operations carried out by any other agencies such as the CIA.

CIVILIAN CASUALTY MITIGATION: A LIFECYCLE APPROACH

Larry Lewis has conducted several rigorous analyses of civilian casualties for the US government over the past decade or so, beginning with a 2010 study he did with Sarah Sewall on casualties in Afghanistan for US Central Command and the NATO International Security Assistance Force (ISAF).[82] Lewis says that a lifecycle approach "reflects care in civilian protection being taken at all points in the planning and use of military force, and includes learning loops so that militaries can adapt and improve to overcome challenges."[83]

The 2010 study was the first to use this concept and the stages that comprise it. Lewis recently has reframed the stages in terms slightly different from the original study. His *Protecting Civilians: A Comprehensive Approach* describes the stages in this way:

- Mission and Mandate. Designating and allocating needed capabilities and authorities to conduct operations in ways that consider the protection of civilians from the beginning.
- Planning. At strategic down to tactical levels, conducting planning and developing command guidance that factors in risks to civilians and includes feasible steps and alternatives to help mitigate them.
- Tactical Execution. Performing targeting processes that promote accurate identification and delivery of lethal effects while seeking ways to minimize civilian harm and reverberating effects.

- Assessment. Considering all available information, with internal and external sources, to determine the best estimate of civilian harm caused by the use of force.
- Response. Working to mitigate the tragic consequences of civilian harm to affected individuals and populations, including the provision of urgent medical care, making amends to victims, and acknowledgement and apology.
- Learning and Adapting. Using assessments, including patterns of harm and trend data, to identify operational refinements to better protect civilians. These assessments also identify institutional requirements that can help address observed challenges.
- Institutional Capacity. Designing the force to reduce risks to civilians: addressing observed challenges and requirements across the military institution (e.g., doctrine, training, materiel solutions) in order to strengthen the ability to protect civilians over time.[84]

This lifecycle includes two learning loops: operational learning, in which identification of causes and trends directly informs an ongoing operation, and institutional learning, in which lessons from operations inform "doctrine, policy, organization, training, and leadership, together with equipment and facilities."[85] These loops are applicable to all operations in which there is risk of civilian casualties, but are particularly important for air-to-ground operations because these pose an especially high risk of such harm.

An essential foundation of this process is the compilation of accurate data on civilian casualties and analysis of their root causes. Lewis emphasizes that this should rely on information from a wide range of sources, including international organizations, NGOs, and local residents. Root cause analysis differs from what the military calls an "after action report" (AAR) following a mission. In an AAR, "any root cause analysis is done for a single incident in isolation, and lessons are typically not effectively shared across different units or operations."[86] This makes it difficult to discern larger patterns across all operations, which is the purpose of root cause analysis.

Awareness of such patterns in the Uruzgan incident, for instance, could lead to improvements such as greater attention to including crucial details and using consistent terminology in air-to-ground coordination, emphasis on drone crew tactical patience, and consideration of including imagery analysts in voice communications with the ground. These represent possible responses to a single incident, but it is important to analyze a larger set of incidents in order to address their root causes across a range of operations.[87]

A lifecycle approach thus can be crucial in realizing the potential for drone strike precision and meeting the requirement of near certainty of no civilian casualties. The US military first began compiling information on civilian casualties in 2006, and has periodically engaged in initiatives since then to reduce civilian casualties. A short review of these initiatives is useful in appreciating what a lifecycle approach involves and the challenges in adopting it. It also will clarify how these initiatives have fostered operational but not necessarily institutional learning. Initiatives to reduce civilian casualties in manned aircraft operations provide the most immediately applicable lessons for reducing casualties from drone strikes. Analyses of other military operations, however, also are valuable in clarifying the basic organizational and institutional components necessary to reduce casualties on an ongoing basis. While these examples are drawn from the military, they are relevant to strikes conducted by the CIA as well.

US MILITARY CIVILIAN CASUALTY INITIATIVES

Beginning in early 2006, the US began to compile figures on deaths and injuries to Iraqi civilians in incidents at checkpoints, in response to criticism of significant casualties in these incidents.[88] An early effort to collect data on civilian casualties across operations was the 2008 creation of a Civilian Casualty Tracking Cell (CCTC) by the International Security Assistance Force (ISAF) in Afghanistan. The Cell initially was created so that ISAF could respond effectively to civilian casualty allegations. Prior to this, ISAF did not systematically record such allegations. Notifications of suspected casualties, with varying amounts of detail, were passed up the chain of command, with follow-up mainly at the tactical level consisting of condolence payments and legal investigations to assess possible culpability. Data collection was not standardized, and there were discrepancies between ISAF data and those of other organizations such as the United Nations Assistance Mission in Afghanistan (UNAMA).

The CCTC began operating in October 2008, with civilian personnel recording every case of suspected or confirmed civilian casualties reported by the troop level to higher command. Countries contributing troops to ISAF continued separately to investigate allegations of civilian casualties by their personnel to identify possible legal violations. In July 2009, Standard Operating Procedure 307 (SOP 307) designated the CCTC the "authoritative repository of civilian casualties" in the Afghanistan theater, and established a procedural checklist for collecting information.[89]

A 2014 study of the CCTC by CIVIC based on interviews with those involved from 2007 to 2014 found that for almost a year staff often lacked enough information to evaluate allegations.[90] ISAF did not have archival data on civilian casualties, and it took time to emphasize the need to record information at lower levels and to transmit it to regional commands in Afghanistan, coalition states, and ISAF headquarters. By the end of 2009, however, the CCTC had compiled enough data to begin analyzing it for trends, and using this analysis to make recommendations for mitigating civilian casualties.

In 2011 ISAF created the Civilian Casualty Mitigation Team (CCMT), of which CCTC data collection was one part. Data collected by the CCTC was sent to various working groups, which used it to make recommendations to the chain of command on matters such as tactical directives, training, and use of force protocols. These recommendations were based on trends identified in aggregated data, rather than root cause analysis, since the CCMT did not have the time nor staff to conduct the latter.[91]

CIVIC noted that the project encountered some challenges. First, it took time to determine how much information the CCMT would share. Eventually, it became clear that establishing trust in the mission by the Afghan government, the media, partners working with the Afghan population, and the population itself required as much transparency as possible. CCMT thus provided greater access to its data and methodology, as well as video footage and evidence collected in investigations. Such transparency enhanced the ability to compare ISAF data with those of other organizations. As one former member of ISAF leadership observed, "We needed third-party validation. Military tracking and nonmilitary tracking are both important."[92] One focus of criticism was that ISAF was willing to revise its data when it discovered new information, but not when such information came from outside sources.

A second challenge was ensuring that collecting information was a priority at the troop level. ISAF was aware that troops and commanders facing the demands of kinetic operations might regard this task as peripheral. There was no coordinated effort at the troop level to explain the importance of the CCTC. Revisions of tactical directives, dissemination of lessons learned, and field visits by senior ISAF leadership, however, appear to have increased appreciation of the importance of collecting and reporting information.

Another challenge was that regional commands separately tracked civilian casualties in addition to the tracking done by the CCTC. This enabled them to respond to allegations of such casualties at the local level, while CCTC tracking enabled responses to allegations at the national level. As CIVIC observed, "While separate systems may be appropriate, there was no systematic way to pass lessons from the Regional Command's tracking to the theater-wide tracking mechanism or to other Regional Commands."[93]

CIVIC drew four lessons from its review of the project. First, casualty tracking needs to be guided by the goal of reducing civilian harm rather than simply collecting data. Second, the importance of casualty tracking must be emphasized and reiterated to troops at the tactical level in order to ensure comprehensive and accurate data collection. Third, reporting should rely on standard clear definitions, and should include sufficient detail to allow subject matter experts and statisticians to conduct root cause analysis. Finally, a tracking mechanism ideally should be in place before a mission begins.[94]

In 2009, the ISAF and US Central Command sought to obtain a more systematic understanding of civilian casualties in Afghanistan by authorizing a team headed by Sarah Sewall and Larry Lewis to analyze such casualties in this theater. This project was "the first comprehensive examination of civilian casualties in ongoing US military operations."[95]

The study was prompted by concerns that US forces were harming civilians at a rate that jeopardized the mission. General McChrystal issued a Tactical Directive in July 2009 that sought to reorient operations to reduce civilian casualties, especially by restricting use of close air support in operations on compounds. This appeared to have some effect, but forces did not always employ tactical patience, nor were best practices identified and disseminated throughout the force. The study focused in particular on conducting a root cause analysis of civilian casualties that could inform operational guidance.

The analysis found that through 2009 airstrikes were the largest contributor to civilian casualties caused by the US. Casualties declined from these operations after the July 2009 Tactical Directive. The study found, however, that there were a number of airstrikes that targeted gatherings of people not inside compounds. Refinement of guidance clarified that the intent of the Directive was to exercise caution in these strikes as well, which resulted in further reduction of civilian casualties.

A second adjustment that reduced civilian casualties involved the use of close air support to assist self-defense of ground forces under fire. Analysis of these cases indicated that airstrikes sometimes continued after the need for self-defense no longer existed, without approval under rules of engagement (ROE) for situations other than self-defense. Guidance then clarified that strikes in support of self-defense should only be used for this purpose and not for offensive operations without additional prior approval.

Finally, analysis indicated that some civilian casualties were caused by follow-up airstrikes based on an assessment that the first strike did not accomplish the mission. Ironically, this sometimes occurred because the first strike used a lower-impact bomb designed to minimize civilian casualties. The second strike sometimes resulted in the deaths of persons attempting to help those harmed in the first response. Guidance based on the study emphasized the importance of conducting a new CDE before conducting a second strike, drawing on all surveillance capabilities.

The report noted that US and ISAF forces developed several best practices to mitigate civilian casualties at the tactical level, but these efforts "were limited by their ad hoc nature and the frequent absence of timely ground truth."[96] There were few standards to guide reporting or means to validate its accuracy, which meant that "[m]any data needed to address important issues were simply not available."[97] Lessons learned often were not shared across the force because of ineffective integration and dissemination both in theater and among US institutions. Finally, when forces devised solutions, there was insufficient assessment of their effectiveness. All these factors, said the report, "limited operational and institutional change regarding civilian casualties."[98]

Building on the study by Sewall and Lewis and on additional studies by Lewis, in 2012 the Center for Army Lessons Learned issued the handbook *Afghanistan Civilian Casualty Prevention: Observations, Insights, And Lessons*. The handbook stated that civilian casualties caused by ISAF declined by 20% in 2010 and 2011 compared to 2009.[99] The handbook listed common factors contributing to civilian casualties, including those specifically related to casualties from aerial operations that are described earlier in this chapter; provided examples of tactical alternatives that had been used to avoid such casualties; and described vignettes illustrating how consideration of these alternatives could inform the use of force.

The handbook included a chapter on how lessons could be captured and shared in other theaters and with other units. This emphasized the importance of forces providing detailed reports on civilian casualties. It suggested that an investigating officer extract and share key lessons from casualty incidents, and ensure that the details of an investigation are used to update a civilian casualty assessment report. The latter report enables identification of trends and recurring issues, which can then be used to take corrective action.[100]

While the CALL report applied to Afghanistan, a month later the Army provided guidance for all operations. It issued *Army Tactics, Techniques, and Procedures (ATTP) 3-37.31*, "to provide doctrinal guidance for minimizing CIVCAS incidents and managing their consequences."[101]

Notably, one of the two chapters was on the "Civilian Casualty Mitigation Cycle."[102] The stages of this cycle were identical to the ones described in the Sewall and Lewis 2010 report on Afghanistan. The chapter provided detailed guidance supporting each stage of the cycle. It noted, "Lessons learned do not come solely from CIVCAS incidents, but also from occasions in which there was a high risk of CIVCASs but they were avoided. 'Near misses' can offer valuable lessons and illustrate best practices."[103] It also urged leaders to ensure that lessons are shared "across the entire area of operations and implemented wherever appropriate, to maximize the benefit and minimize the tendency to create ad hoc or disparate procedures."[104]

Lewis continued to work with the US military on the issue of civilian casualties for four years after the initial project in Afghanistan in 2009. Two Joint and Coalition Operational Analysis (JCOA) papers in 2013 discussed lessons drawn from this work. In *Reducing and Mitigating Civilian Casualties: Enduring Lessons* Lewis said that leaders should identify civilian casualties during operational planning as a critical vulnerability.[105] He also emphasized the importance of tracking and analyzing civilian casualties in order to identify their root causes, and the need for training and education on general principles and specific risk factors related to civilian casualties. With respect to air-to-ground operations, the report said that special consideration should be given to addressing the risks of these operations when there is no supporting ground force.

A second 2013 JCOA paper, *Drone Strikes: Civilian Casualty Considerations*, said that the 2010 study identified specific factors "that contributed to the relative propensity of drones to cause civilian casualties."[106] The paper acknowledged that operations in a declared theater of armed conflict (DTAC) such as Afghanistan can differ from those outside such a theater (ODTAC) (the latter is the focus of this book). Nonetheless, lessons learned from conducting a root cause analysis of civilian casualties in the former can be valuable in the latter.

The JCOA recommended drawing on lessons and best practices regarding civilian casualties in Afghanistan, since "[a]irstrikes in support of operations [ODTAC] appear to have some common elements with operations in Afghanistan."[107] More generally, it recommended a review of civilian casualty levels in operations ODTAC, and of the process for classifying casualties as enemy combatants versus civilian casualties. This underscores that the goal of minimizing civilian casualties from drone strikes can be informed by some common lessons from civilian casualty mitigation efforts across a wide range of operations.

In 2018 National Defense University, at the request of the Chair of the Joint Chiefs of Staff, assessed civilian casualties resulting from US air and artillery strikes in Syria, Iraq, Libya, Somalia, and Afghanistan from 2015 to 2017.[108] The report noted that dynamic rather than preplanned strikes comprised the vast majority of strikes in Operation Inherent Resolve (OIR) against the Islamic State in Iraq, Syria, and Libya. Some interviewees, it said, estimated that the vast majority of civilian casualties resulted from strikes in support of troops in contact in urban environments.

The report concluded that commander guidance, intent, and oversight was clear, and that the priority of minimizing civilian casualties was widespread at all levels of command. It found, however, several areas of concern. These were that:

- Feedback to subordinate commands on the cause of and/or lessons learned from a civilian casual incident is inconsistent;
- NGOs consulted on this study are frustrated with what they see as decreased transparency in US government reporting. USCENTCOM's public release of assessment and investigation findings offers little detail as to why a CIVCAS allegation is considered "not credible";
- US military standards for verifying third party allegations vary significantly, and some may be construed as restrictive;

- Details and information included in Army Regulation 15–6 investigative reports varied, as did alignment with ongoing NGO investigations; and
- There are limits to existing policy, doctrine, and guidance on how regional commands should respond to CIVCAS incidents.[109]

With regard to verification of casualty incidents, the study reviewed 191 incidents from the OIR civilian casualty database. It compared civilian casualties confirmed by the US military in OIR with data from Airwars, which was chosen because it was the only NGO that provided consistent reports for Iraq and Syria during the study period. The report acknowledged that there was "a considerable gap" between US and Airwars data.[110] While allegations from external sources comprised 23 of the 191 incidents, they accounted for 58% of the total number of dead and wounded civilians.

The report also said that local populations may be prevented from reporting an incident in timely fashion because of conflict conditions, cultural constraints, and the lack of access to reporting channels. It noted complaints by NGOs that when they send information about an incident to the military and offer additional data such as munitions remnants, photos, satellite imagery, and witness statements they seldom received a response.[111]

The report recommended that the US "systematically seek out additional sources of information on potential civilian casualties as part of the self-reporting process," including social media and NGOs.[112] It also recommended devoting greater attention to civilian casualties in the BDA process, and considering standardizing the civilian casualty review process across combatant commands. The latter, said the report, "may include review boards for civilian casualty incidents overseen by the next echelon of command," which could "serve as an alternative to official administrative investigation" to provide feedback and lessons learned.[113]

The report also recommended expanding combatant command level civilian casualty cells to include persons responsible for reconciling US military and external reports, and broadening the geographic area and period of inquiry for initial assessment reports designed to determine whether a full investigation is warranted. With respect to investigations, the report recommended that the US military should "institutionalize" the civilian casualty investigation process, which includes closer engagement with NGOs where feasible.[114] Adoption of the report's recommendations would move the US considerably closer to a lifecycle approach to minimizing civilian casualties.

Different elements of the US military thus periodically have focused attention on reducing civilian casualties, have had some success in doing so, and have identified best practices to guide these efforts. As the next section describes, however, there remain challenges to institutionalizing a lifecycle approach across all entities in a position to cause such casualties.

CHALLENGES IN ADOPTING A LIFECYCLE APPROACH

Lewis' 2021 paper identifies two key challenges in adopting a lifecycle approach by the US military: (1) ensuring accurate detection of civilian casualties and (2) addressing the difficulties of institutional learning in the military.[115]

Detection

With respect to detection of casualties, Lewis notes that almost 60% of the civilian harm resulting from operations in Mosul against the Islamic State was not detected by internal military sources, but from an allegation presented by an outside organization. Similarly, he says, analysis of 13 cases of civilian casualties caused by airstrikes in Afghanistan indicated that in 11 cases the assessment conducted by the attacking aircraft did not detect civilian harm from the strike. Thus, "militaries can struggle to accurately estimate the level of civilian harm based on their own information."[116] This echoes findings from the 2018 National Defense University report described above.

A 2020 report on military investigations of civilian casualties by CIVIC and the Columbia Law School Human Rights Institute describes features of investigations that can prevent accurate detection of casualties. The researchers reviewed public records of 228 assessments and investigations into civilian harm, mainly from Afghanistan and Iraq, from 2002 to 2018.[117] It also "reviewed applicable laws, military regulations, protocols, and standards; conducted interviews with military, government, and civil society experts with relevant experience; and conducted four workshops with military personnel and non-governmental organization (NGO) representatives."[118] The report's overall conclusion was that "over the last eighteen years, examples of good practice in investigating civilian harm have been overshadowed by the inconsistency—and, too often, inadequacy—of the overall record of military investigations."[119]

The study found that internal military records in many cases were incomplete and not consistently maintained, leading to erroneous dismissal of external allegations. It also found that the military often tended to rely only on its internal records in assessing such allegations rather than attempting to check them against other sources of information such as survivors, witnesses, civil society organizations, and the media. It noted that civil society organizations complained that a major obstacle to reporting civilian casualties was the absence of a readily identifiable accessible channel for doing so.[120]

The report said that the military rarely interviewed civilian witnesses or conducted investigations at the site of strikes. Site visits are important, the study emphasized, because they allow investigators to "discover evidence that is not visible through aerial footage or remote observation, inspect weapons fragments and damage at the site, collect forensic evidence, and otherwise learn the details of the incident and the resulting harm."[121] Civilian witnesses interviews and site visits, said the report, should be standard practice, When in-person interviews are not possible, there should be arrangements for alternative methods, such as "interviewing by secure telecommunications, relaying questions and answers through third parties, or meeting in locations other than the site of harm."[122]

Finally, the study said that lessons learned from civilian casualty investigations are not systematically transmitted or implemented across the Department of Defense. The report recommended that the Department create a single database on civilian casualties to ensure that lessons are shared across all branches of the military on an ongoing basis.

Institutionalization

Lewis listed the failure to institutionalize prevention and mitigation of civilian casualties as a second key obstacle to adopting a lifecycle approach. This underscores that systematic compilation and dissemination of data are ultimately dependent upon acceptance at all levels of the importance of civilian casualties.

What factors can prompt such acceptance and affect its durability? Sarah Sewall's study of efforts in the US Air Force (USAF) to reduce civilian harm since the 1990s suggests some answers to these questions.[123] Sewall describes how political concern about civilian casualties imposed significant constraints on the use of air power in several operations beginning in the 1990s. Operations in Operation Desert Storm in Iraq and coalition air operations in the Balkans, she says, "revealed that civilian casualties could be highly costly for political or operational reasons. When such harm occurred, US leaders routinely responded by imposing further operational restrictions on airpower."[124]

Sewall observes that giving priority to minimizing civilian casualties initially faced resistance from proponents of the view that using overwhelming force would enable conflicts to end sooner. Three factors, however, enabled the Air Force to overcome this resistance. First, the consistency of the constraints during both Republican and Democratic administrations "indicated that concern about civilian casualties had become an enduring factor in using airpower."[125]

Second, responding to these constraints was consistent to some extent with the USAF focus on greater precision and the use of effects-based targeting that sought to achieve maximum effect with minimal damage. Finally, the USAF came to realize that minimizing civilian casualties "offered a route toward regaining greater operational freedom and ensuring airpower's role in future conflicts."[126] In this respect, casualty minimization served organizational goals.

As a result, the Air Force took steps such as refining pre-strike CDEs, improving weapon precision, and developing low civilian casualty weapons with reduced blast and fragmentation radii. Operations also began to require referral to higher authority if anticipated civilian casualties exceeded a certain number, regardless of the value of the military target. As Sewall notes, this decouples consideration of civilian casualties from the law of war standard of proportionality, reflecting that casualties are a concern in their own right, not simply if they are excessive.[127] In this way, there was learning across the Air Force at the organizational level.

There was not, however, necessarily learning at the level of the military as an institution. Sewall notes that ground forces did not become sensitive to civilian casualties until counterinsurgency operations in the mid-2000s. Furthermore, although "[c]ollateral damage prevention became part of the airpower sales pitch," the process of change even within the USAF "remains tentative and fragile."[128]

Sewall concludes that the fundamental issue facing the US military is "the need for institutional change – internalization within the services that civilian casualty reduction is not something that automatically happens but rather requires dedicated attention: technology, tactics, training, and so forth."[129] She identifies several key steps that could help the military move in this direction. The first is the development of a standardized process for collecting and assembling data, which would include information on best practices for avoiding civilian harm, all of which would be shared across services.[130] The second challenge is the need to build on the 2011 establishment of civilian casualties as a distinct category in the US military database on lessons learned.

Third, says Sewall, the military needs to build a cadre of experts on civilian casualties. The study she did with Lewis was the first comprehensive analysis of civilian harm in US military operations, but there has not been similar analysis in other theaters nor were its lessons systematically applied elsewhere. Furthermore, while several organizations outside the US government gather and analyze data on civilian casualties, the military often dismisses or fails to follow up on this data. "[U]ntil the military develops its own civilian casualty expertise," she says, "civilian analysis of civilian harm is likely to set the terms of the debate."[131]

Next, Sewall emphasizes the importance of a permanent institutional entity within the military focused on reducing civilian harm. As she puts it, "Whose promotion is enhanced if the military fights effectively with fewer unintended deaths?"[132] There is now an office in the Department of Defense responsible for civilian casualty mitigation, but it is too early to know whether it will serve this purpose.

Sewall cautions that, while attitudes have evolved, "there is nothing inexorable about the military's institutional prioritization of civilian casualty mitigation."[133] In particular, there is a risk that the importance given to minimizing such casualties will depend upon the extent this is regarded as integral to accomplishing military missions. An important impetus for the USAF measures that she describes, for instance, was the desire to preserve the operational freedom of airpower in the kinds of conflicts in which the US has been involved since the 1990s. Similarly, ground force sensitivity to civilian casualties in Afghanistan and Iraq was seen as crucial to counterinsurgency success.

This means that attention to civilian casualties may depend upon the kinds of conflicts that the US anticipates, and the extent to which avoiding civilian harm is seen as helping or hindering those operations. Movements away from population-centric operations such as counterinsurgency may limit the perceived need to make changes that limit civilian casualties across all types of operations.

With respect to drone strikes, the controversy over these operations outside war zones means that avoiding civilian harm may be important to the perceived legitimacy of these operations. At the same time, unforeseen circumstances may alter US perceptions of the extent to which minimizing casualties furthers or hinders these kinds of operations. Furthermore, the US does not consider the requirement of near certainty of no civilian casualties a binding legal obligation but a policy choice that can be overridden if need be.

A fundamental challenge to institutionalizing concern for civilian casualties therefore is ensuring that preventing civilian harm is regarded as intrinsically important rather than important only insofar as it contributes to successful operations. What might provide a more durable foundation for internalizing an ethos of civilian protection that is not contingent on its alignment with operational demands?

Neta Crawford suggests one possibility, which is informed by the concept of "normal accidents."[134] Such accidents predictably occur in the course of routine operations by organizations engaged in risky activities that require complex coordination among many actors. Such accidents are unintended but foreseeable, and thus distinguishable from accidents that arise in situations that are unusual and unlikely, which Crawford calls "genuine accidents."[135]

We expect large organizations in which normal accidents are foreseeable, such as hospitals, power plants, and airlines, to adopt organizational structures and processes to minimize their occurrence. As Dennis Thompson puts it, "In bureaucracies, certain patterns of failure are common enough that we should expect any competent official to anticipate them and to take reasonable precautions to avoid them or at least to minimize their harmful consequences."[136] In this respect, the fact that no one in an organization intended a harmful outcome does not absolve an organization of responsibility.

Based on her work studying civilian casualties caused by the US in Afghanistan, Iraq, and Pakistan, as well as drone strikes in Yemen, Crawford suggests that in many cases civilian casualties can be seen as normal accidents in the sense that "many civilians are harmed in ways that were foreseeable and either were, or should have been, foreseen."[137] For many years, she argues, the military emphasized that such casualties were unintentional and inevitable, without taking systematic steps to minimize them other than to ensure that they were not excessive under the law of war. Once it became clear, however, that such casualties were harming counterinsurgency efforts in Iraq and Afghanistan, the military revised "priorities, roles, decision-making knowledge and structure, organizational capacity and training" to foster a process of organizational learning and adaptation in order to minimize civilian casualties.[138] These efforts helped produce demonstrable reductions in casualties.

Thus, as Crawford says, "Once minimizing civilian harm and protecting civilians was deemed an urgent military necessity, it was gradually internalized and institutionalized."[139] In other words, the US has demonstrated that it is capable of engaging in the kind of institutionalization that Lewis says is crucial, albeit limited to specific theaters, types of operations, and, to some extent, service branches. These efforts treated civilian casualties as normal foreseeable accidents, which the US has a responsibility to prevent as much as possible. It is internalization of this understanding of casualties and responsibility across all operations that would lead to genuine institutionalization. This would reflect adoption of the ethos described in the 2012 Army Civilian Casualty Mitigation Manual: "Protection of civilians is at the heart of the profession of arms."[140]

Crawford describes how attention to minimizing civilian casualties waned in recent years in operations in Afghanistan as the US sought to demonstrate strength in bargaining with the Taliban.[141] Concerted efforts to minimize civilian casualties reduced casualties from 552 in 2008 to 104 in 2014. In 2017, however, the US announced relaxation of rules of engagement for airstrikes. There had been 250 civilian casualties from pro-government strikes in 2016. These rose to 295 in 2017, 548 in 2018, 700 in 2019, and 239 through September 2020.

While many factors may affect the incidence of casualties, Crawford concludes, "When the United States tightens its rules of engagement and restricts airstrikes where civilians are at risk, civilian casualties tend to go down; when it loosens the restrictions, civilians are injured and killed in greater numbers."[142] The US therefore is capable of reducing civilian casualties when it focuses on doing so.

While this section has discussed efforts to minimize civilian casualties in a variety of military operations, it is important to appreciate that targeted strikes against high-value targets generally provide greater opportunities to minimize such casualties than are available in many other types of operations. I have cautioned that strike precision should not be automatically assumed based on features of the platform, but that it depends on a concerted focus and coordination among multiple components. Nonetheless, as Dan Mahanty has noted:

> The government's confidence in the precision of planned operations is not entirely misplaced... [T]he resources needed for pre-planned operations normally limit their use to circumstances where the United States has a higher degree of confidence, based on its own intelligence, that it has correctly identified a member of an armed group that it may target... These operations incidentally afford more time for greater precaution in the targeting process itself, such as the choice of ordnance, the trajectory of a projectile, and assuring that civilians such as family members are not present.[143]

In addition, unlike with the use of drones for close air support, targeted strikes generally do not require balancing civilian casualties against the need for force protection. The US thus is in a position to come closer to ensuring near certainty of no civilian casualties from targeted strikes outside war zones if it institutionalizes efforts to meet this standard.

Conclusion

This chapter has assessed the US claim of drone strike precision by examining both the technology and the complex organizational processes that are involved in conducting a strike. Evidence indicates that realizing the promise of precision requires adopting a lifecycle approach to minimizing civilian casualties that includes adequate investigation to identify casualties that draws on multiple sources of information, analysis of the root causes of casualties, communication and incorporation of this analysis into operations to improve performance, dissemination of lessons learned across all entities that may cause casualties, creation of a common database on such lessons, and ongoing learning that keeps the cycle continuously operating. Commitment to this process is likely to be strengthened by internalization of a sense of responsibility to prevent unintended but foreseeable civilian casualties as much as possible, consistent with achieving mission objectives.

The US regards the requirement of near certainty of no civilian casualties for targeted strikes outside war zones as a policy rather than a legal obligation. The distinction may not matter, however, if public expectations make this a precondition for the perceived legitimacy of such strikes. Indeed, it was criticism of US strikes based on NGO reports of civilian casualties that was the impetus for adopting this policy. The US has refined its targeted strike operations, but evidence suggests that there is still significant room for improvement if it is consistently to meet the near certainty standard outside war zones.

As the next chapter discusses, targeted strikes can have impacts on local populations beyond causing deaths and injuries. Accurate information on these impacts can be very difficult to acquire, but some organizations have conducted investigations of individual strikes that provide an indication of the kinds of consequences that can occur. These include damage to homes and businesses, as well as social and psychological effects. In addition, there is an extensive debate about the extent to which drone strikes generate hostility on the part of the local population, and whether they lead to greater support for militant groups. A substantial portion of the next chapter discusses efforts to assess these claims.

NOTES

1. The operational details of missions described in this section are drawn from Lee, P. (2019). *Reaper force: The inside story of Britain's drone wars*. John Blake; Martin, M. J., with Sasser, C. W. (2010). *Predator: The remote-control air war over Iraq and Afghanistan: A pilot's story*. Zenith Press; McNeal, G. S. (2014). Targeted killing and accountability. *Georgetown Law Journal, 102*(3), 681–794; Woods, C. (2015). *Sudden justice: America's secret drone wars*. Oxford University Press.
2. McNeal, 731.
3. Mehta, A. (2014, May 13). Ready for retirement, can predator find new home? *Defense News*. https://archive.ph/20140517154223/http://www.defensenews.com/article/20140513/DEFREG/305120020/Ready-for-Retirement-Can-Predator-Find-New-Home.
4. Woods, 2.
5. Military.com, Joint Direct Attack Munition. https://www.military.com/equipment/joint-direct-attack-munition-jdam.
6. Gregory, D. (2013, September 8). Theory of the Drone 12: 'Killing Well'? *Geographical Imaginations*. https://geographicalimaginations.com/tag/hellfire-missile/.
7. Id.
8. Id.

9. Congressional Research Service, Precision-Guided Munitions: Background and Issues for Congress, June 11, 2021.
10. GlobalSecurity.org, Guided Bomb Unit-12 (GBU-12) Paveway II. https://www.globalsecurity.org/military/systems/munitions/gbu-12.htm.
11. US Air Force, Joint Direct Attack Munition GBU—31/32/38, June 18, 2003. https://www.af.mil/About-Us/Fact-Sheets/Display/Article/104572/joint-direct-attack-munition-gbu-313238/.
12. F-16.net: https://www.f-16.net/f-16_armament_article9.html. Kris Osborne notes, "'In its most accurate mode, the JDAM system will provide a weapon circular error probable of 5 m or less during free flight when GPS data is available. If GPS data is denied, the JDAM will achieve a 30-m CEP or less for free flight times up to 100 seconds with a GPS quality handoff from the aircraft,' an Air Force statement said." Osborne, K. (2017, May 9). The MQ-9 reaper is now wielding these deadly new weapons. *The National Interest*. https://nationalinterest.org/blog/the-buzz/the-mq-9-reaper-now-wielding-these-deadly-new-weapons-20572.
13. Goldstein, S. J. (2019, June 24). Nothing kept me up at night the way the Gorgon Stare did. *Longreads*. https://longreads.com/2019/06/21/nothing-kept-me-up-at-night-the-way-the-gorgon-stare-did/.
14. McNeal, 742.
15. Chairman of the Joint Chiefs of Staff, No-Strike and the Collateral Damage Estimation Methodology, February 13, 2009, D-1.
16. McNeal, 741.
17. Id. 742.
18. Schmitt, M. (2012). Unmanned combat aircraft systems and international humanitarian law: Simplifying the oft benighted debate. *Boston University International Law Journal*, 595–619, 615. http://www.bu.edu/law/journals-archive/international/volume30n2/documents/symposium_schmitt.pdf.
19. Gross, G., Llinias, J., & Nagi, R. (2015, July 6–9). Application of multi-level fusion for pattern of life analysis. In *18th International Conference on Information Fusion* (p. 1): Washington, DC. https://c4i.gmu.edu/~pcosta/F15/data/fileserver/file/472061/filename/Paper_1570113673.pdf.
20. Lewis, L. (2018). Redefining human control: Lessons from the battlefield for autonomous weapons (p. 11). https://www.cna.org/CNA_files/PDF/DOP-2018-U-017258-Final.pdf.
21. US Air Force. (1998, February 1). *Intelligence targeting guide*, 72. https://irp.fas.org/doddir/usaf/afpam14-210/index.html.
22. Lee, Peter, 146–149.

23. Lewis, L., & Vavrichek, D. M. (2014). *Rethinking the drone war*. CNA and Marine Corps University Press, 20–21. https://www.cna.org/cna_files/pdf/RethinkingTheDroneWar.pdf.
24. Id. 20.
25. Lewis, L. (2014). *Improving lethal action*, 50. CNA. https://www.cna.org/CNA_files/PDF/COP-2014-U-008746-Final.pdf.
26. Id. 32.
27. Woods, 2015; Kindle, 363.
28. Center for Army Lessons Learned (CALL). (2012, September). *Afghanistan civilian casualty prevention: Observations, insights, and lessons*, 31. https://info.publicintelligence.net/CALL-AfghanCIVCAS.pdf.
29. Id.
30. Id.
31. Lewis & Varichek, 15–16.
32. CALL, 5.
33. Id.
34. Sewall, S. (2017). *Chasing success: Air force efforts to reduce civilian harm*. Air University, 156.
35. Lewis, L., & Goodman, R. (2018, March 22). *We need better estimates—Not just better numbers, just security*. https://www.justsecurity.org/54181/civilian-casualties-estimates-not-numbers/.
36. Amnesty International, 2019, 28.
37. Id.
38. Kahn & Gopal.
39. Lewis, 2014, 46.
40. United States Department of Defense. (2021, November 3). *Investigation into 29 Aug CIVCAS in Afghanistan*. https://www.washingtonpost.com/context/air-force-inspector-general-s-findings-of-errant-drone-strike-in-kabul-on-aug-29-2021/a7d9edaf-b8d3-497b-9be1-8db427ca7cf6/?itid=lk_interstitial_manual_5; Copp, T. (2021, September 17). *'Horrible mistake': Pentagon admits drone strike killed children, not terrorists, defense one*. https://www.defenseone.com/threats/2021/09/horrible-mistake-pentagon-admits-drone-strike-killed-children-not-terrorists/185440/.
41. Copp, 2021.
42. Id.
43. Id.
44. US Department of Defense, *Investigation into 29 Aug CIVCAS in Afghanistan*.
45. Id.
46. Hartig, L. (2021, November 10). Reexamining the Fundamentals of the Drone Strike Program After the Kabul Strike. *Just*

Security. https://www.justsecurity.org/79168/reexamining-the-fundam entals-of-the-drone-program-after-the-kabul-strike/.

47. Id.
48. Id.
49. Id.
50. United States Forces Afghanistan, Headquarters. (2010, May 21). AR 15–6 Investigation, 21 February 2010 U.S. air-to-ground engagement in the vicinity of Shahidi Hassas, Uruzgan district, Afghanistan. On file with author.
51. Id. 000032.
52. Id. 000024.
53. Id.
54. Id. 000043.
55. Id. 00012.
56. Id. 000021.
57. Id. 000033.
58. Id. 000022.
59. Id.
60. Id.
61. Id. 000029.
62. Id. 000032.
63. Id.
64. Id. 000033.
65. Id.
66. Id.
67. Id.
68. Id.
69. Id. 000022.
70. Id.
71. Id.
72. Id. 000037.
73. Id. 000022.
74. Id. 000023.
75. Id. 000032.
76. Id. 000037.
77. Id.
78. Id.
79. Id.
80. Id. 144–145.
81. Lewis, L. (2021). Protecting civilians: A comprehensive approach, 1 [Unpublished manuscript]. Center for Autonomy and AI, CAN.
82. Sewall, S., & Lewis, L. (2010). Joint civilian casualty study: Executive summary.

83. Lewis, L. (2021). Protecting civilians: A comprehensive approach [Unpublished manuscript]. Center for Autonomy and AI, CNA.
84. Lewis, 2021, 3.
85. Id.
86. Lewis & Varichek, 125.
87. Id. 144–146.
88. Montgomery, N. (2006, March 18). U.S. seeks to reduce civilian deaths at Iraq checkpoints. *Stars and Stripes.* https://www.stripes.com/news/ u-s-seeks-to-reduce-civilian-deaths-at-iraq-checkpoints-1.46403.
89. Center for Civilians in Conflict. (2014). *Civilian harm tracking: Analysis of ISAF efforts in Afghanistan* (p. 5). https://civiliansinconflict.org/wp-content/uploads/2017/09/ISAF_Civilian_Harm_Tracking.pdf.
90. Id. 6.
91. Id. 8.
92. Id. 11.
93. Id. 16.
94. Id. 21–23.
95. Sewall & Lewis, 3.
96. Id. 10.
97. Id.
98. Id. 11.
99. CALL, 1.
100. Id. 51.
101. Headquarters, Department of the Army. (2012, July). *ATTP 3–37.31 civilian casualty mitigation.* Army Tactics, Techniques, and Procedures, 3. https://fas.org/irp/doddir/army/attp3-37-31.pdf.
102. Id. 2–1 to 2–24.
103. Id. 2–24.
104. Id.
105. Joint and Coalition Operational Analysis. (2013a, April 12). *Reducing and mitigating civilian casualties: Enduring lessons.*
106. Joint and Coalition Operational Analysis. (2013b, June 18). *Drone strikes: Civilian casualty considerations,* 1.
107. Id. 2.
108. National Defense University, Executive Summary, Civilian Casualty (CIVCAS) Review. (2018, April 17). https://games-cdn.washingto npost.com/notes/prod/default/documents/e39c5889-6489-4373-bd8e-ac2ca012e03d/note/6c60bba4-5781-4874-acdf-87e199f6e31b. pdf.
109. Id. 3–12.
110. Id. 11.
111. Id. 10.
112. Id. 3.

322   M. REGAN

113. Id. 4.
114. Id.
115. Lewis, 2021, 12–14.
116. Id. 13.
117. Center for Civilians in Conflict & Columbia Law School Human Rights Institute. (2020). *In search of answers: U.S. military investigations and civilian harm.* https://civiliansinconflict.org/wp-content/uploads/2020/02/PDF-Report-for-Website.pdf.
118. Id. 1.
119. Id.
120. Id. 4.
121. Id.
122. Id.
123. Sewall, 2017.
124. Id. 104.
125. Id. 149.
126. Id.
127. Id. 167.
128. Id. 178.
129. Id. 178–179.
130. Id. 182.
131. Id. 155.
132. Id. 183.
133. Id. 187.
134. Crawford, N. C. (2013). *Accountability for killing: Moral responsibility for collateral damage in America's post-9/11 wars* (p. 8). Oxford University Press.
135. Id.
136. Thompson, D. (1980). Moral responsibility of public officials: The problem of many hands. *American Political Science Review, 74*(4), 905–916, 913. https://doi.org/10.2307/1954312.
137. Crawford, 2013, 11.
138. Id. 380.
139. Id. 83.
140. Headquarters, Department of the Army, 1–1.
141. Crawford, N. C. (2020, December 7). Afghanistan's rising civilian death toll due to airstrikes, 2017–2020. *Costs of war.* https://watson.brown.edu/costsofwar/files/cow/imce/papers/2020/Rising%20Civilian%20Death%20Toll%20in%20Afghanistan_Costs%20of%20War_Dec%207%202020.pdf.
142. Id. 1.
143. Mahanty, D. (2020, April 21). *Great Expectations: AFRICOM's New Quarterly Report on Civilian Casualties.* Just security. https://www.justsecurity.org/69785/great-expectations-africom-new-quarterly-report-on-civilian-casualties/.

CHAPTER 11

Effects on Local Populations

There has been increasing attention in recent years to what is called the "reverberating effects" of armed conflict, especially from the use of explosive weapons in urban areas. These are indirect consequences caused by the impact of weapons. As the United Nations has described, these may include effects on "transportation networks, electricity, waste and water management, public health, education, food security, housing and shelter, displacement, culture and identity, economic opportunity, environmental standards, and gender equality."[1] Drone strikes potentially may cause fewer of these impacts because of their more limited blast and fragmentation radius, at least when they use Hellfire missiles, and their use in relatively remote areas. Nonetheless, it is reasonable to assume that they produce some reverberating impacts.

Determining these impacts can be very challenging. Investigations by NGOs of individual strikes provide some indication of them, although there is no way to know how representative they are. The first part of this chapter discusses findings from such investigations.

The impact of strikes on local population attitudes also has received considerable attention. Some critics claim that strikes generate hostility toward the US that makes it more difficult to meet the goal of weakening terrorist groups. This hostility must be considered in a full assessment of strike effectiveness. Furthermore, some argue that resentment of strikes increases support for terrorist groups and helps them recruit. If so, this

M. Regan, *Drone Strike–Analyzing the Impacts of Targeted Killing*, https://doi.org/10.1007/978-3-030-91119-5_11

would undermine US goals even more. Unfortunately, there has been little rigorous empirical investigation to inform this debate.

Given prominent debate on this issue, the second part of the chapter spends considerable time reviewing and assessing research on the impacts of strikes on local population attitudes. The aim is to clarify what we do and don't know about such impacts, and to suggest lines of inquiry that can enhance our understanding of them.

PHYSICAL, SOCIAL, AND PSYCHOLOGICAL IMPACTS

Determining the physical damage caused by US strikes is extraordinarily difficult, and there are no reliable estimates of it. Investigations by NGOs, however, provide information about the effects of individual strikes, even if there is no way to know if these effects are representative. One form of property damage is the destruction of housing. A study by Stanford and NYU law schools notes that extended families in North Waziristan in the Federally Administered Tribal Areas (FATA) in Pakistan live together in compounds that often contain several smaller individual buildings. "Many interviews told us," said the report, "that often strikes not only obliterate the target house, usually made of mud, but also cause significant damage to three or four surrounding houses."[2] Another study by Open Society describes how 19 persons in Yemen lived together in a house struck by a missile that caused two explosions.[3]

Destroying a single house thus can leave several people homeless. A house also "constitutes a massive financial investment, representing years of saving and building, and is often a family's greatest financial asset."[4] Rebuilding it is a major financial burden and in many cases may be impossible. Those who lose housing must then turn to family members for shelter, but those relatives may already live in crowded conditions.

A strike also may destroy businesses, shops, crops, livestock, and other property on which residents rely to make a living. As one study observes, "Even the loss of a few cattle can be devastating."[5] One resident reported that the bakery he owns with his brother was destroyed in a drone strike, depriving them and their employees of their livelihood. "Four tractors were working all the day to clean the debris, all at our own expense," said one of them.[6] Such losses and expenses can impose significant hardship in a society in which families have few assets and sources of income.

Another study by CIVIC noted that destruction of shops and businesses can increase health risks of those who lose their jobs, and can also have effects beyond the individuals directly affected. It can hurt producers in the agricultural sector, and "banks shut down, markets halt, and only goods essential to people's livelihoods are traded."[7]

Research by James Marsh and John Williams in eastern Nangarhar province in Afghanistan bordering Pakistan also documents residents' concerns about economic impacts of drone strikes.[8] The study conducted interviews with 37 members of the Murad Khel sub-tribe of the Mohmand and the Miyagan, which is spiritually connected to the Mohmand, in the Lal Pur district, and the Sangu Khel sub-tribe of the Shinwari in southern Nazian district. One interviewee said, "[I]n [the] past we had worked in our land and take animals to mountain but when these drones start. . .bombing in our village. . .we can't go to our lands, we can't take our animals to mountain so no one go outside of village and home because everyone scare[d] that the drone will shoot."[9] Others mentioned how fear of being mistakenly targeted as Taliban has caused them to stop herding animals or tending fields in remote areas where they normally would carry a firearm for protection.[10]

Research by Paolo Bertolotti, Fotini Christia, and Ali Jadbabaie examines the effects of 74 drone strikes in Yemen between 2010 and 2012 on social networks in strike locations.[11] They review 12 billion records of phone calls and texts by six million subscribers to analyze communication and mobility patterns after strikes occurred. The authors confirm that key militant activities that could affect behavior did not overlap with the dates of strikes.

The study finds that information about a strike diffuses quickly through significant increases in calls by "proximal individuals" in the "strike region," defined as within 15 miles of the strike. These individuals call persons who in turn call others in an extended chain of multiple notifications. Proximal individuals' calls increase by 104% after a strike compared to calls five weeks before and after a strike. Calls by those whom they contact increase by 168% forty minutes after a strike, with calls by the next two persons in the chain respectively increasing by 70% within sixty minutes after a strike, and 46% within seventy minutes. Strikes that cause civilian casualties so spark large cascades, with increases in calls by the person first contacted by a proximal individual increasing by 115% for strikes that kill ten civilians.

The authors conclude that information about a strike thus circulates quickly to persons several steps removed from the first caller in the strike region. They acknowledge, however, that "we lack the content of the communications and are thus unable to analyze exactly how opinions and loyalties shift around these events."[12] Such information would be valuable in assessing the impact of drone strikes on local population attitudes.

The location estimates provided by the call records also enable the authors to analyze travel patterns in response to strikes. These indicate that some displacement occurs after a strike. Compared to average daily distance traveled by proximal individuals 14 days prior to a strike, these individuals increase their travel distance by an average of 7.6 km on strike days, or 27% over the pre-strike average. Of the 74 strikes, 58% resulted in statistically significant increases in mobility on strike days.

Further examination of the data indicates that many individuals flee the region of the strike. Some 4519 proximal individuals who live within the region leave it within the first 24 hours after a strike and remain away for at least 24 hours. Of those who flee, 51% return within five days, but 23%, or 1046 individuals, do not return to their hometowns within 30 days. Strikes that kill 10 civilians result in 41 more individuals fleeing who do not return within 30 days, compared to strikes with no civilian casualties. The authors note, "As the majority of strikes take place in sparsely populated districts, the number of individuals displaced, even in our sample, is substantial and is an order of magnitude larger than the roughly 250 militants targeted in the 74 attacks."[13] The authors suggest that their findings establish "a disruptive impact on civilians" that is not limited to the immediate strike region.[14] They note that "an open question remains of whether the disruption induced by strikes increases or decreases militant recruitment."[15]

Marsh and Williams' research described above also indicates that some displacement has occurred in eastern Afghanistan because of drone strikes. One interviewee reported: "'Most of the people in (a region within Lal Pur) left their homes and went to other areas since their lives and personal assets were in danger. . . [T]hey have their animals with them, but they don't have their own fields in those places to feed their animals."[16] Another resident said of drone strikes, "The biggest influence it had on our people is they (inhabitants) started leaving the village and now we don't have even 50 homes nearby in the village."[17]

Some investigations report that residents in areas of strikes avoid gathering in large groups. This includes in areas such as household guestrooms and mosques, and at events such as weddings and funerals. One resident told researchers, "People are scared of the drone attacks, they don't walk together; they sit only in pairs and if they gather in large groups, it would be only for a very short time."[18]

One consequence in the FATA and nearby areas can be to weaken the local informal Pashtun dispute resolution gathering known as a *jirga*. One resident reported, "Everybody, all the mothers, all the wives, they have told their people not to congregate together in a *jirga*."[19] The *jirga* is an important element in ordering Pashtun community and political life, which means that its disruption can weaken the social fabric in areas in which drone strikes occur.

Marsh and Williams' study also examines the effects of strikes on other local informal social governance processes. Interviewees, they say, "strongly self-identified with their respective tribes and sub-tribes, and customary behaviours."[20] Marsh and Williams argue that characterizing these areas as "ungoverned" fails to consider ways in which cultural institutions can maintain and regulate identity and behavior. Largely hereditary *maliks* traditionally have exercised influence in villages through the "complex interplay of governance institutions and processes at multiple levels," which includes dispute resolution mechanisms such as *jirgas*.[21] Analysis of drone strikes, the authors argue, does not consider the effect on these institutions and processes, which "can allow other political forces than the Taliban to play a stronger role."[22]

Interviews indicated how strikes had affected local informal governance. "Every interviewee," report the authors, "described disruptions from drones damaging customary governance, consequently weakening customary relations, cultural boundaries, behaviour, community cohesion and security."[23] Elders were hindered in their ability to "obtain, deliver and distribute moral and material goods; and, to fulfil, maintain and regulate customary roles, influence and governance."[24] Fewer people are willing to gather in large numbers, which weakens cultural practices by providing fewer opportunities for social interaction.

Marsh and Williams also report, "*Maliks'* lack of a relationship with drones and those using them is not lost on the local populace. Consequently, maliks' influence in moderating behaviours and balancing religious figures in the area has been impacted, weakening customary governance."[25] This is problematic for US interests because local customary practices are opposed to radical and extremist jihadist political groups. "Numerous elders and parents stated since drone strikes had begun youth were more open to radical and extreme views. They noted community means of managing these views had been circumscribed by drone activity restricting gatherings."[26]

It seems reasonable to attribute fewer social gatherings, including the *jirga*, to drone strikes. The decline of local informal governance, however, likely also reflects the control exercised by the Taliban, which has been enabled in part by killing moderate *maliks*.[27] The fact that *maliks* are unable to prevent the Taliban from pressuring unwilling families to provide food, shelter, and perhaps other assistance, as well as Taliban regulation of daily life, also likely contributes to their decline in influence.

Some interviewees told NGO investigators of anxiety and psychological distress from living in areas in which drone strikes occur. One resident in the FATA said, "God knows whether they'll strike us again or not. But they're always surveying us, they're always over us, and you never know when they're going to strike and attack."[28] Others say the continuing background buzz from drones can serve as a constant reminder of this risk. Some fear they may be the target of an attack because incorrect information is given to drone operators. Others report that their stress is compounded by the feeling that they have no way to affect when or where a strike might occur. As one report put it, "Interviewees describe the experience of living under constant surveillance as harrowing."[29]

A Stanford/NYU Law School study interviewed 69 former residents of North Waziristan who "were witnesses to drone strikes or surveillance, victims of strikes, or family members of victims."[30] None of the interviews occurred in the FATA. The project also interviewed a similar number of journalists, activists, Pakistani government officials, and health professionals. The report concluded that drone presence "terrorizes men, women, and children, giving rise to anxiety and psychological trauma among civilian communities."[31] The report said that mental health professionals interviewed by the project confirmed these symptoms.

Some support for this claim comes from *New York Times* reporter David Rohde, who was kidnapped by the Taliban in the FATA. He wrote that in the FATA "[t]he drones were terrifying. From the ground, it is impossible to determine who or what they are tracking as they circle overhead. The buzz of a distant propeller is a constant reminder of imminent death."[32] Marsh and Williams' interviews in eastern Afghanistan also indicated that people were "experiencing immense stresses, reflecting their fear of strikes."[33] A study by Aqil Shah also finds that drone strikes

increase anxiety and stress, especially among children.[34] As one interviewee put it, "the drones are always hovering, watching us and can strike
any time."[35]

Psychiatrist Metin Basoglu has argued that residents who face continuing exposure to the risk of drone strikes face conditions that are similar
to those who are victims of torture.[36] What he describes as a "learning
theory" of torture highlights that the stress occurs not simply because
of physical abuse but because an individual is subject to unpredictable
and uncontrollable stressful events that create anxiety and fear, leading
eventually to a feeling of helplessness.[37]

Basoglu suggests that residents of the FATA are comparable to torture
victims because they have no idea when or where the next strike will occur
or who will be targeted. They also may not be certain of how militants are
distinguished from civilians. They cannot exercise control by moving to a
safer location because of poverty, restrictions on travel out of the FATA,
military checkpoints, and risk of attack by militants.

The Stanford/NYU study has been subject to criticism for a lack of
methodological rigor. Christine Fair and her colleagues, for instance,
note that interviews with a majority of the 69 experiential victims were
arranged through the Foundation for Fundamental Rights (FFR), which
is "the leading opponent of drones in Pakistan and thus is a party to
the debate."[38] Fair and her colleagues conclude, "Much of the report's
evidence is thus derived from interviews fielded among a small sample
that is deeply tainted by selection bias."[39]

With respect to the report's findings regarding distress, they question the report's conclusion that mental distress is because of drones
and not the larger situation in the FATA. They argue, "Although the
strikes are carried out in areas that are also tormented by enormous
terrorist violence, restrictive and violent social regimes enforced by the
local Taliban, [and] extensive Pakistani military and paramilitary and intelligence presence, the authors simply assume that any such instances of
depression can be attributed to drones alone."[40] Marsh and Williams find
that distress is attributable to anxiety not only about drones, but also
because of "disruption to marginal subsistence livelihoods based on agri-
culture and limited trade."[41] Fair et al. conclude, "[T]he authors arrive at
sweeping conclusions that are fundamentally unsupported by the report's
thin and dubious empirical foundation."[42]

Investigations such as the Stanford/NYU study can illuminate how
living in an area where drone strikes occur can cause psychological

distress. It is difficult to know, however, how representative interviewee reactions are, and how much this is attributable to drones apart from other sources of stress in these areas. As a review of the literature on the psychological dimensions of drone strikes observes, most reports include "fairly small numbers of individuals. . . that oversample individuals directly exposed to drone strikes" who suffered some type of injury from them or had family members harmed by them.[43] Such persons "might naturally be expected to have high levels of anticipatory anxiety and it is difficult to generalize these feelings to communities at large."[44] What would be helpful are "[l]arger, quantitative, community-based studies."[45]

Basoglu's "learning theory" seems plausible, but the evidence he cites in support of its application to residents in areas with drone strikes is the Stanford/NYU Law School study, which has the limitations described above. In addition, as Fair and her colleagues point out, it is very difficult to isolate the impact of strikes from the broader context of ongoing violence and instability in areas such as the FATA. This context, apart from drone strikes, is likely to contribute to the kind of learned helplessness that Basoglu describes.

None of these observations is meant to diminish the distress of persons who have been interviewed in reports. Individual stories cannot substitute for systematic research on the entire local population in areas of strikes, but one can imagine anxiety from the presence of drones, uncertainty about when they may strike, and the fact that they sometimes kill civilians. It would be valuable for rigorous research to provide clearer insights into the nuances of psychological reactions to living in areas of instability, physical hardships, terrorist attacks, and periodic drone strikes.

Retaliatory Attacks

Some of the quantitative studies described in Chapter 6 find that strikes can cause retaliatory attacks in or near the locations in which they occur. Lyall provides the most refined analysis to support this claim, based on difference-in-differences methodology in his study of Afghanistan. Lehrke and Schomaker, as well as Carson, also find increases in attacks associated with successful targeting, although their focus on the global level complicates drawing inferences about causality. In addition, Shire finds increases in attacks by Al-Shabaab after the death of its founder. His focus on broad trends, however, creates the risk that confounding variables may account to some extent for the changes he describes. Hepworth did not find a significant relationship between the deaths of four AQ leaders and attacks by the AQ network, which he regards as indicating the absence of any retaliatory effect. Finally, Jaeger and Siddique suggest that short-term increases but longer-term declines in attacks after strikes may reflect a change in the timing of attacks rather than an overall escalation of violence.

Explanations for retaliation include a group's desire to signal its continued strength to the local population (Lyall) and to seek vengeance (Jaeger & Siddique). Lehrke and Schomaker, however, find that an increase in attacks is associated more strongly with the number of strikes than militant deaths from them, and not at all with civilian deaths. This leads them to conclude that retaliation reflects less desire for personal vengeance than anger toward what is regarded as a radically asymmetric tactic. This is consistent with Carson's suggestion that the perceived illegitimacy of drone strikes may play a role in triggering retaliation. Finally, Jaeger and Siddique's study may provide some support for this theory, in that they find that short-term increases in attacks are associated with unsuccessful, but not successful, drone strikes.

Wilner also found an increase in violence following the successful targeting of four Taliban leaders in Afghanistan. He argues, however, along with Abrahms and Mierau, that research on retaliation should focus not simply on the level of attacks following a targeted strike, but on whether the features of such attacks indicate that the ability of the group to conduct sophisticated operations has been impaired. These authors find evidence of this based on the types and targets of attacks after targeting, noting in particular an increase in attacks on civilians in Afghanistan and in Pakistan.

Rigterink's study of the FATA found that after a successful strike there was an increase in attacks outside Pakistan, excluding the West, as well as an increase in attacks against civilians. She attributes this to the greater influence of less sophisticated group members after the loss of a leader. Shire's research also indicates a decline in sophisticated attacks, although he emphasizes high fatalities from them. There is thus some evidence that a successful strike in some cases may have the unintended effect of increasing risk to civilians.

In sum, as several of the studies conclude, the net impact of targeting may reflect on one hand the effect of weakening and disrupting a terrorist organization's ability to conduct attacks in an area, while on the other hand the effect of creating incentives and opportunities for retaliatory attacks in response. As Jaeger and Siddique put it, the question is the extent to which "the incapacitation/deterrence effect dominates the vengeance effect," to which we can add Lyall's point about a group's desire to signal its resolve. Decisions about strikes will need to take these respective impacts into account.

LOCAL POPULATION ATTITUDES

Attitudes Toward the US

Some critics of targeted strikes claim that they undermine the efficacy of the US counterterrorism campaign in the long run by generating resentment and hostility toward the US. Such attitudes, the argument goes, can lead to less cooperation from residents, greater support for militants, and increases in militant recruitment. Counterinsurgency expert David Kilcullen and former Army officer Andrew Exum, for instance, have written that "every one of these dead noncombatants represents an alienated family, a new desire for revenge, and more recruits for a militant movement that has grown exponentially even as drone strikes have increased."[46] Some also claim that strikes reduce residents' confidence in the capacity of the host state to protect them, which hinders the fight against militants.[47]

Several reports, most of which relate to the FATA, suggest that there is opposition to US drone strikes in countries in which they occur. There is, however, a paucity of empirical research that rigorously tests the claim that this increases the number of people who join or provide assistance to terrorist groups. This section discusses research on the effect of strikes on attitudes toward the US, while the following section discusses research on whether strikes increase terrorist group recruitment.

The study by Mahmood and Jetter described in Chapter 6 that analyzes the impact of drone strikes from 2006 to 2016 in Pakistan on subsequent terrorist attacks considers the impact of strikes on Pakistani population attitudes. The authors conduct sentiment analysis of US-related articles in *The News International,* the English language newspaper with the largest circulation in Pakistan. They find that their model predicts that one drone strike "increases negative emotions and anger by approximately three standard deviations in the following week," which continues for several weeks.[48] It also predicts that "one drone strike results in two to four additional protests against the US per day in the following days and weeks."[49]

The Pew Research Center reported in 2014 that two-thirds of Pakistanis oppose drone strikes, 3% approve, and 30% offer no opinion.[50] Two-thirds also believe that drone strikes kill innocent people, 9% disagree, and 24% said that they don't know. Some 21% said that they are necessary to protect Pakistan, 46% disagree, and 33% don't know.

Pew's 2010 report contained slightly different questions.[51] In that survey, 2% said that drone strikes are a very good thing, 3% said good, 31% said bad, and 62% said very bad. Some 32% agreed that they are necessary to protect Pakistan, 56% disagreed, and 11% did not know or refused to answer. Finally, 90% agreed that drone strikes kill too many innocent people, 5% disagreed, and 5% did not know or refused to answer. It is notable that the percentage of those who agreed with the latter statement declined significantly to two-thirds in 2014. This finding may reflect the fact that strikes in the FATA began to decline in 2013.

The New America Foundation conducted interviews in the FATA from June 30 to July 20, 2010, surveying 1000 residents age 18 or older in 120 villages in all seven of the FATA agencies. New America did the interviews in conjunction with the Community Appraisal and Motivation Programme (CAMP), a locally-based group that works with underprivileged communities and government agencies in Pakistan to provide social services and humanitarian assistance.[52]

The survey found that more than three-quarters of FATA residents oppose American drone strikes. Only 16% think such strikes accurately target militants, while 48% think they largely kill civilians and another 33% believe that they kill both civilians and militants. Almost 90% of respondents opposed US military operations against Al-Qaeda and the Taliban in the FATA, while almost 70% wanted the Pakistani military alone to fight the Taliban and Al-Qaeda there. Interestingly, the responses suggest that opposition to drone strikes may reflect general disapproval of US operations more than drone strikes themselves. Some 38% of residents said that the Pakistani military should launch drone strikes in the FATA, while 34% disagreed.

Resentment of the US also was reflected in the fact that 38% of respondents regard the US as a threat to safety in the FATA, while 16% regard the Pakistani Taliban as a threat. Some 87% of residents surveyed have a somewhat or very unfavorable view of the US military, and the same percentage oppose US military presence in the FATA. In addition, while only 12% said that suicide bombings are often or sometimes justified against Pakistani military and police, 59% said that they are often or sometimes justified against the US military.

A 2011 survey in the FATA by CAMP, the group that assisted with the New America survey, indicated that only 6% of those surveyed believed that drone attacks are always or sometimes justified, while 63% said that they are never justified.[53] Some 60% strongly or somewhat supported the Pakistani military alone pursuing the Taliban, Al-Qaeda, and foreign fighters inside the FATA. Consistent with the New America data, 79% strongly opposed US military presence in the FATA, while 68% did with respect to Arab and foreign fighters, 64% for the Afghan Taliban, and 63% for the Pakistani Taliban.

World Public Opinion conducted a survey of the national population of Pakistan from May 17–28, 2009, an effort coordinated by the Program on International Policy Attitudes at the University of Maryland and carried out by SEDCO (SocioEconomic Development Consultants, Islamabad, Pakistan).[54] SEDCO consultants conducted the interviews face-to-face in respondents' homes. They conducted 1000 interviews across 100 sampling units in both rural and urban areas. Asked about "the current US drone aircraft attacks that strike targets in northwestern Pakistan," 82% of the respondents called them unjustified, while only 13% regarded them as justified.

The Center for Research and Security Studies in Islamabad conducted a survey of current and displaced residents of the FATA.[55] The report from December 2017 finds that of the 132 responses, the majority were from the Khyber Agency in the tribal areas. The author acknowledges that the sample cannot be regarded as representative of the entire FATA region. Approximately 90% of the respondents were male and 57% were between 18 and 29 years old.

When asked if they support US drone strikes in the FATA, 28% strongly disagreed and 40.9% disagreed, while 15.9% strongly agreed and 9.8% agreed. The majority of those opposing strikes did so because they believed that they cause high civilian casualties. When asked which counterterrorism strategies they would support in the area, 53% said traditional means of conflict resolution—e.g., *jirga*—; 16.6% said military occupations by Pakistan; 9.6% said US drone strikes; and 7.8% said drone strikes by Pakistan.

Marsh and Williams' study of residents in eastern Afghanistan also indicates resentment of drones. All of their 37 interviewees had seen drones, 25 had directly witnessed strikes or visited strike sited within an hour of a strike, and 18 reported the daily presence of drones. Strikes reinforced accusations of US unwillingness to face or communicate with local residents, and resentment of the Afghan government for its compliance with US wishes. Some also noted that the charred remains of strike victims reflected a violation of Islam's proscription of burning bodies. The authors say that such comments reflect "'popular backlash' via drone strikes' culturally and religiously condemned effects, even in circumstances where respondents supported strikes against the 'right' people."[56]

Reporter Christopher Swift reviewed "extensive published and unpublished source[s]," and conducted 40 structured interviews in Sana'a and Aden, Yemen in May and June 2012 to gain insight into Al Qaeda in the Arabian Peninsula (AQAP) activity and US drone strikes in that country.[57] Interviewees included tribal leaders, Islamist politicians, Salafi clerics, and other persons from 14 of Yemen's 21 provinces. Swift described them as "older, more religious, and far more skeptical of Western influence" than Arab Spring activists.[58]

Swift found considerable Yemeni anger about US drone strikes. While some were based on concern over civilian casualties, many Yemenis "view drones as an affront to their national pride."[59] He quotes a member of the Yemeni Parliament as saying, "'Drones remind us that we don't have the ability to solve our problems by ourselves. If these were Yemeni drones, rather than American drones, there would be no issue at all.'"[60] This resentment can undermine public support for a fragile local government. As Swift puts it, while drones avoid a major US presence, "local reaction to foreign military intervention still resonates in counterproductive ways. This is particularly true when covert actions and civilian casualties are involved," which can animate anti-imperialist sentiments and fuel long-standing conspiracy theories.[61]

Some researchers contest the claim of widespread opposition in Pakistan to US drone strikes, or at least that such strikes are the cause of anti-US sentiment. Christine Fair, Karl Kaltenthaler, and William J. Miller question whether Pew data can be taken to establish "Pakistanis' universal opposition to the drones."[62] They note that in the 2010 survey, only 35% of the survey respondents said that they had heard of the drones, with only 14% saying that they had heard "a lot."[63] (The 2014 survey does not ask this question.)

Among those who said they had heard of the program, "nearly one-third said drone strikes are necessary to defend Pakistan from extremist groups," while "[a] slight majority (56 percent) of the one third who were familiar with drones said that drone strikes are not necessary to protect Pakistan."[64] They conclude, "Pakistani public opinion is less informed, and much less unanimous, than is often presumed."[65] This is a useful point, although it still is notable that a majority of people who are aware of drone strikes disapprove of them.

Fair and her co-authors analyze the 2010 Pew Research survey to examine what may account for differences among Pakistanis in attitudes toward drones. Their dependent variable is whether someone would support or oppose the US conducting drone attacks in coordination with the Pakistani government against leaders of extremist groups, or whether they say they don't know or refuse to answer. The independent variables are education level, attitude toward the US, belief in the superiority of democratic government, assessment of the threat that Al-Qaeda poses to Pakistan, and how large a role someone believes Islam should play in the political life of Pakistan.

The only statistically significant variables affecting attitudes toward drone strikes were hostility toward the US and education. Not surprisingly, those with more hostile attitudes were more likely to oppose drone strikes. Those with more education were more likely to favor them. The authors regard the latter variable as especially important because it is an indication of how diverse a person's sources of information about the drone program are. The less educated a Pakistani, the fewer sources of information he or she will have, and the more likely that those sources will be nationalist Urdu media. As Fair, et al. note, the Urdu media in Pakistan are "almost universally anti-drone."[66]

Highly-educated Pakistanis, however, will have access to English-language media, which contains more diverse opinions on drone strikes. While most of the coverage of drones in Pakistani English-language media is negative, the English-language media gives space to pro-drone views that are completely absent from the Urdu language media. The authors propose that "[t]he fact that so few Pakistanis have fixed attitudes about the program shows that there is, in fact, room for a genuine struggle over Pakistani public opinion."[67] This leads them to suggest that if the US were more transparent about its drone operations it might gain more support for it.

The study by Fair and her co-authors is useful in challenging the view that a large percentage of the Pakistani population are both knowledgeable about drones and are opposed to them. Public opinion may be more fluid than is typically supposed, and may depend on more general attitudes toward the US and on the sources of information on which a person relies than on considered opinion about drones.

At the same time, the authors concede that "Pakistani outrage [over drone strikes] has steadily deepened since 2008, when the United States increased the frequency of the strikes."[68] Furthermore, while Urdu media may be ardently nationalist and relentlessly critical of drone strikes, it is hard to know how much this coverage not only shapes but reflects public attitudes.

Fair and her colleagues also suggest that even if there is considerable opposition to drone strikes in Pakistan, this is not necessarily the reason for hostility toward the US. They note that there has been significant antipathy toward the US in Pakistan for many years, in part based on the perception that the US tends to favor India over Pakistan. Pew Research Center data indicate that in 2002 and 2003, before drone strikes began in Pakistan, the percentage of Pakistanis having an unfavorable view of the US was 69% and 81%, respectively. From 2004 to 2010, Pew data indicate that the percentage of Pakistanis having an unfavorable view toward the US was as follows, with the number of drone strikes that year in parenthesis:

2004: 60% (1)
2005: 60% (3)
2006: 56% (2)
2007: 68% (4)
2008: 63% (36)
2009: 68% (54)
2010: 68% (122)

Fair et al. thus conclude, "Most Pakistanis were anti-American before the drones became a subject of public discourse. The drone strikes definitely did not help America's image with most Pakistanis, but they are not the primary cause of anti-Americanism in the country."[69] This suggests that hostility toward drone strikes may be based on hostility to the US, rather than vice versa. This would be consistent with the finding in the New America report that 38% of Pakistanis would support drone strikes by the Pakistani military, while 33% would not.

A 2009 survey by the Aryana Institute for Regional Research and Advocacy (AIRRA) indicated somewhat favorable views by FATA residents of drone strikes.[70] The survey was conducted in the North and South Waziristan agencies, which is where the vast majority of strikes in Pakistan occurred. It administered structured questionnaires to 550 residents of these areas.

Some 45% agree and 55% disagree that drone strikes "bring [] about fear and terror in the common people." Fifty-two percent say drones strikes are accurate, while 48% say they are not. Forty-two percent say that anti-American feelings in the area had increased because of drone strikes, while 58% disagree. Sixty percent say that militant groups incur damage from the strikes, while 40% say they do not. Finally, 70% say that Pakistani military should carry out targeted strikes against militants, while 30% say that they should not.

The AIRRA apparently is no longer in existence, but it was an organization that conducted research in the FATA and the Northwest Frontier Provinces of Pakistan. It described itself as "independent both ideologically and organizationally."[71] Its main researchers were three academics at universities in Pakistan with several publications in the areas of Pakistani history, culture, and politics, as well as linguistics, terrorism, and international cooperation.[72]

Detailed information on the survey methodology is not available, so it is impossible to know the basis on which its survey subjects were solicited. Professor Farhat Taj of the University of Oslo, a native of northwest Pakistan, wrote not long after the survey that it was consistent with her own contacts that she maintained with over 2000 people in the FATA.[73] More than two-thirds of these people, she said, did not regard US drone strikes as an infringement on Pakistan's sovereignty. Rather, she said, her contacts regard Al-Qaeda and the Taliban as having violated Pakistan's sovereignty. It is unclear how representative these people are, but the AIRRA survey and Taj's column provide at least some indication that attitudes in the FATA are not as monolithic as some contend.

Another indication of some Pakistani support for the drone campaign is the Peshawar Declaration issued in January 2010.[74] This was the product of a two-day conference on terrorism sponsored by Aman Tehrik (Peace Movement), a group of civil society organizations. The Declaration said, "[T]he current wave of terrorism emanates mainly from two sources i.e. Al-Qaeda and the Strategic Depth Policy of Pakistan."[75] The goal of the latter "is to use Jihadi culture in order to counter India, protect nuclear weapons, subjugate Afghanistan," and make Central Asian Muslim states client states of Pakistan.[76] As a result, "the people of the war-affected areas think that the army and Taliban are not enemies but friends."[77] The Declaration stated:

> The issue of Drone attacks is the most important one. If the people of the war-affected areas are satisfied with any counter militancy strategy, it is the Drone attacks which they support the most. . . Even some people in Waziristan compare Drones with Ababeels (The holy swallows sent by God to avenge Abraha, the intended conqueror of the Khana Kaaba). A component of the Pakistani media, some retired generals, a few journalists/analysts and pro-Taliban political parties never tire in their baseless propaganda against Drone attacks.[78]

While there appears to be considerable opposition to US drone strikes in the FATA, many local residents also resent the Taliban presence there. Marsh and Williams' research found that no respondents expressed support for insurgent groups' political goals. "Most rejected them," he says, "and all reported experiencing disruption" that was caused both "by insurgent and terrorist presence and drone operations."[79] Interviewees said the Taliban place pressure on local families "to provide hospitality, including tea, food, and accommodation" in accordance with local customs of hospitality. One *malik* elaborated:

> The Taliban are coming. . . to our homes, we are not inviting them. [T]hey are coming by force. . . and the people have to provide them some food and other things and also sit with them and behave properly. . .

> [W]henever you sit with them inside your home, you are always afraid that we might come under the target of the drones, and if we don't sit with the Taliban. . . they would. . . most probably say that you are American's spy or agent and that is why [they] would not let you live.[80]

In sum, considerable, although not uniform, evidence suggests there is substantial opposition to drone strikes by residents of areas where they occur. This can undermine both counterterrorism and counterinsurgency operations by reducing residents' willingness to provide information, to identify militants, and to cooperate in other ways. Opposition also poses a particular threat to counterinsurgency because it can alienate local populations from their government, erode confidence in its ability to protect them, and undermine its perceived legitimacy.

Terrorist Recruitment

Does local opposition to drone strikes also cause increases in recruitment by terrorist groups? The work by Basoglu described above, which claims that residents in areas with drone strikes suffer psychological consequences comparable to victims of torture, also includes the claim that such residents are likely to become radicalized because they seek revenge. Basoglu bases this argument on the fact that he found in a previous study that persons who experienced the four-year-long siege of Sarajevo had responses on the Emotions and Beliefs After War questionnaire that were similar to those of torture victims.[81]

In that study, the questionnaire includes "questions relating to cognitive and emotional responses to perceived impunity for those held responsible for trauma." Based on the scale from zero ("not at all") to eight ("very true"), with four indicating "moderately true," individuals were presented with questions such as "I feel angry when I think of what they did to me and my loved ones"; "I feel distressed by the thought of the perpetrators of such atrocities getting away with what they have done"; "There is nothing I want more in life than seeing the perpetrators punished"; and "Sometimes I daydream that I take revenge from the perpetrators."[82]

Basoglu found that "[c]omparing the mean scores, the Sarajevo civilians did not differ from torture survivors in their cognitive and emotional responses (except for dreams about revenge)."[83] If residents of areas where drone strikes occur also are comparable to torture victims, he suggests, conditions there "possibly play an important role in radicalizing people," and "could well contribute to the motivational processes behind retaliatory violence."[84]

The questionnaire, however, is meant to elicit responses to questions about attitudes toward perpetrators by persons who have suffered harm or have had "loved ones" suffer harm. One can imagine that these respondents' answers might be similar to those of torture victims. It is less clear, however, that the similarity would extend to the entire population of an area where drone strikes occur.

In addition, with respect to radicalization specifically, the responses on the questionnaire to the three questions dealing with the desire personally to seek revenge, rather than the desire to have perpetrators punished, were the lowest on the scale of any of the responses. Even if we assume that all residents in areas of drone strikes would have responses similar to Sarajevo survivors, those responses do not suggest a desire for revenge that would lead to joining a terrorist group. Basoglu's work thus may provide some insight into the potential psychological and emotional experiences of residents in areas of drone strikes, but does not support the claim that such strikes lead them to become radicalized and seek revenge.

The study by Mahmood and Jetter described above also attempts to estimate the effect of drone strikes on indicators of radicalization. The authors use as indicators Google searches that use as search terms "jihad," "Taliban video," and "Zaarb-Momini/Zarb-o-Momin (ZeM)," which translates to "strike of a devout Muslim," and is "a weekly magazine published in Pakistan, expressing radical beliefs and religious extremism."[85] They estimated that one drone strike increases searches for jihad by 37 percentage points, Taliban video by 33 percentage points, and ZeM by 22 percentage points in the following week.

The authors acknowledge that Google searches are not an ideal measurement of radical attitudes, since "an online search for a radical term does not make a terrorist."[86] They nonetheless say that these results are consistent with the claims that drone strikes turn Pakistanis toward radical groups. Their caution is well-founded, however, and it would be useful to have more precisely targeted research that addresses this question.

The Stanford/NYU Law School report described above concluded that "US strikes in Pakistan foster anti-American sentiment and undermine US credibility not only in Pakistan but throughout the region. There is strong evidence to suggest that US drone strikes have facilitated recruitment to violent nonstate armed groups, and motivate attacks against both US military and civilian targets."[87]

In addition to the criticism of this study by Fairet al., Mohammad Taqi notes that the NGO Reprieve that commissioned the study has close ties to the Pakistani political party Tehreek-e-Insaf.[88] This party has called for an end to drone strikes, and in 2013 organized a protest against the drone program that blocked a road in northwest Pakistan that was used to transport NATO troop supplies and equipment in and out of Afghanistan.

Daniel Silverman has offered a nuanced analysis of reactions to drone strikes by persons in Pakistan outside the FATA, which indicates that they increase support for the Pakistani Taliban but not for the Afghan Taliban or other groups.[89] Relying on six interview "waves" of the Pew Global Attitudes Project, he compared attitudes on various issues 14 days before and after seven US drone strikes between 2005 and 2013. The primary dependent variables were four-point favorability scales regarding opinions of the American people, the Pakistani president and opposition leaders, various militant groups, perceptions of the threat that militants pose, and US and Pakistani counterterrorism policies. The sample was balanced with respect to several individual variables regarding the participants.

While respondents were not residents of the FATA, Silverman argues that the opinions of Pakistani citizens outside of the tribal areas are quite important. First, he notes that militant organizations in Pakistan are not restricted to the FATA. To the extent US drone strikes affect attitudes toward these groups, these attitudes can affect the government's policies toward them. Second, residents of the FATA tend to be marginalized in Pakistani politics, which means that the attitudes of the broader Pakistani population may have more influence on government policy.

Silverman finds that a drone strike increases unfavorable attitudes toward Americans by about 10 percentage points, and also significantly increases opposition to the Pakistani president and support for the opposition leader. A strike increases anti-American sentiment among those closest to the location of a strike, with the effect decreasing with distance and losing significance at about 400 kilometers.

The study finds that a strike does not generate additional support for Al-Qaeda or the Afghan Taliban, but does produces a positive and near-significant increase in support for the Pakistani Taliban. He suggests this indicates that the strikes "appear to be fueling support for militant organizations with an internal as opposed to an external focus."[90] Civilians thus "differentiate clearly between different targets of repression – perhaps only perceiving some as victims – as opposed to simply responding in a pro-(or anti-) militant fashion across the board."[91] This is consistent with the work of Jacob Schapiro and Christine Fair that emphasizes the importance of analyzing the bases of support for specific militant groups rather than "militants" generally.[92]

With the exception of Silverman, most claims that drone strikes increase terrorist recruitment are not based on rigorous research that directly addresses the issue. Mahmood and Jetter's study is well-done and suggestive, but their dependent variables are weak indicators of increased support for terrorist groups. By contrast, other more focused rigorous research casts doubt on the claim that strikes increase terrorist recruitment or support for terrorist groups.

While the New America study described above found disapproval of the US military, it did not indicate that many residents had been radicalized and came to support terrorist groups. The percentage regarding the Pakistani Taliban somewhat or very unfavorably was 63.8% and the Afghan Taliban 57.1%. The percentage who opposed the presence of Arab and foreign Al-Qaeda members in the FATA was 76.5%, with 68.7% opposing the Pakistani Taliban and 61.% the Afghan Taliban.[93]

Given a list of eleven possible problems in the FATA, 69.2% said that the Taliban was a very important or somewhat important problem, and 68.5% said that foreign fighters are. If Al-Qaeda or the Pakistani Taliban were on the ballot in an election, less than 1% of FATA residents would vote for either group. The absence of longitudinal data makes it impossible to know whether these attitudes changed from the first drone strikes in 2004 to the time of the report in 2010. Nonetheless, high disapproval of terrorist groups is notable in light of the fact that the program was very active at the time of the survey.

Similarly, the WorldPublicOpinion.org survey found that opposition to drone strikes did not translate into greater sympathy for the Taliban or terrorist groups. In September 2007, 34% thought the "activities of Islamist militants and local Taliban in FATA and settled areas" were a serious threat.[94] By 2009, this number had increased to 81%. In 2007, 38% thought the "activities of religious militant groups in Pakistan" were a critical threat.[95] By 2009, 67% thought so.

Three-quarters of the respondents said that it would be mostly bad if the Pakistani Taliban "took control over all of Pakistan," with 67% regarding it as "very bad." One question asked, "If the Pakistani government were to identify bases in Pakistan of Taliban groups who are trying to overthrow the Afghan government, do you think the government should or should not close these bases even if it requires the use of military force?" Some 78% percent said the government should close such bases, while only 13% disagreed. These results suggest that opposition to US drone strikes in the FATA did not lead to radicalization of the local population.

While Christopher Swift's study described above found considerable opposition to drone strikes in Yemen, he found no evidence that such resentment resulted in recruitment to AQAP. Interviewees said that

AQAP's affiliate Ansar al-Shari'ah recruits by providing economic bene-fits and some measure of status to impoverished individuals. With almost half the population subsisting on less than two dollars per day, "'joining Al Qaeda represents the best of several bad options,'" according to an Islamist member of Parliament.[96] In addition, tribal elders and commu-nities may recruit fighters for Ansar al-Shari'ah in return for new wells, irrigation systems, and food. In some cases, the group's ability to provide benefits displaces traditional forms of tribal patronage, resulting in a significant shift in personal allegiances. "Drones," says Swift, "play no discernible role in these dynamics."[97] As he summarizes, "[N]one of the subjects interviewed for this study believed that targeted strikes were the proximate cause for AQAP's growing ranks. Nor were they a necessary condition. Even if drone strikes were to cease, noted one tribal militia commander, the economic and social conditions that facilitate terrorist recruiting in Yemen, would still remain."[98]

Swift emphasizes that this does not discount Yemeni anger about US drone strikes and its potential consequences. It is important, however, to "distinguish generalized resentment from the specific pathways that bring individuals, families, and villages into AQAP's domain."[99]

Two careful studies of attitudes in Pakistan also conclude that drone strikes do not lead to greater support for terrorist groups. Aqil Shah conducted 167 interviews with residents of North Waziristan (NWA) who had been displaced to nearby districts by Pakistan military operations in June 2014.[100] Since a random sample was infeasible, he used a "snowball" approach in which initial contacts suggest additional persons to interview. Shah acknowledged this creates a risk that residents are likely to recom-mend people with similar views, but he sought to reduce this by choosing as diverse a set of initial interviewees as possible.

Shah's interviews were with "legislators, masharan (elders), maliks (headmen), clerics, local officials, reporters, lawyers, traders, shop owners, human rights activists, teachers, university students, and local leaders and activists from seven political parties. . .covering the full spectrum of party ideologies in Pakistan."[101] He conceded that the sample size was not large enough for a rigorous quantitative sample. He pointed out, however, that it was the same order of magnitude as used in the Stanford/NYU report, without the concerns about selection bias that have been raised about that study. In addition, the study did not rely on translators or inter-preters. Nonetheless, "Although the interview sample is large compared with those of all similar studies, one caveat is in order: there is no way of knowing how representative the interviewees are of the entire population of NWA."[102]

Shah concluded that there is little evidence to indicate that drone strikes result in "blowback" on the local, national, and transnational level that enhances terrorist recruitment. One basis for this conclusion is interviews with 167 displaced residents of North Waziristan. Some 75% of drone strikes in Pakistan since 2004 have occurred in North Waziristan, and Shah notes that virtually every family from there has been affected by the death of a relative, property destruction, or displacement. Most inhabitants are members of Pashtun tribes and sub-tribes with extended clans or families. As a result, inhabitants are "enmeshed in dense social networks, which makes them uniquely informed about the effects of drone strikes in the community."[103]

Most interviewees said that they knew or were aware of someone in their clan or village involved in militant activity. When asked if opposition to drone strikes led to persons becoming militants, 71% of the people disagreed, 11% agreed and 18% were uncertain or had no opinion. With respect to property damage, 84% had more concerns about Pakistani military operations than drone strikes.[104] One owner of a business in North Waziristan said, "Drones are precise in most cases. After the military comes, nothing is left."[105]

Shah conceded that this latter sentiment might be overrepresented in the sample because subjects had been displaced by the June 2014 Pakistani military offensive. They were consistent, however, with sentiments expressed in the Peshawar Declaration that preceded the offensive. More generally, they reflected the deep alienation of many residents from the Pakistani government based on the harsh provisions of the Frontier Crimes Regulation, the use of draconian policing and military measures in the FATA, and the government's perceived appeasement of militants through periodic peace agreements that enabled militant subversion of social authority by killing elders and attacking *jirgas*. As one interviewee said, "We were trapped between the tanks and the Taliban, between bombardment from [fighter] jets and Taliban terror. The Americans killed the militants for their own interests. But it restored some normalcy to our lives."[106]

Shah questioned the common claim among proponents of the blowback thesis that the Pashtun honor code compels persons to see grievances against those who have killed family members. That code, he said, deals with revenge in the context of disputes between families, not with regard to civilians and security forces that are militant targets. It also provides opportunities in local traditions for peaceful resolution of disputes. More generally, tribal membership is only one dimension of identity, and is continually negotiated and reconstructed. Shah argued that his interviews indicate that "the notion that drone strikes turn aggrieved relatives into bloodthirsty militants is deeply problematic because it essentializes an entire ethnic group and reduces their choices to primordial urges, mores, and customs."[107]

Given the dense social and kinship ties of inhabitants, Shah said, "finding evidence of blowback from well-informed locals should be relatively easy."[108] Instead, "In my interviews, experts with deep knowledge of the Federally Administered Tribal Areas, especially North Waziristan, in addition to well-informed local elders and others deeply embedded in social networks, reject the claim that drones provide a recruitment card for militant organizations."[109]

Shah also found little evidence of blowback on the national and transnational level. On the national level, his conclusions were based upon interviews with experts on terrorism and analysis of the 2017 Sindh Province Counterterrorism Department survey of 500 detained militants. These indicated that militant groups outside the FATA mobilize support by castigating "a range of domestic and international enemies, including India/Hindus, the West, the United States, and, in some cases, minority Muslims such as Shias."[110]

On the transnational level, Shah examined: (1) trial testimony and public statements by US-based captured terrorists believed to have been motivated by drone strikes; (2) court documents and secondary sources relating to Somali- American men charged with terror-related offenses in the US; and (3) scholarly accounts of the motivations for militant Islamism in Europe.[111] He identified only a handful of cases in which terrorists claimed that drone strikes were one of the sources of their motivation. In addition, scholarship indicates a that wide range of perceived grievances against the West, along with personal experiences of alienation, drive recruitment to radical jihadist causes.

"In conclusion," said Shah, "the blowback thesis offers a simplistic, monocausal explanation of a complex process of radicalization and jihadist recruitment at the local, national, and transnational levels."[112] He emphasized that his research is not meant to serve as an endorsement of the use of drone strikes nor to deny the risk of civilian casualties, but to clarify with empirical evidence the accuracy of claims about one of their effects.

A thoughtful perspective on attitudes in the FATA is also presented in a 2013 report by the International Crisis Group, an NGO in Brussels.[113] The report is based mainly on interviews in Pakistan with persons in the legal, political, and NGO communities, along with activists, journalists, and researchers working on FATA.

The report states that responses in the FATA to questions about drones are shaped and influenced by fear of both the military and terrorist groups. Factors include the extent of "dependence on patronage and protection from particular militant or criminal groups," as well as the fear of being labeled a Taliban supporter by expressing opposition to drones.[114] The drone program therefore "has become as much a political football as a security issue for FATA communities. It is in this context that opinion polls conducted in FATA should be assessed."[115]

With respect to purported radicalization because of drone strikes, the report indicates that militant recruitment is a complex process that often is influenced more by economic than ideological concerns. "FATA residents," the report observes, "often rely on various militant jihadi and criminal networks for patronage in the absence of a functioning state, civil society, and traditional tribal structures that have been decimated by militants."[116] Forced recruitment is also common, as households are required to contribute men to terrorist groups in areas they control. The report concludes, "Any voluntary enlistment in response to drone strikes may well be comparatively minimal."[117]

More broadly, the report says that "the main causes for the spread of militancy in FATA are not drone strikes but domestic factors. These include the absence of the state and insecurity due to the resulting political, legal and economic vacuum; and the military's support of, provision of sanctuaries to, and peace deals with militant groups."[118] The report maintains that drone strikes need to be seen in the larger context of Pakistan's failure to integrate the FATA into its political and legal structure. "Distorted through hyper-nationalistic segments of the Pakistani media and hijacked by political hardliners," the report says, "the domestic Pakistani debate on the impact of drone operations has overshadowed a more urgent discussion about the state's obligation to its citizens in FATA."[119]

An excerpt from Adrian Levy and Catherine Scott-Clark's book *The Exile*, a detailed account of Al-Qaeda's activities from 9/11 until the death of bin Laden, also suggests that drone strikes may have reduced support for Al-Qaeda at least in the FATA. The book is based on extraordinary access to the bin Laden family and Al-Qaeda leaders and operatives. It says that by July 2010, "Al Qaeda's local support was also hemorrhaging. The villages inhabited by 'supporters' were almost all ghostly ruins. . . Pashtun codes of honor and protection had been eroded by aerial intimidation."[120]

Asfandyar Mir's interviews with Al-Qaeda and Taliban members also indicated that there was no surge in recruitment in response to strikes or civilian casualties. As one Al-Qaeda operative stated, "When I see the news that drone strikes have helped the militants to recruit more people, I consider it false analysis . . . [both] al-Qaida and Pakistan Taliban had serious manpower shortages."[121] Indeed, several interviewees said that strikes created a pervasive fear of spies that led groups to turn away possible new members, "which had an especially detrimental effect on recruitment."[122]

Finally, while civilian casualties from targeted strikes may spur opposition to strikes, rigorous empirical studies by Rigterink, Mir & Moore, Lehrke and Schomaker, and Jaeger and Siddique, and two such studies by Carson, find that civilian casualties are not associated with increases in terrorist attacks.[123] This belies a common claim that the desire to avenge such casualties is an important incentive for terrorist attacks. Other research described above, however, indicates that these casualties are an important source of opposition to strikes, with potential counterproductive results for counterterrorism efforts. In addition, of course, the loss of innocent lives is an intrinsic concern apart from whatever effect it may have on local motivations and attitudes.

In sum, there is reason to be skeptical of the claim that the US drone program has radicalized a significant number of persons in areas affected by strikes. At the same time, local opposition to strikes nonetheless could hinder counterterrorism efforts by making the local population unwilling to provide intelligence and cooperate with counterterrorism activities, and by undermining support for the host government by fostering the perception that it is incapable of protecting residents. Such consequences need to be taken into account in assessing the overall efficacy of strikes.

Since most of the research on local population attitudes focuses on strikes in the FATA, it is also important to acknowledge the distinctiveness of that region. As Chapter 5 describes, the FATA are a remote, mountainous area in northwest Pakistan on the border with Afghanistan. While Pakistan in now undertaking efforts to integrate it more into the country, the area has never been fully under Pakistan's control, and the Pakistan constitution historically has not applied to it. It has been governed instead by a colonial governance instrument called the Frontier Crimes Regulation. There historically has been no police force in the FATA; security has been provided by paramilitary, military, and tribal militia forces. The Pakistani army has periodically engaged in military operations against foreign Islamic militants that have involved home demolition, the seizure of businesses, property forfeiture, and denial of access to roads out of the area. In addition, Pakistan has periodically entered into truces with terrorist groups that have allowed them to expand their influence in the region.

Attitudes by residents toward drone strikes at the time of the studies therefore may be shaped by the perception that undesirable Pakistani military operations are the only alternative to the strikes. For this reason, it may be perilous to extrapolate findings about local population attitudes toward targeted strikes beyond this region. The broader lesson is that any consideration of the use of targeted strikes must be highly sensitive to local conditions that are likely to influence attitudes. This underscores the need for more rigorous empirical research on local population attitudes in areas in which strikes occur.

CONCLUSION

Drone strikes may cause harm to local populations even when they do not cause civilian casualties. Any accounting of their effects needs to take such harm into account. Investigations of individual strikes that include residents affected by them can provide important information about the nature of these impacts. They indicate that residents may lose homes and sources of livelihood, may limit or cease gathering with others and participating in community events, and may suffer psychological distress. Documenting these effects deepens our understanding of the consequences of drone strikes.

Without discounting the significance of these stories, it is important to recognize that obtaining a full account of the impacts of strikes requires more systematic empirical investigation. The myriad consequences of full-scale armed conflict for local populations have been well documented, even if they do not receive the attention they deserve. Various challenges make it difficult, however, to gain accurate and impartial information that would enable us to evaluate the impacts of targeted strikes apart from instability and other forms of violence in strike locations. Nonetheless, there is room for more refined investigation and analysis of the impact of strikes on local populations.

Whether one such impact is to radicalize residents and increase the ranks of terrorist groups has been a subject of heated contention. Much of the debate, however, has reflected reliance on a priori reasoning and unexamined extrapolation from implicit assumptions. The most reliable empirical work suggests that, while local populations do oppose drone strikes, this does not result in greater support for militant groups or increasing enlistment in their causes. As with other types of impacts, however, more focused research would shed greater light on the accuracy of these findings.

NOTES

1. Willie, C., & Baldo, A. M. (2021). *Menu of indicators to measure the reverberating effects on civilians from the use of explosive weapons in populated areas, 1.* United Nations Institute for Disarmament Research. https://unidir.org/publication/menu-indicators-measure-rev erberating-effects-civilians-use-explosive-weapons-populated.
2. Cavallero, J., Sonnenberg, S., & Knuckey, S. (2012, September 25). *Living under drones: Death, injury and trauma to civilians from US drone practices in Pakistan, 76.* International Human Rights and Conflict Resolution Clinic, Stanford Law School, NYU School of Law & Global Justice Clinic. https://law.stanford.edu/wp-content/uploads/sites/default/files/publication/313671/doc/slspublic/Stanford_NYU_LIVING_UNDER_DRONES.pdf.
3. Open Society Justice Initiative. (2015). *Death by drone: Civilian harm caused by US targeted killings in Yemen, 73.* https://www.justiceiniti ative.org/uploads/1284eb37-f380-4400-9242-936a15e4de6c/death-drones-report-eng-20150413.pdf.
4. Center for Civilians in Conflict (CIVIC). (2010). *Civilian harm and conflict in Northwest Pakistan, 46.* https://civiliansinconflict.org/wp-content/uploads/2017/09/Pakistan_Report_2010_2013.pdf.
5. Id. 45.
6. Amnesty International. (2013, October). *"Will I be next?": US drone strikes in Pakistan, 39.* https://www.amnestyusa.org/files/asa330132 013en.pdf.
7. CIVIC, 2010, 47.
8. Marsh, J. M., & Williams, J. (2021). Drones, Afghanistan and beyond: Towards analysis and assessment in context. *European Journal of*

International Security. https://www.cambridge.org/core/journals/eur opean-journal-of-international-security/article/drones-afghanistan-and-beyond-towards-analysis-and-assessment-in-context/479E5F71A567 2B7A5A78ABB93C53DAB0.

9. Id. 15.
10. Id.
11. Bertolotti, P., Fotini, C., & Jadbabaie, A. (2019). *The social network effects of drone strikes* [Unpublished manuscript]. Institute for Data, Systems, and Society, Massachusetts Institute of Technology.
12. Id. 13.
13. Id. 12.
14. Id.
15. Id. 13.
16. Marsh & Williams, 15.
17. Id.
18. Amnesty International, 2013, 29.
19. Cavarello et al., 99.
20. Marsh & Williams, 10.
21. Id. 12.
22. Id.
23. Id. 17.
24. Id.
25. Id. 18.
26. Id. 19.
27. Williams, B. G. (2010). The CIA's covert Predator drone war in Pakistan, 2004–2010: The history of an assassination campaign. *Studies in Conflict & Terrorism, 33*(10), 871–892. https://doi.org/10.1080/1057610X.2010.508483.
28. Cavarello et al., 81.
29. Id.
30. Cavallero et al., 2.
31. Id. 2.
32. Rohde, D. (2012, January 26). The drone wars. *Reuters Magazine.* https://www.reuters.com/article/us-david-rohde-drone-wars/reu ters-magazine-the-drone-wars-idUSTRE80P11I20120126.
33. Marsh & Williams, 14.
34. Shah, A. (2018). Do U.S. drone strikes cause blowback? Evidence from Pakistan and beyond. *International Security, 42*(4), 47–84, 57. https://doi.org/10.1162/isec_a_00312.
35. Id.
36. Başoğlu, M. (2012a, November 25). *Drone strikes or mass torture?—A learning theory analysis. Mass Trauma*, Mental Health & Human Rights. https://metinbasoglu.wordpress.com/2012/11/25/drone-warfare-or-

mass-torture-a-learning-theory-analysis/?preview=true&preview_id=
298&preview_nonce=c9913cca07.
37. Id.
38. Fair, C. C., Kaltenthaler, K., & Miller, W. J. (2014). Pakistani opposition
    to American drone strikes. *Political Science Quarterly, 129*(1), 1–33, 21,
    note 63. https://christinefair.net/pubs/Fair_KM_PSQ_Drones.pdf.
39. Id.
40. Id.
41. Marsh & Williams, 14.
42. Fair et al., 21 n. 63.
43. Hijazi, A., Ferguson, C. J., Richard Ferraro, F., Hall, H., Hovee, M., &
    Wilcox, S. (2017). Psychological dimensions of drone warfare. *Current
    Psychology, 38*(5), 1285–1296, 1291. https://doi.org/10.1007/s12
    144-017-9684-7.
44. Id.
45. Id.
46. Kilcullen, D., & Exum, A. M. (2009, May 16). Death from above,
    outrage down below. *The New York Times.* https://www.nytimes.com/
    2009/05/17/opinion/17exum.html.
47. Boyle, M. J. (2013). The costs and consequences of drone warfare.
    International Affairs, 89(1), 1–29. https://doi.org/10.1111/1468-
    2346.12002.
48. Mahmood, R., & Jetter, M. (2019, April). *Military intervention via
    drone strikes* (Discussion paper no. 12318, 28). IZA Institute of Labor
    Economics. http://ftp.iza.org/dp12318.pdf.
49. Id. 30.
50. Pew Research Center. (2014, August 27). *Global attitudes project: A less
    gloomy mood in Pakistan.* https://www.pewresearch.org/global/wp-con
    tent/uploads/sites/2/2014/08/PG-2014-08-27_Pakistan-FINAL.pdf.
51. Pew Research Center. (2010, June 17). *Global attitudes project: Obama
    more popular abroad than at home, global image of U.S. continues to
    benefit.* https://www.pewresearch.org/wp-content/uploads/sites/2/
    2010/06/Pew-Global-Attitudes-Spring-2010-Report-June-17-11AM-
    EDT.pdf.
52. New America Foundation. (2010, September). *Public opinion in
    Pakistan's tribal regions.* http://www.terrorfreetomorrow.org/upimag
    estft/FATApoll1.pdf.
53. Shinwari, N. A. (2011). *Understanding FATA: Attitudes towards
    governance, religion and society in Pakistan's Federally Adminis-
    tered Tribal Areas* (Vol. V). Community Appraisal & Motivation
    Programme. http://crossasia-repository.ub.uni-heidelberg.de/2715/1/
    Understanding_FATA_Vol_V_11.pdf.

54. Ramsay, C., Kull, S., Weber, S., & Lewis, E. (2009, July 1). *Pakistani public opinion on the Swat Conflict, Afghanistan, and the US*. World Public Opinion. https://worldpublicopinion.net/wp-content/uploads/2017/12/WPO_Pakistan_Jul09_rpt.pdf.

55. Yousaf, F. (2017, December 1). *CIA drone strikes in Pakistan: History, perception and future*. SSRN. http://dx.doi.org/10.2139/ssrn.3160433.

56. Marsh & Williams, 14.

57. Swift, C. (2014). The boundaries of war? Assessing the impact of drone strikes in Yemen, 72. In P. Bergen & D. Rothenberg (Eds.), *Drone wars: Transforming conflict, law, and policy* (pp. 71–88). Cambridge University Press.

58. Id.

59. Id. 81.

60. Id.

61. Id.

62. Fair et al., 3.

63. Id. 24.

64. Id. 4.

65. Id.

66. Id. 13.

67. Id. 33.

68. Id. 1.

69. Id. 18.

70. Taj, F. (2011). A critical perspective on a recent survey of opinion in Pakistan's tribal zone. *Small Wars & Insurgencies, 22*(2), 402–413. https://dx.doi.org/10.1080/09592318.2011.573425.

71. AIRRA—Aryana Institute for Regional Research and Advocacy. (2009). Aryana Institute for Regional Research and Advocacy. https://web.arc hive.org/web/20091010044825/http://www.airra.org:80/home/.

72. https://web.archive.org/web/20091010044825/http://www.airra. org:80/home/.

73. Taj, F. (2010, January 2). Analysis: Drone attacks: Challenging some fabrications. *Daily Times*. https://web.archive.org/web/201406142 05708/http://archives.dailytimes.com.pk/editorial/02-Jan-2010/ana lysis-drone-attacks-challenging-some-fabrications-farhat-taj.

74. Aman Tehrik. (2010, January 16). *Peshawar declaration: Eliminating terrorism and establishing sustainable peace in the region*.

75. Id.

76. Id.

77. Id.

78. Id.

79. Marsh & Williams, 14.

80. Id. 27.
81. Başoğlu, M., Livanou, M., Crnobarić, C., Frančišković, T., Suljić, E., ĐUrić, D., & Vranešić, M. (2005). Psychiatric and cognitive effects of war in former Yugoslavia. *JAMA, 294*(5), 580. https://jamanetwork.com/journals/jama/fullarticle/201331.
82. Id., E1–E2.
83. Başoğlu, M. (2012b, December 9). *Do drone strikes increase risk of revenge attacks?—A behavioral science perspective.* Mass Trauma, Mental Health & Human Rights. https://metinbasoglu.wordpress.com/2012/12/09/do-drone-strikes-increase-risk-of-revenge-attacks-a-behavioral-science-perspective/.
84. Id.
85. Mahmood & Jetter, 30–31.
86. Id. 33.
87. Cavarello et al., 125.
88. Taqi, M. (2012, October 6). *Shooting down drones with academic guns?* Pakistan Defence. https://defence.pk/pdf/threads/shooting-down-drones-with-academic-guns.211586/.
89. Silverman, D. (2016). *Drone strikes and "hearts and minds": A quasi-experimental analysis in Pakistan* [Manuscript in preparation]. Institute for Politics and Strategy, Carnegie Mellon University. https://danielmsilvermandotcom.files.wordpress.com/2018/09/drones-attitudes-silverman-2016.pdf.
90. Id. 21.
91. Id. 30.
92. Shapiro, J., & Fair, C. C. (2009/10). Understanding support for Islamist militancy in Pakistan. *International Security, 34*(3), 79–118. https://scholar.princeton.edu/sites/default/files/jns/files/understanding_support_for_islamist_militancy.pdf.
93. This finding seems at odds with the findings in Silverman's study.
94. Ramsay et al.
95. Id.
96. Swift, 79.
97. Id. 80.
98. Id.
99. Id.
100. Shah.
101. Id. 54.
102. Id. 55.
103. Id. 56.
104. Id. 58.
105. Id.
106. Id. 60.

107. Id. 82.
108. Id. 60.
109. Id. 82.
110. Id.
111. Id. 76.
112. Id. 84.
113. International Crisis Group. (2013, May 21). *Drones: Myths and reality in Pakistan.* https://d2071andvip0wj.cloudfront.net/drones-myths-and-reality-in-pakistan.pdf.
114. Id. 25.
115. Id.
116. Id. 23.
117. Id.
118. Id. 24.
119. Id. 11.
120. Levy, A., & Scott-Clark, C. (2017). *The exile: The stunning inside story of Osama bin Laden and Al Qaeda in flight*, 350. Bloomsbury.
121. Mir, 2018, 81.
122. Id. 73.
123. Carson, J. V. (2017). Assessing the effectiveness of high-profile targeted killings in the "War on Terror." *Criminology & Public Policy, 16*(1), 191–220. https://doi.org/10.1111/1745-9133.12274; Carson, J. V. (2018). Assessing the nuances of counterterrorism programs: A country-level investigation of targeted killings, *Crime & Delinquency, 65*(9), 1262–1291. https://journals.sagepub.com/doi/abs/10.1177/001112 8718784742; Rigterink, A. (2021). The wane of command: Evidence on drone strikes and control within terrorist organizations. *American Political Science Review, 115*(1), 31–50. https://doi.org/10.1017/S00 03055420000908; Mir, A., & Moore, D. (2019). Drones, surveillance, and violence: Theory and evidence from a US drone program. *International Studies Quarterly, 63*(4), 846–862. https://doi.org/10.1093/isq/sqz040; Lehrke, J. P., & Schomaker, R. (2016). Kill, capture, or defend? The effectiveness of specific and general counterterrorism tactics against the global threats of the post-9/11 era. *Security Studies, 25*(4), 729–762. https://doi.org/10.1080/09636412.2016.1220199; Jaeger, D. A., & Siddique, Z. (2018). Are drone strikes effective in Afghanistan and Pakistan? On the dynamics of violence between the United States and the Taliban. *CESifo Economic Studies, 64*(4), 667–697. http://www.djaeger.org/research/wp/Jaeger-Siddique.pdf.

PART IV

Conclusions

CHAPTER 12

Analyzing the Impacts of Targeted Killing

US targeted strikes against Al-Qaeda and associated groups (AQ) outside war zones over the last two decades have generated intense debate about their effectiveness, legality, and ethical justifiability. The preceding chapters have not analyzed in depth the legal and ethical issues raised by these strikes. They have, however, examined quantitative and qualitative evidence on the impacts of strikes on AQ and civilians, along with other studies on targeted killing, with the goal of ensuring that the legal and ethical debate is informed by our best understanding of these impacts. This concluding chapter briefly summarizes key conclusions from this review of the evidence. It then suggests how these conclusions, and research on other targeted killing campaigns, can inform future decisions about whether and when to conduct strikes against terrorist groups outside war zones.

As a preliminary matter, it is important to recognize that the best available evidence indicates that AQ consists of four elements:

1. Top leadership, or Al-Qaeda Core (AQC), which provides broad strategic guidance to the larger network;
2. Formal affiliates whose leaders have sworn *bayat,* or allegiance to AQC, such as Al-Qaeda in the Arabian Peninsula (AQAP) and Al-Shabaab in Somalia, which have wide discretion to determine when and where to conduct attacks;

© The Author(s), under exclusive license to Springer Nature Switzerland AG 2022
M. Regan, *Drone Strike–Analyzing the Impacts of Targeted Killing,*
https://doi.org/10.1007/978-3-030-91119-5_12

3. Groups not formally affiliated with AQ that sometimes receive assistance from it and collaborate on particular operations, such as Jemaah Islamiyah in Indonesia, which received funding from AQ for its 2002 bombings of Western tourist sites and a US consulate in Bali; and
4. Individuals inspired by AQ but who are not members of the group.

The first conclusion is that strikes against AQC leadership in Pakistan, mainly in the Federally Administered Tribal Areas (FATA), deprived AQC of several capable important leaders, many of whom were difficult to replace with people of comparable experience and skill; caused AQC to restrict movement of leaders and their communication with the rest of AQ; disrupted to some extent those leaders' ability to plan and coordinate operations; and deprived AQC of a relatively safe haven in the tribal areas that it was using to organize attacks in the US and the West.

Second, studies find that these impacts on AQC did not lead to the demise of AQ nor reduce the total number of attacks by the AQ network as a whole. This is consistent with research findings on various other leadership targeting campaigns that strikes against leadership are unlikely to have an impact on the survival or activity of well-established terrorist groups that are religious in orientation, and those that are neither traditional hierarchical organizations nor inspired by a single charismatic figure. AQ has always been an organization in which groups have considerable autonomy to conduct operations, within broad strategic guidelines articulated by AQC. It grew after 9/11 by assembling an even larger collection of groups under its banner, with further decentralization of operations that increased such autonomy. Strikes against AQC therefore will not eliminate the AQ network, and likely will not reduce the number of attacks that the network as a whole conducts.

While this book does not discuss what would accomplish these goals, there may be non-kinetic ways to weaken the network, such as through information campaigns that sow discord within it or turn the local population against it. More ambitiously, some thoughtful observers have suggested that an important step in weakening AQ in the long term would be serious efforts to address the grievances of communities in various countries in which the failure to do so has led to support for Al-Qaeda.[1] The US may be able to assist some local governments in meeting this challenge, but it cannot be the central driving force in this effort. At the same time, we must acknowledge that we do not fully understand all the factors that contribute to support for terrorist groups, so any prescriptions must be offered with caution. Consistent with the approach of this book, counterterrorism decisions should be based as much as possible on insights drawn from empirical evidence.

Third, quantitative studies do not squarely address whether strikes against AQC in Pakistan contributed to lowering the risk of major AQ attacks in the US and the West. Adoption of defensive counterterrorism measures probably made the biggest contribution to reducing this risk, and AQ's strategy after 9/11 of expanding by focusing on the local concerns of various affiliates also has helped reduce this threat.

Nonetheless, qualitative evidence indicates that strikes against AQC weakened the element of AQ most focused on conducting attacks in the US and the West by depriving it of leaders and resources that it could deploy for such attacks, and a safe haven in which it could conduct training for them. This has made AQC more dependent on affiliates to conduct attacks against the "far enemy" on the US and the West. In addition, there is some evidence that strikes that induced AQC to deemphasize attacks in the US and the West in recent years, and to focus more on local issues, so that the network could grow with less concern about being targeted by the US. Local groups may occasionally launch external attacks, but they also must devote time and resources to conflicts in their own regions that are their primary concern. It is therefore reasonable to conclude that strikes in Pakistan that weakened AQC made some contribution to reducing the risk of attacks in the US and the West.

Fourth, strikes against AQC at this point may not have much effect on the risk of such attacks. The role of strikes against AQC in Pakistan in helping to reduce the risk of attacks in the US and the West reflected the role of AQC at a particular point in the evolution of AQ. Conditions now are different. Defensive counterterrorism measures, the evolution of the network toward greater decentralization, the current role of AQC in providing general guidance and less material assistance, and the absence of a safe haven for AQC all have lessened core leadership's ability to serve as the main impetus for attacks that are of especially important concern to the US.

It is conceivable that strikes might not reduce the risk of attacks, but could at least ensure that it does not increase, by exerting continuous pressure on AQC that prevents it from becoming more effective and influential. This would reflect the approach that some in Israel call "mowing the grass"—that is, using strikes to not to eliminate a group but to keep it from becoming strong enough to pose a serious threat. There is no rigorous research on whether periodic strikes would achieve this goal, however. Some research on the local effects of strikes suggests that reducing attacks requires an intensive campaign that combines detailed local intelligence collection with rapid exploitation of information to conduct persistent operations. This may not be feasible in all places in which a more dispersed AQC membership is now located. Whether periodic strikes against AQC members in various locations would reduce the risk of attacks in the US and the West thus is far more speculative than the claim that strikes against AQC in the FATA did so.

In addition, using strikes in this way would raise legal and ethical issues with which the US would need to contend. With respect to law, the US could claim that members of AQC are enemy combatants, but this would require that it continue to regard itself as engaged in an armed conflict against Al-Qaeda—a position that may not continue amid calls for an end to the "forever war." Even if this is the asserted legal basis for strikes, there is controversy over whether killing a nonstate enemy outside a war zone without first attempting to capture them is permissible.

This controversy led the Obama administration to adopt the policy that such strikes could be conducted only against "continuing imminent threats" to the US or US persons. While the Trump administration relaxed this standard, the US could re-institute it, or it may claim that strikes are acts of self-defense against an imminent threat outside of armed conflict. It may claim that the threat is imminent because AQC has made clear its persistent intention to conduct attacks in the US. Is this enough, or must AQC possess the capability to act on this intention? If strikes are meant to prevent AQC from acquiring such capability, is it plausible to say that core leaders pose an imminent threat to the US?

In addition, relying on targeting to maintain a low risk of attacks raises ethical issues. To mention just one, is it justified for the US to keep the risk to itself as low as possible by using strikes that impose costs on people elsewhere? As Chapters 9–11 describe, these costs can include civilian casualties and disruption of local communities. Strikes also may cause resentment of the US that hinders attempts by local governments regarded as US allies to engage in counterterrorism and establish political stability. This can increase the risk of violence for local populations. Furthermore, would it be ethically justified for the US to engage indefinitely in targeted killing operations without any end in sight? Decision-makers contemplating the use of strikes will need to engage in ethical deliberation to consider whether the putative benefits of strikes are outweighed by these costs.

This analysis of the impacts of conducting strikes against AQC may change if this group of leaders is able to reacquire a safe haven in which it is able to plan, coordinate, and establish training camps for attacks in the US and the West. This would enable AQC to organize such attacks itself, with less need to rely on affiliates to do so, and thus increase the risk of such attacks. It is not clear at this point whether the Taliban's ascension to power in Afghanistan will result in creation of such a safe haven, but it may be difficult to ensure that it does not. Conditions in Afghanistan are different from those in the FATA, however, where the US was able to draw on Pakistani intelligence, arrests, and military operations to enhance the effects of targeted strikes. The absence of comparable assistance from the Taliban means that the US would be conducting strikes under far less favorable conditions than in Pakistan. This could require greater reliance on other counterterrorism measures to reduce the threat of attacks in the US and the West.

In addition, fewer US intelligence sources because of the withdrawal of US forces, combined with the lack of a cooperative local government partner, could create significant risk of civilian casualties from strikes. Such risk is reflected in the drone strike targeting mistake that killed ten civilians in Kabul in August 2020 based on faculty intelligence.

One or more groups in the AQ network could come to pose a serious threat of attacks in the US in the West. Some research, mainly on strikes in Pakistan, indicates that targeted strikes can temporarily weaken the ability of a group to conduct attacks. This can occur both through kinetic effects that deprive it of personnel and resources, and anticipatory effects that lead it to take steps to avoid future strikes that impair its ability to conduct attacks. Strikes thus could lower the threat that a group poses for some period of time, especially if combined with local government law enforcement or military operations. A more permanent decrease, however, may require fundamental local political reform that reduces the appeal of extremist groups. For various reasons, this is likely to be a formidable task in many areas in which groups in the AQ network operate. A more feasible goal for the US may be to use strikes to reduce the long-term threat from a group by inducing it to focus its attention solely on local concerns. At the same time, this approach could raise legal issues similar to those raised by targeting AQC, as well as ethical questions about using strikes to maintain a low risk to the US at the expense of increasing the risk of harm to civilians elsewhere.

Chapters 9–11 discuss in detail evidence on the nature and extent of such harm. With respect to civilian casualties, the US has taken steps to reduce such casualties from strikes outside war zones, but it has consistently underestimated their number compared to estimates by other reputable organizations. Fully realizing the potential precision of drone strikes requires appreciating that precision is determined not simply by technological capability, but how organizational processes deploy that technology.

Precision that minimizes civilian casualties entails more systematic attention to accurately determining the number of casualties caused by strikes, conducting root cause analysis of the reasons for them, widely disseminating this analysis across all relevant agencies and departments, and drawing on these lessons to revise operations to reduce the risk of future casualties. More generally, it would involve accepting some responsibility for preventing unintended but foreseeable civilian casualties on the ground that they are "foreseeable accidents." This would enable the US to move closer to compliance with its own standard of near certainty of no civilian casualties for strikes outside war zones (and could reduce civilian casualties from strikes within them as well). Until the US takes such steps, the claim that the use of strikes outside areas of conflict represents reliance on a "small footprint" is a dubious one.

Civilian casualties also can affect persons beyond the direct victims of a strike. The death or serious injury of breadwinners who support several families in some locations can leave a number of people destitute. In addition, strikes in some cases may leave people homeless, destroy sources of livelihood, or force them to relocate. Strikes also can disrupt local community social relationships and informal governance processes that are important to individuals' daily lives. The persistent presence of drones, and uncertainty about when they will fire, also may be a source of ongoing anxiety in areas in which strikes occur.

Research indicates that another cost of drone strikes is local population resentment of them and of the US more generally. The most rigorous research on US strikes does not support the claim that resentment of strikes results in recruitment to terrorist causes, or that civilian casualties cause retaliatory attacks. Some research indicates, however, that there can be increases in local terrorist attacks immediately after a strike, which may be because a group wants to assure the population of its resolve. This may reflect a change in the timing of attacks, however, rather than an increase in their overall number.

Even if local population resentment of strikes does not result in retaliatory attacks or more support for terrorists, it nonetheless can impair US counterterrorism efforts by reducing willingness of the local population to provide assistance, and by undermining the perceived legitimacy of a local government ally. Audrey Kurth Cronin's work emphasizes that counterterrorism campaigns involve competition for public support between terrorists and counterterrorists. This means that the effects on local population attitudes should be an important consideration in a full assessment of the impacts of drone strikes.

The US is likely in the future to conduct targeted strikes in response to what it regards as the threat of an attack in the near future. It may also consider strikes against terrorist group leaders and key operatives in other situations, based on the belief that strikes will reduce the risk of attacks in the US by groups that are committed to conducting them. Decisions about whether and when to conduct strikes raise practical, legal, and ethical issues that must be informed as much as possible by empirical evidence, not based on broad unexamined assumptions about the impacts of strikes. This book has carefully reviewed the best available empirical evidence on such impacts. I have acknowledged the limits of this evidence where appropriate, and offered my assessment of the most reasonable conclusions we can draw from it. I have clearly identified the material on which I have relied, so that others can draw their own conclusions. These may differ from mine. The important thing, however, is that discussion be based on genuine engagement with the empirical evidence.

Unexamined assumptions tend to generate sweeping claims: that targeted strikes have failed to reduce the risk of terrorist attacks, and that they are the main reason why there has been no large-scale attack in the US for two decades; that strikes kill civilians in large numbers that vastly exceed the number of militant deaths, and that they only rarely kill any civilians at all because strikes are so precise; that strikes cause local resentment that enhances terrorist recruiting, and that local populations welcome strikes because they kill terrorists who impose serious hardships on their communities. This book suggests that the truth is more nuanced than any of these claims. The fact that my conclusions do not completely vindicate either critics or supporters underscores that decisions about strikes require that we squarely confront difficult trade-offs, and wrestle in clear-eyed fashion with the weight to assign to diverse sets of values.

This book has focused mainly on what the evidence tells us about US targeted strikes against AQ, but this evidence, along with other research on targeted killing discussed in the book, also can help guide decisions about the use of strikes against other groups and by other countries. Basing these decisions on the best evidence available rather than on firm convictions with no empirical grounding is important not just for practical reasons, but for more rigorous legal and ethical analysis. To paraphrase a quotation attributed to more than one American writer, it's not only what we don't know that gets us into trouble. It's what we know for sure that just isn't so.[2]

NOTES

1. Cronin, A. K. (2011). *How terrorism ends: Understanding the decline and demise of terrorist campaigns. Princeton University Press*; Zimmerman, K. (2019, October). *Beyond counterterrorism: Defeating the Salafi-jihadi movement*. American Enterprise Institute. https://www.aei.org/wp-content/uploads/2019/10/Beyond-Counterterrorism.pdf?x91208.
2. Quote Investigator, It ain't what you don't know that gets you into trouble. It's what you know for sure that just ain't so. https://quoteinvestigator.com/2018/11/18/know-trouble/. (visited September 5, 2021).

REFERENCES

ABC News. (2007, December 29). *Taliban sacks key rebel commander*. https://www.abc.net.au/news/2007-12-30/taliban-sacks-key-rebel-commander/998852

Abrahms, M., & Mierau, J. (2015). Leadership matters: The effects of targeted killings on militant group tactics. *Terrorism and Political Violence, 29*(5), 830–851. https://doi.org/10.1080/09546553.2015.1069671

Ackerman, S. (2014, November 24). 41 men targeted but 1,147 people killed: US drone strikes—The facts on the ground. *The Guardian*. https://www.theguardian.com/us-news/2014/nov/24/-sp-us-drone-strikes-kill-1147

Africa File: Al Shabaab member charged with plotting 9/11-style attack. (2020, December 18). Critical Threats. https://www.criticalthreats.org/briefs/africa-file/africa-file-al-shabaab-member-charged-with-plotting-9-11-style-attack

AIRRA—Aryana Institute for Regional Research and Advocacy. (2009). Aryana Institute for Regional Research and Advocacy. https://web.archive.org/web/20091010044825/http://www.airra.org:80/home/

Airwars. (2020, October). *Eroding transparency: US counterterrorism actions in Yemen under President Donald Trump*. https://airwars.org/wp-content/uploads/2020/10/Eroding-Transparency-Trump-in-Yemen.-Airwars-October-2020.pdf

Airwars. (2021). Retrieved August 3, 2021, from https://airwars.org/

Al Jazeera. (2015, May 28). *Nusra leader: Our mission is to defeat Syrian regime*. https://www.aljazeera.com/news/2015/5/28/nusra-leader-our-mission-is-to-defeat-syrian-regime

M. Regan, *Drone Strike–Analyzing the Impacts of Targeted Killing*, https://doi.org/10.1007/978-3-030-91119-5

Aman Tehrik. (2010, January 16). *Peshawar declaration: Eliminating terrorism and establishing sustainable peace in the region.* https://preetlari.wordpress.com/2011/05/09/pakistanpress-peshawar-declaration/

American Enterprise Institute. (2020, September). *A conversation with commander of US Special Operations Command Africa, Major General Dagvin Anderson* (Panel discussion). The crossroad of competition: Countering the rise of violent extremists and revisionist powers in Africa, Washington, DC. https://www.aei.org/events/the-crossroad-of-competition-countering-the-rise-of-violent-extremists-and-revisionist-powers-in-africa/

Amnesty International. (2013, October). *"Will I be next?": US drone strikes in Pakistan.* https://www.amnestyusa.org/files/asa330132013en.pdf

Amnesty International. (2019). *The hidden US war in Somalia: Civilian casualties from airstrikes in Lower Shabelle.* https://www.amnesty.org/download/Documents/AFR5299522019ENGLISH.PDF

Anderson, K. (2009, May). *Targeted killing in U.S. counterterrorism strategy and law.* Brookings Institution. https://www.brookings.edu/wp-content/uploads/2016/06/0511_counterterrorism_anderson.pdf

Arquilla, J., & Ronfeldt, D. (2001). *Networks and netwars: The future of terror, crime, and militancy.* RAND. https://www.rand.org/pubs/monograph_reports/MR1382.html

Arsenault, E., & Bacon, T. (2015). Disaggregating and defeating terrorist safe havens. *Studies in Conflict & Terrorism, 38*(2), 85–112. https://www.tandfonline.com/doi/abs/10.1080/1057610X.2014.977605?journalCode=uter20

Bacon, T. (2018, September 11). Deadly cooperation: The shifting ties between Al-Qaeda and the Taliban. *War on the Rocks.* https://warontherocks.com/2018/09/deadly-cooperation-the-shifting-ties-between-al-qaeda-and-the-taliban/

Barela, S. J., & Plaw, A. (2016, August). *The precision of drones: Problems with the new data and new claims.* https://www.e-ir.info/2016/08/23/the-precision-of-drones-problems-with-the-new-data-and-new-claims/

Başoğlu, M. (2012a, November 25). *Drone strikes or mass torture? A learning theory analysis.* Mass Trauma, Mental Health & Human Rights. https://metinbasoglu.wordpress.com/2012a11/25/drone-warfare-or-mass-torture-a-learning-theory-analysis/?preview=true&preview_id=298&preview_nonce=c9913cca07

Başoğlu, M. (2012b, December 9). *Do drone strikes increase risk of revenge attacks? A behavioral science perspective.* Mass Trauma, Mental Health & Human Rights. https://metinbasoglu.wordpress.com/2012b/12/09/do-drone-strikes-increase-risk-of-revenge-attacks-a-behavioral-science-perspective/

Başoğlu, M., Livanou, M., Crnobarić, C., Frančišković, T., Suljić, E., ĐUrić, D., & Vranešić, M. (2005). Psychiatric and cognitive effects of war in former

Yugoslavia. *JAMA, 294*(5), 580. https://jamanetwork.com/journals/jama/fullarticle/201331

Bauer, V., Reese, M., & Ruby, K. (2021, September 29). Does insurgent selective punishment deter collaboration? Evidence from the drone war in Pakistan. *Journal of Conflict Resolution,* 1–30 (original manuscript). https://journals.sagepub.com/doi/abs/10.1177/00220027211041158

Becker, J., & Shane, S. (2012, May 29). Secret 'kill list' tests Obama's principles. *The New York Times.* https://www.nytimes.com/2012/05/29/world/obamas-leadership-in-war-on-al-qaeda.html

Bergen, P. L. (2011). *The longest war: The enduring conflict between America and Al-Qaeda.* Free Press.

Bergen, P. L. (2021). *The rise and fall of Osama bin Laden.* Simon & Schuster.

Bergman, R. (2018). *Rise and kill first: The secret history of Israel's targeted assassinations.* Random House.

Bertolotti, P., Fotini, C., & Jadbabaie, A. (2019). *The social network effects of drone strikes* (Unpublished manuscript). Institute for Data, Systems, and Society, Massachusetts Institute of Technology.

Bin Laden, O. (2010, August 7). *Letter from "Zamarai" (Usama bin Ladin) to Mukhtar Abu al-Zubayr.* Reference Number: SOCOM-2012-0000005. Combating Terrorism Center at West Point, West Point, NY. https://ctc.usma.edu/harmony-program/letter-from-usama-bin-laden-to-mukhtar-abu-al-zubayr-original-language-2/

Boghani, P. (2021, April 2). Syrian militant and former Al Qaeda leader seeks wider acceptance in first interview with U.S. journalist. *Frontline.* https://www.pbs.org/wgbh/frontline/article/abu-mohammad-al-jolani-interview-hayat-tahrir-al-sham-syria-al-qaeda/

Boyle, M. J. (2013). The costs and consequences of drone warfare. *International Affairs, 89*(1), 1–29. https://doi.org/10.1111/1468-2346.12002

Brennan, J. O. Prepared statement of John O. Brennan. In Senate Committee on Intelligence, *Nomination of John O. Brennan to be Director of the Central Intelligence Agency, S. Hrg. 113-31* (pp. 28–31). Federation of American Scientists. https://fas.org/irp/congress/2013_hr/brennan.pdf

Brennan, J. O. (2020). *Undaunted.* Adfo Books.

Burt, R. S. (2009). *Structural holes: The social structure of competition.* Harvard University Press.

Byman, D. (2006, March/April). Do targeted killings work? *Foreign Affairs, 85*(2), 95–111. https://doi.org/10.2307/20031914

Byman, D. (2011). *A high price: The triumphs and failures of Israeli counterterrorism.* Oxford University Press.

Byman, D. (2013). Why drones work. *Foreign Affairs, 92*(4), 32–43.

Byman, D. (2014). Buddies or burdens? Understanding the Al Qaeda relationship with its affiliate organizations. *Security Studies, 23*(3), 431–470. https://www.tandfonline.com/doi/abs/10.1080/09636412.2014.935228

Byman, D. (2015). *Al Qaeda, the Islamic State, and the global jihadist movement: What everyone needs to know.* Oxford University Press.

Byman, D. (2021). The good enough doctrine: Learning to live with terrorism. *Foreign Affairs, 100*(5), 32–43. https://www.foreignaffairs.com/articles/middle-east/2021-08-24/good-enough-doctrine

Byman, D., & Mir, A. (2021, May). *Assessing Al-Qaeda: A debate* (Working Draft).

Carson, J. V. (2017). Assessing the effectiveness of high-profile targeted killings in the "war on terror." *Criminology & Public Policy, 16*(1), 191–220. https://doi.org/10.1111/1745-9133.12274

Carson, J. V. (2018). Assessing the nuances of counterterrorism programs: A country-level investigation of targeted killings. *Crime & Delinquency, 65*(9), 1262–1291. https://journals.sagepub.com/doi/abs/10.1177/0011128718784742

Carvin, S. (2012). The trouble with targeted killing. *Security Studies, 21*(3), 529–555. https://doi.org/10.1080/09636412.2012.706513

Cavallero, J., Sonnenberg, S., & Knuckey, S. (2012, September 25). *Living under drones: Death, injury and trauma to civilians from US drone practices in Pakistan.* International Human Rights and Conflict Resolution Clinic, Stanford Law School, NYU School of Law, & Global Justice Clinic. https://law.stanford.edu/wp-content/uploads/sites/default/files/publication/313671/doc/slspublic/Stanford_NYU_LIVING_UNDER_DRONES.pdf

Center for Army Lessons Learned. (2012, September). *Afghanistan civilian casualty prevention: Observations, insights, and lessons.*

Center for Civilians in Conflict. (2010). *Civilian harm and conflict in Northwest Pakistan.* https://civiliansinconflict.org/wp-content/uploads/2017/09/Pakistan_Report_2010_2013.pdf

Center for Civilians in Conflict. (2013, July 2). *Drones more likely to harm civilians than manned aircraft in Afghanistan.* https://civiliansinconflict.org/press-releases/drones-more-likely-to-harm-civilians/

Center for Civilians in Conflict. (2014). *Civilian harm tracking: Analysis of ISAF efforts in Afghanistan.* https://civiliansinconflict.org/wp-content/uploads/2017/09/ISAF_Civilian_Harm_Tracking.pdf

Center for Civilians in Conflict & Columbia Law School Human Rights Clinic. (2012). *The civilian impact of drones: Unexamined costs, unanswered questions.* https://web.law.columbia.edu/sites/default/files/microsites/human-rights-institute/files/The%20Civilian%20Impact%20of%20Drones.pdf

Center for Civilians in Conflict & Columbia Law School Human Rights Institute. (2020). *In search of answers: U.S. military investigations and civilian harm*. https://civiliansinconflict.org/wp-content/uploads/2020/02/PDF-Report-for-Website.pdf

Clarke, C. P., & Asfandyar, M. (2020, September 11). *Is Ayman al-Zawahiri really the future of Al-Qaida?* RAND. https://www.rand.org/blog/2020/09/is-ayman-al-zawahiri-really-the-future-of-al-qaida.html

Clarke, C. P., & Lister, C. (2019, September 4). *Al Qaeda is ready to attack you again*. Foreign Policy. https://foreignpolicy.com/2019/09/04/al-qaeda-is-ready-to-attack-you-again/

CNN Wire Staff. (2010, November 5). *Yemen-based al Qaeda group claims responsibility for parcel bomb plot*. CNN. http://edition.cnn.com/2010/WORLD/meast/11/05/yemen.security.concern/index.html

Coll. S. (2018). *Directorate S: The C.I.A. and America's secret wars in Afghanistan and Pakistan*. Penguin Books.

Columbia Law School Human Rights Clinic. (2012, October). *Counting drone strike deaths*. https://web.law.columbia.edu/sites/default/files/microsites/human-rights-institute/files/COLUMBIACountingDronesFinal.pdf

Copp, T. (2021, September 17). *'Horrible mistake': Pentagon admits drone strike killed children, not terrorists, defense one*. https://www.defenseone.com/threats/2021/09/horrible-mistake-pentagon-admits-drone-strike-killed-children-not-terrorists/185440/

Crawford, N. C. (2013). *Accountability for killing: Moral responsibility for collateral damage in America's post-9/11 wars*. Oxford University Press.

Crawford, N. C. (2020, December 7). *Afghanistan's rising civilian death toll due to airstrikes, 2017–2020*. Costs of War. https://watson.brown.edu/costsofwar/files/cow/imce/papers/2020/Rising%20Civilian%20Death%20Toll%20in%20Afghanistan_Costs%20of%20War_Dec%207%202020.pdf

Critical Threats, Africa File. (2020, December 18). *Africa File: Al Shabaab member charged with plotting 9/11-style attack*.https://www.criticalthreats.org/briefs/africa-file/africa-file-al-shabaab-member-charged-with-plotting-9-11-style-attack

Cronin, A. K. (2006). How al-Qaida ends: The decline and demise of terrorist groups. *International Security, 31*(1), 7–48. https://doi.org/10.1162/isec.2006.31.1.7

Cronin, A. K. (2011). *How terrorism ends: Understanding the decline and demise of terrorist campaigns*. Princeton University Press.

Cronin, A. K. (2013). Why drones fail: When tactics drive strategy. *Foreign Affairs, 92*(4), 44–54.

Cruickshank, P. (2011, July). *The militant pipeline between the Afghanistan-Pakistan border region and the West*. New America Foundation. https://newamerica.org/documents/887/the-militant-pipeline

Dahir, A. L. (2019, December 30). Somali terror group Al-Shabab remains resilient despite setbacks. *The New York Times.* https://www.nytimes.com/2019/12/29/world/africa/somalia-attack-shabab.html

David, S. R. (2002, September). *Fatal choices: Israel's policy of targeted killing.* BESA: The Begin-Sadat Center for Strategic Studies, Bar-Ilan University. https://besacenter.org/wp-content/uploads/2002/09/msps51.pdf

David, S. R. (2003). Israel's policy of targeted killing. *Ethics & International Affairs, 17*(1), 111–126. https://doi.org/10.1111/j.1747-7093.2003.tb0 0422.x

Dell, M., & Querubin, P. (2017). Nation building through foreign intervention: Evidence from discontinuities in military strategies. *Quarterly Journal of Economics, 133*(2), 701–764. https://doi.org/10.1093/qje/qjx037

Dilanian, K. (2011a, June 29). U.S. counter-terrorism strategy to rely on surgical strikes, unmanned drones. *Los Angeles Times.* https://www.latimes.com/pol itics/la-xpm-2011a-jun-29-la-pn-al-qaeda-strategy-2011a0629-story.html

Dilanian, K. (2011b, February 22). CIA drones may be avoiding Pakistani civilians. *Los Angeles Times.* https://www.latimes.com/world/la-xpm-2011b-feb-22-la-fg-drone-strikes-2011b0222-story.html

Dilanian, K. (2019, March 14). CIA drones may be avoiding Pakistani civilians. *The Los Angeles Times.* https://www.latimes.com/world/la-xpm-2011-feb-22-la-fg-drone-strikes-20110222-story.html

Dilanian, K., Nichols, H., & Kube, C. (2017, March 14). *Trump admin ups drone strikes, tolerates more civilian deaths: U.S. officials.* NBC News. https://www.nbcnews.com/news/us-news/trump-admin-ups-drone-strikes-tolerates-more-civilian-deaths-n733336

Dugan, L. (2010). The series hazard model: An alternative to time series for event data. *Journal of Quantitative Criminology, 27*(3), 379–402. https://doi.org/10.1007/s10940-010-9127-1

Emmerson, B. (2013). *Report of the Special Rapporteur on the promotion and protection of human rights and fundamental freedoms while countering terrorism.* U.N. Human Rights Council. https://digitallibrary.un.org/rec ord/751002?ln=en

Emmerson, B. (2014). *Report of the Special Rapporteur on the promotion and protection of human rights and fundamental freedoms while countering terrorism, Ben Emmerson.* U.N. Human Rights Council. https://digitallibrary. un.org/record/766937?ln=en

Epifanio, M. (n.d). *Appendix A: "Codebook," legislative responses to international terrorism dataset.* Peace Research Institute of Oslo. http://www.polsci.org/epifanio/codebook.pdf

Everton, S. F. (2012). *Disrupting dark networks.* Cambridge University Press.

Eviatar, D. (2020, May 14). *The fatal flaw in DOD's latest civilian casualties report*. Just Security. https://www.justsecurity.org/70139/the-fatal-flaw-in-dods-latest-civilian-casualties-report/

Exec. Order No. 13732, United States policy on pre- and post-strike measures to address civilian casualties in U.S. operations involving the use of force, 3 C.F.R. 499. (2017). https://www.govinfo.gov/content/pkg/CFR-2017-title3-vol1/pdf/CFR-2017-title3-vol1-eo13732.pdf

Exec. Order No. 13862, 3 C.F.R. 8789. (2019). https://www.federalregister.gov/documents/2019/03/11/2019-04595/revocation-of-reporting-requirement

F-16 Armament—GBU-31 and GBU-38 JDAM. (2021). F-16.Net. https://www.f-16.net/f-16_armament_article9.html

Fair, C. C., Kaltenthaler, K., & Miller, W. J. (2014). Pakistani opposition to American drone strikes. *Political Science Quarterly, 129*(1), 1–33. https://christinefair.net/pubs/Fair_KM_PSQ_Drones.pdf

Falk, O. (2015). Measuring the effectiveness of Israel's 'targeted killing' campaign. *Perspectives on Terrorism, 9*(1), 1–26. https://www.jstor.org/stable/2629732

Falk, O., & Hefetz, A. (2017). Minimizing unintended deaths enhanced the effectiveness of targeted killing in the Israeli-Palestinian conflict. *Studies in Conflict & Terrorism, 42*(6), 600–616. https://doi.org/10.1080/1057610x.2017.1402429

Finkelstein, C., Ohlin, J. D., & Altman, A. (2012). *Targeted killings: Law and morality in an asymmetrical world*. Oxford University Press.

Fisk, K., & Ramos, J. M. (2016). *Preventive force: Drones, targeted killing, and the transformation of contemporary warfare*. NYU Press.

Gartenstein-Ross, D., & Barr, N. (2018, June 1). How Al-Qaeda works: The Jihadist group's evolving organizational design. *Current Trends in Islamist Ideology*. https://www.hudson.org/research/14365-how-al-qaeda-works-the-jihadist-group-s-evolving-organizational-design

Gibbons-Neff, T. (2019, April 5). U.S. acknowledges airstrike in Somalia caused civilian deaths. *The New York Times*. https://www.nytimes.com/2019/04/05/us/politics/us-civilians-somalia-airstrikes.html

Giordano, G. N., & Lindström, M. (2015). Trust and health: Testing the reverse causality hypothesis. *Journal of Epidemiology and Community Health, 70*(1), 10–16. https://doi.org/10.1136/jech-2015-205822

Girma, S., & Gor, H. (2007). Evaluating the foreign ownership wage premium using a difference-in-differences matching approach. *Journal of International Economics, 72*, 97–112. https://www.sciencedirect.com/science/article/abs/pii/S0022199606001139

Goldstein, S. J. (2019, June 24). *Nothing kept me up at night the way the Gorgon Stare did.* Longreads. https://longreads.com/2019/06/21/nothing-kept-me-up-at-night-the-way-the-gorgon-stare-did/

Gordon, R. (2016, July 18). How the US military came to embrace extrajudicial killings. *The Nation.* https://www.thenation.com/article/archive/how-the-us-military-came-to-embrace-extrajudicial-killings/

Greenwald, G. (2011, July 19). *New study proves falsity of John Brennan's drone claims.* Salon. https://www.salon.com/2011/07/19/drones/

Gross, G., Llinias, J., & Nagi, R. (2015, July 6–9). *Application of multi-level fusion for pattern of life analysis.* 18th International Conference on Information Fusion, Washington, DC. https://c4i.gmu.edu/~pcosta/F15/data/fileserver/file/472061/filename/Paper_1570113673.pdf

Gunaratna, R., & Nielsen, A. (2008). Al Qaeda in the tribal areas of Pakistan and beyond. *Studies in Conflict & Terrorism, 31*(9), 775–807. https://www.tandfonline.com/doi/full/10.1080/10576100802291568

Gunneflo, M. (2016). *Targeted killing: A legal and political history.* Cambridge University Press.

Hafez, M. M., & Hatfield, J. M. (2006). Do targeted assassinations work? A multivariate analysis of Israel's controversial tactic during Al-Aqsa uprising. *Studies in Conflict & Terrorism, 29*(4), 359–382. https://doi.org/10.1080/10576100600641972

Hardy, J., & Lushenko, P. (2012). The high value of targeting: A conceptual model for using HVT against a networked enemy. *Defence Studies, 12*(3), 413–433. https://doi.org/10.1080/14702436.2012.703845

Hartig, L. (2021, March 12). *Part II: The muddy middle: Challenges of applying use of force policy guidance in practice.* Just Security. https://www.justsecurity.org/65819/part-ii-the-muddy-middle-challenges-of-applying-use-of-force-policy-guidance-in-practice/

Headquarters, Department of the Army. (2012, July). *ATTP 3–37.31 Civilian casualty mitigation.* Army Tactics, Techniques, and Procedures. https://fas.org/irp/doddir/army/attp3-37-31.pdf

Helfstein, S., & Wright, D. (2011). Covert or convenient? Evolution of terror attack networks. *Journal of Conflict Resolution, 55*(5), 785–813. https://doi.org/10.1177/0022002710393919

Hepworth, D. P. (2013). Analysis of Al-Qaeda terrorist attacks to investigate rational action. *Perspectives on Terrorism, 7*(2), 23–38. https://www.jstor.org/stable/pdf/26296922.pdf?refreqid=excelsior%3Acdfa5604f8cba1452d74945be1ee7b0b

Hepworth, D. P. (2014). Terrorist retaliation? An analysis of terrorist attacks following the targeted killing of top-tier al Qaeda leadership. *Journal of Policing, Intelligence and Counter Terrorism, 9*(1), 1–18. https://doi.org/10.1080/18335330.2013.877374

Hijazi, A., Ferguson, C. J., Richard Ferraro, F., Hall, H., Hovee, M., & Wilcox, S. (2017). Psychological dimensions of drone warfare. *Current Psychology, 38*(5), 1285–1296. https://doi.org/10.1007/s12144-017-9684-7

Himes, K. R. (2016). *Drones and the ethics of targeted killing.* Rowman & Littlefield.

Hoffman, B. (2009, January 29). The myth of grass-roots terrorism. *Foreign Affairs, 87*(3), 133–138.

Hoffman, B. (2020, March 12). *Al-Qaeda: Threat or anachronism?*https://hoffmangroup.global/terrorist-threats/al-qaeda-threat-or-anachronism/

Hoffman, B., & Reinares, F. (Eds.). (2014). Conclusion. In *The evolution of the global terrorist threat: From 9/11 to Osama bin Laden's death* (pp. 618–640). Columbia University Press.

Hoffman, B., & Ware, J. (2021, January). Terrorism and counterterrorism challenges for the Biden administration. *CTC Sentinel, 14*(1), 1–12. https://ctc.usma.edu/wp-content/uploads/2021/01/CTC-SENTINEL-012021.pdf

Hovee, M., & Wilcox, S. (2019). Psychological dimensions of drone warfare. *Current Psychology, 38*(5), 1285–1296. https://doi.org/10.1007/s12144-017-9684-7

Human Rights Watch. (2013, October 22). *"Between a drone and Al-Qaeda:" The civilian cost of US targeted killings in Yemen.* https://www.hrw.org/report/2013/10/22/between-drone-and-al-qaeda/civilian-cost-us-targeted-killings-yemen

Huntley, T., & Regan, M. (2022). From armed conflict to countering threat networks: Counterterrorism and social network analysis. In F. C. Finkelstein, J. Ohlin, & M. Regan (Eds.), *Between policing and armed conflict: Hybrid legal frameworks for asymmetric conflict.* Oxford University Press.

Institute for National Strategic Studies, National Defense University. (2018, April 17). *Executive summary: Civilian casualty review.* Just Security. https://www.justsecurity.org/wp-content/uploads/2019/02/Civ-Cas-Study-Redacted-just-security.pdf

International Committee of the Red Cross. (2009). *Interpretive guidance on the notion of direct participation in hostilities under international humanitarian law.* https://www.icrc.org/en/doc/assets/files/other/icrc-002-0990.pdf

International Crisis Group. (2013, May 21). *Drones: Myths and reality in Pakistan.* https://d2071andvip0wj.cloudfront.net/drones-myths-and-reality-in-pakistan.pdf

Islamic Republic of Pakistan. (2012, September). *Details of attacks by NATO forces/predators in FATA.*

Jacobson, D., & Kaplan, E. H. (2007). Suicide bombings and targeted killings in (counter-) terror games. *Journal of Conflict Resolution, 51*(5), 772–792. https://doi.org/10.1177/0022002707304814

Jaeger, D. A., Klor, E., Miaari, S., & Paserman, M. D. (2012). The struggle for Palestinian hearts and minds: Violence and public opinion in the second Intifada. *Journal of Public Economics, 96*(3–4), 354–368. https://www.scienc edirect.com/science/article/abs/pii/S0047272711001708

Jaeger, D. A., & Paserman, M. D. (2009). The shape of things to come? On the dynamics of suicide attacks and targeted killings. *Quarterly Journal of Political Science, 4*(4), 315–342. https://doi.org/10.1561/100.00009013

Jaeger, D. A., & Siddique, Z. (2018). Are drone strikes effective in Afghanistan and Pakistan? On the dynamics of violence between the United States and the Taliban. *CESifo Economic Studies, 64*(4), 667–697. http://www.djaeger.org/research/wp/Jaeger-Siddique.pdf

Johnsen, G. D. (2012). *The last refuge: Yemen, al-Qaeda, and America's war in Arabia.* W. W. Norton Company.

Johnson, J. (2012, November 30). *The conflict against Al Qaeda and its affiliates: How will it end?*https://www.lawfareblog.com/jeh-johnson-speech-oxf ord-union

Johnston, P. B. (2012). Does decapitation work? Assessing the effectiveness of leadership targeting in counterinsurgency campaigns. *International Security, 36*(4), 47–79. https://doi.org/10.1162/isec_a_00076

Johnston, P. B., & Sarbahi, A. K. (2016). The impact of US drone strikes on terrorism in Pakistan. *International Studies Quarterly, 60*(2), 203–219. https://doi.org/10.1093/isq/sqv004

Joint and Coalition Operational Analysis. (2013a, April 12). *Reducing and mitigating civilian casualties: Enduring lessons.*

Joint and Coalition Operational Analysis. (2013b, June 18). *Drone strikes: Civilian casualty considerations.*

Joint Chiefs of Staff, 'Countering Threat Networks' (Department of Defense Joint Publication 3-25, 21 December 2016).

Joint direct attack munition. Military.com. Retrieved August 2, 2021, from https://www.military.com/equipment/joint-direct-attack-munition-jdam

Jones, S. G. (2021). The evolution of Al-Qaida: 1988 to present day. In M. Sheehan, E. Marquardt, & L. Collins (Eds.), *Routledge handbook of U.S. counterterrorism and irregular warfare operations* (pp. 41–53). Routledge.

Jones, S. G., Liepman, A., & Chandler, N. (2016). *Counterterrorism and counterinsurgency in Somalia: Assessing the campaign against Al Shabaab.* RAND. https://doi.org/10.7249/RR1539

Jordan, J. (2009). When heads roll: Assessing the effectiveness of leadership decapitation. *Security Studies, 18*(4), 719–755. https://doi.org/10.1080/09636410903369068

Jordan, J. (2014a). Attacking the leader, missing the mark: Why terrorist groups survive decapitation strikes. *International Security, 38*(4), 7–38. https://doi.org/10.1162/isec_a_00157

Jordan, J. (2014b). The effectiveness of the drone campaign against Al Qaeda central: A case study. *Journal of Strategic Studies, 37*(1), 4–29. https://doi.org/10.1080/01402390.2013.850422

Jordan, J. (2019). *Leadership decapitation: Strategic targeting of terrorist organizations.* Stanford University Press.

Joscelyn, T. (2010, June 23). *Times Square bomber discusses Taliban ties at plea hearing.* FDD's Long War Journal. https://www.longwarjournal.org/archives/2010/06/times_square_bomber.php

Joscelyn, T. (2013, July 18). *Global al Qaeda: Affiliates, objectives, and future challenges.* FDD's Long War Journal. https://www.longwarjournal.org/archives/2013/07/global_al_qaeda_affi.php

Joseph, D., & Maruf, H. (2018). *Inside Al-Shabaab: The secret history of Al-Qaeda's most powerful ally.* Indiana University Press.

Kaplan, E. H., Mintz, A., & Mishal, S. (2006). Tactical prevention of suicide bombings in Israel. *Interfaces, 36*(6), 553–561. https://doi.org/10.1287/inte.1060.0242

Kaplan, E. H., Mintz, A., Mishal, S., & Samban, C. (2005). What happened to suicide bombings in Israel? Insights from a terror stock model. *Studies in Conflict & Terrorism, 28*(3), 225–235. https://doi.org/10.1080/10576100590928115

Keating, J. (2020, May 10). *What do you learn at a terrorist training camp?* Foreign Policy. https://foreignpolicy.com/2010/05/10/what-do-you-learn-at-terrorist-training-camp/

Kendall, E. (2018, July). *Contemporary Jihadi Militancy in Yemen: How is the threat evolving?* Middle East Institute. https://www.mei.edu/sites/default/files/publications/MEI%20Policy%20Paper_Kendall_7.pdf

Kendall, E. (2020, February 14). *Death of AQAP leader shows the group's fragmentation—And durability.* The Washington Institute for Near East Policy. https://www.washingtoninstitute.org/policy-analysis/death-aqap-leader-shows-groups-fragmentation-and-durability

Khan, A., & Gopal, A. (2017, November 16). The uncounted. *The New York Times.* https://www.nytimes.com/interactive/2017/11/16/magazine/uncounted-civilian-casualties-iraq-airstrikes.html

Kilcullen, D., & Exum, A. M. (2009, May 16). Death from above, outrage down below. *The New York Times.* https://www.nytimes.com/2009/05/17/opinion/17exum.html

Kirchofer, C. (2016). Targeted killings and compellence: Lessons from the campaign against Hamas in the second Intifada. *Perspectives on Terrorism, 10*(3), 16–25. https://css.ethz.ch/en/services/digital-library/articles/article.html/169c2bcb-5b01-40b5-86c4-2eff8a2801b9

Knickmeyer, E., & Gorman, S. (2012, May 10). Behind foiled jet plot, stronger Saudi ties. *The Wall Street Journal*. https://www.wsj.com/articles/SB1000 14240527023045439045773943739456627482

Knoll, D. (2017, October). *Al-Qaeda in the Arabian Peninsula (AQAP): An Al-Qaeda affiliate case study*. CNA. https://www.cna.org/cna_files/pdf/DIM-2017-U-016116-2Rev.pdf

Knuckey, S. (2014). *Drones and targeted killings*. International Debate Education Association.

Knuckey, S. (2016, October 24). *The good and bad in the US government's civilian casualties announcement*. Just Security. https://www.justsecurity.org/31785/good-bad-governments-civilian-casualties-announcement/

Kober, A. (2007). Targeted killing during the second Intifada: The quest for effectiveness. *Journal of Conflict Studies, 27*(1), 76–93. https://journals.lib.unb.ca/index.php/JCS/article/view/8292

Krebs, V. E. (2002). *Mapping networks of terrorist cells*. American Civil Liberties Union. https://www.aclu.org/sites/default/files/field_document/ACL URM002810.pdf

Lahoud, N., Caudill, S., Collins, L., Koehler-Derrick, G., Rassler, D., & al-'Ubaydi, M. (2012, May 3). *Letters from Abbottabad: Bin Ladin sidelined?* Combating Terrorism Center at West Point. https://www.ctc.usma.edu/wp-content/uploads/2012/05/CTC_LtrsFromAbbottabad_WEB_v2.pdf

Langdon, L., Sarapu, A. J., & Wells, M. (2004). Targeting the leadership of terrorist and insurgent movements: Historical lessons for contemporary policy makers. *Journal of Public & International Affairs, 15*(Spring), 59–78. https://jpia.princeton.edu/sites/jpia/files/2004-4.pdf

Lee, K. (2015, January). Does Al Qaeda central still matter? *UNISCI Journal, 37*, 15–48.

Lee, P. (2019). *Reaper force: The inside story of Britain's drone wars*. John Blake.

Lehrke, J. P., & Schomaker, R. (2016). Kill, capture, or defend? The effectiveness of specific and general counterterrorism tactics against the global threats of the post-9/11 era. *Security Studies, 25*(4), 729–762. https://doi.org/10.1080/09636412.2016.1220199

Levitt, M., & Zelin, A. (2020, December 11). *Al-Qaeda's external operations one year after the Pensacola attack*. The Washington Institute. https://www.washingtoninstitute.org/policy-analysis/al-qaedas-external-operations-one-year-after-pensacola-attack

Levy, A., & Scott-Clark, C. (2017). *The exile: The stunning inside story of Osama bin Laden and Al Qaeda in flight*. Bloomsbury.

Lewis, L. (2013, April 12). *Reducing and mitigating civilian casualties: Enduring lessons*. Joint and Coalition Operational Analysis. https://info.pub licintelligence.net/JCOA-ReducingCIVCAS.pdf

Lewis, L. (2014). *Improving lethal action*. CNA. https://www.cna.org/CNA_files/PDF/COP-2014-U-008746-Final.pdf

Lewis, L. (2018). *Redefining human control: Lessons from the battlefield for autonomous weapons*, 11. https://www.cna.org/CNA_files/PDF/DOP-2018-U-017258-Final.pdf

Lewis, L. (2021). *Protecting civilians: A comprehensive approach* (Unpublished manuscript). Center for Autonomy and AI, CNA.

Lewis, L., & Holewinski, S. (2013). Changing of the guard: Civilian protection for an evolving military. *Prism, 4*(2), 57–66. https://cco.ndu.edu/Portals/96/Documents/prism/prism_4-2/prism57-66_Lewis_and_Holewinski.pdf

Lewis, L., & Varichek, D. M. (2014). *Rethinking the drone war*. CNA and Marine Corps University Press. https://www.cna.org/cna_files/pdf/RethinkingTheDroneWar.pdf

Lewis, L., & Goodman, R. (2018, March 22). *We need better estimates—Not just better numbers*. Just Security. https://www.justsecurity.org/54181/civilian-casualties-estimates-not-numbers/

Lister, C. (2018, February). How Al-Qa'ida lost control of its Syrian affiliate: The inside story. *CTC Sentinel, 11*(2), 1–9. https://ctc.usma.edu/wp-content/uploads/2018/02/CTC-Sentinel_Vol11Iss2-2.pdf

Loidolt, B. (2012, May 18). Managed risks, managed expectations: How far will targeted killing get the United States in Afghanistan? *War on the Rocks*. https://warontherocks.com/2021/05/managed-risks-managed-expectations-how-far-will-targeted-killing-get-us-in-afghanistan/

Loidolt, B. (2022). Were drone strikes effective? Evaluating the drone campaign in Pakistan through captured Al-Qaeda documents. *Texas National Security Review, 5*(2), 53–79. https://tnsr.org/2022/01/were-drone-strikes-effective-evaluating-the-drone-campaign-in-pakistan-through-captured-al-qaeda-documents/

Long, A. (2014). Whack-a-mole or coup de grace? Institutionalization and leadership targeting in Iraq and Afghanistan. *Security Studies, 23*(3), 471–512. https://doi.org/10.1080/09636412.2014.935229

Luft, G. (2003). The logic of Israel's targeted killing. *Middle East Quarterly, 10*(1), 3–13.

Lyall, J. (2017, September 3). *Bombing to lose? Airpower, civilian casualties, and the dynamics of violence in counterinsurgency wars*. SSRN. http://dx.doi.org/10.2139/ssrn.2422170

Mahanty, D. (2020, April 21.) *Great expectations: AFRICOM's new quarterly report on civilian casualties*. Just Security. https://www.justsecurity.org/69785/great-expectations-africom-new-quarterly-report-on-civilian-casualties/

Mahanty, D., & Siemion, R. (2020, May 7). *Grading DOD's annual civilian casualties report: "Incomplete."* Just Security. https://www.justsecurity.org/70063/grading-dods-annual-civilian-casualties-report-incomplete/

Mahmood, R., & Jetter, M. (2019, April). *Military intervention via drone strikes* (Discussion paper no. 12318). IZA Institute of Labor Economics. http://ftp.iza.org/dp12318.pdf

Mannes, A. (2008). Testing the snake head strategy: Does killing or capturing its leaders reduce a terrorist group's activity? *Journal of International Policy Solutions, 9*(4), 40–49. https://doi.org/10.2139/ssrn.2988670

Marsh, J. M., & Williams, J. (2021). Drones, Afghanistan and beyond: Towards analysis and assessment in context. *European Journal of International Security.* https://www.cambridge.org/core/journals/european-journal-of-intern ational-security/article/drones-afghanistan-and-beyond-towards-analysis-and-assessment-in-context/479E5F71A5672B7A5A78ABB93C53DAB0

Martin, M. J., with Sasser, C. W. (2010). *Predator: The remote-control air war over Iraq and Afghanistan: A pilot's story.* Zenith Press.

Mazzetti, M., & Schmitt, E. (2015a, April 12). Terrorism case renews debate over drone hits. *New York Times.* https://www.nytimes.com/2015a/04/13/us/terrorism-case-renews-debate-over-drone-hits.html

Mazzetti, M., & Schmitt, E. (2015b, June 16). For U.S., killing terrorists is a means to an elusive end. *New Yok Times.* https://www.nytimes.com/2015b/06/17/world/middleeast/al-qaeda-arabian-peninsula-yemen-nasser-al-wuh ayshi-killed.html

Medact. (2012). *Drones: The physical and psychological implications of a global theatre of war.* https://www.medact.org/wp-content/uploads/2012/10/rep ort-drones-2012.pdf

Megerian, C. (2021, September 3). The U.S. war in Afghanistan is over—But the war on terror continues. *Los Angeles Times.* https://www.latimes.com/politics/story/2021-09-03/afghanistan-counterterrorism-challenges

Mehta, A. (2104, May 13). Ready for retirement, can predator find new home? *Defense News.* https://archive.ph/20140517154223/http://www.defensenews.com/article/20140513/DEFREG/305120020/Ready-for-Ret irement-Can-Predator-Find-New-Home

Meisels, T., & Waldron, J. (2020). *Debating targeted killing: Counter-terrorism or extrajudicial execution?* Oxford University Press.

Melzer, N. (2008). *Targeted killing in international law.* Oxford University Press.

Miller, G. (2018, February 7). John Brennan CIA hearing exposes skepticism about U.S. antiterrorism efforts. *The Washington Post.* https://www.was hingtonpost.com/world/national-security/brennan-defends-drone-strike-pol icies/2013/02/07/f7384950-7145-11e2-ac36-3d8d9dcaa2e2_story.html

Mir, A. (2018). What explains counterterrorism effectiveness? Evidence from the U.S. drone war in Pakistan. *International Security, 43*(2), 45–83. http://doi.org/10.1162/isec_a_00331

Mir, A. (2021, September). Twenty years after 9/11: The terror threat from Afghanistan post the Taliban takeover. *CTC Sentinel, 14*(7), 29–43. https://ctc.usma.edu/twenty-years-after-9-11-the-terror-threat-from-afghanistan-post-the-taliban-takeover/

Mir, A., & Clarke, C. (2020, September 9). Al Qaeda's franchise reboot. *Foreign Affairs.* https://www.foreignaffairs.com/articles/afghanistan/2020-09-09/al-qaedas-franchise-reboot

Mir, A., & Moore, D. (2019). Drones, surveillance, and violence: Theory and evidence from a US drone program. *International Studies Quarterly, 63*(4), 846–862. https://doi.org/10.1093/isq/sqz040

Montgomery, N. (2006, March 18). U.S. seeks to reduce civilian deaths at Iraq checkpoints. *Stars and Stripes.* https://www.stripes.com/news/u-s-seeks-to-reduce-civilian-deaths-at-iraq-checkpoints-1.46403

Morag, N. (2005). Measuring success in coping with terrorism: The Israeli case. *Studies in Conflict & Terrorism, 28,* 307–320. https://www.tandfonline.com/doi/abs/10.1080/10576100590950156

Mtwana for Human Rights. (2021, March). *Death falling from the sky: Civilian harm from the United States' use of lethal force in Yemen January 2017-January 2019.* https://mwatana.org/wp-content/uploads/2021/03/Death-Falling-from-the-Sky-22.pdf

Nasr, W. (2019, May 30). *Exclusive: FRANCE 24 questions AQIM jihadist leader.* France 24. https://www.france24.com/en/20190530-aqmi-jihadist-leader-maghreb-france-terrorism-al-qaeda-islamic-youssef-al-Aanabi

National Commission on Terrorist Attacks Upon the United States. (2004a). *The 9/11 commission report.* https://www.govinfo.gov/content/pkg/GPO-911REPORT/pdf/GPO-911REPORT.pdf

National Commission on Terrorist Attacks Upon the United States. (2004b). *Monograph on terrorist financing.* https://govinfo.library.unt.edu/911/staff_statements/911_TerrFin_Monograph.pdf

National Defense Authorization Act Fiscal Year 2018, § 1057(a). Pub. L. No. 115-91, 131 Stat. 1283. (2017). https://www.congress.gov/115/plaws/publ91/PLAW-115publ91.pdf

National Defense Authorization Act Fiscal Year 2019, § 936. Pub. L. No. 115-232, 132 Stat. 1636. (2018). https://www.congress.gov/115/plaws/publ232/PLAW-115publ232.pdf

National Defense Authorization Act Fiscal Year 2020, § 1723. Pub. L. No. 116-92, 133 Stat. 1198. (2019). https://www.congress.gov/116/plaws/publ92/PLAW-116publ92.pdf

National Defense University, Executive Summary, Civilian Casualty (CIVCAS) Review. (2018, April 17). https://games-cdn.washingtonpost.com/notes/prod/default/documents/e39c5889-6489-4373-bd8e-ac2ca012e03d/note/6c60bba4-5781-4874-acdf-87e199f6e31b.pdf

National Public Radio. (2012, May 1). *John Brennan delivers speech on drone ethics.* https://www.npr.org/2012/05/01/151778804/john-bre nnan-delivers-speech-on-drone-ethics

New America Foundation. (2010, September). *Public opinion in Pakistan's tribal regions.* http://www.terrorfreetomorrow.org/upimagestft/FATApoll1.pdf

New America, America's Counterterrorism Wars. https://www.newamerica. org/international-security/reports/americas-counterterrorism-wars/method ology/#counting-the-strikes

Nichols, C. P., III. (2014). *Counterterrorism strategies: Leadership decapitation vs mid-tier elimination.* Baccalaureate dissertation, Pennsylvania State University. https://honors.libraries.psu.edu/files/final_submissions/2614

Noble, D. (2015, November 9). Reaper madness: Obama's Whack-a-Mole killing machine. *Counterpunch.* https://www.counterpunch.org/2015/11/09/reaper-madness-obamas-whack-a-mole-killing-machine/

Office of the Director of National Intelligence. (2016). *Summary of information regarding U.S. counterterrorism strikes outside areas of active hostilities between January 20, 2009 and December 31, 2015.* https://www.dni.gov/files/doc uments/Newsroom/Press%20Releases/DNI+Release+on+CT+Strikes+Out side+Areas+of+Active+Hostilities.PDF

Office of the Director of National Intelligence. (2017). *Summary of 2016 information regarding U.S. counterterrorism strikes outside areas of active hostilities between January 1, 2016 and December 31, 2016.* https://www. dni.gov/files/documents/Newsroom/Summary-of-2016-Information-Reg arding-United-States-Counterterrorism-Strikes-Outside-Areas-of-Active-Hos tilities.pdf

Office of the Director of National Intelligence. (2021, April 9). *Annual threat assessment of the US intelligence community.* https://www.dni.gov/files/ODNI/documents/assessments/ATA-2021-Unclassified-Report.pdf

Open Society Justice Initiative. (2015). *Death by drone: Civilian harm caused by US targeted killings in Yemen.* https://www.justiceinitiative.org/uploads/1284eb37-f380-4400-9242-936a15e4de6c/death-drones-report-eng-201 50413.pdf

Osborne, K. (2017, May 9). The MQ-9 Reaper is now wielding these deadly new weapons. *The National Interest.*https://nationalinterest.org/blog/the-buzz/the-mq-9-reaper-now-wielding-these-deadly-new-weapons-20572

Pakistan Body Count, Drone Strikes, Pakistan. https://www.kaggle.com/zusmani/pakistandroneattacks?select=PakistanDroneAttacksWithTemp+Ver+11+%28November+30+2017%29.csv

Pettyjohn, S. (2021, November 7). *Over-the-horizon does not have to mean next door.* Lawfare. https://www.lawfareblog.com/over-horizon-does-not-have-mean-next-door

Pew Research Center. (2010, June 17). *Global attitudes project: Obama more popular abroad than at home, global image of U.S. continues to benefit.* https://www.pewresearch.org/wp-content/uploads/sites/2/2010/06/Pew-Global-Attitudes-Spring-2010-Report-June-17-11AM-EDT.pdf

Pew Research Center. (2012, June 13). *Global attitudes project: Global opinion of Obama slips, international policies faulted.* https://www.pewresearch.org/global/wp-content/uploads/sites/2/2012/06/Pew-Global-Attitudes-U.S.-Image-Report-FINAL-June-13-20123.pdf

Pew Research Center. (2014, August 27). *Global attitudes project: A less gloomy mood in Pakistan.* https://www.pewresearch.org/global/wp-content/uploads/sites/2/2014/08/PG-2014-08-27_Pakistan-FINAL.pdf

Plaw, A. (2008). *Targeting terrorists.* Routledge.

Plaw, A., & Fricker, M. S. (2012). Tracking the predators: Evaluating the US drone campaign in Pakistan. *International Studies Perspectives, 13,* 344–365. https://academic.oup.com/isp/article-abstract/13/4/344/1786989

Plaw, A., Fricker, M. S., & Colon, C. (2015). *The drone debate: A primer on the U.S. use of unmanned aircraft outside conventional battlefields.* Rowman & Littlefield.

Pratt, S. F. (2013). "Anyone who hurts us": How the logic of Israel's "assassination policy" developed during the Aqsa Intifada. *Terrorism and Political Violence, 25*(2), 224–245. https://doi.org/10.1080/09546553.2012.657280

Price, B. C. (2019). *Targeting top terrorists: Understanding leadership removal in counterterrorism strategy.* Columbia University Press.

Quote Investigator, It Ain't What You Don't Know That Gets You Into Trouble. It's What You Know for Sure That Just Ain't So. https://quoteinvestigator.com/2018/11/18/know-trouble/. Accessed 5 Sep 2021.

Ramsay, C., Kull, S., Weber, S., & Lewis, E. (2009, July 1). *Pakistani public opinion on the Swat Conflict, Afghanistan, and the US.* World Public Opinion. https://worldpublicopinion.net/wp-content/uploads/2017/12/WPO_Pakistan_Jul09_rpt.pdf

Rigterink, A. (2021). The wane of command: Evidence on drone strikes and control within terrorist organizations. *American Political Science Review, 115*(1), 31–50. https://doi.org/10.1017/S0003055420000908

Rinehart, C. S. (2016). *Drones and targeted killing in the Middle East and Africa: An appraisal of American counterterrorism policies.* Lexington Books.

Robertson, N., Cruickshank, P., & Lister, T. (2012, April 30). *Document shows origins of 2006 plot for liquid bombs on planes.* CNN. https://www.cnn.com/2012/04/30/world/al-qaeda-documents/index.html

Roggio, B. (2007, December 29). *Taliban dismisses senior Afghan commander [Updated]*. FDD's Long War Journal. https://www.longwarjournal.org/arc hives/2007/12/taliban_dismisses_se.php

Roggio, B. (2008, January 2). *Mullah Omar confirms firing of Mullah Mansoor Dadullah*. FDD's Long War Journal. https://www.longwarjournal.org/arc hives/2008/01/mullah_omar_confirms.php

Roggio, B., & Mayer, A. (2010, January 5). *Analysis: US air campaign in Pakistan heats up*. FDD's Long War Journal. https://www.longwarjournal. org/archives/2010/01/analysis_us_air_camp.php

Rohde, D. (2012, January 26). The drone wars. *Reuters Magazine*. https:// www.reuters.com/article/us-david-rohde-drone-wars/reuters-magazine-the-drone-wars-idUSTRE80P11I20120126

Ross, A. (2014, January 29). *Leaked official document records 330 drone strikes in Pakistan*. Bureau of Investigative Journalism. https://www.thebureau investigates.com/stories/2014-01-29/leaked-official-document-records-330-drone-strikes-in-pakistan

Rowlands, D., & Kilberg, J. (2011). *Organizational structure and the effects of targeting terrorist leadership*. Centre for Security & Defence Studies, Paterson School of International Affairs, Carleton University. http://www3.carleton. ca/csds/docs/working_papers/RowlandsKilbergWP09.pdf

Sageman, M. (2008a). Does Osama still call the shots? Debating the containment of Al Qaeda's leadership. *Foreign Affairs, 87*(4), 163–165.

Sageman, M. (2008b). *Leaderless jihad*. University of Pennsylvania Press.

Savage, C. (2021, May 6). Trump's secret rules for drone strikes outside war zones are disclosed. *New York Times*.https://www.nytimes.com/2021/05/ 01/us/politics/trump-drone-strike-rules.html

Savage, C., & Schmitt, E. (2017a, March 12). Trump administration is said to be working to loosen counterterrorism rules. *The New York Times*. https://www.nytimes.com/2017a/03/12/us/politics/trump-loosen-counterterrorism-rules.html

Savage, C., & Schmitt, E. (2017b, September 21). Trump poised to drop some limits on drone strikes and commando raids. *The New York Times*. https://www.nytimes.com/2017b/09/21/us/politics/trump-drone-strikes-commando-raids-rules.html

Schmitt, M. (2012). Unmanned combat aircraft systems and international humanitarian law: Simplifying the oft benighted debate. *Boston University International Law Journal*, 595–619, 615. http://www.bu.edu/law/jou rnals-archive/international/volume30n2/documents/symposium_schmitt. pdf

Schmitt, E., & Dahir, A. (2020, March 21). Al Qaeda branch in Somalia threatens Americans in East Africa—And even the U.S. *The New York*

Times. https://www.nytimes.com/2020/03/21/world/africa/al-qaeda-som alia-shabab.html

Schmitt, E., & Latif, A. (2020, March 21). Al Qaeda branch in Somalia threatens Americans in east Africa—And even the U.S. *The New York Times.* https://www.nytimes.com/2020/03/21/world/africa/al-qaeda-somalia-shabab.html

Schmitt, E., & Shanker, T. (2011). *Counterstrike: The untold story of America's secret campaign against Al Qaeda.* Times Books.

Senate Select Committee on Intelligence. (2014, January 15). *Review of the terrorist attacks on US facilities in Benghazi, Libya, September 11–12, 2012.* https://www.intelligence.senate.gov/sites/default/files/press/benghazi.pdf

Sewall, S. (2017). *Chasing success: Air Force efforts to reduce civilian harm.* Air University.

Sewall, S., & Lewis, L. (2010). *Joint civilian casualty study: Executive summary.*

Shah, A. (2018). Do U.S. drone strikes cause blowback? Evidence from Pakistan and beyond. *International Security, 42*(4), 47–84. https://doi.org/10.1162/isec_a_00312

Shahidi News Team. (2021, March 30). Wanted Kenyan pilot linked to Al-Shabaab escapes to Somalia. *Shahidi News.* https://shahidinews.co.ke/2021/03/30/wanted-kenyan-pilot-linked-to-al-shabaab-escapes-to-somalia/

Shahzad, S. S. (2007, August 11). Taliban a step ahead of US assault. *Asia Times.* https://web.archive.org/web/20070818133337/http://www.atimes.com/atimes/South_Asia/IH11Df01.html

Shane, S. (2011, August 11). C.I.A. is disputed on civilian toll in drone strikes. *The New York Times.* https://www.nytimes.com/2011/08/12/world/asia/12drones.html

Shane, S. (2016, July). The enduring influence of Anwar al-Awlaki in the age of the Islamic State. *CTC Sentinel, 9*(7), 15–19. https://ctc.usma.edu/wp-con tent/uploads/2016/08/CTC-SENTINEL_Vol9Iss710.pdf

Shapiro, J., & Fair, C. C. (2009/10). Understanding support for Islamist militancy in Pakistan. *International Security, 34*(3), 79–118. https://sch olar.princeton.edu/sites/default/files/jns/files/understanding_support_for_islamist_militancy.pdf

Shiel, A., & Woods, C. (2021, June 7). *A legacy of unrecognized harm: DoD's 2020 civilian casualties report.* Just Security. https://www.justsecurity.org/76788/a-legacy-of-unrecognized-harm-dods-2020-civilian-casualties-report/

Shinwari, N. A. (2011). *Understanding FATA: Attitudes towards governance, religion and society in Pakistan's Federally Administered Tribal Areas* (Vol. V). Community Appraisal & Motivation Programme. http://crossasia-reposi tory.ub.uni-heidelberg.de/2715/1/Understanding_FATA_Vol_V_11.pdf

Shire, M. I. (2020). *How do leadership decapitation and targeting error affect suicide bombings? The case of Al-Shabaab.* Studies in Conflict & Terrorism. https://doi.org/10.1080/1057610X.2020.1780021

Shortell, D., & Perez, E. (2020, May 19). *FBI finds al Qaeda link after breaking encryption on Pensacola attacker's iPhone.* CNN. https://edition.cnn.com/2020/05/18/politics/pensacola-shooting-al-qaeda/

Silverman, D. (2016). *Drone strikes and "hearts and minds": A quasi-experimental analysis in Pakistan* (Manuscript in preparation). Institute for Politics and Strategy, Carnegie Mellon University. https://danielmsilvermandotcom.files.wordpress.com/2018/09/drones-attitudes-silverman-2016.pdf

Singh, R. (2013, October 25). Drone strikes kill innocent people: Why is it so hard to know how any? *New Republic.* https://newrepublic.com/article/115353/civilian-casualties-drone-strikes-why-we-know-so-little

Smith, M., & Walsh, J. I. (2013). Do drone strikes degrade Al Qaeda? Evidence from propaganda output. *Terrorism and Political Violence, 25*(2), 311–327. https://doi.org/10.1080/09546553.2012.664011

Strawser, B., & McMahan, J. (Eds.). (2013). *Killing by remote control: The ethics of an unmanned military.* Oxford University Press.

Stuart, E., Huskamp, H., Duckworth, K., Simmons, J., Song, Z., Chernew, M., & Varry, C. (2014). Using propensity scores in difference-in-differences models to estimate the effects of a policy change. *Health Services and Outcomes Research Methodology, 14,* 166–182. https://link.springer.com/content/pdf/10.1007/s10742-014-0123-z.pdf

Swift, C. (2014). The boundaries of war? Assessing the impact of drone strikes in Yemen. In P. Bergen & D. Rothenberg (Eds.), *Drone wars: Transforming conflict, law, and policy* (pp. 71–88). Cambridge University Press.

Szuba, J. (2020, March 31). *Promising transparency, US Africa Command to begin reporting civilian casualty claims.* Defense Post. https://www.thedefensepost.com/2020/03/31/us-africom-report-civilian-casualties/

Taj, F. (2010, January 2). Analysis: Drone attacks: Challenging some fabrications. *Daily Times.* https://web.archive.org/web/20140614205708/http://archives.dailytimes.com.pk/editorial/02-Jan-2010/analysis-drone-attacks-challenging-some-fabrications-farhat-taj

Taj, F. (2011). A critical perspective on a recent survey of opinion in Pakistan's tribal zone. *Small Wars & Insurgencies, 22*(2), 402–413. https://doi.org/10.1080/09592318.2011.573425

Taqi, M. (2012, October 6). *Shooting down drones with academic guns?* Pakistan Defence. https://defence.pk/pdf/threads/shooting-down-drones-with-academic-guns.211586/

Terrill, W. A. (2013, June 1). *The struggle for Yemen and the challenge of Al-Qaeda in the Arabian Peninsula.* United States Army War College. https://press.armywarcollege.edu/monographs/523/

Thompson, D. (1980). Moral responsibility of public officials: The problem of many hands. *American Political Science Review, 74*(4), 905–916. https://doi.org/10.2307/1954312

Tominaga, Y. (2018). Killing two birds with one stone? Examining the diffusion effect of militant leadership decapitation. *International Studies Quarterly*, *62*(1), 54–68. https://doi.org/10.1093/isq/sqx055

Tominaga, Y. (2019). Evaluating the impact of repeated leadership targeting on militant group durability. *International Interactions*, *45*(5), 865–892. https://doi.org/10.1080/03050629.2019.1647836

Tucker, J. (2013, June 14). Is theory getting lost in the "identification revolution"? Monkey Cage. https://themonkeycage.org/2013/06/is-theory-getting-lost-in-the-identification-revolution/

United Nations Security Council. (2019, November 1). *Letter dated 1 November 2019 from the Chair of the Security Council Committee pursuant to resolution 751 (1992) concerning Somalia addressed to the President of the Security Council.* https://www.securitycouncilreport.org/atf/cf/%7B65BFCF9B-6D27-4E9C-8CD3-CF6E4FF96FF9%7D/S_2019_858_E.pdf

United Nations Security Council. (2020, January 20). *Letter from the Chair of the Security Council Committee pursuant to resolutions 1267 (1999), 1989 (2011) and 2253 (2015) concerning Islamic State in Iraq and the Levant (Da'esh), Al-Qaida and associated individuals, groups, undertakings and entities addressed to the President of the Security Council.* United Nations Digital Library. https://digitallibrary.un.org/record/3848705?ln=en

United Nations Assistance Mission in Afghanistan. (2019, February). *Afghanistan: Protection of civilians in armed conflict: 2018 annual report.* https://unama.unmissions.org/sites/default/files/unama_annual_protection_of_civilians_report_2018_-_23_feb_2019_-_english.pdf

United Nations Assistance Mission in Afghanistan. (2020, February). *Afghanistan: Protection of civilians in armed conflict: 2019 annual report.* https://unama.unmissions.org/sites/default/files/afghanistan_protection_of_civilians_annual_report_2019.pdf

United Nations. (2021, April 28). *Letter dated 28 April 2021 from the Analytical Support and Sanctions Monitoring Team addressed to the Chair of the Security Council Committee established pursuant to resolution 1988 (2011).* https://undocs.org/pdf?symbol=en/s/2021/486

United States Africa Command. (2019, March 20). *Statement on the Amnesty International report.* Joint Chiefs of Staff. https://www.jcs.mil/Media/News/News-Display/Article/1790860/us-africa-command-statement-on-the-amnesty-international-report/

United States Air Force. (1998, February 1). *Intelligence targeting guide.*

United States Central Command. (2021, April 20). *Letter to Ms. Radhya A-Mutawakel & Ms. Priyanka Motaparthy.* Mwatana for Human Rights. https://mwatana.org/wp-content/uploads/2021/06/CENTCOM-Mwatana-Response-4-20-2021.pdf

United States Department of Defense. (2016a). *Law of war manual.* https://tjaglcspublic.army.mil/documents/27431/61281/DoD+Law+of+War+Man ual+-+June+2015+Updated+Dec+2016/5a02f6f8-eff3-4e79-a46f-9cd7aa c74a95

United States Department of Defense. (2016b). *Law of war manual June 2015 (updated December 2016).* Homeland Security Digital Library. https://www.hsdl.org/?view&did=797480

United States Department of Defense. (2017, February 13). *Combined Joint Task Force, Operation Inherent Resolve, CIVCAS allegation closure report.*

United States Department of Defense. (2018). *Annual report on civilian casualties in connection with United States Military operations in 2017.* Federation of American Scientists. https://fas.org/man/eprint/civcas2018.pdf

United States Department of Defense. (2019). *Annual report on civilian casualties in connection with United States Military operations in 2018.* https://media.defense.gov/2019/May/02/2002126767/-1/-1/1/ANN UAL-REPORT-CIVILIAN-CASUALTIES-IN-CONNECTION-WITH-US-MILITARY-OPERATIONS.PDF

United States Department of Defense. (2020a). *Lead Inspector General report to the United States Congress, East Africa counterterrorism Operation; North and West Africa counterterrorism Operation: July 1, 2020–September 30, 2020.* https://media.defense.gov/2020/Dec/04/2002546287/-1/-1/1/LEAD% 20IG%20EAST%20AFRICA%20AND%20NORTH%20AND%20WEST%20A FRICA%20COUNTERTERRORISM%20OPERATIONS.PDF

United States Department of Defense. (2020b). *Annual report on civilian casualties in connection with United States Military operations in 2019.* https://media.defense.gov/2020/May/06/2002295555/-1/-1/1/SEC-1057-CIVILIAN-CASUALTIES-MAY-1-2020.PDF

United States Department of Defense. (2021a). *Annual report on civilian casualties in connection with United States Military operations in 2020.* https://media.defense.gov/2021/Jun/02/2002732834/-1/-1/0/ANN UAL-REPORT-ON-CIVILIAN-CASUALTIES-IN-CONNECTION-WITH-UNITED-STATES-MILITARY-OPERATIONS-IN-2020.PDF

United States Department of Defense. (2021b, November 3). *Investigation into 29 Aug CIVCAS in Afghanistan.* https://www.washingtonpost.com/con text/air-force-inspector-general-s-findings-of-errant-drone-strike-in-kabul-on-aug-29-2021/a7d9edaf-b8d3-497b-9be1-8db427ca7cf6/?itid=lk_interstitial_manual_5

United States Department of Justice. (2020, December 16). *Sealed indictment, United States v. Abdullah, Criminal Docket No. 20-677, United States District Court for the Southern District of New York.* https://www.justice.gov/opa/press-release/file/1345286/download

United States Department of Justice, United States Attorney for the Eastern District of New York. (2015, February 15). Letter to the Honorable Raymond J. Dearie regarding motion in limine to admit Bin Laden documents, in *United States v. Abid Naseer*, Criminal Docket No. 10–19 (S-4) (RJD). http://kronosadvisory.com/Abid.Naseer.Trial_Abbottabad.Doc uments_Exhibits.403.404.405.420thru433.pdf

United States Forces Afghanistan, Headquarters. (2010, May 21). *AR 15-6 Investigation, 21 February 2010 U.S. air-to-ground engagement in the vicinity of Shahidi Hassas, Uruzgan District, Afghanistan.* On file with author.

Usmani, Z., & Bashir, H. (2014, December 4). *The impact of drone strikes in Pakistan.* Costs of War. https://watson.brown.edu/costsofwar/files/cow/imce/papers/2015/The%20Impact%20of%20Drone%20Strikes%20in%20Pakistan.pdf

van Linschoten, A. S., & Kuehn, F. (2011). *Separating the Taliban from al-Qaeda: The core of success in Afghanistan.* New York University Center on International Cooperation. https://cic.es.its.nyu.edu/sites/default/files/gregg_sep_tal_alqaeda.pdf

van Linschoten, A. S., & Kuehn, F. (2012). *An enemy we created: The myth of the Taliban-al-Qaeda merger in Afghanistan.* Oxford University Press.

White House. (no date). *Principles, standards, and procedures for direct action against terrorist targets.* American Civil Liberties Union. https://www.aclu.org/foia-document/psp-foia-document-april-30-2021

White House. (2010, January 7). *Summary of the White House review of the December 25,2009 attempted terrorist attack.* https://obamawhitehouse.archives.gov/realitycheck/the-press-office/white-house-review-summary-regarding-12252009-attempted-terrorist-attack

White House. (2013a, May 22). *U.S. policy standards and procedures for the use of force in counterterrorism operations outside the United States and areas of active Hostilities.* American Civil Liberties Union. https://www.aclu.org/sites/default/files/field_document/presidential_policy_guidance.pdf

White House. (2013b, May 23). *Fact sheet: U.S. policy standards and procedures for the use of force in counterterrorism operations outside the United States and areas of active hostilities.* https://obamawhitehouse.archives.gov/the-press-office/2013/05/23/fact-sheet-us-policy-standards-and-procedures-use-force-counterterrorism

White House. (2013c, May 23). *Remarks by the President at the National Defense University.* https://obamawhitehouse.archives.gov/the-press-office/2013/05/23/remarks-president-national-defense-university

White House. (2016a, July 1). *Executive order—United States policy on pre- and post-strike measures to address civilian casualties in U.S. operations involving the use of force.* https://obamawhitehouse.archives.gov/the-press-office/2016/07/01/executive-order-united-states-policy-pre-and-post-strike-measures

White House. (2016b). *Report on the legal and policy frameworks guiding the United States' use of military force and related national security operations.*https://fas.org/man/eprint/frameworks.pdf

White House. (2020). *Notice on the legal and policy frameworks guiding the United States' use of military force and related national security operations.* Federation of American Scientists. https://fas.org/man/eprint/frameworks-soleimani.pdf

White House, Background Press Call by a Senior Administration Official on Afghanistan, April 13, 2021. https://www.whitehouse.gov/briefing-room/press-briefings/2021/04/13/background-press-call-by-a-senior-administration-official-on-afghanistan/

Williams, B. G. (2010). The CIA's covert Predator drone war in Pakistan, 2004–2010: The history of an assassination campaign. *Studies in Conflict & Terrorism, 33*(10), 871–892. https://doi.org/10.1080/1057610X.2010.508483

Williams, B. G. (2013). *Predators: The CIA's drone war on Al Qaeda.* Potomac Books, 93.

Wilner, A. S. (2010). Targeted killings in Afghanistan: Measuring coercion and deterrence in counterterrorism and counterinsurgency. *Studies in Conflict & Terrorism, 33*(4), 307–329. https://doi.org/10.1080/10576100903582543

Woods, C. (2011, July 18). *US claims of 'no civilian deaths' are untrue.* Bureau of Investigative Journalism. https://www.thebureauinvestigates.com/stories/2011-07-18/us-claims-of-no-civilian-deaths-are-untrue

Woods, C. (2013, July 22). *Leaked Pakistani report confirms high civilian death toll in CIA drone strikes.* Bureau of Investigative Journalism. https://www.thebureauinvestigates.com/stories/2013-07-22/leaked-pakistani-report-confirms-high-civilian-death-toll-in-cia-drone-strikes

Woods, C. (2015). *Sudden justice: America's secret drone wars.* Oxford University Press.

Yousaf, F. (2017, December 1). *CIA drone strikes in Pakistan: History, perception and future.* SSRN. http://dx.doi.org/10.2139/ssrn.3160433

Youssef, N. A. (2007, July 11). *Pentagon: U.S. troops shot 429 Iraqi civilians at checkpoints.* McClatchy Washington Bureau. https://www.mcclatchydc.com/news/nation-world/world/article24466393.html

Yusufzai, R. (2007, May 18). Spies in their ranks worry Taliban. *The News International.*

Zawahiri, A. (2018). *America is the first enemy of Muslims.* English translation: https://www.longwarjournal.org/wp-content/uploads/2018/03/18-03-20-Zawahiri-22America-is-the-First-Enemy-of-Muslims22-translation.pdf

Zenko, M., & Wolf, A. M. (2016, April 25). *Drones kill more civilians than pilots do.* Foreign Policy. https://foreignpolicy.com/2016/04/25/drones-kill-more-civilians-than-pilots-do/

Zimmerman, K. (2013, September 18). *Statement before the House Committee on Homeland Security Subcommittee on counterterrorism and intelligence on "Understanding the threat to the Homeland from AQAP, AQAP's role in the al Qaeda network"*. https://docs.house.gov/meetings/HM/HM05/201 30918/101315/HHRG-113-HM05-Wstate-ZimmermanK-20130918.pdf

Zimmerman, K. (2019, October). *Beyond counterterrorism: Defeating the Salafi-jihadi movement*. American Enterprise Institute. https://www.aei.org/wp-content/uploads/2019/10/Beyond-Counterterrorism.pdf?x91208

Zimmerman, K. (2021). Al-Qaeda after the Arab Spring: A decade of expansion, losses, and evolution. *Current Trends in Islamist Ideology*, *28*(1), 1–27. https://www.aei.org/wp-content/uploads/2021/04/Current-Trends-28_1-Zimmerman-al-Qaeda-After-the-Arab-Spring.pdf?x91208.mir

Zussman, A., & Zussman, N. (2006). Assassinations: Evaluating the effectiveness of an Israeli counterterrorism policy using stock market data. *Journal of Economic Perspectives*, *20*(2), 193–206. https://doi.org/10.1257/jep.20.2.193

INDEX

CPSIA information can be obtained
at www.ICGtesting.com
Printed in the USA
LVHW101701250422
716945LV00003B/1

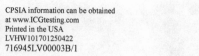

9 783030 911188